To Kathleen,
Our views may change, but our friendship thrives.
Love,
Shauna

Washington Siren

Washington Siren

A woman's journey through scathing scandals, lies, and secrets inside the FDIC, HUD, IRS and other agencies, with a love story that survives it all

Shannon O'Toole

This memoir / political exposé is based on my experiences throughout my career. Names have been changed and characters combined, with the exception of named elected public figures, Shaun Donovan, HUD Secretary, Carol Galante, FDIC Commissioner, LaMar Kelly and Ricky Tiggert, FDIC, Tom Stack OMB and Vicky McDowell, US Treasury. Additionally, Kathleen Zadareky, Charles Coulter, Joy Hadley, and Jason Burch are exceptional HUD managers and deserve to be recognized as such. Some events have been compressed. Certain episodes are imaginative recreation, and those episodes are not intended to portray actual events.

Washington Siren
Copyright 2017 by Shannon O'Toole

First Edition 2017
First Printing February 2017
Printed in the United States of America

ISBN: 10: 0692801723
ISBN 13: 9780692801727
Library of Congress Control Number: 2016917964
Washington Siren, San Juan Capistrano, CA

To contact the author, write to washingtonsiren@yahoo.com and visit the website www.Washingtonsiren.com. If you would like to be placed on the author's list for future books, please use the contact information above.

About the Author

Shannon O'Toole appeared before the U.S. Congress to present the National Government Lien Recovery Program and developed a pilot plan for government lien recoveries for the U.S. Treasury.

Ms. O'Toole developed the pilot plan for government lien recoveries for the California State Treasury and developed a program for the State of California, Department of Insurance, examining fraud, waste and abuse carried out by title insurance and escrow companies.

As executive director for the U.S. Department of Housing and Urban Development (HUD), she was responsible for 175 staff members and managed five distinct divisions to identify fraud, waste and abuse in government programs and transform the way each division conducted business. She developed a future staffing model for HUD/ FHA throughout the nation, reorganized field operations, improved asset recoveries, developed risk management policies, and managed during sequestration and a federal government shutdown.

As quality assurance director for HUD, responsible for risk management and oversight of FHA lender activity, she developed the first FHA lender servicing reviews of the largest national lenders, exposing fraud and lack of required foreclosure loss mitigation and loan restructures, which became the foundation for the largest global servicing settlement agreement with the five largest lenders in the nation. She contributed to pending mortgage rule making and legislation.

Ms. O'Toole received the HUD secretary's award for developing compliance management training risk models to prevent fraud and reduce HUD/FHA losses that contributed to removing HUD from the GAO high-risk report and is a frequent invited industry speaker.

As Federal Deposit Insurance Corporation/ Resolution Trust Corporation (FDIC/RTC) department head of real estate, she resolved over $45 billion in real estate and loans (REO and investment holdings from failed thrifts and banks). She also developed FDIC and RTC real estate auction programs.

The author lives in Laguna Beach with her husband, who stole her heart on the golf course and while kayaking in the Pacific Ocean.

Contents

Washington DC Congressional Testimony

"I, Shannon O'Toole, swear to tell the truth, before this United States Congress, and the Subcommittee for Government Reform and Oversight, so help me, God," she promised as she held up her right hand.

"Thank you for coming here today, Ms. O'Toole, and appearing before this Subcommittee, to put forth your findings and recommendations concerning certain government debt collections, namely by the Internal Revenue Service. I thank you, and the committee thanks you for testifying today. I think we are ready, and rather anxious, to hear your expert recommendations in this matter," Steven Horn, the serious Republican Committee Chairman from Long Beach, California, said to open the meeting. He leaned back in his high-backed, black leather chair while his colleagues did the same. There were about ten other congressmen sitting along the raised platform.

Shannon was excited to have finally been invited to present her Government Lien Program to congress, and Congressman Horn had been excited as well to finally share the plan with his committee about IRS inefficiencies including their inability to know where they had placed billions of dollars' worth of liens. She stood at the lectern, feeling confident, with her hands folded across the lengthy report she had been working on for over a year, which she was at long last about to present.

"Thank you, Congressman Horn. It is an honor to be invited here today, to speak to you and your distinguished colleagues on this most important issue of the inefficiency of the Internal Revenue Service or, rather, its lack of lien and redemption collections that is cheating the American public and the Treasury out of billions of dollars each year that could be put into the national budget. This is not a new finding. unfortunately, these gross mistakes and this mismanagement have-been occurring for at least twenty years, with billions of dollars being lost each and every year, while taxes are being raised because the IRS and other government agencies do not manage and collect their debts efficiently. I will present a plan for improving revenue collections by the IRS. I will explain now."

With her opening remarks, Shannon O'Toole turned the page of her twenty-six-page prepared statement, looked down at the first item on the outline, took a deep breath, and reached for her reading glasses. She spread her fingers and patted the podium table top but did not find the reading glasses. She flashed a tight smile at Congressman Horn while she quickly glanced at the floor to see if she had dropped the glasses and then moved her name card on the testimony podium, thinking maybe they had slid under there. She slipped her hands into her jacket pockets, searching for them, but felt nothing except the metro ticket she had used that morning to come to the congressional hearing. No reading glasses meant no reading the reports. Her confidence quickly turned to near panic. She quickly squinted down at the now-seemingly very blurry, very small print and could see the circles she had drawn around the most important points and the color-coded paragraphs so she wouldn't lose her place when reading the paper to the congressional committee. But she could not see the print. She could not read a word—pretty colors, though. She felt butterflies in her stomach and found that she was holding her breath. The Congressmen were waiting. And suddenly, it became very, very warm on this rainy spring day in March 1996 in Washington, DC, as she was standing at the witness table before the United States Congress.

Congressman Horn cleared his throat, signaling Shannon to begin. *I can do this,* Shannon told herself to try and calm down. *I know the material, I researched it, and I wrote it. So what if I can't see it? I can recite the reports with my eyes closed.*

Shannon lifted her head and gently tossed her shoulder-length blond hair, smiled through her Lancome cherry-red lips, and stared through her blue eyes at the serious congressmen, noting that there were two or three additional people seated behind each of the congressmen, whom she assumed were various aids, consultants and clerks. It was three people deep all around the raised platforms where the congressional committee sat, with additional people to the side and below the platforms to handle documents and exhibits for the congressmen.

She ran her damp hands across her black-and-white houndstooth wool suit skirt, smoothing the black collar and cuffs.

She stood as tall as her five-foot, three-inch, 125-pound figure would stretch, squared her shoulders, straightened her back and firm, full bosom, and said, "I'm sure you would be bored if I merely read my report to you, so, instead, I'm going to tell you a story about how a very broken government program requires immediate triage to stop billions of dollars in IRS and other government agency ongoing collection losses each and every year. Some of these government liens are against our elected leaders in Congress. These are losses that the American people deserve to have recovered and paid into the Treasury to reduce our national budget deficit. We wouldn't even need to cut many of the present programs if you will listen to my plan."

She leveled her eyes at the center of the dais, where Congressman Horn sat, moistened her lips, and took a very deep breath.

"That is, if the IRS and other agencies could find where they put the liens. Unfortunately, the IRS and other agencies can't report to you about these liens, because they've lost them."

And so began the ad-libbed testimony of Shannon O'Toole, on the most important day in her career, before the United States Congress.

First Week in the Federal Government

"Are You a Player?" and "Kitchen Passes"

Shannon had a queen-sized knot in her stomach and was nearly hyperventilating as she entered the Federal Deposit Insurance Corporation's (FDIC) two-story office building in Costa Mesa, California. She was scared, apprehensive, and wondering how she would ever fit into what she perceived to be a tightly woven government maze or make sense of the bags full of government-orientation materials that had been mailed to her house over the last two days. There were so many rules and regulations that a new employee was cautioned not to violate. With all the executive rules, judicial rules, administrative rules, and ethical rules, it was hard to determine where one area started and the next ended.

Newly divorced at thirty-four, she knew she would have to get through all the paperwork as she had full responsibility for raising her ten-year-old daughter, Jennifer, and helping her son, Toby, finish high school and get through college. She needed this job.

She approached the receptionist and gave her a small smile, juggling her briefcase full of government forms and new-hire information. She quickly took in the worn carpeting, sagging and peeling wallpaper and tape across the torn carpet in one area of the adjacent hallway. The name "FDIC" had been hand written on a paper sign and taped to the front door.

However, before Shannon could introduce herself, the receptionist answered one of two ringing telephone calls and hurriedly informed the caller, "Hello, FDIC. We don't have any information on that failed bank yet; it usually takes several weeks before we have a complete list of assets for sale. Please hold." Then she answered the second ringing line.

"Hello, FDIC." As the harried receptionist listened to the caller, she consulted a list beside her phone and replied, "Yes, we closed that bank about two months ago. No, I don't have any information yet on the loans that will be sold. I can't give you any information yet on the closed bank branches. I can give you the account officer who is handling that bank. If you will hold a moment, I will transfer you." And she pushed another button on her busy phone consul to send the call to someone else who hopefully could give the caller the information they needed.

The receptionist picked up the first line again and continued. "Thank you for holding. No, we don't have any appraisal information on any of the real estate yet from that failed bank. You can write in and request a list of the properties that are available. Yes, you can come down and pick up the list. We are on Paularino Street in Costa Mesa. Yes, thank you for calling."

The two lines rang again immediately, and the receptionist seemed to pause to catch her breath before reaching for the first line again. Shannon smiled again at her and said quickly,

"I'm here to see Bradley Donner and Fin Jenner," appreciating the obviously busy and stressed receptionist.

Without returning Shannon's smile and barely looking up from her desk, the receptionist pointed over her left shoulder and said, "Go down that hall. You'll see their names on their doors," and she returned to her phone calls.

Shannon followed the receptionist's directions, and while finding her way down the hallway, looked around at her new colleagues and peers. She listened to a cacophony of ringing telephones that rang unanswered because everyone was already on the phone with another caller. She also noted that there were sometimes three people in each office, nearly shoulder to shoulder, with their mismatched desks nearly touching. She took measure of the disorganized activity: piles of files in boxes on the floor in the hallways, piled on top of file cabinets, on desks and spilling onto what floor space remained in the office. The furniture was scratched and dented throughout the offices.

While proceeding down the hall, looking for her appointed office, she noted that no one seemed to be able to answer a caller's question. She heard, "I don't know"; "We have too many failed banks to know about all their real estate holdings this soon"; "It will probably be three or four months before we can tell you anything about any of the failed banks properties"; "We don't have an appraisal or asking price on that property yet"; "We need to order an environmental study on that property"; and "No, I can't take your number; you'll have to call back in two weeks."

The sound of ringing telephones that rang unanswered was continuous, because as soon as an employee hung up their phone, it rang again. There was no silence between calls.

It appeared that there were no firm rules, guidelines, or processes yet in place at this office to guide the staff in assisting the public with getting the information they requested.

It seemed that the callers were asking questions that no one could answer because the FDIC was experiencing historical failed bank activity and was trying to staff up quickly to manage all the real estate, loans and other assets from the failed banks.

She knew that the Federal Deposit Insurance Corporation had just experienced a historical boom in growth due to the recent failure of banks in 1984. Such a failure of banks had not happened since the organization was created by Congress in 1933 with the Glass-Steagall Act, when the FDIC had been created to provide insurance to cover limited dollar amounts of deposits to encourage the public to place their money into banks, with the government insuring those deposits in the event of the bank's failure. In 1984, the amount guaranteed or covered by the FDIC was $100,000 per deposit. Of course, there were loopholes, including the law that allowed for one person to be insured up to $100,000 for an account in his or her name only and another $100,000 for accounts held jointly with a child and so on.

However, due to the 1984 economic collapse of the nation's banking system from bad loans and real estate losses, the FDIC was in a frenzy to hire new people to attempt to handle and process the many insured deposits, failing banks and the assets acquired or held by those banks.

Some of those assets included loans secured by real estate, actual real estate owned by the banks for investment or in partnership for profit, bank branches and real estate that had been foreclosed on when a debtor defaulted and no longer paid on his or her loan.

The job of the FDIC in part was to liquidate the failed banks' assets and recover the maximum amount of money to first pay back the FDIC for its administrative costs and then to collect revenue from the sale of the failed bank assets to pay back the depositors and stockholders. The FDIC had been reasonably successful in paying back depositors who had more than $100,000 in their accounts when their bank failed, and in paying back stockholders. Often the FDIC issued "receivership certificates", a sort of promissory note against the failed bank that was converted into a receivership when it failed, and redeemed when the FDIC recovered sufficient money from the sale of the failed bank's assets.

The Office of the Comptroller of the Currency (OCC) and the Office of Thrift Supervision (OTS) placed the failing institution into a Receivership legal category and appointed the FDIC as Receiver over the institution to manage its affairs and collect its debts. This Receivership status also protected the FDIC from personal liability or lawsuits, as any claims arising from incidents pertaining to the failed bank would be assessed against the failed bank, not the FDIC. And any claims against the FDIC were usually pushed back against a Receivership. Failing banks and thrifts were also placed into Conservatorships, allowing the institution to continue operating, although on a limited basis, until it could be sold in whole or in parts to other solvent lending institutions or investors.

When Shannon reached an office with the name Bradley Donner on the door, she knocked lightly and introduced herself. "Hello, Mr. Donner, I'm Shannon O'Toole. I'm a new account officer, and I was told to ask for you this morning."

Sitting behind his large, dented, old, oak banker's desk, Bradley Donner made no attempt at disguising his visual examination of her, sliding his eyes up and down, pausing at her breasts, and then finally looking up at her face.

"Hello, and do come in." He smiled and motioned for her to have a seat. "I have your personnel file right here," he said and reached to the corner of his desk to pull a manila file toward him.

He looks like WC Fields, Shannon thought, including the rather red, bulbous nose. He was a large man, definitely over six feet, and in his fifties. His office also had piles of files on the floor and his desk, while his walls were covered with pictures of boats, and pictures of Bradley as the captain with a variety of attractive women smiling at the camera.

Bradley interrupted her thoughts and said, "I want Fin Jenner to come in and meet you too. He's the real estate branch chief for real estate assets from all the failed banks. You'll report to him as your Chief." As he walked around his desk toward the door he casually ran his hand over Shannon's shoulder, and said, "I'll be right back," then left his office. Shannon jumped in her chair. She was surprised by his forwardness and determined to keep her distance from him as much as possible in the future.

He returned a moment later with a rather slight, small man with thinning gray hair, about 135 pounds and in his mid-fifties.

"Hello. I'm Fin Jenner," he said, and extended a thin hand. Shannon shook his hand while Bradley Donner returned to his desk and sat down. "I remember your résumé," Fin continued.

"You're the one with the real estate license, construction and legal experience, right? I was really interested in your knowledge of title insurance and real estate contracts. We have quite a 'black hole' here with real estate properties encumbered with title issues and exceptions that we can't market, and we're looking at you to work with our legal department to work them out."

Shannon was pleased that he remembered her application information and that he seemed genuinely happy to have her on board. She was also pleased that he had discussed legal workouts.

She enjoyed real estate law and found it fascinating, though challenging. Before she could answer Fin, Donner interrupted.

"I guess you're one of those pretty real estate ladies who like to go around and show expensive homes so you can get good decorating ideas," he said, leaning forward and leering at her.

Shannon was taken aback and surprised herself by saying, "Oh, I would much rather build them than decorate them."

Fin Jenner chuckled while Donner frowned with a lack of understanding.

"I have designed and built several custom homes, and prepared all the legal documents for the zoning, lot splits, variances, building permits, and modifications for city councils and state regulatory agencies. I enjoy resolving title exception issues and obtaining expungements and quiet title actions when necessary, and examining chains of title for lien information."

Fin Jenner's smile broadened, while Donner looked a little confused. Fin offered, "She's the one we discussed that could help us out with partial construction loans, encumbered titles, and raw land sales and resolve all the pending litigation and cases tied up in legal." He paused. "She has a legal background and also has a real estate license."

That information seemed to help Donner remember Shannon's qualifications, and he sat back in his chair. His demeanor seemed to become more professional, and he said,

"Oh, OK, then. I guess Fin can show you around the office and give you some new files to start you working."

Shannon's FDIC career was ready to begin.

Fin Jenner showed Shannon to an office with two other real estate account officers already at work. She had to squeeze sideways between the three desks in order to reach her assigned chair. She wasn't sure she could open the drawers on her desk all the way because of the lack of space in the overfilled office.

"This is Phil," Fin indicated a dark-haired, slender man in his mid-forties. "And this is Karen," he added about a young woman, about twenty five years old, with curly dark hair.

"Here are your first few files," Fin said as he handed her ten files. "These have been carefully selected by the other account officers for you from their asset portfolios to get you started. You will quickly learn *why* the other account officers have chosen these files for you." Fin smiled, and his eyes twinkled. "They will probably have some unresolvable legal problem, title matter, or are just about impossible to market or sell," he chuckled. "But you can go into the files and read over the appraisals, if there are any, and look at the cases in there to see how we write up the reports to get authority to take certain actions concerning the real estate asset. Your cases will go before a committee for approval. I'll come and check on you later."

He winked at Shannon as he left her with her stack of problematic and impossible files.

Shannon smiled at her officemates. They briefly returned her smile and immediately turned back to their open files and the ringing telephones on their desks. She once again questioned herself and what she had gotten herself into with this new job, and then quickly reminded herself that there was no room for doubt about accepting this position because she had her two children, Toby and Jennifer to support, and did not receive child support.

She looked outside her office door at the mismatched desks, chairs, filing cabinets, and credenzas, wondering which failed banks all this office furniture had come from. Absolutely nothing in the entire FDIC matched anything else, and it added to the disorganized, flying-by-the-seat-of-your-pants atmosphere that seemed to permeate the place. There were desks of heavy Spanish oak, light maple, gray metal, mahogany and light-blond wood, sometimes with one bank of drawers and sometimes two. There were heavy, dark oak, light-blond fiberboard or medium walnut credenzas, some short, some long. File drawers were in every conceivable color and size, including modern, early colonial, old Spanish designs and metal. And the chairs were in every kind of style and pattern, some solid black or brown wood, some molded plastic with bucket seats, and some fabric with blue, green or red geometric patterns. It appeared that the furniture had come from a combination of failed banks, each with its own distinctive style. There were extra desks and file drawers lined up along the hallways, with boxes of files teetering on their surfaces. She read the names of recently failed banks on the boxes: Heritage Bank, West Valley, and others.

Everyone seemed to either be talking on the telephone or to each other, but no one seemed to be working on or reading from their desk files, and the noise level was palpable. She decided that she might as well start on her impossible files and see just what she was up against. She opened up the top file to begin reading about a parcel of vacant land in Malibu, California. She became involved with the file as she read about its' oceanfront location in a prestigious area of Malibu primarily with very expensive custom-built homes overlooking the Pacific Ocean. Most of the adjacent homes were owned by Hollywood movie stars, who cherished the privacy of the prestigious Malibu enclave and ocean front views. Having designed custom homes in the past, including her own in Anaheim Hills, Shannon was familiar with obtaining required hydrology, soil, and topography reports to obtain building permits, variances and modifications. She was intrigued with the easy access to this parcel of land and its location right on the sandy beach of Malibu. To add to its desirability, it was a level lot, a luxury that Shannon had never experienced in designing and building her collection of hillside custom homes throughout Southern California. It was a dream property.

Thinking that the parcel was a gem, she couldn't understand why this piece of ocean front land was still in the unsold inventory of bank foreclosed properties. It should have never even gone through foreclosure, as it was such a valuable piece of land. She continued to read over the preliminary title report to see if there were any unreasonable restrictions against the property that could have made it undesirable or unbuildable, but couldn't find anything to discount the value of the property, or explain why it hadn't already been sold by one of the other account officers.

She began to devise a marketing strategy for the parcel to expose it to the public for purchase, and had just decided on designing and placing a small advertisement in the *Los Angeles Times*, when Fin Jenner returned to her desk. He came to retrieve Shannon shortly before lunchtime to introduce her to some of her other colleagues and took her across the open-office area where more vacant desks sat awaiting newly hired staff, to an office similar to Shannon's that was occupied by three women.

Fin approached a pleasant-looking woman in her early forties with short blond, curly hair, wide, broad cheekbones and pretty green eyes. "Tanya Glasser, I would like you to meet Shannon O'Toole, who is starting with us today," Fin stated as he ushered Shannon over to one of three women sharing one office.

"Hello," Tanya said and smiled. "Welcome to the FDIC. It's nice to meet you. Where are you sitting?"

Shannon returned Tanya's smile and told her she was across the open area, also sharing an office.

"Tanya's been here just a little longer than you," Fin informed Shannon. "She started about two months ago."

Shannon noticed a photograph on Tanya's desk with two attractive young men and Tanya smiling out from the frame. Tanya noticed Shannon's gaze at the picture and offered,

"These are my two sons, Zack and Ian. Do you have any children?"

"Yes," Shannon responded. "A son and a daughter. My son looks about the same age as your boys…"

But before Tanya could respond, Fin pulled on Shannon's arm and took her toward a second woman in the same office.

"Joan, I would like you to meet Shannon O'Toole. She will be working on some of the files you all donated to her, and I'm sure she will be coming over to ask questions about the file documents," Fin said, laughing as he introduced the two women.

"Hello," Joan smiled up at Shannon from her desk. Shannon quickly looked down at the thirty-something-year-old, thin, brunette woman and returned her greeting.

Before the two women could begin any conversation, Fin pulled Shannon around to face the third desk, where a forty-something, brassy blond woman sat with overdone makeup and a tight dress and who was using exaggerated hand motions while she talked on the phone.

"I'm telling you, darling," she was saying into the telephone to some unseen person, "That's just the way it is, because this is the Government, and because I'm the Government, and that's just the way we do it." She rolled her heavily mascaraed eyes around to let Fin know how irritated she was with the unfortunate caller. "If you don't want to do it my way, then the deal's off, darling. There's just no way I'm going to recommend anything else. If you don't want the property, that's OK because there's someone else who will. It doesn't matter to me."

Shannon blanched at the brassy woman's unprofessional attitude. She looked at Fin to see what his reaction would be to the woman's lack of professional demeanor, expecting disapproval or embarrassment, and instead saw him devouring the woman with his eyes.

"And this is Laurie Morgan," Fin said as he held out one hand to indicate Laurie's presence, as if there was anyone else who might have had her name in the room.

"Oh, hi," Laurie said quickly in Fin and Shannon's direction, without attempting to offer a welcoming smile to Shannon, but instead glued her eyes onto Fin. "Oh, Fin, sweetie, how do you expect me to work with these full-moon jerks?" she exclaimed, throwing her hands up in the air to accentuate her words to make sure she didn't lose his attention. "I swear, the full moon brings out the weirdos, Fin, and I seem to get them all," she purred at him, leaning toward him across her desk and revealing a full bosom for his inspection. "I don't know why you give me all the really dumb files, Fin, and give Karen Louve all the good houses in Newport Beach. You know I have friends that have the money to buy those homes, but instead you give me all this junk—the junk the whackos call me about. You know Fin, we really need to redistribute the workload around here," she continued, and finally sat back in her chair.

"Laurie, this is Shannon O'—"

"Yes, hi," Laurie interrupted Fin with an all-but-dismissing greeting directed at Shannon.

"But, Fin," she began again, and this time Fin interrupted her.

"Just do the best you can with your portfolio, Laurie." Fin smiled down at the aggressive woman. "And come see me later about the case you wrote and gave me yesterday. We need to go over it."

"Oh, OK, sweetie." Laurie tipped her head and smiled up at Fin. "I'll be in to see you after lunch. Richard is coming to pick me up for lunch and take me to Nordies, so I'll come and see you when I get back."

Laurie looked over at Shannon, quickly taking her in and measuring her new perceived competition.

"We've brought Shannon on board to handle all the 'Black Hole' litigation assets. So if you have any problems with your contracts or title policies, just see Shannon."

Laurie still kept her eyes glued on Fin and responded, "Oh, you know that won't be necessary. I have everything worked out on my files. You know that, Fin. My portfolio is completely under control, and I really want to get more new assets in Newport..." She began accentuating her words with her hands going up into the air again.

"All right Laurie," Fin said, cutting her off. "I know what you want, and we'll be looking at the portfolios with Brad in the next couple of days to see what we're going to do and if anything needs changing."

"My portfolio needs changing," she exclaimed to Fin. "And I don't see why you've given all this junk..."

"OK, Laurie." Fin gave her a wink and turned to leave the over-crowded room.

He then took Shannon in tow across the hall into another office to meet two additional account officers, two Asian men in their mid-thirties.

"This is Ken Ito and Mat Pham," Fin announced to Shannon.

She looked into the eyes of two not-very-warm faces. The two men merely looked at Fin and then briefly over at Shannon. "This is Shannon O'Toole," Fin continued with his introductions.

The first man, named Ken, gave brief eye contact to Shannon with an even briefer "hello." The second man, Mat, actually looked at Shannon and gave her a very small smile and a "Hi," without any offer of welcome or interest.

Shannon wasn't comfortable with the aloofness or coldness she was encountering with these two men and decided she wouldn't attempt to try to start up any kind of conversation with them right away. They obviously weren't interested in meeting her, and she decided that was OK for now; she had enough to learn at the present and other new people to try and get to know. She would try to approach these two colleagues later and begin an office dialogue with them. She knew how important it was to be a team player and get along with everyone.

The next day, Shannon attended her first office meeting and was amazed by the demeanor of the Department Head, Bradley Donner. Still looking like WC Fields to Shannon, with a large, bulbous nose that was perpetually red and swollen, either from drinking or too much sun—or probably both, she soon realized. His first order of business was a discussion about his afternoon martini lunch and his weekend plans to go fishing on his boat. But it was his behavior that astounded her. He was going around the room, asking all the women if they would like to come out on his boat that coming weekend. He said he had several other friends coming along to go fishing, and they could be his serving wenches. Shannon was once again taken aback, and this time appalled, while the other women just didn't make eye contact and giggled nervously.

The meeting format was a roundtable sort, with Bradley asking each account officer about the real estate assets in their respective portfolios, and going over a summary report tallying all of the departments' assets with their status. Each account officer gave an update on the work he or she was doing on each property asset, and discussed any major problems they were encountering.

When it came for Shannon's new friend Tanya Glasser's turn, Tanya started off a little shaky.

"Well, I have ordered the appraisals for three properties, and I've talked with some brokers about their market value opinions..."

"That's broker opinion of values, dumpling," Laurie broke in, flipping her wrist at Tanya to emphasize the "darling" part. "We call them BOV's around here. You'll learn all the lingo pretty soon," she said and rolled her eyes over at Bradley and Fin, as if saying, "The poor little thing just can't seem to catch on."

Fin Jenner interrupted Laurie's performance and looked directly at Tanya with,

"That's good. You've gotten the appraisals ordered already because they can take a month or longer to get back."

Tanya smiled shyly at Fin. "Thank you, and I'm starting to draft the listing cases for three residential assets now, while I'm waiting for the appraisals and broker opinions to come in."

"Have there been a lot of calls from the public for those houses?" Fin asked her.

"Oh, yes," Tanya responded. "The phone doesn't seem to stop just because the appraisals aren't ready." She laughed. "I'm making a list of interested buyers that I will get back to when the properties are ready to market."

"That's good, Tanya," Fin assured her. "You've got those residential properties under control."

Fin then went around the table continuing to discuss each account office's portfolio of real estate properties.

"Ken, what's happening on the Western Bank Building?" Fin directed his question to Ken Ito, one of the Asian men Shannon had met earlier.

"Well, uh, you know, I have been kinda busy with some of the other assets," he began.

"How long have you had this property in your portfolio?"

"About four months now."

"And you've ordered an appraisal and preliminary title report?" Fin continued his questioning.

"Uh, well, I was gonna do that next, 'cause I thought I would get some broker opinions of value first. But I will see why they are taking so long," Ken muttered without a smile.

Fin moved on to a discussion of another property.

"And what about the Crenshaw Commercial Building?" he asked Ken.

"It's still tied up in the legal department. Something about a parking easement. I'm waiting for the legal department to get back to me with their opinion about the legal description and the parking easement issue."

"How long have you been waiting for an opinion?" Fin asked.

"About three months now."

"And you've sent follow-up memos to the legal department on this?" Fin continued his questioning.

"Uh, well, I was gonna do that next 'cause I thought they were going to get a legal opinion to me by now. But I will make up a memo and get it over to legal to see why they are taking so long," Ken muttered.

"We have to stay on top of the legal department and our asset portfolios," Fin announced to the room full of account officers. "I have some good news and some bad news. First the bad news: The assets tied up with legal problems seem to be in a 'Black Hole', they go in but never come out. Every time we send a new property to the legal department, it seems like four to six months before we ever see the asset again it just stays tied up, and the legal issues are never resolved. Then our inventory becomes very stale, and Washington DC Headquarters and Congress want to know why and what's taking so long to get these properties cleared up and ready for the public to view. I don't like answering those questions to Washington DC and telling them I don't know what's wrong, or when the legal problems will be resolved. You guys tell me that the legal department has been pretty much nonresponsive to the real estate department, and we need to keep after them all the time. I want a list of legal requests any of you have out right now, so I can track our legal requests and follow up in our department head meetings to see what's taking so long. Everyone get me a list of your open legal items by tomorrow."

Fin took a breath.

"OK, now for the good news. Our newest staff person here, Shannon O'Toole," Fin said, turning and extending an arm in Shannon's direction, "Will be unraveling all the legal problems and write the cases to resolve the legal action hindering the real estate from selling. She has an excellent legal background, and will be handling all of the legal problems from now on. Any questions?"

No one said a word. The account officers just made their appropriate notes to themselves to get this information to Fin as requested.

At the end of the meeting, Donner fell into step with one of the account officers Shannon had not yet met, Karen Louve', while Shannon walked just behind them. Karen was an attractive blonde with short hair and a very trim yet curvy body, which seemed to have caught Donner's eye. He leaned over to Donna and said in a seductive sotto voice, "I have a kitchen pass tonight. What do you think about us getting together later?"

Karen pushed her shoulder up against Bradley's and smiled at him, answering "You don't need a kitchen pass with me. I'm just happy to see you when you can get away. What time?"

"After work. I'll be at the Love Boat, same booth, waiting for you."

"OK, I'll find you there," she responded with a peculiar little laugh, something like a huh-huh-huh-huh sound.

As the two apparent lovers walked away after making their rendezvous plans, Shannon wondered which of the laws they were about to break: the executive, judicial, administrative, or surely the ethical rules, with a kitchen pass for cheating on an unsuspecting wife.

Shannon went back to her desk and picked up a file that had some notes in it pertaining to an eviction that was underway, and she decided to go and discuss the action with Mike Doogan, the new section chief of property management, who was also a personal old friend of Bradley Donner's, as she had overheard Laurie telling Tanya Glasser earlier that morning in the staff meeting. The property management department supported Shannon's sales division in handling needed repairs to the properties as well as clean-ups, lawn maintenance and eviction matters.

As she approached Mike's office, she noted that the fifty-something-year-old, slightly balding, and paunchy man was laughing over something private with a young secretary, who was just turning around and leaving his office.

"You really should get a matching coconut for the women to enjoy, Mike," she said, laughing. "You know, something with some cocoa-nuts."

Mike shook his head in laughter as the young woman walked away from his door.

"Hello," Shannon said cautiously as she approached his open door.

"Hello. Come in." Mike motioned to Shannon with one arm as he rested his other arm on his desk. "Come on in here," he continued, while his eyes roamed up and down Shannon's curvy figure and then finally met her eyes. "You're new here, and I'm here to help everyone, especially the pretty new women. I'm at your service."

Shannon noticed a slight Southern drawl, and didn't like the way Mike's eyes kept sliding up and down from her breasts to her toes.

Doogan motioned for Shannon to take a seat, and she sat on the edge of one of his visitors chairs.

"Um, Mr. Doogan, I would like to ask you for a little more information about this file I've been reviewing," she began, trying to get comfortable with this new manager and to bring his attention back to the property file and away from her body.

"And I want to help you," Mike answered with a laugh and a nod of his head. "What can I do for you?" he asked with a big smile.

"Well, I just wanted to understand how long the eviction process takes here, and what stage this action is in, who should I see about the court appearance, and—"

"Well, now, you see, it's like this," he began, leaning back in his chair. "We send a request up to legal when we have a legal problem, like this here eviction one, and they either do the eviction inhouse, or they choose an outside law firm to handle it for us, like Katz and Block. They do most of the eviction work for us now."

"OK, I see," Shannon responded, nodding her head. "So I should find out from our legal department who is actually handling the matter?"

"Yeah, that would work out fine," Mike continued, and then Shannon didn't hear another word he said as her eyes came across a coconut on Mike's desk that had the shape and distinct characteristics of a woman's private lady-parts, sitting proudly upon his desk for all who would care to look.

Mike saw the surprised look on Shannon's face and laughed.

"Yep, it's kinda funny how Mother Nature sometimes imitates itself on hard nuts the same as soft, fuzzy peaches, ain't it?"

Shannon felt herself beginning to burn with a blush that was about to make a sunburn look pale.

"Oh, lookee that." Mike laughed again. "You're turning red just like this here coconut." He leaned back in his chair while he continued to watch her and chuckle.

Shannon didn't know how to respond when Mike continued, "Well, now, tell me, Shannon, are you a player?"

Shannon wasn't sure what he meant, but decided to answer with as safe a response as she could offer. "Well, I do play softball, soccer, and volleyball, but I never could play tennis."

Mike stopped laughing, but he kept a smile on his face. "That's not what I meant." He leaned up from his chair and looked Shannon directly in the eyes. "I mean that around here, we sometimes travel a lot, you know, when banks fail, or we have to go out and inspect some of the properties." He paused to give Shannon a moment to catch on. "And it's kinda fun sometimes to just, you know, play a little game when we're out there traveling, sorta like a room key exchange thing, you know what I mean?"

Shannon couldn't quite believe what she was hearing. "Uhm, I don't think I'll be traveling much," she offered weakly, not knowing what to say or do.

"Well, we'll just have to see about that," Mike joked.

Shannon stood up quickly. "Thanks for your help with this file," she said and turned to quickly back out of his office.

She quickly made her exit from Mike Doogan's office, and was proceeding back to her cubicle when she heard Bradley Donner's voice coming from another female account officer's cubicle.

"Don't those braces ever bother you?" Brad was asking Kelly. Kelly was a tall, pretty brunette in her late twenties with a full figure curvy body and big smile.

"Oh, you know, you just kind of have to get used to them. I guess I don't eat much steak, though, since they're new, and I'm still getting used to them."

Bradley leaned in closer to Kelly and leered. "Oh, so you can't eat much meat, huh? I guess your braces could really hurt the men—I mean meat. You know, I mean, you could really hurt a guy with those things. You must have to be pretty careful, huh?"

Kelly didn't smile. She just shook her head and said, "Brad, I think your wife is calling you."

Bradley didn't take the hint and continued. "I guess those braces could get stuck in a guy's zipper, now, couldn't they? Then you might have to call out a locksmith and have a threesome to, um, straighten things out!" and he laughed at his own humor.

Kelly didn't think it was so funny. "I think I need to get back to work now, Bradley, if you'll excuse me," and she turned her back on her boss.

Brad just chuckled as he walked away at his own amusement, laughing with, "Maybe I'll get a kitchen pass, and we can talk about it some more."

A few weeks later, Shannon was crossing the office and stopped by Mat Pham's desk. "Have you seen Mike Doogan today? I haven't seen him for the last three or four days," she asked. "I need to get a budget from him on one of my properties."

Mat laughed and answered, "You know, he's probably down in Mexico at the dog races again, and Brad's covering for him. He's probably either on a gambling binge or drinking binge, and I bet Brad is telling everyone he's out inspecting properties or something like that again."

Shannon couldn't believe what Mat was telling her, and she blurted out, "You're kidding! You're not serious!"

"Oh, yes, I am," Mat replied. "Every time Mike disappears for a few days like this, you can bet he's out getting drunk, getting laid, and gambling like he always does, and Brad will always cover up for him."

"I can't believe they would do that," Shannon exclaimed, shaking her head.

"Oh, sure they can, and they do," Mat informed her. "Brad just fills out Mike's timesheet and signs it, and then nobody knows any difference, and nobody cares, except maybe for Mike's wife. Sometimes she calls the office looking for him too."

3

Single Parenting

It was Monday, and Shannon had had a particularly tough weekend with her ex-husband not showing up to pick up their daughter as he had promised or paying any child support as he had promised, as usual. Jennifer needed new glasses, and Shannon's budget just didn't stretch far enough.

She packed up her briefcase after working late while her daughter was at dance class and put the files she planned to work on later that night at home in the car. She drove to Jennifer's class to pick her up. It broke her heart that Jenny had to ride her bike to dance class because she couldn't get off work early enough to take her. Sometimes the guilt of not being a stay-at-home mom was so strong. Dance was Jennifer's passion; moving to music was her love. She was on pointe now in ballet, and so beautifully graceful. She had developed exceptional skills with her arm and leg extensions, and held her neck and head so elegantly. Her posture was perfect, elongating her slender body, with her waist-length blond hair in a chignon at the base of her neck. She also played the flute like an angel. Whenever Jennifer performed in a ballet or music recital, Shannon had tears for Jennifer's artistic beauty in the flow of the dance or her touch in the music she played. One of Shannon's favorite songs was 'I Am Sixteen Going On Seventeen' and the sheer innocence and wistfulness of the song as Jenny performed it moved her to tears.

But the performances were expensive in terms of costumes, musical instruments, rehearsals, ballet shoes that wore out in a few weeks, and special training. Shannon was thankful for the overtime she earned while working weekends when banks failed; it helped her afford those things.

She was so sad that she couldn't give her son, Toby, the college campus he so wanted. He had discussed with her several college options, including his favorite, Santa Cruz. It was a natural fit, after all, being right on the Pacific Ocean. Toby loved the water, loved surfing, and played on his high school water polo team, which had helped develop his broad shoulders and strong swimmer's V-body. His hair was curly and sun-bleached blond. But Santa Cruz would mean finding the cash for housing, an additional cost, and meals. If he stayed close to home, she could help with the tuition and books, but wouldn't have to find the means or take out loans for the additional room and board. It was a tough decision: give Toby his first choice, or compromise because of limited financial resources.

Toby was such a good-natured, funny young man, with an outrageous sense of humor and lots of friends. He was equally bright, able to get great grades seemingly without much effort. He had been tested and found to be in the genius IQ range and deserved to go to a good college.

Shannon parked and put her head back on the headrest in the car while she waited for Jenny to finish her dance class. Throughout the day she worked in a corporate world, fast paced and political. Although the single parenting was hard, it kept her grounded, humble, and human. Her work challenged her mind and honed her business skills, but her personal life with Jenny and Toby touched her heart. The unlimited depth of love she felt for her children was beyond words, without boundaries, and was the source of her energy and strength.

Jenny came out to the car and leaned into the front seat, placing her dance shoes carefully into the backseat. Shannon stepped out of the car to put Jennifer's bike onto the bike racks on the back of the little sports car.

"How was dance class?" Shannon turned to her pretty daughter and asked with a smile.

"The dancing part was fine, I loved it as usual. But the parts in the upcoming ballet, Little Mermaid, were given out, and I didn't get the little mermaid part, one of the older girls got it." She sighed. Jenny helped Shannon secure the bike to the rack, and they both got into the car.

Shannon turned toward her daughter and asked, "Remember when you were just a little girl, about three, and we would go to the beach?"

Jenny smiled and answered, "Yes, and I didn't like it much, because I always got sand all over and it stuck to me."

Shannon laughed and said, "Well yes, that does usually happen when you sit in the suds, where the waves break into the sand." She remembered her little towheaded daughter in-sisting on going no deeper into the water but sitting where the waves tickled her feet and the damp sand stuck to her legs. "I also told you that you were a real little girl when we parked the car and walked through the tunnel under the coastal train tracks in San Clemente to go to the beach, but that when you came out the end of the tunnel onto the beach, you were a little mermaid, so you wouldn't be afraid of the water."

Jenny giggled and said, "Yes, I remember that too! And it worked, it really did. I wasn't afraid anymore. Toby would go straight out into the water with his surfboard, you would read a book, and I would play in the suds. You also told me that the mermaids swam where the water sparkled the brightest."

"That's right. Where the sun danced on the water and made sparkly water diamonds. It was a really sweet time," Shannon reminisced and then asked, "So what part did you get in the Little Mermaid ballet?"

Jenny sweetly groaned and tipped her head to one side. "I'm a crustacean."

"A what?" Shannon inquired as she started the car.

"I'm a crustacean with a shell and big red claws."

"Your costume will have claws?" Shannon echoed.

"Yes. Because I'm a big red lobster!" Jenny burst out laughing.

Shannon began to laugh with her. "Well, Jenny, I just know you will be the most delightful, adorable, musical lobster on ballet pointe toe shoes there's ever been!" They both laughed and talked about the upcoming dance performance on the drive home.

When Shannon and Jenny arrived home, Toby greeted them in the kitchen and said with his usual wit and charm, "Hello, lovely ladies. Welcome home."

Shannon looked around the kitchen and smelled something wonderful cooking.

"Did you start dinner, honey?" she asked Toby, trying to see around him, but he was blocking the stove.

"I might have," he answered in his usual sassy and easy way. "But you won't find out what it is until you put your briefcase down and relax a minute. Jenny, you can help me set the table. I want you to be really, really relaxed tonight mom. I have some important stuff to talk to you about." He continued to block the stove when Shannon tried to peek around him.

"What sort of important things that would prompt you to start dinner?" she asked suspiciously.

"Really good things, college things," he said, continuing to evade her questions.

So she left the kitchen with a smile at the son she so adored and went to drop her briefcase by the living room sofa, while she could hear her two beloved children laughing and banging pots around in the kitchen. It was a very sweet sound and music to her ears—and so very far from the office.

4

The Government's Interpretation of Equal Rights

The FDIC had finally outgrown its earlier office space with the mismatched furniture in the hallways and taped-over, torn carpeting and had moved to the Fluor Building in Irvine, California. The space was more professional and had been built out with conforming cubicles, although some of the mismatched furniture had made its way through the transition, including the many varieties of file drawers and credenzas, which broke up the monotony of the sea of teal green cubicle sections.

"Did you hear that they finally posted the Team Chief's grade-thirteen position?" Tanya Glasser walked into Shannon's coveted window-facing cubicle, sat down, crossed her pretty legs, leaned toward Shannon, and continued in a conspiratorial whisper. "Now that Mike is banished to Arizona to dry out, they have to fill the position, and you know Karen Louve is the best candidate. She has been reading all the real estate cases for Brad Donner for the last year and marking them up for him before he goes to committee, telling him what's wrong with the cases so he can look good in committee. She's also been doing most of his reports for the department, and she knows what's going on better than he does since he's out of the office so much on his boat and with managing his twenty-five personal rental properties."

"So, then, we can expect Karen to be our next team chief?" Shannon asked innocently.

"Are you kidding?" Tanya exclaimed. "Brad can't pick her, even if she is the most qualified and has been doing the job for the last year. It would look like favoritism, since he's been having an affair with her all that time."

"I have seen them talking together about meeting up at the Love Boat," Shannon said thoughtfully. "How long have they been seeing each other?"

"For over a year that I know of. Karen actually hopes and thinks that Brad will leave his wife and marry her, and she really loves him. I feel awfully sorry for her. First she gets screwed by Brad, literally, and now she's getting screwed professionally and figuratively."

"Let's see what's wrong with this picture." Shannon shook her head. "Karen is the most experienced one here, she's been here the longest, she's been doing the work of the team chief and also Brad's department head work, and she isn't going to get a fair chance at the promotion because of Brad's concern that it might make him look bad? He *is* bad! He is awful, he cheat's around all the time, and now it's going to hurt Karen's chance for a promotion to grade thirteen. That is incredibly unfair and lousy."

"I know it is," Tanya agreed with Shannon. "It is really crummy, but Karen knows Brad is married and what she is getting into with him, and she says he's told her he's ready to leave his wife, and she believes that he will marry her, and so the promotion doesn't matter to her so much. Brad's more important to her than a grade thirteen. I just hope it doesn't backfire on her. If she doesn't get the promotion after doing all his work for him for the last year, and then Brad doesn't leave his wife for her, that would be a double whammy for Karen."

Shannon's eyebrows shot up. "You're kidding?"

"No, not at all. Karen and I have gone out after work a couple of times, and she always has a file of cases to read for Brad with her. She even writes down questions for him to ask during the committee meetings."

"I think this place is a sorry excuse for a government business," Shannon said in a disgusted voice. "Nothing changes. Mike goes out and parties, and Brad covers for him. Karen covers for Brad and does his work. We come in ten minutes late, and there's a note on our desk."

"Well, Shannon," Tanya offered philosophically, "We knew we were going into a man's world when we came here, and we're lucky to work so close to home and make the salaries we do. We're never going to have the same conditions as men, and so don't expect it, or you're going to keep on getting disappointed." Tanya unwound her legs, shook a finger at Shannon, and left.

Senior Credit Review Committee (SCRC)

The senior credit review committee was a formal process for requesting management approval to expend funds for the repair and maintenance of corporate-held properties from failed banks, and to take certain actions like entering into contracts, paying property maintenance expenses, accepting sales offers, and commencing evictions.

Shannon was presenting an operating budget case to the senior credit review committee (SCRC) for a property estimated to be valued at over a half a million dollars, so as not to waste any more time with this expensive property being held off the market. She had arranged for two current broker price opinions and suggested listing prices to present to the committee as well. When the appraisal was received, she would decide if the property would be listed with a local real estate broker or sold directly by herself. FDIC initially added all new market-ready properties to a list of available assets that was released to the public. The FDIC real estate account officers sold the properties directly to the public. As the number of bank failures increased and the number of foreclosed real estate increased, FDIC began listing the properties with local real estate brokers to advertise, show, market, and bring offers to the FDIC for consideration and acceptance. After the budget was approved, she would order the formal appraisal, environmental report, and title policy. When they were received and accepted, she would market the property for hopefully a quick sale since it was in a very desirable location.

The property case she would be presenting that day was for a file she had been given from another account officer, as were all her cases. This property was a commercial piece with a year-old appraisal of $550,000. The property was located in Cerritos, a small bedroom community just south of Los Angeles, in highly coveted Orange County, California. It was an attractive property, a small strip center with several storefront spaces and additional professional office space. It was all brick on the front and side exteriors and had semimature landscaping, which finished the property off nicely. The brick was a definite upgrade because all the surrounding office buildings were plain stucco. The property stood out prominently, and the corner location would garner great visibility for the future tenants. From Shannon's past experience with construction and zoning, she knew she had to insure there was sufficient parking for the property for it to be desirable. She had seen a few too many commercial properties fail because they had insufficient parking, and potential customers would not wait for someone to leave so they could find a parking space. Typically, the cities had tightened up on their zoning rules requiring more parking for the newer properties, and she noted that this property had more than the required number of parking spaces. She also noted that the property was vacant. For a commercial property, the primary value was usually in the income stream, the rent, paid by tenants. With no tenants, there was no income and thus a lesser value for the asset.

Shannon hadn't been able to find any information on what marketing or advertising had been done on the half-a-million-dollar property. She didn't see an operating budget case that would provide authorization and approval to expend funds for an appraisal, title report, environmental reports or to pay the property taxes, or to pay for the landscaping that surely was dying or very overgrown by then. She also couldn't find any real estate broker price opinions indicating the previous account officer had worked on the file to get the property ready to market and sell. It looked like the property had been in the previous account officer's portfolio for over six months without any activity or work being done on it. She wondered how this one had slipped through the cracks and had not been noted by either Fin Jenner or Brad Donner during the roundtable real estate property update meetings.

Shannon was still a little nervous about the SCRC meeting she was attending that afternoon. She had presented a few other cases and had received SCRC approval for the actions she recommended. She had learned from the other account officers in her group that if the cases were written well and were thorough, they usually were approved for the action requested. All the cases listed the 'bookvalue' for the property and the amount on the failed bank's books for the asset, with a separate listing for the current appraised value, and the date of the appraisal, to ensure the committee was considering current valuations. FDIC considered any appraisal approaching six months old, as not a fair indicator of its current market value because the real estate market was constantly changing, and an appraisal of six months or more was considered expired by the committee. The cases also provided a marketing summary page, detailing all offers on the subject property, the terms of the offers and the final dispositions. That way the committee could see the effort expended by the account officers, the timeliness of their actions, and the activity that had taken place on the property.

Shannon sat down in one of the chairs along the walls of the long committee room, reserved for the staff presenting cases during the senior credit review committee. She looked around the room at the many managers attending the SCRC. Ron Turner, the office managing agent, the highest-ranking official, sat at the opposite end of the table, chairing the meeting. At his right was his secretary, to take the minutes of the meeting and to his left was his special assistant. Along the sides of the table sat the various department heads from the several FDIC divisions including Brad Donner from the real estate sales department and mangers from the commercial loan, residential loan, collections and other departments. Ron Turner's assistant read from the prepared agenda.

"Ms. O'Toole is next, presenting an REO budget case."

Shannon moved from her seat along the wall to the presenter's chair at the end of the very long conference table, and smiled at Ron.

"Hello, Shannon." Ron Turner smiled down the length of the table at her. "Nice to see you again. How are you enjoying your new work here at the FDIC?" he said in a pleasant manner.

Shannon had presented a few other cases to the SCRC. She had been nervous when she presented her first case for the sale of the Malibu vacant land to a Hollywood radio station mogul. It had been a quick sale once she had placed the marketing advertisements in the local paper, and she had received multiple offers, which she had detailed in her case. She had presented a sale case for a custom million-dollar gate-guarded home in an exclusive neighborhood in Newport Beach, two commercial properties with parking and zoning issues she had cleared, and an apartment building with some complicated legal and title issues she had expunged and resolved. She had experienced very favorable responses to her sales efforts and offer acceptance recommendations from the SCRC members each time.

"I am enjoying my work very much, Mr. Turner," she answered.

"And we enjoy your cases, Shannon, and your effective efforts to unlock some of the legal issues that have kept certain properties off the market for way too long."

Shannon was flattered that the managing agent had acknowledged her efforts with the legally encumbered properties.

Ron Turner continued saying, "Our legal department tells us that you generally do their work for them, preparing draft expungements to clear exceptions from the title reports, or clearing chains of title and liens. They tell me you can resolve bankruptcy issues as well."

Shannon was pleased to hear that the legal department had accepted and approved of her legal work, although she was a little uncomfortable with all the attention, and answered, "Some of the bankruptcies permit the real estate to be dismissed from the pending BK action; others can be more protracted," she offered.

"You are still the newest account officer for REO, and we've seen you in committee often with assets that you have unraveled from the depths of the legal department's black hole. We enjoy reading well-written cases, and several of yours have been particularly well written. I think we all learn something from your discussion of the legal issues at hand, how you have resolved the matters or problems and the alternatives you propose. Keep up the good work."

Shannon could feel her face beginning to blush, and she answered the managing agent, "I appreciate your encouraging words, Mr. Turner."

"So, shall we hear the case you are presenting today, Ms. O'Toole?"

She was concerned about the budget case she was presently presenting, since it was for a property file that had not been worked on for several months by the previous REO account officer. At a minimum, an operating budget should have been prepared to pay the utilities, property taxes, appraisal and title report fees when it was first received into the REO inventory after the foreclosure. However, the previous account officer had not taken the initial steps to prepare the property for marketing, and it had been reassigned to Shannon.

She opened the manila file she had brought to the committee meeting, and began discussing the half-a-million-dollar commercial building. She detailed the proposed marketing plan and explained the information she had gained from the local real estate brokers.

"The property is in a highly desirable location in Cerritos, California, on a busy intersection with heavy traffic flow, and it has great visibility. It has a red brick exterior in contrast to the ordinary stucco exteriors in the surrounding area, which sets it apart."

"And you are requesting an operating budget of eighty thousand dollars for this property, we see," said the commercial real estate loan department head.

"Yes, you can see that the budget covers operating costs, marketing, and property taxes," she began, but before she could say anything more, the commercial real estate loan department head interrupted her.

"Why are the property taxes so high?"

"They cover past due and current property taxes," she responded in an even voice.

"Why are these property taxes overdue? Why aren't we paying them on time to avoid paying the penalties and interest?" the commercial loan department head queried her.

Shannon was a little surprised at his curt question, but he was right: paying the operating expenses was a priority to avoid needless penalties and fines.

"A portion of the property taxes was unpaid by the previous owner, and a portion was unpaid by the failed bank. We are now bringing the property taxes current with this operating budget case."

The commercial loan manager was not satisfied with this answer and continued to ask Shannon, "It looks like REO has had this asset in its inventory for over nine months now. My division foreclosed on it then, and sent it over to REO nine months ago. Why haven't we seen a case for this asset before now?"

She knew he had a valid question, but she did not have a valid answer. She didn't know why the previous account officer had not worked on the file before her. She only knew that she had received the property file three weeks ago and had ordered the broker opinion of values immediately. She did not want to get argumentative and offered,

"I've had the file for three weeks, and have received three broker opinions of value and a title preliminary report, which looks clear. The brokers suggest that the property is in a great local with high visibility and will sell quickly for about five hundred and fifty thousand, well above the book value. With the approval of the operating budget, I will immediately order a new appraisal, pay the property taxes, and order a general cleanup."

"Can you tell me if the property has been maintained during the last nine months, or has it been allowed to deteriorate?"

"It will have a general cleanup and landscaping maintenance performed once this budget is approved," she answered honestly.

The commercial loan manager made a few *hhrrgghh* sounds and then directed his next comments to Brad Donner, Shannon's department head for REO.

"Brad, can you tell me why this property had not been managed or prepared to sell for the last nine months, let alone not having its property taxes paid to avoid the penalties and interest?"

Shannon had heard that there was some tension between the loan collections division and the REO division as they competed for staffing and resources. The loan collection manager constantly complained that his staff efficiently foreclosed on the unpaid, defaulted loans in the failed banks portfolios, but the REO department sat on them too long before selling the properties. One of the issues was the amount the loan collections division paid for the property at the trustee's sale. The foreclosure bid amount was often compared to the amount the REO department sold the property for in the fair and open market. If the REO was left to deteriorate, the value would decrease, and the loan collection group would be criticized for paying too much at the foreclosure sale.

Though Shannon was glad the question had not been asked to her, she felt uncomfortable that it had been shot at her manager. Brad was ultimately responsible for his department's operations, but she still felt a little sorry for his being put on the carpet like this. Brad had been given a copy of the case before she had submitted it to the SCRC, but he had not had any questions about the case for her. She wondered then if he had even read the case or if this was one of the cases Karen had read over for him.

Brad glanced over the case in front of him and began, "Well, it may be that there were some other problems with the property—"

The commercial loan manager interrupted again. "I don't see any mention of legal problems in this case, or title restrictions, or anything else that would delay the management and sale of this property."

Brad tried again. "Well, it could be there were some other things going on, like maybe some parking or other problems…"

"This is an awfully expensive property to just have sitting around for nine months," the commercial loan officer repeated.

"Well, you know, commercial properties are more complicated than residential properties," Brad sputtered.

This time Ron Turner spoke up. "Tell you what, Brad. We're going to approve this budget so Shannon can pay the property taxes and stop the interest from accruing, avoid any further penalties, and get the property ready to market. But I want you to report back to me what delayed the managing and marketing of this property before Shannon received it and who was supposed to be managing it."

Shannon wanted to save Brad from further embarrassment but didn't want to say anything to antagonize the committee.

"When do you think you will be able to market and sell this property, Shannon?" Ron Turner asked.

She tried to redirect the committee's attention to the positive nature of her case.

"I anticipate bringing a full-price offer to committee in a few weeks," she said confidently.

"Well, that certainly is the best answer we've heard today," grumbled the commercial loan manager, and the meeting was adjourned.

Later that afternoon, Shannon saw Brad bring Ken Ito and Fin Jenner into his office. A few minutes later, Ken walked by her cubicle and slapped the side hard to make a loud noise that startled Shannon, and she jumped in her chair and turned around to see a very angry Ken glaring at her.

"Don't *ever* embarrass me like that again," he spat out.

"What are you talking about?" Shannon exclaimed.

"You know damn well what I'm talking about," he said and glared at her with narrowed eyes.

"Ken, I *don't* know what you are talking about," he eyed him squarely, now annoyed at his threatening behavior.

"In committee, not covering for me with the Cerritos property."

She understood then, his embarrassment and anger. She had barely given any thought to who the previous account officer had been for the property. Now she knew it was Ken. She had been focused on getting done what she could to get the property ready to market. In reality, several of her new portfolio of assets had been Ken's, and none of them had had operating budgets written or legal follow-up where warranted.

"Ken, I didn't say anything in committee about you," she responded evenly.

"Yeah, well, you didn't have to. Brad just called me into his office and reamed me royally. You could have said something about me working on the file with you or helping you or something. But you didn't."

"Ken, you gave me the file. Remember? Did you have any cases or budgets in the file that I missed?"

"That's not the point."

Shannon didn't think there was anything she could say that would make Ken less angry. He leaned toward her and continued to glare and then turned and stomped away.

The team chief position was posted and went to another candidate, Ken Ito, since Karen couldn't be promoted in order to protect Brad's career. Ken was married to a woman who stayed home with their two children, and she catered to and supported Ken. Ken often spoke about the lists of tasks he left for his wife to complete, so that when he came home he didn't have to be bothered with domestic chores. He boasted that his work was in the office, and only in the office.

To establish his new control over the FDIC real estate group, Ken "redistributed" the files according to skills level and ability. That meant that the other officers got 25-45 files, and Shannon got 50-75, including most of the "Black Hole" legal cases.

When Shannon received her new portfolio of real estate assets to work, she was more than a little surprised at the load that had been bestowed upon her. She was further concerned to find that the majority of files had legal problems that had not been updated or resolved by the other FDIC account officers who had previously worked on the assets. That would mean that her portfolio would quickly become "stale" without new activity, and she would be answering to FDIC Washington DC about why the properties were not ready to market to the public. She was inheriting the other account officers' oldest and most legally encumbered files. She was going to have to unlock the legal department's deadlock on these cases, and she was going to have to do it fast, because these cases had been sitting around unworked for several months.

Since this was the first remix and redistribution of the real estate files by the new team chief, she thought there may have been an oversight or mistake with the allocations and decided she would check. She knocked on Ken's door when it appeared that he wasn't busy.

"Hi, Ken. Got a minute?"

"Sure, yeah, come on in, but my carpool is leaving in ten minutes," he said abruptly.

She was a little taken aback by his tone, but proceeded conversationally with,

"Oh, when did you start the carpool?"

"Uh, last week."

She tried to think of something neutral to say and remembered another colleague's description of the corporate vans that carried up to ten people. "I've heard the corporate vans are really comfortable. Do you have to make a lot of stops?"

"No, it's just two of us. Me and Mat."

Oh, she thought—Mat Pham, his friend from kindergarten and the same friend he had been in business with before he came to the FDIC who had a much lighter case load than she did. Ken and Mat had tried to operate a mortgage broker business, taking loan applications and then placing them with various lenders to earn a commission. But the business had not been successful, and Ken had found his position with FDIC and brought Mat in as soon as he could.

Before she could answer, Ken continued, "But, uh, you probably wanted to talk to me about something else, right?" he cut her off.

"Well, yes." She tried to smile but found it difficult. "I wanted to discuss the portfolio distribution with you if you have time." *There now*, she thought. *That was pretty benign and not negative. Let him pick up the ball and explain how he distributed the files.*

"What about the portfolios?" he answered, again abruptly.

"Well, I seem to have a more files than the other account officers..." she began.

"And you can't handle it?" he finished for her.

"No, that's not the issue," she replied firmly but quietly. "I'm concerned that many of the files have legal issues, and they all need immediate budgets and cases to be written, and that with the double number of files I'm carrying now..."

Ken cut her off again and leaned back in his chair, crossing his legs at the ankle. "You don't have double the number of files, not really. Some of your files are inactive, aren't they? So they don't count."

"If you mean that they have legal issues or they need appraisals or title policies and other documents, that is correct. But you know, Ken, that it takes longer to unwind the legal issues and to order, review, and track the start-up documents for a new file. It takes a lot longer to start up a new file than to monitor an active case that is listed with a broker."

"Like I said, if you can't complete your assignments..." Ken seemed to be enjoying himself.

Shannon tried again. "Ken, I've noticed that a large number of my new files have lien redemption rights where the previous account officers didn't take any redemption actions..."

"What are you talking about? I mean, we don't do that here," Ken interrupted.

Shannon flinched this time. "I think there are federal and state rules and laws about that..." she began, and Ken stopped her.

"What do you mean, redemption rights?"

Shannon tried to remain calm, although Ken seemed to be badgering her. "It is federal law that when an agency, say the IRS, places a lien against a property, they are supposed to be notified if there is a sale or foreclosure pending on the property so they can respond with their payoff demand or, in the case of foreclosure, decide if they want to bid at the foreclosure sale and purchase the asset and then resell it for their lien recovery value," she began to explain. "There are numerous states that have redemption rights through which the previous owner can 'buy back' their foreclosed property for up to six months or more, and we can't sell the property during the redemption period."

"I've never seen that before," he retorted.

"The IRS has certain 'redemption rights' they can exercise wherein they can come back after the foreclosure sale and purchase the property from the person who bought the property at the foreclosure sale."

"No one else at the FDIC has ever discussed any redemption rights," Ken snorted.

"I don't know how often the IRS bids at our FDIC foreclosure auctions..." she started, and then Ken jumped in.

"We don't get involved in that sort of thing. I want you to drop it now. What else did you want to talk to me about?"

She was taken aback at Ken's abrupt response and attitude about the government liens, but continued with her concerns about the volume of her workload.

Ken barely listened. "You had better take another look at your portfolio. I don't think there's any problem." He stood up to get ready to leave his office and catch a ride home with Mat.

Shannon wondered why he was so upset with her. Was it the commercial building case she had taken to the senior credit review committee, and he was still carrying a grudge? He hadn't worked the property, and she hadn't lied for him. She thought to herself, *The government even pays for his gas because he and Mat listed themselves as a carpool! How convenient.*

Shannon stayed late again that night, reviewing some additional new cases that Ken had assigned to her that day, delighting in telling her that the senior credit review committee had asked him about them that day and were expecting a fast case submitted for their review.

She opened the first file and noticed the high book value, the amount of unpaid loan balance the failed bank had on its books, of nearly a million dollars. The property was a three-story, oceanfront house located on Balboa Island, Newport Beach, California, near the famous Wedge surfing beach. It had been the home of a well-known rock-and-roll surf guitarist, whose music she had danced to as a teenager. The home also had a dock floating out into the canal that led directly out to the Pacific Ocean.

It was another gem of a property, and she was surprised it was still in the FDIC's inventory of unsold properties. The old appraisal in the file showed custom mosaic tiles on the floors, a beautiful curving staircase, and one room with mirrors on the walls and ceiling. She noted that the property had been handled by a male colleague who had made an exorbitant number of 'field' visits to the ocean front property, but somehow, was not able to sell it. His signature was on the REO reports, and a female property inspector's signature was on the property management inspection reports on the same days. The property seemed to have been inspected weekly and jointly. They had been visiting the beach property together for the last nine months, but the property had never been marketed or put on the market to sell to the public.

Shannon didn't need to think any longer about the tryst that the FDIC managers had missed or tolerated for so long—she didn't know which—and ordered a new updated appraisal for the property and updated brokers' opinions of value, as the previous were over a year old. Immediately, she was informed by the brokers that the property was worth over a million dollars, even though its' current condition was abundant with deferred maintenance. They advised it would sell very quickly due to its' attached private boat dock and ocean front location. Another very expensive property that had not been managed well although it was a highly visible and marketable property, it had been instead used as a lovers' meeting place. Shannon sketched out a case for the senior credit review committee detailing the new value, real estate listing, and public marketing that would commence within five days, which later resulted in a sale the same week.

Shannon ended up working late nearly every night or brought work home just to stay current on her bulging portfolio. When she approached the FDIC attorneys with her request for office appointments to discuss the pending litigation cases, they were very receptive. She discovered that her previous experience working for real estate law firms prepared her to summarize the subject litigation and lay out the options and alternatives, which she could then discuss with the attorneys and then plan the best legal strategies with timelines to complete the pending litigation. She wrote cases that were thorough and well written, to convey her rationale for recommending various actions to be taken for the particular property. She was actually unwinding the litigation that had encumbered these assets for months and even years. Each case was a unique challenge: sometimes a first right of refusal, sometimes an encroachment, often liens that affected the title to the property. She enjoyed the challenges and the satisfaction of resolving each of the cases.

She had just unwound a lis pendens against a desirable property on a bluff overlooking the Dana Point Harbor in Southern California, and the city had placed liens for weed abatement on the parcel. The lis pendens had been placed but not perfected, by a contractor who alleged that he was owed payment for work he had performed on the parcel. However, after much research and negotiations, it was determined that he had done the work on an adjacent neighbor's property and erroneously extended the work onto Shannon's parcel, without approval or filing required notices for mechanics' liens. Shannon was able to negotiate payment with the city for the weed abatements and have the lis pendens expunged, or removed, clearing the title to the property.

With the title now clear, the property was ready to market and sell. It was a beautiful piece of land, overlooking the Pacific Ocean and the Dana Point harbor, with unobstructed views clear to the horizon. The bluff was about two hundred feet above the ocean, creating magnificent vistas. From the property, a person could watch the sailboats leave the harbor and navigate out into the ocean, with flocks of seagulls and pelicans often trailing. Or watch the old wooden tall ships come in and out of the harbor, with their impressive masts and sails. The ocean reflected the sky, a different color each day. The currents drew beautiful curved lines and designs in the water. And clouds floated gently on the sea breeze. She knew the property well, as she often kayaked in the harbor below. It had an old shack on the property that had no value and would need to be removed before it became a hazard and potential liability. It was a level parcel, over an acre in size, and would be suitable for a commercial bed and breakfast, inn or hotel. The very popular Quiet Cannon and Chart House restaurants were next door. Shannon was laying out a marketing brochure for the property, including pictures from the current appraisal and detailed legal description. She had started a case to present to the SCRC for approval to sell the property and pay the city for the weed abatements and removal of the shack.

Ken came by Shannon's cubicle after lunch.

"Uh, Shannon, come to my office when you're done with that file."

Shannon looked up from her work, surprised to see Ken standing there, and said, "All right, I'll be right there."

She closed the file she was working on, and walked over to Ken's office.

"Come on in," he offered, "and close the door."

She didn't like the "close the door" part, but couldn't think of anything she might have done to cause a problem.

Ken continued, "I've been reading over some of your cases here," he indicated a stack of paperwork on his desk, "And I want to talk to you about your case writing."

"OK," she answered tentatively.

"I think that you seem to go on too much, they are too long, and there's too much information in here that is not useful," he began.

She was surprised. The committee chairman, Ron Turner, several grades higher than Ken, had always complimented her on her case writing, her analysis, and thoroughness. She worked well with the legal department, getting their consensus and often their sign-off on her cases when they contained litigation workouts.

"I'm surprised, Ken," she began. "I usually have legal review my cases if they are involved with the asset, and they have never said anything about changing the cases."

"Well, I don't care what legal thinks," he began curtly. "I'm telling you that we don't need all this extra information, and I think you should leave it out."

"Maybe my cases are longer because they usually involve legal problems and activity. But I can certainly try to condense the information."

"Condense it or just leave it out," he challenged.

"SCRC always wants to know why a property wasn't offered for sale, so I give them an explanation of the legal issues that delayed the sale."

"You don't have to go into so much detail," he growled.

She didn't want to argue with Ken and offered, "All right, maybe it's my legal training that sets my writing standards and my cases apart from the others, but if you want the cases to be shorter, then that's what I'll do."

"Good." He seemed satisfied with her answer. "And listen Shannon," he continued, "I just don't want the cases coming out of my section looking inconsistent. And your cases are clearly different. You are kind of making the rest of the account officers look bad. I want everyone's cases to be consistent, all right?"

She wasn't really sure that she had heard him correctly, but it sounded like he wanted her to write a weaker case and stop doing such a thorough job, so she would be writing at the same level as the other staff in her group. It was clear that he didn't want her to continue writing the same style case she had been submitting to committee for the last year.

Just then, Mat Pham knocked quickly and stuck his head in the door of Ken's office.

"Excuse me, Shannon. Ken, I just need to know if you've approved those budget cases I gave you yesterday."

"Sure, Mat," Ken answered quickly, as he reached below the stack of Shannon's cases and handed Mat about six or eight cases he had approved and signed off.

"Thanks, Ken, and sorry to interrupt your meeting, Shannon."

She gave Mat a small smile. When Mat had left the office and closed the door behind him, Shannon turned to Ken.

"You have a couple of my cases there too," she said, indicating the stack in front of him. "I'm afraid they are going to get stale since they've been here for about a week now, and I'd like to get them into committee this week." She also didn't want to rewrite the several cases he had had on his desk for over a week.

As she feared, he pushed her cases toward her and said,

"Here. Why don't you start with these cases and change them? I want to see them more simplified."

"Couldn't we start with any new cases I write?" she asked. "I have about four new cases I'm writing now, and I can work on them to simplify them for your review," she offered.

"No, I don't think so," Ken countered. "I want you to re-write these cases now."

Shannon knew that rewriting the cases would put her several days behind and would delay her handling of the other cases needing attention on her desk. But she didn't seem to have any choice.

She reached out and picked up her cases from Ken's desk and started to leave his office.

"I would like to see those cases back in here by the end of this week," he said evenly.

She didn't even look back at Ken, she just said, "I'll try."

Later that week, Ken and Brad announced a new "performance evaluation program" by which all the account officers would be measured and ranked for most productivity. The criterion was the number of cases each account officer wrote and had approved by Ken.

Mat Pham was the top producer.

❦

"Did you hear that our department is getting a new account officer liquidation-grade LG thirteen position?" Tanya asked Shannon, as she slid into Shannon's cubicle carrying a cup of steaming coffee and leaned against Shannon's desk.

Shannon's small cubicle office held the standard desk and overhead storage unit; however, what was unusual about Shannon's area were the two additional four-drawer file cabinets she squeezed into her cubicle to hold the additional files she managed, while most of the other grade-twelve real estate officers could keep their workload in their desk drawers.

"No, I hadn't heard," Shannon answered curiously. "Tell me about it."

"Well, I just heard that the new organizational charts are coming down from Washington, DC, and our department is getting a new grade thirteen. And I hear it's a two-year contract instead of the usual one-year contracts we have now. You should go for it, you know, because of the extra load of files you carry. You deserve it."

"Right. I know about the extra work. Sometimes I think I live here at the office instead of home, but we also know how the FDIC 'Old boys Club' works too, Tanya," Shannon sarcastically answered.

"That's true, but this time you can use your case numbers, and they can't mess with the numbers, you know."

"No, they may not be able to change the numbers around, but they can still play politics and favorites."

Tanya leaned forward toward Shannon and whispered, "Ken and Brad are so mean. They just torture you with all the extra work and problem files and then the extra projects. I'm telling you, Shannon, they just don't like smart women, especially one as smart as you. You threaten them, you know. I'm not a threat to them because I just do my work, keep my files up to date, and follow the rules. That way, they just leave me alone."

Shannon smiled at her new best friend in the office, understanding fully well how Tanya operated. "You can do that, Tanya, because you don't have to play 'catch up' the way I do. Almost all of my files were with other account officers before they were reassigned to me, and have legal issues, encumbered titles, evictions, liens or other problems. And I volunteer to work on the failed bank closings because I need the money. When you were divorced, you received a settlement, remember, and enough money to put a down payment on your house and some in the bank too. I, on the other hand, came out of a seventeen year marriage with $10,000 of debt, and no child support. So I have to ride a faster horse to try to get ahead and catch up. And I still can't contribute to the 401k retirement plan yet, I need all of my salary to take care of the kids. You know that."

"Oh, I know." Tanya sighed. "I just wish they would give you the recognition and grade thirteen that you deserve. It's only right."

"Well, thanks for your support, Tanya." She smiled and pulled another file from her crowded file drawer to begin working.

Later that night, Shannon stayed late and decided to work on her application for the LG grade-thirteen promotion since her daughter was at ballet class and wouldn't miss her. She listed the extra volume of caseload she carried and listed her successful closed files for the last year, knowing that she had the best and strongest performance record in the department, despite Ken's attempts to hold back her cases and make her rewrite them. After feeling that her application was as good as it could be, she began to think that there might be a chance of her actually getting the promotion. Her application and reputation with the legal department and committee were very strong as well.

The next day, Shannon approached Ken with her application for the LG grade 13 and asked him to sign it off. He looked at her with apprehension.

"Uh, there's no grade thirteen available right now," he advised her.

"Oh, well, that's not what our new organization chart shows," she answered directly and remembered to smile even though she was beginning to have a pain in her stomach again from his confrontations.

"No, there's no opening now," he repeated. "There may be a grade thirteen on the org chart, but we've decided to hold it for a while."

"Why are you holding it?" she asked, confused.

"Well, Brad and I just think that this isn't the time to post the position."

"Do you know when it will be posted?" she asked.

"No, but not for a couple of months at least."

Shannon also knew that the much-coveted GG, or government grade, positions were about to be released. The GG positions were career positions, offering permanent government status with full retirement benefits, whereas the LG, or liquidation-grade employee, as Shannon was, was a year-to-year employment contract. Shannon also knew that her supervisor's recommendation had to be obtained to apply for the much-sought-after GG positions.

"Ken," she began again, "I would like to post for one of the GG positions when they become available. It would give me more security, with a GG permanent position. I need to know where I will be working down the road."

"You know the Federal Deposit Insurance Corporation hires mostly LGs, or Liquidation grade staff. They want to be able to downsize at any time since they never know which or how many banks are going to fail. The GG is a special grade and is usually not handed out lightly. It could require travel and even relocation. Besides, you're a single mother, and you shouldn't be traveling with Jennifer at home and so young."

Once again, Shannon bristled at Ken's arrogant behavior toward her and his out-of-line opinions. "I have carefully considered the possibility of travel and reassignment, Ken, and I think I can make my own good decisions regarding my career and Jennifer's well-being. Besides, I travel a lot now on the bank closings and to handle the inspections for the properties in my portfolio. I think converting to GG would be a good career move, and I would like your support."

"I'm going to be honest with you, Shannon. I don't like the idea of you converting to GG for the reason I've already given you, and I would have a hard time, in good conscience, making such a recommendation. Why don't you concentrate on your at-home and personal life instead of making such a big deal out of a career. You know what I mean?"

Shannon stiffened, and responded, "You know, Ken, if I choose to pursue a career as a GG, then that's my choice."

She began to leave his office when he responded, "I meant what I said, I am not willing to make the supervisor's recommendation. You are a single mother, and I don't think you should be thinking about converting to a GG."

Shannon left his office, and again realized that the chauvinistic ideas and sexual attitudes at the FDIC were larger hurdles than she had imagined, and she tried hard to hold back her tears of frustration. She didn't understand why they would hold back on posting the new higher LG grade-thirteen position until a few months later, when Ken hired another one of his friends, Farley Tripp, also his neighbor and colleague he had been in business with in addition to Mat Pham. Farley, Mat, and Ken had all lived on the same street or within a couple of blocks from each other for many years. Farley was the third partner that had operated the now-defunct mortgage business that had failed prior to Ken's joining the FDIC and then bringing in Mat and now Farley. Farley was given the LG grade-thirteen position, while the women all remained in LG-twelve positions.

Farley was a short, round, balding man who would come into the female account officers' cubicles and visit with them, asking them about their love lives and their current boyfriends. Shannon tried to avoid him, but it was not always possible.

Farley walked by Shannon's cubicle one Monday morning, and sat down. He leaned close to her chair, and said in a low, presumable caring voice, "Hey, are you OK today? You look kind of sad."

Shannon looked at Farley, and felt that he had no business asking her anything, especially since she knew he was really insincere, and Tanya had told her she had overhead Farley repeating things other women had told him to Ken and Mat.

"You know, you kind of wear your heart on your sleeve," he told her, observing her like a hawk.

"Well, you know Farley," she said slowly, "I guess I just need a wife like you have. You know, someone to cook and clean and have the kids ready for bed when I get home. Maybe that would help." She hoped that by giving him a sarcastic answer he would go away.

"Or maybe you just need a man," he leered.

Shannon's eyes narrowed, and she gave him a drop-dead look. He took the hint and left her office, smirking.

Ken announced that he was going to redistribute the real estate files again. Shannon had worked diligently and many long hours to get the litigation cleared from the assets by working closely with the legal department. Ken would call Shannon into his office and ask her how certain litigation processes worked, and what laws or statutes applied to legislation, and about title expungements. He took the clean or cleared files and transferred them to the men and took the encumbered files that required a lot of cleanup work and gave them to the women.

Tanya came into Shannon's cubicle and sat down, rubbing her tired shoulder. "Well, did you get your new portfolio files from Ken yet?" she asked in a grumpy voice.

"Oh, yeah," Shannon answered. "I got a lot of stale files where the guys didn't order the appraisals and title reports for a few months or left the legal problems without even trying to approach FDIC legal for resolution. They just sent the case upstairs and never followed up."

"I know," Tanya fumed. "I've got a bunch of stupid vacant land that needs to be listed, and the appraisals are all ready to expire. I don't know what these guys were doing or, rather, *not* doing with these properties. You know, Shannon, we just don't have the right equipment," Tanya quipped, putting her index finger out straight and wiggling it in front of her groin. "I guess it takes one of these if you're to be treated fairly."

"Why don't you file an EEO complaint? You certainly have the grounds after Ken's harassment and the size of your portfolio, just to name two things."

"Because winning an EEO award is only a couple of years' salary; I would rather have a lifelong career. Anyplace I would want to work for later, would see me as a problem person, and I don't want that. So I have to work a little harder, Tanya. I guess I'm used to it."

"It's not right."

"I know, but I have Jennifer to support, and Toby is in college. I can't take the chance of ruining my future career opportunities. FDIC is not forgiving."

"You know more than they do about the legal cases, and you write better than any of them. Do you have to work late again tonight?"

"Yes. I'll be here about an hour or two to get these cases done while Jenny is at ballet, but it will make tomorrow that much easier."

"You're working late a couple nights a week now, aren't you?"

"I have to, Tanya. I usually take the work home so I can be with Jenny. There's no way to keep up with my load any other way."

Shannon dug into her new stack of properties previously handled by Ken's old friends, Mat and Farley, and the other men in her department, and again became interested in a trend she was finding concerning government liens placed against the failed bank real estate owned (REO) properties. She noticed that government agencies like the Small Business Administration (SBA), U.S. Dept. of Housing and Urban Development (HUD), California State Franchise Tax Board and the IRS had placed liens against the owners' property while they still owned the asset. These liens might have been placed voluntarily with the permission of the debtor who borrowed the money as collateral for the loan, as an advanced partial claim, or involuntarily, when the debtor stopped paying on the government loan or when the previous owner of the property didn't pay his or her taxes.

Shannon knew that the current real estate law provided that each of the government agencies were to be sent notice of the pending foreclosure, so they could determine what action they should take regarding collection of their lien/loan money from the property.

If the property were being sold through a regular real estate sale transaction, the title to the property could not be cleared or transferred to a new owner until the government lien was either paid off or would be paid off from the proceeds of the sale. However, when the property was *foreclosed* on, the government liens were then wiped out, or erased from the title, and canceled by the foreclosure process. The money owed to the government agency from the equity in the real property was no longer a lien against the property, but the debtor was usually still responsible for the loan or debt. For instance, the IRS would continue to pursue a debtor for ten years to recover their tax lien money when, in fact, the IRS could have bid for the property at the foreclosure sale, purchased it, and then resold it to recover their lien. The other government agencies had the same opportunity to purchase the property at foreclosure sale and resell it to recover their government lien money.

Shannon also knew that the law provided that the IRS could redeem the property for *120 days following the foreclosure sale. That meant that for 120 days after the day of the foreclosure, the IRS could come back to whoever bought the property at the foreclosure sale, and buy the property back for the same amount paid at the foreclosure sale*, and resell the property to recover the IRS tax debt. However, she knew that the IRS rarely redeemed their properties; in fact, she had never seen them purchase a property at foreclosure or redeem a property with an IRS tax lien against it since she had worked at the FDIC. She had never seen any government agency purchase a property at foreclosure to recover its government loan money. The taxpayers were not getting a fair return or service by these nonresponsive government agencies.

The government agencies were allowing the banks to foreclose on properties where the government agencies had a lien interest for an unpaid debt, and by not exercising the agencies' rights to recover or redeem the properties and thus recover their lien amount, the banks or buyers of the properties at foreclosure were keeping all the equity that should have gone to the government agencies, back to the US and California State Treasuries, and thus reduce the state or national debt.

Shannon had watched this failure of government agencies to act to recover their lien money through foreclosures for over four years, and she estimated that the amount of unclaimed lien repayments to state and federal governments was in the billions of dollars every year.

She considered her previous conversation with Ken about property liens and redemption rights, but decided to approach him with a different angle with her thoughts about the unclaimed government liens. She knocked lightly on his office door.

"Yeah, what is it?" Ken barked out without looking up from the newspaper he was reading while sitting with his heels crossed on his desk.

"Ken, I have been going through the new files you just assigned to me, and I see a pattern concerning government liens against some of the foreclosed properties that I'd like to discuss."

"So, what do you want?"

Shannon wasn't happy with Ken's lack of interest or rude behavior, but continued with her question, "In your experience here at the FDIC or before, with your mortgage business, did you ever have a government agency redeem a foreclosed property or otherwise try to get their lien money from the property?"

"What are you getting at?"

"I have been watching the preliminary title reports and trustees' sale guarantees come across my desk, and have noticed the various government liens from, say, the IRS, the SBA, and California State Franchise Tax Board, for example. These agencies have billions of dollars in liens against the foreclosed properties from the failed banks, and yet I don't see one government agency coming forward to redeem the property or bid at the foreclosure sale to recover their lien amount and debt. Do you know if FDIC is sending the required notice to these agencies before we foreclose on a defaulted loan, or have you ever had a government agency act on recovering their debt from a foreclosure?" she asked.

"Don't start putting your nose into the FDIC loan foreclosure process!" Ken roared. "And, no, I never have seen any liens paid, and I doubt I ever will. If you just stay quiet, and don't say anything or try to contact the government agencies, their liens will be removed from the property title after foreclosure. That's all I care about—getting the property title clear and ready to sell."

Ken seemed to be finished, but then he continued. "And don't start nosing around the loan collection and foreclosure department asking questions, or go calling any of those government agencies or start trying to negotiate with them to redeem any FDIC controlled properties, because I don't want you wasting time, and because it's not your job to do that. You just stay quiet until the government liens are expired or erased from the title to the property. I don't care if the IRS chases a guy for the next twenty years, it really doesn't matter to me. I just don't want you taking it upon yourself to notify those agencies and try to start something, understand me?" He slapped his newspaper on his desk, and glared at Shannon, anticipating her agreement.

"It doesn't seem right, that's illegal," she began and was quickly cut off by Ken.

"I don't care what you think is right. I'm telling you to just drop it, right here and now."

She looked at the narrow-minded man, frustrated that he hadn't even listened to her comments before he issued his directive to ignore her findings.

Shannon felt the hot tears burn behind her eyes, her usual response to an unfair situation that she couldn't change. The unfairness of Ken's demands, the nepotism and preference for the male staff in her department, the nearly double caseload assignments, and the unethical and very sexually suggestive behavior exhibited by the managers toward the young women that Mike and Brad had recently hired as their secretaries were no longer tolerable. She felt that the behavior of the real estate managers and especially Ken's behavior toward her were insurmountable, and she needed to make a change.

∽

FDIC brought in a new EEO person, for the purpose of making a supposedly unbiased person available to staff on any equal employment complaint issue. New posters had been hung around the office announcing the new EEO officer's services and office hours. Pamphlets had been given to each employee discussing FDIC's corporate message for no tolerance for sexual harassment or violation of equal employment rules.

Tanya came by Shannon's cubicle and waved one of the new EEO pamplets at her,

"You know, you should go and talk to this guy. He's supposed to be impartial and unbiased. I think you should make an appointment."

Shannon looked up at her good friend from a case she was writing and answered,

"Tanya, I told you that I want a long, successful career..."

"I understand tht, but you could at least ask for some input, some information, and then decide what you want to do, if anything."

"I have work to do," Shannon smiled and waved away her friend, and returned to the case she was writing.

After evaluating the intolerable conditions, Shannon concluded that she would consider asking the advice of the new EEO officer. She sought out the new equal employment officer, Harold Jackson, only to find out that this avenue was also unavailable.

She tried for three weeks to make an appointment with the EEO officer, but never received a return call to set an appointment. Shannon walked over to the facility area where Harry's office was located, and ran into another good friend, Sara Leon, one of the FDIC receptionists, and a very vivacious, friendly redhead.

"Who are you looking for?" she smiled at Shannon.

"I'm trying to find Harry," Shannon answered. "I've been trying to get a hold of him all week, and he hasn't returned my calls. Do you know if he is in?"

"Oh, Harry, huh. I think he's out for a while—out of his mind, I think."

"Excuse me?"

"Well, you know what he's done, don't you?" Sara asked.

"I guess not, because I thought he was here."

"Well, you know Maria, the other receptionist?"

"Of course I do, Sara. She's a sweetheart. She's young, single, cute, maybe a little naive, and is raising at least two kids on her own. She's always so helpful and positive up at the front desk. I've had several clients comment on how pleasant she is. She's a good kid."

"Yes, she is. And she's pregnant."

"Maria? No way. She's sort of pious; she's always going to church and going to events with her kids at school."

"It's true. I work with her. And she's really torn up about it. She doesn't know if she'll have the baby or not, or put it up for addoption. I think abortion is probably out of the question for her, but then she'll have to explain it to her kids and go through the whole thing here at work."

"How, I mean, who—" Shannon stumbled.

"Who?" Sara exclaimed in an angry voice. "It's Harold, the sterile EEO officer, of course! The creep transferred here a few months ago and started hanging around Maria. I was working at the front desk with her, and he just kept hanging around her all the time, and then he started taking her out to dinner after work, and obviously he took her someplace nice and quiet too."

"What's this about him being sterile?"

"He told Maria he was sterile, and had been for a long time. I guess Maria thought he was serious about her and was considering marrying him. She wanted a father for her kids so much, you know. And she was struggling so hard, to make it on her salary and pay all the bills and raise her kids. She's had it really hard on her own, and he seemed to say all the right things to make her think he was her knight in shining armor. Except he was really just a horny old man!"

"Do you mean he's not taking responsibility?"

"I know he denied making Maria pregnant at first. But now he's admitted his affair with her, and I don't know what they are going to do about the baby."

Shannon shook her head. She looked at the irony of the whole situation.

"Now let me get this right. I'm here to see Harry, our revered EEO officer, who is supposed to be righteous and ethical and represent us as employees if there should be any allegations of sexual harassment or other unfair labor practices. Except he's not available because, as a sterile man, he just got our little receptionist pregnant?! This is obscene."

Sara widened her eyes. "Yup, that's our one and only EEO officer, all right!"

5

Singles Dating

Jennifer had made plans to spend the night at her girlfriend's house, and Shannon's friends decided to set her up with a blind date, Peter, from New York. Shannon had objected with excuses like "I don't have time for dating," "I need to get caught up on my work," and the classic "I don't have anything to wear." But her friends persisted, and she was soon looking at the clock, anticipating the New Yorker's arrival to take her to dinner. But she had had early concerns when he had first called, and she could barely understand him with his strong New York accent.

Peter was of medium height with tight, curly brown hair, a tweed jacket, a big smile, and a whiny, nasal accent that began grating on Shannon's usually calm nerves immediately. He began to sneeze the minute he entered the house, looked around, and spotted the gray and white cat, Buckwheat.

"Uh, I didn't know you had a cat," he wheezed. "You never mentioned it on the phone."

"I don't think you asked," she responded evenly.

"Yeah, I get kind of congested, and my eyes get watery—" but he didn't have time to finish his sentence when Buckwheat the cat started to wretch and gag near his foot. Peter jumped back and said, "What is he doing? What's the matter?"

Shannon looked down at Buckwheat, who was now choking with his entire body jerking and was making loud, coughing noises.

Peter said loudly, "Is he dying?"

At that moment, Buckwheat erupted with the largest hairball Shannon had ever seen him emit, which barely missed Peter's shiny shoe—and he had emitted some pretty large hairballs in the past.

"Ewwwwww, what is THAT?" Peter exploded.

Shannon felt herself start to giggle, then she couldn't hold it back any longer, and she laughed out loud. "I think he likes you. He's been saving that up all day."

They went to dinner at a New York-style deli, listened to a little music, and then, mercifully, the evening was nearly over. When Peter returned Shannon home, he asked for a cup of coffee, which she reluctantly prepared for him while trying to hide her yawns. He just wouldn't stop talking—about New York, about himself, about his work, his sports, his...

But he was stopped in midsentence when Buckwheat raced full speed across the room, flew into the air over the couch where he sat, landed next to Peter's head, took a swat at a moth on the wall, and then drug her claws all the way down the wall while pulling the moth in her mouth as she fell. The moth flapped its wings frantically, and landed heavily in Peter's lap. Peter jumped up and spilled his coffee, and Shannon helped him make a fast exit.

6

Closing Failed Banks FDIC Style

Shannon was chosen for a large Southern California bank closing assignment in Los Angeles County, California. She had made arrangements with her mother to have Jennifer spend the weekend with her grandmother so Shannon could work on the bank failure project.

When FDIC staff was chosen for a bank closing, they made reservations at a hotel close to the failed bank under a pseudo name, such as a travel agency or marketing agency, so as not to alert the local community that there was a bank closing about to occur. It was also to prevent a run on the bank, where the majority of its customers would panic and withdraw their cash. This would further reduce the capital of the bank and its value if it lost its' depositors. Before closing the bank, FDIC would try to sell it to another lending institution, in whole, or in parts. They would offer portfolios of real estate, commercial loans, car loans, credit card loans, mortgage loans, and the like. Selling the failing bank as a whole was the least disruptive to the community and depositors. The Office of Thrift Supervision (OTS) and the comptroller of the currency continued to monitor the financial condition of the failing lender. If there were no takers, the bank was declared insolvent, and the FDIC staff was scheduled to close the bank, usually on Friday evenings when the bank normally closed.

Just before six o'clock on Friday evening, Shannon's team of about eighteen FDIC staff entered the bank in Los Angeles in their business suits, each carrying a briefcase, reports on the failed bank, general ledger statements, loan stratification reports, and other bank reports. The FDIC closing manager had entered the bank an hour earlier and had explained to the bank manager the closing process that was about to occur. Often, the bank manager knew the FDIC was coming in and had been present at meetings with the bank's top executives, when the FDIC advised them they were approaching insolvency and had to raise new capital or be closed by the FDIC.

The bank manager and FDIC closing manager locked the bank doors, and asked the thirty bank employees to gather around. By then, the employees were very concerned, and a few began to cry.

The bank manager began. "I want to thank each one of you for giving your all to our efforts to make this bank a successful venture. Your hard work and dedication have made us a community asset. However, our present loan loss situation has caused us to become insolvent, and the FDIC is here now to close this bank."

With that announcement, more employees began to cry, and placed their arms around each other. The bank staff were now facing the uncertainty of losing their jobs without any previous knowledge or notice.

The FDIC closing manager then spoke,

"We will all be working together now, and we ask you to call home if you need to and stay an extra hour or so to help us count out the cash and deposits for today. We will try to balance all accounts through the weekend and, hopefully, open up on Monday morning with a new name. FDIC has been trying to sell this bank's assets to another bank, and if we can complete the transaction, you will all be asked to come back to work here on Monday as an employee of the new assuming bank."

With that announcement, there was an audible sigh from the majority of the bank staff.

"You'll also be talking with the FDIC people here now to discuss your responsibilities and the work you do, so please share with them your reports and knowledge about the accounts and assets you manage. Your assistance is needed to make this transaction run smoothly and successfully."

The bank staff began to move off and make calls to their friends and family, telling them about this unexpected turn of events, and that they would be home late that night.

As was customary, Shannon talked with employees of the failed bank and asked to see their files on real estate the bank had foreclosed on and any real estate litigation files. She reviewed the files and the underlying loans that had been the demise of the failed bank, as they made loans based upon inflated values. Then when the property was foreclosed on by the bank, they could not sell the property for the amount of the loan. They took large losses, and were required to increase their loan loss reserves by the FDIC and Office of Thrift Supervision (OTS).

After reviewing the failed bank records and real estate files, Shannon became interested in one particular piece of property. It was a twelve-unit apartment building that was in the process of being converted into condominiums, and they were located on Los Alamitos Bay in Long Beach, California. The only thing between the condominiums and the water was a six-foot-wide dock, where the owners of the condominiums could dock their boats. Looking out the windows of the condominiums, a person had to look at and through the sailboats and power boats docked only a few feet from the units to enjoy the calm blue waters of the bay.

Shannon recognized the potential value in the twelve-unit property if the condominium conversation was completed. The property would be worth several million dollars if completed, and they were 95 percent done. She would order a formal appraisal and write a case for the senior credit review committee to retain and complete the conversion of the property, and an estimated budget for the required remaining construction, including floor covering and electrical work.

She worked well into the night and throughout the weekend, looking over the other fifty properties the failed bank held as foreclosures, noting the ones that had offers pending and entering the transaction information into her reports. She asked the bank staff to assist her in copying the appraisal and title documents and prepared the real estate files to take back with her to the FDIC office on Monday morning.

Shannon was selected for another bank closing, with their main office in Fullerton, California, because of her legal contract experience and commercial leasing knowledge.

As she normally did, Shannon obtained copies of all the real estate property leases the bank held for its' various branches. The federal government enjoyed certain privileges, including 'disaffirming' property leases if they were found to be unwanted or disadvantageous to FDIC. The leases had to be reviewed and analyzed within a short timeframe of about ninety days from the date of the bank failure, and notice had to be given to the lessor if FDIC was going to walk away from the lease and cease banking operations at any given branch location. FDIC didn't want to be making lease payments at vacant bank branches. Alternately, if another bank agreed to purchase the failed bank, usually with a cash incentive from FDIC, selected branch leases were assigned or assumed by the purchasing bank.

Shannon was evaluating the real estate leases and discovered that the main office in Fullerton, California, covered approximately thirty thousand square feet of commercial office space, with an elevator to the second floor of the garden-style office complex, which totaled over 100,000 square feet. She also read that the lease rate of thirty cents per square foot ran for another twenty-five years. She ran through some calculations and completed a current market evaluation of comparables at current market lease rates for similar properties, and determined that the market rate was somewhere between $1.10 to $1.35 per square foot, and she knew there would be consumer price index (CPI) increases in rental rates over the remaining life of the lease. It was easy math to calculate the annual profit of over one dollar per square foot per month on the property.

She would order an appraisal to support her evaluation, and would prepare a case for the senior credit review committee to affirm the lease. This was one lease the FDIC should hold on to.

Shannon continued reviewing the additional real estate owned by the failed bank through foreclosure, noting the beautiful custom homes that were nearly finished that had been someone's dream home at one time. She reviewed the construction loans and noted the percentage of completion on the bank's reports, and the remaining construction loan balances intended to complete the projects. Each bank failure was unique depending on the types of loans they made; sometimes real estate loans, sometimes jet airliner loans, boat loans, often car loans, and unsecured credit card loans. She knew that the real estate would be discounted in its' present "as is" condition, and that the unsecured loans would be sold at a very steep discount, often at a 50 percent discount and more.

FDIC Faux Pas

Ted Joiner, closing and managing agent for FDIC, assigned to close a bank in the Midwest, watched Sheri Rolo, one of his FDIC staff also assigned to the bank closing, walk into the vault with a drawer of cash and place it on one of the vault shelves. He was impressed that by eleven pm on that Friday night, the cash had all been counted, verified, and balanced. He shut the vault door, spinning the dial and locking the handle. Often the cash counts took into the small hours of the morning.

He turned around with a satisfied smile on his face and said to the FDIC staff standing near him,

"That was a great job! I've never seen the cash counted and balanced so early! Now we can go start sampling that good ol' Midwest beer I've been hearing so much about."

In horror, three of the FDIC women who had been counting the cash gasped in unison, and Sheri squealed,

"Open up the vault, Ted, that's not funny. The cash is right here on the counter."

Ted sped from the vault to the counter where Sheri was standing, and he saw piles of money—singles, fives, tens, and twenty-dollar bills strapped together, with the fifty- and hundred-dollar bills set over to the side.

"How much is there?" He gulped.

"About seven hundred and fifty thousand!" Sheri answered. "You had better go and open up that vault right now," she began to scold. "That wasn't very funny, and we're tired."

Ted looked at Sheri and the other two women standing and guarding the cash, and said, "Where's the vault teller, or the assistant manager? They will have the combination."

"Oh swell, Ted," Sheri's voice rose. "They've both gone home."

"Well, get on the phone right now!" Ted ordered, "And get them back here to open the vault or at least tell us the combination."

Sheri stalked away to get the list of the failed bank's employees' names, positions, and phone numbers. Along the way, she asked several of the remaining failed bank employees if anyone else knew the combination. One very tired woman, who was still in shock from having the bank closed without notice to the bank staff, answered,

"I used to know the combination or at least a portion of it. But it's been quite a while since I used it, and it could have been changed."

Ted overhead the woman, and came scrambling around the counter to where she was sitting and ordered,

"Well, think…think hard! You must remember the combination," he demanded.

The tired woman deliberated, scrunched up her brow, rubbed her forehead with her palm, and said,

"I think it starts with four-eight-six-five, and then there were four or five more numbers."

Ted began to pace, nervously looking around the failed bank, trying to think of a way to open the vault as the frazzled, tired woman watched him.

Sheri came back to Ted, "Neither the vault teller or assistant manager are answering their phones."

"How many times did you try?" he roared.

Sheri just looked at him, steadily, frowning, dropping her voice. "You know Ted, this is all your fault. You locked the vault because you were in such a hurry to get out tonight."

Ted looked as if he were about to explode. "I don't care why it happened. We just have to get that vault combination!"

"Face it," Sheri said evenly. "We aren't going to get it tonight. We are going to have to have double custody of the cash here all night. Two people are going to have to stay here in the bank tonight until we can reach someone tomorrow to give us the combination, or you could call Washington DC and tell them our situation."

"That isn't going to happen," Ted growled at Sheri.

As it turned out, two FDIC staff had to stay all night in the failed bank to provide double custody over the cash that was left out of the vault.

On Sunday morning, after two days of trying to locate the missing failed bank vault teller and assistant manager, Ted was becoming highly agitated and knew that the new, assuming bank VP was coming in later that day to make final arrangements to have all of the assets transferred over to enable the new bank to open on Monday morning.

Another of the FDIC women who had been counting the cash, Karen, offered,

"I once heard that if a person can be hypnotized, they can be coached into remembering something they used to know."

"Like the vault combination?" Ted finished for her.

"Yes," Karen concurred.

"Then go find me a hypnotist!" Ted said through gritted teeth.

"And where do you think we are going to find a hypnotist around here? Maybe the Yellow Pages?" Karen said sarcastically.

"I don't care where you find a hypnotist. Someone find me the Yellow Pages for around here," Ted continued to roar.

Karen couldn't believe she was actually calling a local hypnotist to try to flush out the vault combination from the failed bank staff. She called and found one hypnotist willing to come to the closed bank on a Sunday morning.

The hypnotist arrived, and Karen ushered her into a private office, where the hypnotist worked with the frazzled bank staff until she was able to coax out the secret numbers to the vault. It had taken several tries with different number combinations, but it had finally worked. The failed bank staff remembered the rest of the combination, the vault was opened, and the cash was placed into the vault.

"Now how do we pay the hypnotist?" Sheri asked Ted. "We can't exactly put in a check requisition for two hundred dollars to pay a hypnotist for services rendered to help someone remember the vault combination."

Ted paid the hypnotist, and the vault cash count was somehow two hundred dollars short.

Heritage Bank, Costa Mesa, California

One of first banks to fail in Orange County, California was Heritage Bank. FDIC was careful to keep only those who needed to know informed about a pending bank failure. Of course, there was the 'at risk' list of potential bank failures maintained by the Office of Thrift Supervision (OTS), the comptroller of the currency (OCC), and the FDIC. These banks were at risk of failing because their financial balance sheets were not strong enough to sustain their lending and deposit account liabilities—that is, they were low on cash and had an increasing defaulting loan portfolio. In an effort to disrupt the community as little as possible, and to maintain the deposits, it was easier to sell the bank to an assuming strong bank because they assumed the deposits as well as the other assets consisting of loans and other bank holdings. Additionally, there wouldn't be enough cash on hand to pay out all of the depositors' balances.

However, at this bank, the imminent bank failure had leaked out, and customers lined up around the block to withdraw money, it was a run on the bank. On Wednesday and Thursday before the FDIC closed Heritage Bank, the depositors lined up in the dark hours of the morning, and continued throughout the two days to withdraw all of their money from the failing bank. Additional cash infusions had to be ordered from the Federal Reserve to pay out the depositors, and the cash was drained.

The bank was closed on Friday. Very little money was left, but it was counted, balanced, and the armored truck came to take it away (back to the Federal Reserve) because there was no assuming bank to reopen or take over the accounts on Monday morning.

On Saturday morning at nine am sharp, a bank robber came into the bank, jumped up on the counter, brandishing his pistol, and demanded loudly "Give me all your money."

Initially the FDIC staff and failed bank staff looked up, alarmed. Whether it was the fatigue from working late into the night to balance the bank's assets and bundle all the cash for an armored car pickup in the wee hours of the night, or the irony of the situation that a bank robber was one day late to get any cash, some of the FDIC staff started to laugh, and said, "The bank is closed."

The bank robber said, "No, it's not, it's open. I just came in through that door."

They said, "No, the bank is closed. It failed. We're the FDIC, and there's no money here."

Alaska Bank Closing

Brad came by Shannon's office one Tuesday morning.

"Shannon, what's your caseload like?" *OK*, she thought, this is the department head, who's supposed to read all the reports, and know what his staff is doing, including the distribution of portfolio cases.

"I'm caught up," she answered evenly.

"Ready to go on a bank closing?" he asked quickly.

"Sure. Is it this weekend?"

"Well, this is kind of different. It would be for about three weeks. It would be in Alaska."

"Wow, Alaska!" she exclaimed. She was now managing failed bank properties in over thirty-one states, and Alaska would be a new state to add to her portfolio.

"Yes, they have a very large real estate inventory, and I need to send two of you. I was thinking maybe you and Kelly could go up there."

"It sounds really good to me," Shannon answered, thinking quickly that her next call would be to her mother, who stepped in while she worked out-of-town failed bank assignments. At the same time, she was excited about going to Alaska.

"OK, then," Brad responded quickly. "They're going to have a lot of staff from Washington DC there, too, and I know you will do a great job with them."

"Thanks, Brad," Shannon was pleased with his compliment.

"OK, you're going, and I'll talk to Kelly. I want you to be the lead. And I'll tell Ken," and Brad walked away.

Shannon was looking forward to this assignment, it would be a great opportunity to meet more senior staff from Washington DC, and it would be an adventure as well. Being assigned as the lead by Brad indicated that he had confidence in her since this was going to be such a huge bank failure. Hopefully, it would also get her acknowledgment of her skills and knowledge that would poise her for a grade promotion.

Later that afternoon, Ken approached Shannon's cubicle, leaned one arm against the doorway, and asked,

"Are you sure you can go to Alaska this week, I mean with your daughter at home and all that?"

Shannon was surprised at his question.

"I have everything covered," she answered. She had called her mother and asked if she would be available to stay with Jennifer, and she had happily agreed, but Shannon was not going to offer that information to Ken.

"I guess I'm just not used to working mothers," Ken muttered. "My wife stays home and takes care of the kids and the house she doesn't want to travel around or work. I don't understand why you would want to go and leave your daughter like this. Your priorities—"

Shannon knew about Ken's wife but didn't like his murmuring about her decisions and priorities. She interrupted,

"Well, Ken, you know, some of us women like to work, and need to work. I am looking forward to going to Alaska."

"Are you sure your work is all caught up?" he asked.

"Yes, it is," she assured him.

"Well, I'm going to send Farley Trip with you and Kelly. He doesn't have much experience in bank closings, and I want you to teach him."

She was taken aback that Ken was sending Farley along. It was a big assignment, and Brad had only wanted two account officers to go. It was also highly unusual for three account officers to be at one bank closing at a time, or out of the office for that length of time because it usually caused a burden on the account offices who remained back in the office to service public information calls, and often resulted in a lack of responsiveness to the public when they called in for property asset information.

"Farley's going?" Shannon echoed.

"Yeah, that's what I said," Ken answered her abruptly, and walked away.

About then, Farley Trip came by Shannon's cubicle, and stepped inside.

"Looks like I'm going to be going along to Alaska with you," he said. "Are you sure you can go and leave your daughter like that. I feel kind of sorry for you having to go and leave her. Who's going to watch her while you're gone?"

Shannon looked Farley in the eye. "I have everything under control, Farley, but thanks for your concern."

"Sure, but I think Kelly and I can handle it, and you wouldn't have to go. I hear it's going to be a lot of work—I mean, because the big boys from Washington DC will be there and will be asking for a lot of reports and the real estate asset list is long."

There it was, she realized. Farley wanted to take her place, and have the opportunity to meet and work with the Washington DC people.

"Thanks, Farley," she shook her head. "But I'm going."

"OK, be that way," he said, turned, and continued on to his cubicle.

☙

Alaska was an intense assignment, with very large inventories of real estate to be handled from the failed Bank of the North. Shannon attended meetings every day with the Washington DC management, providing reports and status information pertaining to the real estate portfolio of foreclosed homes and foreclosures in process. She also was responsible for the pending litigation.

As the team lead, she divided the case work among herself, Kelly McKean, and Farley Trip, giving Farley direction on completing checklists to verify if certain documents were available for the new properties. Because the laws in Alaska were different from California, where Farley had most of his real estate experience, she explained the pertinent differences and showed him the significant contract clauses for Alaskan real estate transactions. It was also customary practice to visit with appraisers and real estate brokers who had been hired by the failed bank to see if their contracts should be ratified and extended, or cancelled. She also continued to train the Bank of the North real estate staff in FDIC policies and procedures.

Eventually, Shannon, Kelly and Farley would return to California, and the staff from the failed bank would be expected to continue working on preparing the foreclosed real estate properties for sale, and reporting their results to FDIC in California. FDIC frequently retained staff from failed banks to continue working on liquidating real estate assets, loans and other tangible assets like desks, computers, file drawers and artwork from the failed bank.

Each time Shannon returned from a management meeting, Farley would come over to her desk, and ask what had occurred, what was happening, what did the Washington DC staff have to say about the failed bank operations, and wanted to know what plans they were making.

Shannon returned from a management meeting on the third afternoon, and began to draft management memorandums and reports that she knew would be requested by the Washington DC staff, and Farley approached her again.

"What happened in the management meeting?" he asked.

"The usual, Farley—update statuses, projections, planning, changes to scheduling, recommendations for retaining contracts and disaffirming others, and marketing the failed banks assets."

"That's it?"

She didn't have time for Farley's curiosity but answered him evenly, "We always discuss newly discovered assets and portfolio modifications as well as timeline projections for resolving this bank and resources."

"What else?" he continued.

"Hey, Farley, why don't you work on your case files? If anything comes out of the management meetings that affects your assignment, I'll be sure to let you know. But for now, I need you to finish your interviews with the appraisers and real estate brokers on your files to know if we should retain their services or cancel them, and I need your case file summaries for a report."

After lunch on the fourth day in Alaska, Shannon could not locate Farley. She asked the failed bank staff if they had seen him, and she checked with Kelly to see if she had seen him return from lunch. At about three pm, Farley came back into the bank, and deposited himself into his working office quietly, closing the door behind him.

Shannon walked over to his office, knocked, and walked in.

Farley looked up at Shannon, and she immediately saw the effects of alcohol on the small man, and could smell it strongly as well.

"Farley, where have you been?" she asked him directly.

"Oh, well, I had lunch with some of the boys," he answered without looking at her.

"Um, I guess maybe you guys drank your lunch instead of eating it?" she responded.

Farley became defensive and snarled,

"I introduced myself to the boys from Washington DC when they were getting ready to go to lunch, since you wouldn't introduce me, and I went with them. I was with the guys from Washington DC, and I think whatever they do is OK for me to do, OK?"

"Look, Farley," she said quietly. "I don't care what you do, but I do care about getting this work done on time and having the reports ready when Washington DC asks for it. And that means that we have to be here and be in a condition to work when we are here. I don't care what the Washington DC guys do, but I don't want to see you coming back in here after lunch plastered. We've got to work with the failed bank staff, and this really doesn't look good."

"I was with the Washington DC guys, and you can't tell me what to do. I can still work now," he said, trying to convince her.

"How about some black coffee, or maybe you want to just go and stand outside for a minute? I think it's about twenty degrees out there. It might clear your head."

"I'm fine," he muttered.

Shannon left the office, closing the door behind her.

That night, as Shannon, Kelly and Farley were leaving the failed bank to go back to their hotel, Farley started to walk away from the two women.

"I'm not going to dinner with you two tonight," he announced. "I'm having dinner with the DC boys. See you in the morning." With that, he turned and left.

"What do you think that's all about?" Kelly asked.

"I think Farley is trying to make some new friends," Shannon answered carefully.

"You know I heard that they are going to the topless and bottomless bars around here," Kelly offered. "The hot spot for tonight is called 'The Bush'. Isn't that cute?"

Shannon didn't care, but she answered,

"I just don't want some newspaper reporter to write an article about FDIC staff frequenting those places for three or four-hour lunches instead of doing our job up here. That's all we would need to have it look like taxpayers' dollars are subsidizing the drinking and indulging of FDIC employees."

"I know what you mean," Kelly added. "The way the press likes to follow us around, it isn't too smart to be hanging around those places all the time."

"Oh, well," Shannon answered. "They are big boys, and they can answer for themselves." And she and Kelly continued back to the hotel.

The next morning, Farley was late to work. Shannon was waiting for a summary report he was to have prepared, and couldn't find him. She was walking by the conference room where the

Washington DC staff had set up their office, and heard Farley's voice,

"Yeah, those girls were incredible last night. And they were really bare, you know what I mean? I mean completely naked!" he laughed.

Another male voice added, "Yeah, I know what you mean. That's why they call it 'The Bush' ," and the men continued to laugh.

Shannon didn't want to go in and deal with the men while they were discussing last night's entertainment, and she continued walking past the conference room, hoping not to be called in for any status updates, or participation in their anatomical discussions.

The next night, Farley seemed to be his regular sober self, and he was particularly friendly toward Shannon as they packed up to leave the failed bank for the night.

"Hey, Shannon, why don't you and Kelly join a couple of us for dinner tonight?" he asked.

"I don't think I would be interested in naked dancing women, Farley," Shannon answered dryly.

"Oh, we're going out to a great steakhouse tonight," he explained. "It's supposed to be just about the best steak place in Alaska, and I think you and Kelly would enjoy it. A couple other people might be there; some of the brokers and appraisers that work on the bank's properties might be there too. I've been talking to them a lot today. It would be a good time for you to meet them, I think."

Shannon thought about his offer, and decided it sounded better than sitting in her hotel room for another night or working out in the hotel gym.

"OK," she answered. "I'll go, and I'll mention it to Kelly."

"Oh, don't worry about Kelly," Farley quickly said. "I'll get her to go, I know she'll like it. How about if we meet in the hotel lobby about seven thirty?"

With their dinner plans made, Shannon left for the hotel to get ready.

The dinner was all right, and true to Farley's word, there was an appraiser joining them. Shannon enjoyed talking with the Washington DC management about the current bank's asset base and what opportunities were available for selling or liquidating some of the failed bank's portfolios of real estate and loans. She had briefed them earlier that day on the several pending litigation actions, and was enjoying the more casual atmosphere at the dinner table. The dinner house was also a dance hall, and Shannon was soon left with the appraiser, as Farley dragged Kelly off to the dance floor and to talk with some other Washington DC staff.

Shannon and the appraiser made small talk about Alaska real estate values, the procedures the appraiser used in establishing his market values, and the general condition of real estate in Alaska.

When it was finally time to go back to the hotel, the Washington DC boys said they were stopping for a nightcap at a local bar, and Farley and Kelly said they weren't ready to go yet. As Shannon prepared to leave, the appraiser left with her and walked her to her room, and then asked to use her bathroom. Shannon called home and was saying goodnight to her daughter, when the appraiser came out of the bathroom.

Shannon said good-bye to her daughter and turned around in the hotel chair to encounter a very nude man.

"What are you doing?" she exclaimed.

"I thought we might have a good time," he answered.

"I think you've made a mistake," she responded quickly, standing with a bed between them.

He lay down on the bed, spread eagle, motioning with his arms for her to join him and smiling provocatively, lifting one eyebrow.

"There's no mistake," he assured her. "I've been told you are available for a good time, and I'm here to give it to you."

"Well, you've been told wrong," she responded angrily. "Who the hell told you that?"

"Oh, one of the guys who says he knows you real well," he leered.

"I think you'd better get your clothes and get out of here, now," she warned.

He got up from the bed, reached her and put a hand on her shoulder, smiling suggestively into her face.

She slapped his hand off her shoulder, jumped up, walked across the bed to the bathroom, and came out holding his clothes in her hand.

"I suggest you put these on now, before I call security."

He looked confused. "But I thought you wanted a little action while you were here," he seemed bewildered.

"I want to know who told you to do this?" she demanded.

"Just one of the guys from FDIC."

"Who?"

"He just said that you kinda showed your heart and feelings on the outside, and you needed a little lovin.'"

She was furious. "Who said that to you?"

"I'm not saying."

"I suggest you get out of here while you can," she said angrily

The appraiser took the clothes she held out and tried one last time,

"I'm sure we could have a real good time."

She narrowed her eyes and answered, "In your dreams. Now get out of here."

He pulled on his pants, she opened the door, and he left with his shirt and shoes in his hands.

After the misguided appraiser had left, Shannon locked her hotel room door and realized she was shaking. But whether she was shaking with fear or anger was not altogether clear.

She put her head back against the wall and closed her eyes. She couldn't prove it, but she felt down in her heart that Farley had set up the whole thing. *Does Farley really hate me that much?* she wondered to herself. She rationalized that Farley probably wanted to set her up so that he could then humiliate her to get back at her for finding him drunk and frequenting the nude bars at noon and after work. If he could ruin her reputation, then he could get her out of his way and further his own career goals. The Washington DC men had openly discussed their intention to offer career government-grade, or GG positions soon.

After two and a half weeks in Alaska, Shannon felt that the assignment was just about wrapped up, and she sat down to write the final closing reports to summarize her work. She was just about done and left a few blanks for the final numbers and asked Kelly to fill in the blanks for her at the end of the week when the final real estate activity was tallied. She had worked twelve and fourteen hour days on the final management report for the Bank of the North for Washington DC management. She knew the report was a good one.

"I'm really pleased to submit this report to the Washington DC staff," Shannon informed Kelly as she reviewed the final reports with her. "We did an outstanding job up here," she continued. "I don't think Washington knew just how much inventory we were walking into at this failed bank, and I'm especially proud of the training we were able to give the existing bank staff in preparing the properties for the public in such a short time, not to mention the retention of the best real estate agents, property managers and appraisers. We covered over two hundred properties, with more in the pipeline through foreclosure."

"This is certainly the largest bank failure I know about," Kelly agreed. "I mean, FDIC even started to cater in lunch and dinner so we wouldn't lose any time. They want to try to wrap this project up."

"Well, I think that Washington DC calculated the lost man hours if two hundred employees and FDIC members left for lunch and dinner every day, and it made sense to bring in those meals if we would stay here and work through the lunch and dinner hours. I think it probably was an efficient maneuver."

"Yeah, maybe so, but I think I've gained a few pounds. I look like a stuffed sausage in my sweat suit now."

"I know what you mean. I think my waistband has become some sort of medieval torture!"

The two women laughed and then continued going over the final reports that Shannon had written.

"Now tell me, Shannon," Kelly began. "I don't see anything here about Farley's contribution to this project."

Shannon started to answer,

"I combined all of our work with the litigation reports and recommendations for retaining contractors." Then she looked up to see if Kelly was serious, and burst out laughing when she saw Kelly crossing her eyes and doing a little lascivious dance imitating a topless dancer.

Shannon returned to work in California, and was looking forward to a response from Washington DC regarding the Alaska reports summarizing her work as lead at the Bank of the North failed bank closing, training of the local staff, and resolving the volume of assets, however, no response came from Washington DC. She was certain her reports would demonstrate that she was deserving of one of the upcoming coveted permanent GG positions.

Kelly McKean returned from Alaska the next week, and instead of coming over to talk with Shannon and give her a copy of the final report after she had filled in the blanks with end of the week numbers, Kelly walked into Shannon's cubicle with blazing, narrowed eyes, and her hands made into fists.

"I have to talk to you, Shannon," Kelly spit out between clenched teeth.

"Well, hi, glad to see you too," Shannon tried to make the other woman relax a little.

"You're not going to think this is funny," she answered curtly.

Shannon realized that Kelly was really upset. "OK, Kelly, what's going on?"

"You know those final reports you wrote on the Alaska bank closing? You know all the work you and I did while Farley went out and played nasty little games with some of the Washington DC guys? Remember how he came in hung over and couldn't work at all? Well, guess what that lazy little son of a bitch did?"

"I don't know, but you'd better tell me."

"He took your name off all the reports, and put his name on them instead, and walked them into the Washington DC boys!" she blurted out.

Shannon's blood ran cold. She felt her chest tighten, and her eyes narrowed.

"How..." Shannon started to ask,

"He took them off my desk while I was at lunch, put his name on them, and gave the reports to the Washington guys. I heard the Washington guys congratulating Farley for all the great work and reports when I came back from lunch."

"That bastard," she said quietly.

"But let me tell you what I've done," Kelly interrupted. "I already went upstairs and told our new managing agent, Seth Kent, and his assistant, Mark Long, what Farley did. When Farley gets back here tomorrow, they are going to call him upstairs and put him on the carpet. I don't know what will happen to him, but I hope they bust his butt."

Shannon was stunned. She had never seen such manipulation, laziness, lack of ethics, and outright malicious behavior in her life. *So this is politics?* she asked herself. First the office affairs and cover-ups for Mike Doogan and then manipulating workloads, holding and giving away higher-graded positions to male friends, the naked appraiser, and now stealing credit for extensive and important reports. *If this is politics, I don't think I want to play.*

When Farley Tripp returned from Alaska that week, he was called upstairs, and then came down and made a formal corporate apology to Shannon. She was unable to find out what else was said in the meetings, but one thing was for sure, nothing appeared to happen to Farley by the boys upstairs. In fact, a little later, Ken recommended Farley for a career GG, in the position Shannon had told Ken she would like to apply for, but Farley was one of the Old Boys Club now, and it was not open to single women supporting their children, as Ken had made it very clear.

7

From the FDIC Frying Pan into the RTC Fire of Management

Senior Credit Review Committee

*B*ack in the FDIC office after the bank closings, Shannon was evaluating the case she had written and the final appraisal for the Fullerton failed bank's real estate leases, and concurred with the appraiser's opinion of value based upon the existing long-term lease at thirty cents a square foot and the current market rental rate of $1.35 per square foot. She checked her earlier calculations and completed a current market evaluation. *Wow,* she thought to herself. *Whoever holds on to this lease will be making about thirty thousand dollars per month from the other tenants in this building.* She finished the case for the senior credit review committee to affirm the lease. This was one lease the FDIC should hold on to.

When Ken Ito received her case recommending affirmation of the lease, he informed Shannon in a condescending manner, "This case will never fly. FDIC never holds on to any failed bank leases. They want them all disaffirmed. I've never seen one lease continued. You had better change the case."

Shannon answered calmly, "Perhaps in the past that is how the leases have been handled; however, I don't believe there has ever been a lease as valuable as this one. This is a very important asset for the failed bank, and FDIC has a duty to recover the highest possible value for the assets. FDIC should affirm and hold this lease and retain the thirty-thousand-dollar-a-month income from this property."

Ken shook his head. "I told you, they've never kept any leases from the failed banks. I don't think you understand leasing very well."

Shannon bristled. "You know Ken, leasing is really pretty simple. If you'd like, I can explain the appraisal to you," she said, not caring if he was angered by her response.

Ken gritted his teeth and sneered. "You know, Shannon, maybe you should just take this little case of yours into committee, and while you're at it, you could explain the appraisal to all the committee members too."

The case was presented to the senior credit committee the next week. The committee was astounded at the inherent value in the lease and affirmed the lease. Shannon developed a marketing campaign to expose the valuable asset to investors in the commercial market and negotiated a full value sale. It was one of the largest leasehold asset sales ever accomplished by FDIC.

Shannon pulled out the twelve-unit apartment building file that was in the process of being converted into condominiums on Los Alamitos Bay. The conversion project was about 95% complete. She looked at the pictures of the building and the yachts docked in front. From her previous experience building custom homes, she could quickly determine the cost of completion. She had received the final appraisal for both the "as-is" value of the property and "as completed". The completed value was $3.5 million dollars if sold as individual condominiums, or the "as-is value" was about $900,000 as an apartment building based upon rents and cost to repair and complete.

She wrote a case for the senior credit review committee to retain and complete the conversion of the property, and an estimated budget for the required remaining construction, including floor covering and electrical work.

She had researched the pending State of California approvals, covenants, conditions and restrictions and the status of the nearly formed homeowners' association, all of which she estimated would take about ninety days to finalize.

When she submitted the case for Ken Ito's review, she steeled herself for his assault.

Ken appeared at her cubile, scowling,

"What do you think you're doing with this case recommendation?" Ken began his criticism. "You can't submit this case to the committee."

"I think I've supported the triple value of the property if it is completed, and the committee is always interested in obtaining the best recovery value for every property."

"Yeah, but this has never been done before, and I can't concur with your recommendation."

Shannon had prepared her responses carefully, anticipating Ken's resistance. "I think it will be well received, Ken. It's a highly desirable property, and will…"

But Ken wasn't going to listen anymore and took the case back with him while he stomped into his office.

Shannon's case came up in committee at the end of the week. She learned that while the committee thought it was a tempting opportunity to make triple the asset value and recovery, they didn't want to advance the money to finish the project or the time to complete the necessary legal work. Ken Ito had gone around to each member of the committee and explained the disadvantages of completing the condominium conversion and the advantages of selling the property as is as an apartment complex.

When Shannon later sold the property for just under a million dollars, the investors asked, "Do you have any more properties like this one? We'll take them all."

Shannon returned to her cubicle, and could hardly conceal her frustration, when Kelly came around the corner and sat down.

"Hey, did you hear? I'm going to Washington DC!"

Shannon asked, "What? When?"

"My new husband, Steven, is being transferred to work in the computer programming department for FDIC in Washington DC headquarters, and we're going to be moving there in just a couple of weeks. I'm so excited. I can hardly wait to leave here and get away from Ken and the other male jerks like Farley and Brad!"

"I can't believe you're really going to go. I'm not ready to say good-bye to you and Steven. It sounds like a super career opportunity for Steve, though."

"Oh, it is. He's going to do so well, and I'm already looking for a transfer position too. Hey, what's eating at you?" she asked.

Shannon looked at Kelly helplessly and answered, "You know, Kelly, sometimes it just seems impossible to try to fix this old, broken boys' system around here."

"What happened? As if everything that could happen hasn't already."

"Well, I guess I've just finally had it with Ken. I asked him to approve a GG position, and he refused because I'm single and have Jennifer at home. Then he threw back some cases I had submitted that were initially written by the guys. Now he wants them all rewritten, even though he approved the exact same cases when the men wrote them."

"He can't do that; that's out and out discrimination, or male favoritism, or something like that." Kelly threw her hands in the air and then punched them onto her hips.

"I mean, think about it. The EEO group here is nonexistent, with Harry Jackson getting our receptionist pregnant, so he's been shipped back East again. There is absolutely no support or way to get things changed around here."

"You know I'm just so tired of the way the women in this department have been treated. I'm going to talk to Steven, and then I'm going to write a long letter to our managing agent, Mark Long, so that when I leave here in a couple of weeks, he's going to have it in writing what has been going on down here. And then he'll have to do something about it."

"I wish I believed it would make a difference, Kelly, but I'm just kind of out of hope about now."

Kelly bent her head to one said and said in a subdued voice, "It's going to be better, Shannon. Just wait and see."

Two weeks later, Kelly came into Shannon's cubicle with a mischievous look on her face.

"Well, I did it," she announced.

"What did you do?" Shannon asked her friend.

"I gave my notice to Mark Long, told him I was transferring to Washington DC, and then I handed him a three-page letter listing all the things Ken and Brad had done to us down here. I covered all the bases. I mean, I really laid it all out—how mean they were, how unfair the file distribution was, and I even added that little stunt Farley pulled up in Alaska. And all the harassment we've gone through, including Brad's rude and crude remarks about zippers and braces and such."

"Do you really think it will make any difference?" Shannon wondered out loud.

"It has to. I wrote down the way Ken assigned all the dirty assets to the women to clean up, and the way he assigned the already opened escrows from failed banks to the men so their closing numbers would be higher than ours. I listed the hours the guys worked and the long lunches for working out, and how the women got lectured if we were ten minutes late. I promised that things were going to get better now, didn't I?"

Shannon waited the next week for evidence that Mark Long would respond to Kelly's letter. She was appalled when she learned that Mr. Long's response was to have Ken find Kelly AWOL when she reported that she was preparing to transfer to Washington DC with her husband, Steve, and requested time off for moving. Ken alleged he never received her request for leave, and reported Kelly as insubordinate.

It was all Shannon could do to maintain her composure when she learned about the malicious treatment Ken Ito and Mark Long had meted out to Kelly. With the FDIC EEO ethics officer still out on administrative leave due to the pregnant Mormon receptionist, there would be no investigation or any corrective action. She knew she would finally have to make a change for herself.

❧

Ron Turner, the managing director before Mark Long, had called Shannon previously to discuss various legal actions and remedies for real estate assets he had encountered at his new job with the RTC, the Resolution Trust Corporation.

Congress had just announced the creation of the Resolution Trust Corporation, or RTC, in January 1989, to handle the now-failing Savings and Loans. The RTC was to operate parallel to the FDIC. The assets were much larger with the S&Ls since these lending institutions made loans on a much larger scale for real estate projects and large commercial ventures. Where the FDIC insured banks, the real estate assets were primarily smaller residential properties with a few commercial assets mixed in; the savings and loans real estate inventories were ten times larger or more in terms of value and volume.

The RTC was given a limited lifespan by Congress to fulfill its mission of cleaning up the failed savings and loans and was to sunset, or close down, at the end of 1997. Congress had estimated that with accelerated asset disposition strategies and initiatives such as bulk sales, portfolio sales and auctions, the savings and loan holdings could be sold off in about seven to nine years, as opposed to 360 years if the assets were each negotiated and sold one at a time. Shannon evaluated her opportunities at the FDIC as being limited to none with Ken refusing to authorize her posting for the permanent GG positions, and she felt the future with the RTC had to be better than her present situation with FDIC.

She opened her side desk drawer, pulled out a stack of saved messages, and flipped through them until she found the one she was looking for with Ron Turner's phone number at the RTC. She dialed his number and waited, hoping she was doing the right thing, and knowing she could not work under Ken any longer. When Ron answered the phone, he was pleased to hear from her.

"Well, hello, there, Shannon. I was hoping to be hearing from you soon."

"Oh, is that right, Ron? And just how did you know I might be calling?"

"Because you always did like a good challenge, the hardest cases, the biggest problems to resolve, and a lot of litigation to keep you zooming. I thought I had piqued your interest last time I called, and I hope I'm right."

"Well, you are right in that I'm interested in hearing more about your operation."

"I'm ready to tell all, and I think you should come over here just as soon as you can so I can show you the RTC offices and we can talk about which department you might want to set up."

"Since you know me well and you've seen my work and committee cases, can you tell me now where you would like me to work? In what department did you think I would be the best fit?"

"I've already thought about it, and there are three areas I think you could run. I like your experience with the real estate sales department and the way you work with the public. You have a way of soothing ruffled feathers and facilitating transactions as well as getting the best deal put together. Your negotiation skills are great. So, section chief of the real estate department would be a great fit, plus you have terrific public relation skills, and at the RTC you would have more direct public contact at the sales center. I know you wrote the first FDIC REO training manual, and you've been training all the new FDIC hires and have been conducting the REO training classes for the new staff and staff from the failed banks.

"Then there's the property management division, where you would be a great department head. This is a new section that really oversees outside contractors that do the actual management of the properties. FDIC doesn't use contractors much, but RTC uses them extensively. You would watch over the contractors and manage them to make sure they're doing their jobs right—you know, look over their contracts for acceptable performance and watch their budgets. I know you would be great in this area too.

"Then there's a new department being required by Congress/FIRREA and Washington DC; it's called the new special assets, low-income housing department. You would have a smaller staff with this department, and it requires a lot of outreach with nonprofit and government agencies. I know you would be very good at this, plus you would be conducting a lot of training sessions for the staff and nonprofits. You're a great public speaker, and we could use your talent in this department too."

Shannon had been making notes as Ron talked, and now she looked down at her scribbled paper and thought quickly about the three offers Ron had made her.

"I think I would like to hear more about the special assets department head position, Ron. What do you think?" She knew that this area was becoming more and more important to HUD, Congress, and other State of California politicians, and she recognized that there would probably be a long, challenging career in this area.

"I think you should come over here so we can discuss these options together and make a decision as soon as possible."

She didn't even blink. "How about tomorrow?"

Shannon was almost through packing up her desk when Tanya Glasser came into her cubicle office and sat down.

"Oh, Shannon, I'm going to miss you so much! Who else am I going to talk to about how mean Ken is and how nasty Brad is? I won't have anyone to share with anymore. How will I know if I'm sane, or these guys are finally driving me crazy?"

Shannon smiled at her best friend at the FDIC. They had surely looked out after each other over the past four years and, in doing so, had become very close friends.

"I'm only a phone call away, and a little over five miles down the road. It's not that far, and we can still have lunch together."

"I know, I know," Tanya lamented, shaking her head from side to side. "It's just that it won't be the same around here anymore without you. You always kept trying to change things for everyone, tried to make things fair and better. Now everything's going to get worse, I just know it is!"

"Tanya, you're going to be just fine. You always have your work done, you get along OK with everyone, and I'm not that far away."

"I'm just being selfish," she muttered, and then whispered conspiratorially. "Do you know what they're going to do with your workload? I mean have you heard who they are going to transfer it to?"

"I just know that Marshall Talley has come around to talk to me the last couple of days, and I am guessing that he will be the lucky recipient of my portfolio. It's all in good shape though, and it won't be too hard to pick up where I left off."

"That's easy for you to say," Tanya answered sarcastically. "It will probably take two or three of the men to pick up your load; they're so lazy and spoiled. I doubt Marshall Talley can last with your workload more than two weeks!"

"You know Tanya, that remains to be seen. You'll have to let me know when he starts complaining, and tell me what Ken does then."

"Are you almost done packing? It looks like you have just about everything ready to go."

"Yes, I am. But I have one more stop to make. I'm meeting with Mark Long for my exit interview in a few minutes. I'm looking forward to this being the last time I have to deal with the old boys' network at the FDIC."

"Just be careful, Shannon. Remember what they tried to do to Kelly."

She would later learn from Tanya that two men had to share her old portfolio because it was so large and had so much activity. It was initially assigned to Marshall Talley, who, after the first week of trying to take all the phone calls pertaining to the real estate properties, put his phone in his desk drawer and shut it because he couldn't stand the constant ringing. He immediately complained to Ken that the portfolio was not manageable by one person, and Ken divided it between two male account officers.

Shannon walked into Mark Long's office. He had his head down, reading over some paperwork, and then looked up at Shannon.

"Come in. Sit down," he invited her in and waved his hand toward the chair in front of his desk. "So this is your exit interview, huh? You're really going to transfer to the RTC? I hear it's a real mess over there. They're trying to reinvent the wheel when we have all the policies in place here. You could be going from the frying pan into the fire."

Shannon was determined to make the meeting cordial, "I'm sure it will be different and a challenge, and that's what I'm ready for. I'm looking forward to the opportunity."

"Old Ron got you to come over there, didn't he? He's a sly fox."

"I think Ron was familiar with my work and felt I could contribute a lot of experience to the RTC and—"

Mark cut her off. "Yeah, well, you never know about ol'Ron. He's so queer, you just can't tell what he's up to next. Except that he's hiring other queers, and the whole damn place is going to be climbing over each other with them, if you know what I mean."

Shannon decided it was time to change the subject, redirect the interview, and bring it to a quick close. But not until she had the chance she had been waiting for: a final discussion regarding Ken Ito's and Bradley Donner's management of the REO department.

"Actually, Mark," she began quietly, "I know you have had the opportunity to talk with Laurie Morgan before she left and to read Kelly McKean's letter to you before she went to Washington DC. Both of these women had tried to advise you of certain conditions, and I've talked to you previously about—"

He interrupted her again. "Look, Shannon, there is nothing I want to hear from you about Ken or Brad. I don't want to hear it, I don't want to see it, and I don't want to read it. Understand?"

She was stunned. "You mean you don't want to correct illegal practices by your management, or take action to prevent liability—"

"No, I don't want to know anything about anything you have to say about the real estate department. I think you're making a big mistake by going to work for those faggots, and I'm telling you now that if you think the FDIC is a big, smelly frying pan, you're about to jump into the preverbal RTC fire. I suppose if you wanted to stay here, I could see about moving you…"

She straightened her back and shook her head at the sloppy man sitting in front of her with his silly red-rimmed glasses and balding head. "You know, in spite of the lack of management around here, I really enjoyed the work. We saw the inside of banks and what broke them, we were able to unwind legal cases that had been stuck in the system for years, and working with Washington DC has been an education in itself."

"Yeah, yeah," he sputtered. "We made history here at the FDIC."

She stood up and looked down at the messy man. "Yes," she answered sharply, "And I'm about to be part of another chapter in American banking history. Only this time, I'll be the manager, and it will be a clean operation."

She turned and left his office, relieved to be moving away from the mismanaged federal agency.

8

Singles Dating, Again

She knew she needed to get more balance in her life, and decided to take up golf. It was outdoors, she loved the sun and the beauty of each golf course, and no one could call her, fax her or page her while she was on the course. Shannon enrolled in group lessons at San Joaquin Golf Course in Irvine, California, and discovered she had a natural ability when it came to golf. She might not hit the ball farther than 150 yards, but it was straight. She was soon invited to play golf with one of the instructors, Pat, teaching the class. He was a high school coach and a scratch golfer, which meant he always hit par and could hit the ball a lot farther than Shannon.

Pat was patient, and made a lot of suggestions to Shannon for her golf swing, always reminding her to keep her head down and eye on the ball. Shannon felt fortunate to be getting private golf lessons from such a great golfer. Pat approached the ball and always sent it sailing over three hundred yards toward the green, while Shannon took at least two and sometimes three shots to meet him at the flag. During one play, Pat coached Shannon on approaching the ball. He had her waggle, a sort of wiggle to get her balance, and changed her grip. She took a full swing and hit the ball about 180 yards down the fairway, and she was elated.

"What are you doing?"Pat exclaimed. "The pin's right there!" He pointed to another pin about 125 yards away. When Pat had rearranged her feet and grip, she had turned so that she was facing the wrong hole!

"Hey, the good news is that's the farthest I've ever hit the ball!" Shannon said proudly.

"The bad news is, you could have killed someone," he said, laughing.

Pat began asking Shannon to play golf more frequently, and during the summer, to play after work. When Shannon could, and her work could wait until that evening, and Jenny was in dance class, she would meet Pat and play eight or nine holes at a local course. Then Pat began asking her to dinner after golf. One evening at the end of their golf round, he said,

"I have a gift I've been wanting to give you," then with great flourish, he pulled a club from his golf bag and gave her a new Ping putter.

She was surprised and delighted by the putter, feeling its excellent balance, and thought that it would definitely improve her putting. She thanked him for the generous gift.

Pat leaned in and said, "And I have another gift for you. I want you to enjoy the putter, and I want you to practice a lot, getting the feel of the putter, how it plays, how to swing it and hold it—"

When she looked down, he was demonstrating his imaginary techniques in his crotch with his own personal putter. Shannon was startled, got out of the golf cart, left the clubs Pat had provided for her to play with, took her purse, and stomped off toward her car.

Pat called a few times and then wrote her a note of apology, but Shannon decided he could play by himself without her.

9

The Resolution Trust Corp. (RTC) and Feminine Management

Men on Top in Bed and in the Office

The beautiful Spanish style exterior of the RTC office building in Costa Mesa, California, was stunning. It was the former corporate headquarters building of Pacific Savings and Loan, recently failed and then occupied by RTC to save money on office space. It had a charming courtyard with Spanish tiles and a fourteen-foot-high fountain in the middle, with curved stairways leading up to the second and third stories. But the main feature was a prominent bell tower with windows all the way around and a classic red-tile roof. The building was finished with rough-hewn lumber around all the windows that cranked open and hand-beveled glass panes with heavy, dark Spanish oak doors.

Shannon knocked on Ron Turner's office door and peered inside.

The fifty something-year-old man with thinning white hair looked up at her from behind his desk and smiled.

"I've been expecting you. What's taken you so long?"

Shannon smiled at the aging man. He looked thinner to her than she had remembered, and she replied, "Oh, you know how government paper work takes forever. I've been in personnel taking care of the transfer forms, and I thought I would never get finished. I'm free now."

"Then come in, come in and sit down. We have a lot to go over."

She entered the office and looked around. She immediately noted the worn-out carpeting, taped-up seams, torn thresholds, and chipped and peeling paint. There were extension cords with multiple electrical lines and plugs snaking around the desks for the computers, printers, and other office equipment. She noted that the failing thrift had maintained the exterior of the building to project a successful and profitable savings and loan, while the interior had clearly not been maintained at all. Ron noticed her looking about the office and offered his explanation.

"Congress thought we should watch our budget real closely, so Washington, DC felt we should occupy this building since the savings and loan failed. All their records are here, and we can operate from this building while we are trying to sell it. That way we save tax payers money on rent."

Shannon nodded her head in understanding, and teased the older man, "I especially like the wrinkled carpeting and tape holding some of the seams together." She looked down at the old carpeting with duct tape running across the threshold.

"Now that tape serves two purposes," he teased back. "It holds the carpet together, and it hides the electrical cords we have running all over this place for our computers and other equipment."

They laughed, and then Ron continued. "I want to go over some changes since the last time we spoke and bring you up to date on our operations."

"OK, I'm ready," she agreed, smiling.

"I would like to have you head up the real estate sales section, because I know you can do a great job for us there. It will be different from the FDIC, like I told you before, because there's a public sales center and a lot more public contact. But I'm sure you will train your staff to be the best and do a good job."

She smiled and asked, "Who will I be reporting to?"

"I think you already talked with him last week. His name is Travis Marker."

"That's right. I did. He called and talked to me about how I would set up the real estate sales division. He came over from FSLIC, the Savings and Loan group, didn't he?"

"Yes, he did. He headed up the marketing group there, and is the sales director here now."

"I look forward to meeting him again soon."

"You will, because there's a staff meeting in about twenty minutes, and you'll meet all of the other managers then." Ron got up and came around the side of his desk, and extended his hand toward Shannon. "Welcome on board. Come on. I'll introduce you to Travis Marker first. I'm sure you two will have a lot to talk about."

Shannon was sitting in Travis Marker's office, trying to comprehend the whacky story he was telling her. He was an attractive, well-built younger man, maybe forty years old.

"So Congress makes up these stupid rules about compelling the RTC to hire independent fee contractors to manage and sell the real estate that was foreclosed on or owned by the failed savings and loans, instead of leaving all of that work for us to do at the RTC real estate sales center, like the FDIC had staff do the real estate marketing and sales. Somehow, we are supposed to oversee the fee contractor's work, and make sure they are really getting the properties ready to sell, ordering appraisals, ordering environmental reports for some of the commercial properties, making sure the title is clear and marketable, marketing the assets and taking the best, highest offers. And that they are doing all that in a timely manner too, to reduce RTC's holding costs. They call the fee contractors SAMDA, for Standard Asset Management Disposition group, or something like that.

"But instead, they are just sitting on the properties, because then they can collect their property management fees for months and months, and then they can sell the properties and earn a commission too. They are taking hundreds of thousands of dollars each month to manage the properties, and then millions in sales commissions when they finally sell them. One big commission is more than my entire operating budget for the year. We could do the job so much more efficiently and save the taxpayers millions, but the lobby in Washington, DC for the outside contractors is so strong, we can't get the assets back in house.

"The contractors won't put the properties into the RTC database like they are supposed to so we can track them and oversee their marketing and sales efforts. It's a huge mess."

Shannon shook her head. "Do you mean that the RTC doesn't control any of the real estate from the failed savings and loans?"

"Pretty much the private fee contractors, SAMDA contractors, control the real estate except when there are new properties acquired from new foreclosures or new savings and loan failures, we can sometimes get to the properties first and try and sell them. Except that the REO management group here at the RTC just runs in and gobbles up the assets and puts them under contract as fast as they can."

"It sounds to me like there are too many divisions trying to manage and sell the same assets," she offered in summary. "There just seem to be layers and layers of oversight personnel, all watching but doing nothing."

"And there's more. Washington DC has a capital markets group and national sales center that also tries to grab the real estate and loans for National sales programs. I'm going to give you a folder for the first real estate auction Washington DC is trying to do. I want you to do an analysis on the proposed assets we are supposed to contribute to this event and tell me if they are available and appropriate for an auction." He pushed a blue folder across his desk to her.

She reached out and took the folder into her lap, slowly opening it. She noticed that next to the name of each property there was a fee contractor name as well.

"Should I understand this to mean that these properties are already being managed by one of the outside fee contractors?" she asked.

"Yep, you got that right," he answered. "And if those properties do go to auction, there will be additional expenses to pay the auctioneer in addition to the fee contractors. And real estate commissions too. You'll see it all in the file. I would like you to also do a financial analysis on the fee contractors while you're at it."

"I'll get into this right away and let you know what I find," she answered, still flipping through the file.

"Good. I'm glad you're on board. But first I want you to come with me to a senior credit review committee meeting. I've heard from Ron Turner that you're good at case writing and committee presentations. He said you presented some of the most intelligent cases at the FDIC when he was managing agent over there. You'll have to see this with your own eyes to believe what the property management department is trying to do here at the RTC."

He stood and he ushered Shannon down the corridor, being careful to step over the taped-together torn seams in the worn carpeting and stepping around boxes stacked waist high. They entered a long conference room with floor-to-ceiling glass windows along one wall and a long table with seats for about thirty people or more. There was a chalkboard at one end of the room and a wet bar sink at the opposite end, obviously the executive board room for the previous failed savings and loan. There was no torn or taped-together carpet here, just polished wood floors.

"Have a seat." Travis indicated a chair next to him, and Shannon began to sit down—except she couldn't sit all the way back in the chair or her feet would have been sticking straight out, and if she placed her arms on the armrests of the chair, her shoulders would be pushed up against her chin. The chairs were obviously contoured for very large, overfed, full-bodied men, probably the board of directors of the failed Pacific Savings Bank that had been converted into RTC office space, and not for a five-foot, three-inch petite woman. She moved forward and to one side of the vast chair, propped one elbow up on the armrest, crossed her ankles, and touched the floor with her toes to keep from falling back into the cavernous chair.

Travis looked at her posturing to get comfortable, and whispered, "Does the size of the furniture tell you anything about the size of the egos that occupied them?"

As Shannon was about to reply, the room began to fill with ten men from the real estate management and loan departments. One very large man of at least 250 pounds or more and with greasy hair and glasses slipping down his nose was entering the room as she looked up, and she sucked in her breath involuntarily.

"What's the matter?" Travis said under his breath.

"Do you know that man that just came in, Gary Thomas?" she whispered back.

"Yes."

"What does he do here? I mean what's his position?"

"He's the head of the real estate property management department, the SAMDA group. He's my counterpart. Why?"

"I can't believe he's here after all the trouble he got into at the FDIC. He was investigated for sexual harassment and EEO complaints. He had to leave."

"Well, well, well." Travis smiled. "That seems to add up. He's already got a reputation around here for either lovin' them or hatin' them. He either promotes his favorite women or sends them to the trenches or file rooms."

"I can't believe the RTC has hired him. They either don't know about his problems at the FDIC—"

"Or don't care," Travis finished for her.

She noted that Ron Turner came in and took the seat at the head of the long table, with a female assistant to his right prepared to take minutes of the meeting, and an in house RTC attorney, Vance Netherling, at his left.

Travis leaned over to Shannon and whispered behind his hand, "I know this is your first committee meeting, but try to follow the power plays going on here, especially with the property management department and their cases for paying their SAMDA contractors outlandish fees. They're trying to build an empire out of managing the assets and don't want the sales department to dispose of anything. If Thomas can make a proposal to Washington DC for hiring more staff, his grade and pay go up because his empire increases."

At that moment, Ron Turner cleared his voice; the shuffling of bodies and papers stopped, and the senior credit review committee meeting began.

"We have a full agenda today, a lot of cases to hear, and some new policies and procedures I want to review. So let's keep it short and to the point, and move through the agenda quickly," Ron said to open the meeting. "Mr. Thomas, you're up first."

Gary Thomas was raising his considerable body from his chair to begin presenting his case for committee approval.

"This case is requesting funding for adding eighty new real estate assets valued at thirty-eight million dollars to be added to the Arrow Asset Group SAMDA contract. FIRREA, the Financial Institutions Reform, Recovery, and Enforcement Act of 1989, for those who don't know," and she shot Shannon a searing look, in apparent recognition of their previous acquaintence at the FDIC, "Is our founding and enabling legislation, and calls for the RTC to utilize the expertise of outside-fee contractors, and Arrow Asset Group is one of our standard asset management and disposition contractors that manages and sells properties for the RTC. You will see that we have budgeted for their new asset setup fees, anticipated monthly management fees, and ultimate disposition fees. We would like to receive committee approval to award this contract to Arrow Asset Group immediately."

Shannon leaned over to Travis and asked, "How do you know that none of these properties is already sold or in escrow by the previous failed thrift? The RTC wouldn't want to pay double fees or expenses, I'm sure."

Travis posed the question to Thomas. "Can you assure me that none of these properties are already sold or in escrow, Gary? I don't want to be paying all these fees for setup, management, and closing to a contractor if the sale was done by the employees still out at the failed institution site who are working on these assets. After all, we are paying the salaries of the failed institution's staff, and we don't want to pay twice or pay the contractor when we don't have to."

Thomas glared at Travis. "Now, Travis, you know—"

"And I checked the Real Estate Owned Management System, the new REOMS inventory database, and didn't see most of these assets listed. Why is that?" Travis continued.

"It must just be a glitch in the system," Gary replied defensively. "I'll have someone look into it later."

Ron spoke up at that point. "I'd like to know why the properties are not in the inventory system, too, Gary. I'm going to table this case until the next committee meeting. We need to have an accurate inventory reporting system, or our reports to Washington DC are worthless."

Gary sat down and glared across the table at Travis. He didn't make any attempt to hide his animosity toward his counterpart, and instead deemed Travis as his apparent adversary, to be dueled with for feudal territory. He shot Shannon a harsh look too, through his slitted eyes. The RTC territory to be won would be that of property management, versus property sales. If Travis's department controlled and sold the assets, Thomas's department would have nothing to manage. If Thomas's outside-fee contractors were given control of the properties, Travis's real estate sales department would have no properties to sell. And whoever controlled the real estate assets and inventory would reign and control all the budgetary power.

Shannon returned to the real estate sales center and was about to enter her office when the receptionist stopped her and asked for her help.

"Miss O'Toole, I have a couple in the reception area who wants information on a piece of property that I can't find in the inventory database. They insist that they know which failed savings and loan held the loan against the property and that the foreclosure took place over six weeks ago. I've tried to tell them that we don't show any record of controlling the property, but they won't leave. What should I do?"

Since Shannon had just spoken with Travis Marker about the inaccuracy of the real estate management group in listing the RTC-controlled properties in the REOMS inventory database, she thought she would talk quickly with the inquiring couple about the missing property.

Shannon strode purposefully into the reception area and extended her hand to the young couple.

"Hello. I'm Shannon O'Toole. I understand you are trying to locate a property that you think RTC is controlling."

The young couple shook hands with Shannon, and the young man answered her. "Yes, we've been watching the property for about four months now, and when we saw the notice posted for the foreclosure, we followed up with the title company and learned that the RTC as receiver for Pacific Savings had taken the property back and now owns the property."

With the young man's account of checking with the title company to determine who currently owned the property, she thought he was probably right in his assertions.

"I would like to help you out with this matter and look into it for you. Could you give me the address of the property, and leave me your name and phone number? I'll call you by tomorrow with an answer as to whether the RTC has this property or not."

"We'd really appreciate it if you would do that," the young woman responded, and scribbled down the information Shannon had requested. "We've been trying to get information on this property for over three months now, but every time we tried to talk to someone in the RTC real estate management department, they just brushed us off without even taking down our name or the property information. We're anxious to know if this property is available because we would like to make an offer on it."

Shannon smiled at the couple and then asked, "Can you remember who you talked to in the property management department? It might help me to get started on locating the property."

The young woman pulled some notes out of her purse. "Yes, it was a Mr. Gary Thomas in the property management department. I think he's the manager or something like that. But he wasn't helpful at all."

"Well, I thank you for coming in, and I'll talk with you later today or tomorrow with my findings." And as the couple left the office, her brow began to furrow. The more she learned about the political jockeying for power by the property management section, the less she liked it.

The next thing Shannon discovered was that the database of foreclosed properties was completely inaccurate. It did not report all of the properties held by the RTC, did not reflect their current availability, correct pricing or condition. At least at the FDIC, the real estate database was balanced to the "black book" or general ledger balance from each failed bank. The inventory at the RTC did not balance to any ledger or report and was significantly underrepresented, and thus Congress was not getting a real picture of the failed bank inventory. RTC directors in Washington, DC had already gone back to the US Congress asking for more money to run the new corporation because the initial estimation of failed savings and loans and the number of assets that required management and disposition had been sorely underestimated.

The RTC real estate management group had built a database named REOMS for tracking all real estate assets from the failed savings and loans, and was responsible for inputting and reporting the assets into the database. However, the property management group clearly held back adding the new assets into the database until they had made arrangements for a fee contractor to handle the property, and only then did they show the property in the inventory database. Additionally, the fee contractors were responsible for maintaining their inventory status in the REOMS system as well; however, they were not trained properly by the RTC real estate management group, and thus the SAMDA contractors were not updating the inventory system either. This prevented the sales center from marketing or selling the assets and raised the value of the SAMDA contracts that the management group oversaw, thus providing the basis for this department's staff to receive higher ranking and salaries based upon purported responsibility. They didn't care if they wasted the taxpayers' money by hiding the assets and holding them off the market for several months.

She discovered this when she compared the listing of properties from a specific failed savings and loan to the RTC real estate inventory database reports. She had obtained the list of assets from an acquisitions clerk in Washington, DC working on RTC activity.

Shannon walked into the real estate management department and made her way over to the desk of a friendly man, Pao Heleo, who was responsible for the real estate assets from one of the largest failed banks in California, Imperial Savings and Loan in San Diego.

In earlier committee meetings, Shannon had observed Pao's demeanor to be quiet and attentive. He was a little taller than Shannon and seemed to have the face of an Aztec warrior with a wide, strong jawline.

"Good morning, Pao," she said with a warm smile. "I'd appreciate you running a current report on Imperial Savings real estate properties. Imperial Savings seems to be the only institution that has its real estate listed correctly in the Reoms database. I can't seem to locate the properties from other institutions in the Reoms inventory."

"I'm glad to help out. You're pretty new here, aren't you?" inquired Pao.

"Yes, I am new to the RTC, but I was transferred from the FDIC, where I also worked with the real estate properties. I'm a department head with the RTC sales center, training the staff in marketing, negotiations, and sales of the real estate and in writing the action cases."

"Well, I think you will find the programs here a little different from the FDIC. You had direct control of the properties there, didn't you?"

"Yes, we did. We were directly responsible for analyzing, appraising, listing, marketing and negotiating the highest offers for the real estate. We knew the status of the properties at all times."

"Well, here the properties are sometimes sold by the real estate staff remaining at the failed savings and loan or by the SAMDA contractor, if the property is put under contract with one of the fee contractors."

"What happens if the failed savings and loan has already put the property into a sales contract or into escrow? Does the failed thrift close the sale, or is the property transferred to a SAMDA contractor to close with the SAMDA contractor then earning another fee for closing the sale they didn't make?"

Pao could see where she was going with her question, and he smiled.

"With the institutions I manage, I have the old employees from the failed institution close the sale. For instance, I have Imperial Savings staff close their own transactions. That way I save the "Asset Set-up" fee the SAMDA contractors get paid every time they receive a new property, and I save the monthly management fee and the ultimate closing or transfer fee. That can add up to be a lot of money."

Shannon remembered the cases she had read and heard being presented to the senior credit review committee, and how appalled she had been at the excessive fees the real estate management department wanted to pay their contractors.

She asked, "Isn't the 'set-up fee' something like $500 per asset, and then the monthly management fee a percentage, say ½ percent, of the market value of the property for every month they hold the asset, plus a sales or disposition fee of to three percent of the sales price when the SAMDA sells the property?"

Pao smiled and nodded his head.

"So doing the math, when a savings and loan fails, the SAMDA fee contractor might receive, what, fifty to two hundred real estate properties, so that would be twenty-five to a hundred thousand just for a 'set up' fee, taking in the properties, then with a combined market value of say, three to twenty-five million, they would receive a hundred and fifty thousand to one-point-two million each month while holding the asset, getting the properties appraised, ordering title prelims, and environmental reports, plus another two or three percent of the sales price when they sell the properties?"

Again, Pao nodded.

"Can all the failed savings and loans close their own real estate sales transactions?" she asked.

"Yes, if their staff is retained, like the one I oversee, Imperial Savings in San Diego. I guess that's because I have a pretty thorough real estate background and escrow background, and I have a good handle on all of the properties in the institutions I oversee. But most of the time, the property management group here takes all the real estate away from the failed thrift staff and places the inventory with a SAMDA contractor. I don't like to do that because then you really just lose control of the property, and the SAMDA contractor does whatever they want to with the assets."

"Don't the property management SAMDA oversight people monitor the fee contractor's performance closely?" Shannon queried.

"They're supposed to, but they can't tell the SAMDA contractor what to do because supposedly the SAMDA was hired because they have special experience and know how to manage, market, and sell the property to achieve the best sales prices. And because the RTC contracting department tells us we can't give the SAMDA contractor specific orders, it's supposed to all be in their contract."

"Do you believe that?"

Before Pao could answer, Gary Thomas walked up. "Can I help you?" he asked gruffly.

Not wanting to betray Pao's confidence, she cordially responded,

"Hi, Gary. I was just learning about Imperial Savings real estate assets from Pao. I had a couple come into the sales center today looking for a particular property that I can't locate in Reoms, and I'm trying to find out if we control it."

"If it's not in Reoms, then we don't own it yet, or it's not ready to market and sell."

"I see," she responded evenly. "But my understanding of the inventory system is that all properties are supposed to be listed by their present status, and a new asset that has just been foreclosed on should be listed in Reoms with the code showing it is new but not yet available to sell."

"The system is full of problems," Thomas smirked. "We're trying to fix the system as we go along, but it is a pain in the butt."

"So I would need to go to the oversight person from each institution to get an accurate list of all the real estate assets to determine what is really available for sale?"

"No, I don't want you doing anything like that. We are trying to get the properties into the Reoms database, and we are trying to train our SAMDA contractors on how to do their data inputting too. But it all takes time, and you'll have to wait for the next download."

"And how often do you download?"

"Once a week, usually on Wednesday or Thursday."

"So since today is Wednesday, and I don't see the property in the database, you want me to wait until next week?"

"That's right," he responded in a low voice. "You'll just have to wait."

Shannon saw that she wasn't going to get the information she needed, thanked Pao for his help, and returned to her office.

She sat down at her desk and shuffled through the stack of files and committee cases Travis had given her to analyze. She pulled the committee cases forward first and began reading. She realized that the fees being paid to the SAMDA contractors were a small fortune, much more than a comparative cost for the real estate sales center to handle the sale of the properties.

In the file in front of her, for a portfolio of fifty properties with a total value of $45 million, the SAMDA contractor was paid an initial 'Asset set-up fee' of five hundred dollars for each property upon receipt of the assets. The setup fee totaled about twenty-five thousand dollars for the fifty properties listed in the case. Next, the SAMDA contractors were paid a monthly management fee for each property of about a half percent of the appraised value for the portfolio, or $225,000, almost a quarter of a million dollars every month they held the property! And when the SAMDA contractor finally sold a property, they were paid 2–3 percent of the sales price, the equivalent of $900,000 to $1,350,000 for the portfolio. In addition to these SAMDA fees, there were additional commissions of 2–4 percent to other real estate brokers who brought the buyer to the SAMDA contractor, and other maintenance expenses such as property taxes and repairs paid by the RTC.

In addition to the above costs, were the expenses associated with marketing the property and the expense of the RTC property management staff to oversee the SAMDA contractor. This usually included one oversight manager, two or three clerical staff, and their department managers. One provision Shannon particularly didn't like was the clause paying the contractor a one percent fee in the event the RTC withdrew the asset from the contractor's portfolio for any reason, such as if the sales center had a buyer for the property, or the Washington DC sales center elected to place the property into an auction. This seemed to be free and wasteful money for the contractor for "doing nothing."

Shannon quickly calculated the comparative cost of having the RTC real estate sales center handle the marketing and sale of the same fifty properties, utilizing three sales persons and two support staff, with an approximate expense of less than $375,000 to RTC. This amount was a little more than the 'asset setup fee' to the SAMDA contractor, and about a million less than the contractor's monthly cost for holding the property in addition to the sale or disposition fee of 2–3 percent. And this was only for one failed thrift's inventory; there were hundreds more.

She quickly wrote up her summary analysis for Travis, laying out the figures and cost comparison, and concluded that the case should not be approved but instead that the marketing and sale of the properties be handled by the RTC real estate sales center through a combined marketing campaign and that the management fee be renegotiated with the SAMDA contractor for a lower, more reasonable amount. She had sold similar properties at the FDIC and knew it could be done also at the RTC for much less than the SAMDA contractors were being paid.

As she began skimming the next case, she stopped, leaned her head against her hand, and shook her head. This case was just about the most wasteful use of taxpayer money she had seen yet. This time the RTC property management group was recommending another large portfolio of primarily commercial real estate equaling $75 million dollars be placed into yet another SAMDA contractor's greedy hands. Only this time, the properties were already in pending sales transactions and were ready to close escrow. All of the hard work preparing the assets for sale, clearing up the property title, marketing, and negotiating sales had been done by the staff at the failed institutions. The sales contracts for the properties had been ordered or executed by the institutions staff, and some of the sales were only twenty days away from closing.

Yet here was the RTC real estate property management group again recommending that the SAMDA contractor be given 'setup fees', monthly management fees until the property closed escrow, and then the sales or disposition fee of 1–3 percent for doing nearly nothing. If the case was approved, the SAMDA contractor would be paid about $1.75 million in new asset fees, management fees, and disposition fees for this portfolio in about sixty days. She calculated that the staff at the failed institution could efficiently complete the sales and escrow transactions for an approximate cost of about $400,000, a huge savings to the taxpayers of the United States.

Shannon quickly read through the remaining cases, doing similar analysis on the SAMDA fees versus the cost of the sales center or institutional staff to handle the sale of the assets, and each time recommended that the sales center or failed institutional staff do the marketing and sales of the properties. She further supported her recommendation that the SAMDA contractor not be given the set up fees and that a lower property management fee should be negotiated to a reasonable amount.

She rationalized that the RTC had organized a formal real estate sales center for the purpose of marketing and selling properties and other assets from the failed savings and loans and that the sales center would do the work more efficiently and economically.

Shannon soon began to learn that efficiency and economy were no match for Politics.

The lobbying groups in Washington, DC were pressing Congress and the congressional committees to privatize and to use private companies rather than RTC staff to manage and sell the assets from the failed savings and loans were powerful. It became clear that these lobbying groups were successful when RTC had to go back and ask Congress for more funding, and Congress directed the RTC to contract with the private sector for services. The lobbyists could wine and dine the pertinent congressmen, but the RTC sales staff could not.

❧

Travis called and asked Shannon to come up to his office. When she arrived, he was just finishing a telephone conversation.

"Thanks for coming up so quickly," he said. She noticed that he did not wear his usual easygoing smile, and his voice was measured. "I need to bring you up to speed on some new changes that are coming around, and talk about how they will affect the real estate sales center."

She nodded and waited for Travis to continue.

"I've just talked to the RTC national sales director in Washington DC. It seems that the SAMDA contractors have some powerful pull in Washington and that they have been successful in getting the congressional committees to put the pressure on RTC in Washington, DC to outsource most of the real estate work. Even though we have supported the economics of this as being inefficient, Ben Grey, the RTC director over SAMDA contracts, is issuing a new policy directive giving the property management department the authority to place nearly all the real estate assets into SAMDA contracts. And we can't ask or try to keep or get the assets out of the SAMDA contracts. Our task will become that of a "Traffic Cop", giving direction to interested buyers as to what SAMDA contractor is handling the property."

She listened to his dialogue, and shook her head,

"That's unbelievable! Do you mean that somehow the SAMDA lobbyists have persuaded RTC directors that they should handle all the real estate even though the cost is, say, five or ten times more than if the sales center handled the sale of the properties?"

"I think the SAMDA lobbyists convinced the congressional committees, who convinced the RTC directors that the SAMDAs should get all the work."

"I can't believe it, Travis!", she said, still stunned by the news. "I've seen laziness at the FDIC and some waste but nothing like this. This is beyond reason. It's just plain crazy."

"It's just plain politics," he answered.

"It sounds like the congressmen are giving out their final favors to the SAMDA contractors to me."

"And that, my dear, is politics," Travis sighed. "I'm going to Washington, DC next week, so you can call me there if anything comes up. I will rely on you as usual to keep the sales center running smoothly."

Travis called Shannon from Washington, DC., but she barely recognized his voice. It was heavy and he was clearly upset. He told her that there would be a new Sales Director for the California office, Samuel Franklin. Travis didn't know where he was being transferred.

He warned Shannon, "It seems that the SAMDA industry has been complaining to Headquarters that the real estate sales group has been hindering their efforts to put more assets and properties under their control. They said that they couldn't afford to support the RTC if they weren't promised all the assets from the failed savings and loans to manage. And they had contacted their respective congressmen to talk with our top brass in Washington, DC. I've never seen lobbying to this degree before."

It only took Shannon a moment to realize that the higher the financial stake, the tougher the fee contractors would play and the deeper politics would go. "There's a tremendous amount of money on the table with the SAMDAs," she responded carefully.

"Yes, clearly there is. And where there's that much money, there is equal or more power." He paused, and seemed to be forming his next words. "We haven't worked together very long, but I've enjoyed the time we did share, and I appreciate your candid analysis on the costs for selling real estate by the SAMDAs compared to RTC sales staff. It was an eye opener. Unfortunately, it wasn't what the eyes wanted to see."

The following week, Sam Franklin arrived at the California RTC office as the new Real Estate Sales Director and also introduced Alan Donovan, the new real estate sales coordinator hired by the RTC Regional office. She had heard that Sam was recently retired from the military, and his trim figure confirmed that he practiced military discipline. He was in his late forties, about five-foot-ten with a well-trimmed dark moustache. Alan was a round Irishman, with a ready smile.

Shannon came into work on Monday morning and found a memo on her desk announcing a staff meeting Alan had planned for that morning. She took care of a few pressing matters and organized her days' calendar and went to the conference room for the meeting. As the staff in the sales center settled in for the meeting, Alan entered the room and started,

"I want to give you all a little background on me. I was the area manager for real estate for Security Savings in Texas. My experience includes commercial, multifamily, and some residential work. Then I, um, semiretired, but now I'm back here. I've never worked for a government agency before, but, hey, real estate sales is real estate sales. Maybe a little different form here and there, but I'm sure it's all about the same," and he chuckled at his own humor. "I've made some of the biggest deals on the golf course over a cigar," he continued to guffaw. He sounded like a used car salesman.

Shannon's eyes rolled up to the ceiling, as she crossed her legs and leaned back in her chair, trying not to sigh out loud at this new manager's lack of knowledge in government agency transactions. He might have had the corporate knowledge to sell millions of dollars in bank-owned real estate assets, but he had a very long way to go to learn the RTC government policies and procedures. She guessed that he wasn't familiar yet with the fifty-two-page commercial real estate purchase contract RTC required for each sale or the inch-thick addendums that had to be attached. No, she was sure that Alan Donovan was going to be sorely surprised when he found out the government's methods for managing and selling the real estate, especially through the SAMDA contractors. His golf handicap wasn't going to help him here.

The next morning, Shannon came into her office to find a memo that Alan had prepared and distributed to the real estate sales center staff, stating that the appraisal information in the Reoms system needed updating. He had noticed that many of the properties did not have appraised values or that the appraisals were outdated and new ones were needed.

Shannon knocked quietly on Alan's office door.

"Come in, Shannon. We haven't had a chance to visit yet, but I'm glad to have you here. Please, sit down."

Shannon sat down and crossed her legs and smiled lightly at the very round man with a big Irish grin. "Hello, Alan. Good morning."

"And top o' the mornin' to ya, too, lass," he quipped. "I see you have a copy of the memo I dictated last night. What do you think of my discovery about the appraisals?"

She blinked at Alan and then realized that he obviously was serious and had not been informed about the real estate property management and SAMDA control of the properties.

"Well, Alan, I think maybe I can clear up some of the information you are looking for. Did Sam ever mention that at the RTC we have been directed to use outside-fee contractors to manage and sell most of the real estate assets?"

Alan was still smiling. "Uh, yeah, I think I remember him saying something about paying some real estate management companies for looking after the properties."

"Well, you see, Alan, they do more than just look after the properties. Once the real estate is put into a SAMDA contract, the RTC sales center has no more control over it. The SAMDA has to manage the property and order any environmental or title policies, and they are responsible for ordering the appraisals too. They order cleanup and repair work, if it is warranted. We don't have the authority to do any of those things now. We've brought up the fact that the appraisals, environmental, and title reports are not being ordered timely by the SAMDA contractors to the senior credit review committee, but since the SAMDAs are being paid a setup fee for each asset and monthly management fees, they can actually be paid for doing nothing for a few months. Their contract states that they have sixty to ninety days to open the files, become familiar with the properties, and order necessary documents. Do you have any idea how much money the government is wasting during that time?"

Alan stopped smiling. "Do you mean that I can't sell the properties managed by one of those SAMDA contractors?"

"Unfortunately, that's right." She sighed. "We can't touch the real estate in their contracts."

"So why does the RTC have this sales center here, and the national sales center in Washington, DC, and the employees out at the failed institution trying to compete with the SAMDA contractors for the right to sell the same assets? That's at least FOUR different groups chasing the same sales. It sounds really stupid."

"Somewhere along the line I think the RTC founding fathers and directors just got confused. They started along one line with the sales centers to sell all the assets from the failed savings and loans, and then Congress directed them to use the SAMDA contractors. I guess the big Wall Street real estate firms have the lobbying power that the RTC employees don't have."

"And the SAMDAs have something like ninety days to service a new property?"

"And to get it entered into the Reoms database so that the rest of RTC knows about the asset. The cost to the RTC to hold on to, say, $70 million in real estate assets for about ninety days is something like $775,000 in accrued property taxes, utilities, maintenance, and the SAMDA's fees. Then add the cost of the RTC property management oversight staff salaries and overhead. And that's not even counting the lost opportunity cost if the same $775,000 was invested at even a modest 3%

annual rate of return to provide some earnings, instead of just more expenses. And that's just for one SAMDA contract," she finished.

Alan stood up and started pacing back and forth across his office and his face was turning red. "There must be some way to hold on to some of the real estate so we can sell it. Otherwise, why are we here?"

"Travis mentioned to me that we will now have to just monitor the SAMDA's performance to make sure they perform, and to report to him, or I guess now to Sam Franklin, if the properties are not being handled correctly. I think Travis was trying to get the process changed when he hired you, but Washington, DC made it clear that the private-fee contractors will be paid to handle the real estate assets, not the sales center. Travis used the term 'traffic cop' in directing public inquiry to the appropriate SAMDA contractor handling each property."

"That isn't a sales department's function," he grumbled while he paced. "It's a gosh-damn switchboard function."

"We have to direct the public to the appropriate SAMDA contractor when they come in to make offers on the properties."

"I'm going upstairs to talk to Sam Franklin about all this," and he walked out the door leaving Shannon sitting at his desk.

Sam Franklin came down to the sales center and knocked on Shannon's open door.

"Come in, Sam," Shannon smiled at the new Sales Center Director.

"Got a minute?"

"Sure. What's up?"

Sam had a nervous smile and was obviously deciding how to approach a sensitive subject with Shannon.

"Well, it's about the Special Assets and Affordable Housing division. They will be monitoring the sale of the low-income qualified properties and reporting the sales, but they will have nothing to do with any actual sales. In the other regions, the special assets department head will continue selling the special assets and low-income properties, but not in this region. There will be a new contractor, Technical Assistance Advisors, called a TAA, coming in to help with the oversight. I'm giving the sales of the special assets and low-income properties to you," he finished with a nervous grin, as if he had given her a gift.

Shannon was stunned. She had wanted the special assets department head position originally, when Ron Turner had told her that Cinco had been chosen for the job because of her supposedly great background with special asset housing. Now, she was being told she was supposed to pick up Cinco's sales responsibility along with her own heavy load.

"Wait a minute," Shannon finally said. "Cinco has been reporting to Ron Turner, then to Heim Gerwelder, then Gary Thomas. No one can deal with her. Now she has been passed to you. She gets passed around more than a hot potato."

Sam gave a nervous chuckle.

"So why do I get the feeling that you are now the fourth boss that Cinco has had in less than a year—make that nine months? Are you telling me that her job description is changing, and as a result, so is mine."

"You might say that. Cinco has now been transferred to work under me. Let's just keep this quiet between us, Shannon. No one else seems to know much about how to run an organization like we have here. You and I are the exceptions."

The attempted compliment fell flat. "And I need you to step in right now. Washington, DC is calling for a scrub of all the real estate assets, especially the low-income eligible housing properties. I know you will do it right."

"Let me get this straight. You want me to sell the low-income qualified housing assets, but Cinco will report them as her department's goals and accomplishments?" she asked directly.

"Well, now, Shannon," he looked at the ceiling, "Let's just say that you know real estate sales like the back of your hand, that's why Ron Turner put you here. And I know very well that you can do it, too." He looked back at her and continued, "Besides, you've been interested in the special assets from the beginning, and this way you get to actually work with the properties. You should be glad I'm giving this opportunity and responsibility to you. And I'm going to get you more staff, too."

She squinted her eyes at Sam, ignoring his bait about the additional staffing, knowing how hard it was to hire new employees with the SAMDAs getting all the budget money.

"Have you talked to Alan Donovan about this so he knows what I'll be doing?" She had the feeling that Sam was accustomed to giving orders to his subordinates for other duties as assigned, and she was now receiving new, additional orders.

Sam frowned. "Never mind Alan. I don't think it would make any difference," he said and left her office.

That was a strange comment, she thought to herself. *What is going on between Sam and Alan already? Now I'm starting to think that what Mark Long said might be true. I left the FDIC frying pan for the RTC proverbial fire.*

Alan called Shannon into his office a few minutes later. "Um, little lassie, I need some help with a few reports Sam has asked me for. He wants something called a weekly offer summary report, an escrow tracking report, and something else called an Initiative report. I know what the Initiative report is, but do you know what the other ones are?"

Shannon looked at Alan, surprised that he didn't know what these very basic reports were all about. They were extremely basic real estate logs and reports, that would be utilized in any real estate operation, private, public or government.

"Well, now," she began slowly, "You know how we discussed the need to have everyone here in the sales center log in any offers they received for the real estate properties, so we could track and report all offers? The Government Credit Manual states that we have to respond to those offers with an acceptance, counteroffer, or rejection within about forty-eight hours."

"Oh, that thing. I told the other office staff we didn't have to do that."

Shannon's eyes widened with disbelief. "Alan, are you serious? The offer log is a required document in case anyone ever claims their offer was not fairly considered or responded to. We don't have the option of not doing one."

"I've never heard of anything so stupid, or time consuming. I've never done anything like an offer log before."

"That may be, Alan, but it's a little different here, working for the government. You see, there are auditors and the inspector general who will eventually come in and look over our operation. They will hold us to the credit manual for compliance. I know a lot of it seems like a waste of time, but we have to follow the corporate guidelines, policies, and procedures."

"I want to talk to you about this commercial property sales contract. It looks like it's on steroids. Fifty two pages, I want you to reduce it."

"Well, Alan, the commercial sales contract was developed by our attorneys in Headquarters, and it is the standard commercial property sales contract that is required to be used throughout the nation. I know it can seem confusing sometimes. We just have to be flexible and do the best we can."

Alan changed the subject then. "I'm getting a new secretary, Candy. Anderson in contracting asked me to hire her, she's his girlfriend. She's a real knockout, wait till you see her. It will be nice to have her to look at every day. It's a real coup to get a secretary as great looking as Candy."

Shannon stared at Alan, considering how she should respond to him. "I think we're done here for now," she said and left Alan's office, wondering what his priorities were. Certainly not reports.

"There's a gentleman in the lobby who wants information on this building. He says it's for sale, and he wants to see it today." The sales center receptionist stood in Shannon's doorway. "I didn't know our office was for sale?"

Shannon looked up from her overflowing desk at Connie, the pretty, slender blond woman in her midforties. "I knew that Washington, DC wanted to put it on the market because it would be a big sale and a large book value reduction," she replied to Connie. "But I didn't know when. We need larger office space because of all the failing savings and loans, but I didn't think that new office space had been found yet."

"Will you come out and talk to this man? He's getting kind of impatient because I couldn't give him any information on the building."

"Of course I will, Connie," Shannon responded. "I'm going to make a couple of quick phone calls and see what I can find out first. Please tell him I'm doing just that and I will be out to meet with him in just a few minutes. I'm going to call the SAMDA property management group and see who they've assigned to this property."

Connie left her office, and Shannon picked up the phone to first talk with Alan Donovan.

"Alan," she began hurriedly, "Do you know anything about our offices here being available for sale? I would think that if that were going to happen, we would know about it, or the sales center would naturally be handling the sale?"

Alan sounded tired and answered slowly and absent-mindedly. "Yeah, I was going to bring that up at our last staff meeting, but I forgot. Yeah, our offices are for sale. The appraisal just came in at about $16 to $18 million."

Shannon sat up straighter and frowned into the phone. "Do you mean you knew about this? Who in the sales center is supposed to be handling it? Who have you assigned it to? We have someone in the lobby right now who wants to talk about the building."

He sounded sluggish and fatigued and was beginning to slur his words. "Yeah, well, I know about it. But I guess I forgot to tell you. The sales center is not handling it. I guess the property management, the SAMDA section is. I was in a meeting and—"

Shannon interrupted him. "Alan, what do you mean? Why isn't the sales center handling the sale of our office building? What's going on?"

"Um, well, I guess some fellow over in property management made a pitch during a committee meeting and said that he had done a lot of commercial property work, and so the committee gave the building to a guy named Craig Endive in SAMDA to sell it."

"But I don't understand why the sales center isn't involved? We have terrific commercial sales people in our department, including you...."

"Uh, well, sure, I guess so, but I think I wasn't there for the whole meeting, maybe I've missed a couple of meetings. I-I've had a couple of doctor's appointments. And I had another doctor's appointment that day, and somehow things just got kind of turned around. I got to the meeting late. I thought they were talking about a different building. I guess Ron Turner felt that he knew Gary Thomas and trusted his input, and so when Gary recommended that Craig handle the deal, Ron Turner said OK."

She was concerned with Alan's slow talking and slow thinking about such an important matter, and for "forgetting" to mention such a visible and valuable project.

"Are you alright?" she asked Alan. "Are you feeling ok?"

"I've been having a little blood pressure problem lately. I'll be alright."

"Look, I'll be down to talk to you about this in a few minutes. Right now I have to call Endive and see what he has prepared for due diligence or marketing materials for the building." She hung up the phone with Alan and looked up Craig's phone number and dialed.

"'Lo," a male voice answered.

"Craig, this is Shannon O'Toole in the sales center. I have a gentleman in the lobby right now who wants information on this office building. I understand you are handling the project?"

"Yeah, I am," replied the arrogant voice.

She paused and waited for him to say more. When he didn't, she continued with, "OK, then would you like to come over and meet with this prospective buyer? He would like to tour the building, and he wants specifics as to its size and office count."

Immediately Craig replied. "No, I won't. He doesn't have an appointment, so he'll have to make one and come back."

Shannon could feel her blood pressure begin to rise with one more lazy property management and SAMDA oversight-minded person. "Craig, the man is here now. He's been waiting for over ten minutes already. I think we owe him the courtesy of talking with him and answering his questions. This is a $16 or $18 million dollar deal we're talking about here."

"Uh, well, yeah, it is, but I'm not going to see him without an appointment. That's all there is to it."

Shannon was becoming very angry with this arrogant, lazy man. "All right then," she said between clenched teeth. "Tell me what you know about this building, and I'll try to help him."

"Oh, sure," Craig seemed to finally wake up and come to life now that he had successfully avoided getting off his large back-side to meet with the potential buyer. He gave Shannon some preliminary details and cheerfully said, "Let me know if he wants to make me an offer," and she swiftly hung up the phone.

She went to the lobby and introduced herself to the waiting potential buyer, and gave him a tour of the building and campus, filling in as much detail as possible. When she finally came back and settled in her office again, she began to muse on the extent of waste and abuse that was going on with a growing number of inept RTC and FDIC staff. With the lazy employees and the waste and abuse with paying the SAMDA and TAA contractors for sitting on millions of dollars in properties for months and months, it was no wonder that the original amount of money Congress appropriated for the savings and loan bailout had grown exponentially. It was like dancing on shattered glass, the blood just kept draining out.

This time Sam didn't knock on Shannon's door, he just pushed it open and strode in.

"Hi, Sam," Shannon said as she looked up at her still new boss. One look at his face told her that there was something very wrong.

"Uh, hi, Shannon. There's something I have to talk to you about."

"OK," she said, waiting for him to continue.

Without any preamble, he said, "Uh, there was some conflict that occurred in the general meeting earlier today."

"What happened?" she said quietly.

"Well, Alan and Gary went toe to toe about who was going to handle the new properties coming in from a new failed savings and loan in Arizona, the sales center or SAMDA, and things got a little out-of-hand."

Shannon continued to listen, waiting for Sam to gather his thoughts.

"Alan challenged Gary about the competence of the SAMDA contractors and I thought Gary was going to explode. And it looked like Alan was having trouble breathing. They went back and forth until Ron finally stepped in and called them into his office to finish the discussion privately. After they were finished, Ron called me and told me Alan was going to be working on a special project. He won't be coming to the sales center for a while."

Shannon was about to respond when Sam continued. "I want to put you in charge while we figure things out here. I don't know what we're going to do about Alan. I think he'll be out for a while. I'll talk to you more about this later, but I'll put out a memorandum about you being the sales center coordinator and assistant director in Alan's absence. OK?"

She nodded her understanding and then added, "You know, Sam, after the special assets and low-income housing workload being added here, I'm really overloaded. I really need some help."

He nodded. "I'll try and get you more staff. I'll see what I can do," and he left. He never found her any help.

⚭

The office building on 19th Street sold and the RTC operation moved to new offices in Newport Beach. The sales center was located on the ground floor for easy public access, between two tower buildings where the other RTC departments were housed. About the time of the transfer, Ron Turner retired, and was replaced with two new managers. Frank Atwater was the new top boss. He was in his seventies. Justin Paulson was his second in command, a blond man in his mid to late forties.

Alan Donovan had returned to work after several months' rest, and he and Shannon were summoned up to Justin Paulson's office. They were barely seated when Paulson began.

"I want you both to know that I want the real estate sales increased. I am personally increasing the sales goals for the sales center. There is too much real estate just sitting around and costing the RTC money to hold those properties. I want to see the assets sold and moved out. Do I make myself clear?"

Alan just sat staring at the floor, not saying a word. in California, the SAMDA contractors were stalling and holding the properties to collect their management fees and then taking too long to sell the properties. Sometimes they didn't even get the properties appraised or get the appropriate environmental reports performed as another way to delay the sale of the properties, and to extend their management fees.

Shannon waited a minute more to see if Alan would say anything. When it was clear that Alan wasn't going to speak up, she spoke quietly,

"I see, Justin, what you want. However, here in the California office, most of the real estate is under the control of the SAMDA contractors. We cannot take the properties away from the SAMDAs and sell them. The sales center is ready, willing and able to sell the properties, however, we can't get to them."

"What do you mean, you can't get to the properties?" his voice elevating. Justin had a reputation for yelling, and it appeared his reputation was correct.

Shannon looked over at Alan and saw him continuing to look at the floor, not attempting to respond to Justin. She took a deep breath, and felt her heart flutter a little too fast.

"Well, we have a very strong SAMDA property management group here, Justin, and they won't agree to release any properties to the sales department once they are put under a SAMDA contract. And they put almost everything into a SAMDA contract immediately, before we even know about the property."

"Why don't you just pay the SAMDA their g-damn fees, and sell the property anyway?" he bellowed.

"We would like to have that opportunity, and we are ready to sell the properties, but we are not able to get them released from SAMDA control or to get to the files on the properties."

"Who the hell is in charge of this mess?" he yelled.

"You may want to talk to Gary Thomas, as he heads up the SAMDA property management department."

"And what else do you need to sell the g-damn assets?" he continued to roar, and then he answered for himself. "I'll talk this mess over with Thomas, and issue a written memorandum stating that the assets can be withdrawn from the SAMDA contract for the sales center to sell the properties. Will that do?"

Shannon nodded her head in agreement. "That would be great, and we can go forward immediately selling the SAMDA-controlled assets."

Just as Shannon was beginning to feel that the conversation had turned out just about as good as it possibly could, Justin came around his desk. Alan still had not said a word. Justin glared down at Alan and Shannon and threatened,

"There are over two thousand boxes to be unpacked and inventoried from failed savings and loan sitting in storage. You two will be reassigned to work on those boxes if you can't get the real estate sales to turn around. I want the real estate sold. Do you both understand?"

Alan nodded silently. Shannon's heart was really beating too fast now. She didn't like the lightheaded feeling she was having. She felt like she was caught in a catch 22; she was being ordered to sell assets that she couldn't touch. And she wasn't sure that Justin completely understood the situation.

Shannon looked directly at Justin and answered, "We are ready to sell the properties, Mr. Paulson, and we'll meet your goal if you can get the properties released to us."

"Good!", he exclaimed. "That's what I wanted to hear!"

And the meeting was over.

Sam Franklin came into Shannon's office.

"I want to talk to you about the REO coordinator's position and a few other positions as well," and Sam sat down. "I've been successful at getting approval to hire additional positions for more sales center staff," he began, obviously pleased.

"That's great," Shannon offered. "We sure do need more help, especially with all the new failed savings and loans assets and walk-in traffic we're getting now."

"That's what I figured, and the proforma budget you prepared substantiating the additional staffing was certainly a big help."

"Good, that was the whole purpose of putting the numbers together."

"Yes, right, and of course, I had to finish the overall request and get it just right in order to present it to Atwater and Washington, DC," he boasted. "But it all went together just fine, and now we will be advertising for a few more good people. And that's what I want to talk to you about. There are a few resumes and 171s I want you to look over and consider when interviewing candidates for the new slots." He handed Shannon a short stack of applications. The infamous government form 171 was a lengthy job application document, often taking an estimated six to eight hours to complete.

"I thought that the government hiring rules stated that we had to review all 'veterans preference' applications first, then internal candidates, and, last, outside candidates?" she asked.

"Well, maybe that would be correct if there were any veterans or internal candidates that were qualified," he chuckled. "But can you imagine anyone, *any one* of those people over in property management coming over into the real estate sales department? Can you?" He laughed.

"I do think I've heard that some good people from other RTC and FDIC offices would like to come on board or transfer to our sales center here in California. I think we should take a look at them."

"Well, you can take a look, but before you do anything or hire anyone, I want you to look over three candidates I've just given you."

Shannon glanced down at the first application. "I see that Jacquelin Mason has been a consultant and has been independent for quite a while here. Her salary is also quite a bit lower than our similar job descriptions. Do you think that she will fit into a structured environment like ours with layers of approvals and deadlines? She looks like she has been very independent and may have a problem with all the rules and government regulations here."

Sam turned his chair sideways and looked over his shoulder at Shannon. "Just keep one of the real estate sales positions for her. She made a very good impression on one of our Washington, DC boys during a Headquarters public outreach event."

Shannon looked down at the next application. "Yang Beno has been a commercial leasing agent in New York," she read out load. "I can't find anything on his application about knowing anything about commercial real estate transaction law, environmental law, title reports, sales, or contracts."

Sam turned his chair to the other side and said to Shannon, "Keep a real estate position for him."

Shannon couldn't understand why Sam was taking this position he was taking. "Have you met these two people before, Sam? Are they really good?"

"Yes, I've either met them or Ted Joiner has met them, and we think they will be very good additions to the sales department. Ted and I gave some public seminars to promote the RTC and did some outreach public speeches to let the public know about our operations and assets for sale. Both Jacquelin Mason and Yang Beno attended those seminars and asked about working for the RTC. Ted Joiner and Jacquelin have met several times," he said with a smile and a wink.

Shannon waited for Sam to continue, but he stopped. She looked down at the third candidate's application. "Bennett Kemper," she said out loud, "was a commercial real estate broker then went to Hawaii and ran a surf shop for several years. Looks like he kind of dropped out of active brokerage for a few years there. He used to manage a bank trust portfolio, but I don't see anything current that would lead me to think he would be capable of handling a heavy commercial real estate portfolio or be a superior candidate."

"I want you to hold a position for him too," Sam said without a smile.

"Do you know him or of him too?" Shannon asked.

"He is a friend of Wayne Grey, our western regional director. I will take Wayne's word for it that this fellow is good."

Shannon saw that she would accomplish little by discussing these candidates any further with Sam, but still wanted to discuss the new REO coordinator's position.

"Sam, since I've been carrying Alan's load for quite a while now, I hope I have your support now that the position is open to be filled."

She waited for his response, expecting his support and even a compliment for all her hard work. Sam still sat sideways, and made a steeple with his two hands. He looked out the window.

"You know, Shannon, how things can change in an organization the size of this one. One day you're the director, and the next day you're an asset specialist. The corporations needs change, the political climate changes, and sometimes we have to be flexible and understand that there are obligations and reasons jobs are filled with certain people."

She wasn't sure what he was getting at, but she was sure she was getting brushed off.

"I've been doing the job, Sam," she answered him evenly, looking at his profile.

He finally turned to face her. "I know that, and I appreciate it, you've done a great job. A terrific job. But you're only a grade fourteen. And this is a grade fifteen job."

"Yes, I know. And after being a grade fourteen for a few years, and demonstrating that I have done a good job handling the responsibilities of the coordinator's grade-fifteen job, as well as my own department's responsibilities, I feel I am the best candidate for the job."

Sam nodded his head. "I understand, but politics are politics. Go ahead and throw your hat into the ring, that's OK. But I just want you to know that the grade situation is going to be rough for you to get past."

She thought, *How naïve of me to think that hard work and integrity would pay off with this government work.* It was all politics, and she was an apolitical woman.

Shannon wasn't interviewed for the real estate coordinator's position. Alan Donovan was moved into an internal position, and a new sales center coordinator, Hastings Kemper, was brought in instead. Kemper, who had been managing a failing savings and loan, was appointed into the position. As much as Shannon wanted the job, she found that she enjoyed working with Kemper. He knew real estate inside out and gave her as much freedom and leeway as possible to run her department as she saw fit. She had to admit, it was the first time in a long time she only had to do one job, and it was a relief.

A new format intended to open up the lines of communication between the sales center and the property management section was developed to include weekly meetings to discuss the status of all real estate properties. The intent was a good one, the actual execution a disaster.

Shannon entered the conference room on the second floor of the RTC SAMDA property management department and looked around at the other meeting members. There was only one other woman, a secretary prepared to take notes.

She noted that Gary Thomas was present, with about seven other men from his property management staff. Shannon sat with Ian McNally and Rick Jessup, two of Shannon's colleagues from the real estate sales center.

Gary Thomas opened the meeting, and sat his large 250 pound frame into a chair at the end of the table.

"As you all know, these weekly meetings have been set up to open up the lines of communication between the property management department and the sales center. During the recent 'visitation' from RTC Washington, DC and the internal auditors, it became apparent that there is some friction between our two departments. At these weekly meetings, we will share information and attempt to repair any dissention at this level. Frank Atwater and Justin Paulson want this problem cleared up now, and no further such reports about the two departments not getting along are to occur in any future reports. It's a bad reflection on management. Is that clear?"

Shannon looked around the table and noted that all eight men from the property management department had their eyes diverted down toward the table or at the walls. Ian McNally, one of the other department heads in the real estate sales center, responsible for multifamily sales, sat to Shannon's right. He was about 70 years old, had been an attorney in his earlier years, and was usually a peacemaker. He spoke up.

"I'm sure we all want to do what's best here. There's no need for any more finger pointing. I know the sales center has always wanted to be cooperative, and I think these meetings are going to open a good deal of understanding between our departments."

"I certainly hope so," Gary Thomas responded gruffly. "I'm going to leave now and turn this meeting over to Mark Beneteau to run."

With that, the large man left the room. His other eight property managers seemed to heave a collective sigh of relief. Mark Beneateu, another very large man of around 240 pounds with a deep, bellowing voice, began to speak.

"We all must accept that FIRREA is the founding legislation for the RTC, and that FIRREA instructs us to use outside fee contractors to manage all the properties from the failed savings and loans."

Shannon winced. Was this just going to be another reiteration of excuses as to why the property management department felt they could pay exorbitant fees to the SAMDA contractors and to tie up the real estate assets from the failed institutions? And what about the instructions she had just been given by

Frank Atwater and Justin Paulson to sell the properties? At least headquarters had just released a new memo instructing staff to prepare selected properties for accelerated sales, such as real estate auctions. All across the nation, RTC would be conducting property auctions to reduce holding inventory and paying extensive management and related fees.

"Mark, have you had a chance to read the new Directive that just came out of Washington, DC on accelerated sales and marketing, and especially auctions?" she asked politely.

"Yes, I have. But I don't think auctions work. Nobody in the property management department thinks they work. They tie up the properties for too long, and they don't bring in very good prices. We think that the SAMDA contractors do a better job of selling the properties than an auctioneer." Mark Beneteau retorted loudly. The other men from the property management department nodded their heads in agreement.

"I think the most recent auction results showed that the properties were being sold at about 92-95% of the appraised value. The cost of sales was less than 3%. The average holding time was less than 99 days, and the savings on the holding costs were impressive. Washington, DC has been very pleased with those numbers," Shannon advised calmly.

"I don't believe those numbers are real," Mark roared. "I think they just chose a few good examples and expect us to believe them. Where were those auctions done anyway?"

"The Kansas, Florida, and Atlanta offices have been extremely successful with their auctions, including affordable housing auctions. The press has been favorable, and the results have been great. Auctions are one of the primary sales procedures in those offices."

"Well, that may be fine for those offices," he continued to complain. "But they won't be here. We don't want our SAMDA contractors doing any auctions," he finished.

Shannon decided she wasn't getting anywhere with Mark, and she turned to the one man in the room she felt was more rational and professional. In her past dealings with Stewart VanHuesen, he was fair, honest, and seemed to be the only one in property management with integrity. He read all of the management directives, not just those pertaining to property management, and he was always willing to listen to both sides in the committee meetings. Shannon had recently had the opportunity to meet with Stewart to discuss a comparison of sales methods and their related expenses. She appealed to Stewart, a tall, thin man, with an honest face and a sincere smile.

"Stewart, we were talking about the expenses of an auction versus the fees charged by the SAMDA contractors. And it seems that we came up with a figure of 3% or less to conduct an auction within 60 days, versus 5%-6% for the SAMDA to manage and sell the same properties, after counting their setup fees, contractual right to have 60 days before actually preparing the budget and appraisal for the property, and their sales commission. I don't think we even counted the holding time the RTC pays while the contractors have the properties."

Stewart seemed a little uncomfortable to be singled out as a possible ally to the sales department, but he responded honestly, "We did have the chance to talk about different sales initiatives and strategies, which included auctions, sealed bids, and SAMDA negotiated sales. For some properties, it did seem to make sense that the auction method was the best one. Especially for out-of-the-area properties, it made a lot of sense."

Shannon wasn't altogether pleased with his edited response. Another man from the property management department, Den Tang, a short, plump man with a balding head and glasses then added, "So you mean, Stewart, that the properties outside of California can go into auctions, but not the California properties?"

Before Stewart could answer, Derrick Penner, another property management department head, about sixty years old with a receding hairline and thin moustache, leaned forward. "So, if we give you the out-of-state assets for auctions, you would be satisfied with that? And leave the California assets alone for the SAMDA contractors to sell?"

Shannon was taken aback by this obvious effort to extract an agreement from her, and to tie her hands from working on any California properties. She felt her heart begin to beat too fast again, like a butterfly trying to get out of her chest.

"No, that's not what I'm saying at all," she countered reasonably. The men from the property management department shifted uncomfortably in their chairs. "I'm saying that when our Atlanta, or Kansas, or Florida office is already holding an auction, it is our best sales strategy to put any assets we have in those geographic areas into their auctions. It is a much faster and economical way to sell the properties within 45-60 days, as opposed to having a SAMDA contractor hold the property for 90-120 days before listing the property with a local broker. I would like to see the same thing for California assets," she added, wanting to get her comments regarding the California properties into the minutes for the meeting—however, finding that she was a little short of breath.

The property management men all spoke spontaneously and mumbled among themselves. She caught portions of comments including, "We can't let her do that", and "no way do we want auctions in California" to "We'll put all the California properties into SAMDA contracts as fast as we can to protect them from the sales center and auctions."

About then, Rick Jessup, the third department head from the sales center, cleared his throat. "Hmm," he began. "Let's just say that we have discussed the fact that certain sales strategies and initiatives can sell properties more quickly and economically, and that the sales center will be looking over the real estate inventory for likely candidates for sales efforts..."

Rick was interrupted by Hector Gunther, a small, blond man. "I don't think Washington, DC wants the sales center to take any assets away from the SAMDA contractors for the sale center to sell. Otherwise, the SAMDA contractor would still get his management and sales commission anyway, even if the sales center did the sale."

"Or maybe," Rick countered, "Our two departments should agree as to which properties go into SAMDA contracts and which ones go to the sales center for sale." Rick had just uttered an unthinkable solution to the property management department. Their collective gasp, rumblings, and mumblings were evidence that they would never consider such a recommendation.

Shannon was beginning to see that the SAMDA property management staff had not received the same message that she and Alan Donovan had just received.

"Evidentially you are not aware of the new shift Atwater and Paulsen are taking. They have some different ideas about how they want the real estate properties sold," she informed the group. "I just met with Justin Paulsen earlier this week.

He wants the properties sold through sales center initiatives. I believe we will be seeing a new memorandum coming out on this matter from Justin. I think the sales center can go through the current list of new real estate assets and indicate what sales center marketing programs they can fit into. Those assets should not go into SAMDA contracts; they will be handled by the sales center. I will submit a list of those assets to this committee and to Sam Franklin and Gary Thomas, our respective Directors, for their concurrence. That way, they will see that our two departments are working in concert and cooperation." She smiled, as she felt she had found the common ground between the two departments.

"No way!" began Den Tang. He was interrupted by Mark Beneteau with a curt, "Just let it drop, Den. We'll discuss this with Gary." Then Mark turned to the rest of the room and announced, "This meeting is adjourned."

With that, all the property management men stood up and abruptly began leaving the room. But not before Shannon overheard Den Tang mutter under his breath, "She's a bitch, and we have to stop her."

The men from the property management department went directly to Gary Thomas's office. Den Tang, Stewart Van Huesen and Mark Beneteau sat down across from Thomas' desk. Another four men stood up and moved inside the office.

"Well, how did the first kiss-ass joint department meeting go?" Thomas sneered at his selected managers.

"It was a disaster," Den Tang began.

"It wasn't exactly a disaster," corrected Mark in his booming voice. "But I didn't like the way that bitch, O'Toole, tried to get her claws into our assets," he complained. "She's a real problem."

"She thinks she knows it all because she came from the FDIC over to the RTC. And she keeps talking about inspector general audits, policies and procedures, and all that stuff. But we all came from the private sector, and we know what we're doing here better than she does. She's a bitch-on wheels," Den added.

"So you men were not able to control this one woman, this one person who has been making our lives miserable lately?"

The men looked around at each other helplessly. "What are we supposed to do?" Hector Gunther asked weakly. "She even said that Justin Paulsen was going to issue a new memorandum saying that the sales center can sell the SAMDA assets. Have you heard anything about that?"

"I'll tell you what we are going to do," Thomas announced proudly. "We are going to put the new real estate properties into a pending status in the computer, pending assignment to a SAMDA contractor. That way, the properties will appear to be under a SAMDA's control, and the sales center can't get to them. I will contact Brad Grey in Washington, DC to make sure that he writes a policy that says that once the properties are included in a SAMDA contract, they can't be pulled out by the sales department. He's the director of the SAMDA program, and my bet is he has more power than the head of the sales division! We'll stop Shannon and her cronies once and for all!"

The men smiled and relaxed, feeling that their sacred domain had once again been reinforced to keep the sales center department out.

"What about the new HomeFed and Imperial properties that we are getting this week?" Den Tang asked.

"Include them with a pending SAMDA status," Thomas instructed. "I want you to add a new column to the Reoms reports. I want a column for an A or a B letter. The A will indicate that the property is actually really under a signed SAMDA contract, and the B will indicate that it is pending being added to a SAMDA contract."

"That's a great idea, Gary," Mark Beneteau laughed. "We'll out smart those assholes."

The men stood up, laughing and joking among themselves, convinced they had just won not only a battle, but the war between the two departments.

In the sales center, Hastings Kemper had called a meeting with his three department heads, Shannon, Rick and Ian. "I want you to take one list of all the properties, both SAMDA-controlled and not SAMDA-controlled, and indicate what sales initiative the asset can go into. That means sealed bids, an umbrella marketing program, auctions, and so on. I want to see it back in my office in twenty-four hours. Any questions?"

Shannon advised, "You know, Hastings, the property management group made it very clear that they felt all the properties should still go into a SAMDA contract, and I think they are going to give us a real fight when we indicate that we have a sales program for most of the assets."

"She's right," Ian added. "If you were in that meeting just now with us, you would have seen how strongly they felt about giving up any properties for us to sell."

"Except the out-of-state properties," Rick complained, shaking his head. "They were very generous in offering to consider giving us the hard-to-sell, out-of-state properties. But it was clearly hands-off the local California stuff."

"We'll see about that," Hastings responded. "Sam Franklin is going to Frank Atwater with our sales initiative plan. When he sees that we can put most of the properties into an immediate sales program, I think you'll see a change in attitude and cooperation with the property management department."

"We sure hope so," Ian said wearily.

Shannon brought up the Justin Paulson memo. "Have you heard anything yet about the memo Justin was going to write stating that we can pull properties out of a SAMDA contract and sell the properties through sales center initiatives?"

"I haven't seen it yet. But there is a new directive out, Shannon. Washington, DC wants to see a new sales program for all assets valued at half a million or less. I want you to write the sales initiative plan, and identify the assets."

"I see," Shannon pondered. "I think that about 75% of all our real estate inventory is priced at $500,000 or less."

"Could be," Hastings countered. "But I want every property that can be included in this sales initiative plan identified."

"Whether it is in a SAMDA contract or not?" she asked.

"That's right. I understand there are almost two hundred new assets being added to the Reoms database either tonight or tomorrow from HomeFed and Imperial Bank. I want you to be sure and pick up all of those new assets too. Go ahead and take them for auctions."

"Are you sure?" She was surprised. "We haven't done any California auctions yet, but I will be happy to set them up."

"Good, then you all know what I want, and when I want it?" he stated, rather than asked.

"Yes," was his answer from his three department heads in unison.

Hastings then asked, "Have you heard anything about something called Cash for Keys?"

"It seems RTC has a 'Cash for Keys' program, where residents in a home that is being foreclosed on after the borrowers stop making house payments to the bank, are offered $5,000 to move out and leave the property in clean and undamaged condition," Shannon offered.

"I understand the SAMDA group offers this program. RTC and other lenders are arguing that this is an efficient program because the properties are generally left in decent condition when the owners are given an incentive to move out. When holdover owners are offered the cash for keys, it's an inducement for the old owners to get more money, even after they may have lived in the property for a year or more without making any house payments. However, it could be argued that the previous owners lived in the property for free and shouldn't benefit or receive more money to move out. Additionally, the holdover owners often illegally occupy the property after the foreclosure, which then requires an eviction, and during the eviction process, it takes up to six months to have them removed, so that's additional time they live in the property for free without paying house payments. But, the argument from the SAMDA department is that the old owners trash the house, strip out the plumbing and appliances, punch holes in the walls, and all that if the Cash for Keys is not offered."

"Find out more, O'Toole, and let me know," Hastings said. "I want to understand how the whole Cash for Keys process works."

Shannon walked over to the sales center information services guru, Manny Bracken, and sat down at his desk.

"What can I do you for?" Manny asked. She enjoyed Manny with his unusual, somewhat off-center humor. His sarcasm knew no limits, but he was a genuine great guy.

"You can run a new list of real estate inventory for me, please. Washington has just put out a new memorandum mandating us to put all properties with an appraised value of $500,000 or less into a sales event. I need to see what we have that is either in a SAMDA contract or not in a pending sales contract."

Manny laughed and answered, "You mean you want to see everything, right?"

She smiled and nodded.

"If you want to wait, I can run the report for you in just a minute. I wanted to talk to you about some new enhancements to the system anyway, and now is just as good a time as any to discuss the changes." Manny turned around and hit a few keys on one of the several computers in his office, and then mumbled something to himself as he peered at the screen.

"What is it, Manny?" Shannon asked.

"Hmmm, well, now, it looks like our illustrious friends in the property management department have just added a new field of codes to the Reoms database. I wonder why?"

"A new field of data? What is it supposed to reflect?"

"Well, I don't know just yet, but I'm gonna find out here real quick." Manny entered a few more key strokes and codes into the computer, and with the new program he had just entered, pulled off a couple of newly printed pages of inventory.

"This, Shannon, is the new data field called 'SAMDA.' It seems that every piece of property RTC has in its inventory is under SAMDA control, and each property is indicated with either an A or a B. Now, it seems to be that when I only run the properties with an A in the column, it matches the current list of inventory that is listed with a SAMDA contractor. And when

I run a sample of the B list properties, they are not yet under a SAMDA contractors' control. Now isn't that interesting?"

"Yes it is," she agreed. "What do you think this is all about?"

"I would say that our good friends in property management are trying to give the impression that all the properties are in a SAMDA contract and that the sales center can't touch them or try to sell them. That's what I think they are doing."

Shannon could feel her heart start to beat too fast again, and she felt a little fuzzy. "Manny, do you think you can verify that for me, and let me know as soon as possible?"

"Sure Shannon, I'll get right on it."

She left the computer wizard's office.

Shannon submitted her auction plan to Hastings. She was pleased with her work. She had designated every asset with an appraised value of $500,000 or less for either an auction or a sealed bid, whether they were in the A or B column on the real estate reports. She had prepared a detailed memorandum for Hastings and the property management department noting which properties were to be placed into the several sales initiatives.

Manny reported back to Shannon that his analysis of the new A and B data field was correct.

She had been very careful and detailed with her reports, noting that the A properties were already under a SAMDA contract, and that the B properties were not, and into which sales event each of the real estate properties would go. The report was color coded according to sales event and the geographic location of the assets. Hastings had called a meeting to discuss Shannon's sales plan.

Hastings Kemper opened the meeting with, "Has anyone here noticed a new code column in the Reoms database?"

Shannon looked at Rick and Ian, and neither of them could answer Hastings's question.

"It seems that the B column indicates new properties, like from HomeFed or Western Savings, that are intended to go into a SAMDA, and the A column are those properties that are already signed and under contract with a SAMDA," Shannon filled them in.

Rick Jessup commented first. "I asked the SAMDA department about those codes, and they told me that it indicated which fee contractor was managing and marketing the property." He didn't like being lied to.

"Well, they didn't exactly tell you how their codes worked, and Manny was able to confirm how the codes are being used," Hastings explained.

"That's really deceptive," Shannon commented, surprised at just how far the property management staff would go to control the assets.

"Don't you guys have a joint property management/sales department meeting in three days?" Hastings asked.

The three department heads nodded and began to gather their notes and reports.

"I will distribute this sales center plan to liquidate all of the properties valued at under $500,000 to Gary Thomas, and I will discuss their attempt to hide the assets from our sales events," Hastings informed them.

Shannon turned around and asked Hastings, "We have provided the RTC directors with sufficient information about the lack of cooperation from the property management department and the waste before. Why don't they take some kind of action and correct the problems?"

Hastings sighed. "Because, Shannon, if any of the Directors were to go to Atwater with the problems to get his support, it would appear that they were not capable of doing their own jobs. And if the Property Management Director isn't willing to give up any power or compromise, then the other Directors can't successfully make any changes. None of the Directors wants to be seen as not having the skill or ability to fix the problems, so no one is telling Atwater that the two departments have such serious problems. It's all about ego, power, and control."

"And politics?" Shannon said sarcastically.

"And, most importantly, politics," Hastings agreed.

Shannon was waiting for a large copying project to be completed at the business center. As she waited and leaned against the counter, she noticed a short stack of SAMDA files for commercial properties also waiting for copying. She noticed that these were the same commercial properties that she had tagged for an auction event planned by the sales center. It had been a battle, but she had received support from Atwater to pull the properties for the event.

Well, this is convenient, she thought to herself. She casually opned the first file and began scanning its contents. She was astounded at what she was reading. She quickly left the business center and went into Hastings office.

"Hastings, I need to advise you of more SAMDA property management staff waste and abuse. I just looked at some SAMDA files for about fifty million dollars of old bank buildings that Atwater agreed to have placed into our sales center auction initiative that have been under a SAMDA contract. I looked at all the broker listing agreements for the required cancellation clause that modifies the SAMDA and broker fees and commission in the event the RTC pulls the properties back for a sales initiative. That clause is mandated by a Washington, DC directive for all properties handled by RTC. I have even discussed this clause with the property management department before in meetings and provided them with a copy of the Washington, DC directive giving the language for the cancelation clauses," she paused and took a deep breath. "If these commercial properties go into one of the sales centers' new auctions, because the property management department has elected to ignore the directive, it will be costing the RTC over one million dollars in commissions that should not be paid."

"What?!" Hastings exclaimed and stood up from his chair. "They're not abiding by the broker modification directive from Washington, DC either?"

"That's right." Shannon continued. "I don't know why they think they don't have to abide by the same directives we are given, but they are refusing to go along with this directive. I spoke to some of the remaining bank employees at HomeFed, and they said the SAMDA property management department told them they didn't have to modify their broker listing agreements right now. Maybe in the future, but not now."

"Give me a copy of your memo to the property management department with the broker modification attachment."

"Sure," she replied, and took a deep breath. "The final matter I need to discuss with you is even more important though."

"More property management uncooperation, or should I say sabotage?"

"Actually, it's just plain incompetence this time. Remember all the directives we have been receiving from Washington, DC about environmental studies, surveys, and remediation?

"After I reviewed several SAMDA properties for appraisals and environmental studies, I found that the SAMDAs had not ever ordered the required environmental reports for the commercial properties. Either the property management department hasn't been managing their SAMDA contractors, or they have not given the SAMDAs the memos from Washington, DC about ordering the environmental reports. Either way, it's incompetence. The RTC rules state that the commercial properties cannot be sold without the environmental report completed and a remediation plan in place, if needed. So, there are hundreds of millions of dollars of commercial properties and old bank buildings that cannot be offered for sale because they don't have the required environmental surveys completed."

Hastings rolled his eyes back, shook his head, sat back down and leaned far back into his chair. "I can't believe all this! I mean I do believe you, of course. But what the hell have all those property management people been doing? Shit! They know we can't sell the property until the appraisals and environmental studies are done. I think they are purposefully holding up the sale of all these damn properties! I think they know exactly what they are doing."

"Rather, what they *haven't* been doing," she echoed his thoughts. "So the SAMDA contractors are billing for six months or so for their fees, even though they are not doing their job. And we can't sell the properties. They are delaying our sales. When I call the SAMDA directly, they tell me they have up to sixty days to order the appraisal, and it sometime takes a month or two to get the appraisal, so they are holding up the property for four months that way, too. But they want their fees paid, for doing nothing."

"Just get a memo to me on this right away," he said between clenched teeth. "I've had just about as much of this maleficence and incompetency as I can take. Sam Franklin is going to have to take this to Atwater; it's gone on too long and too far."

"So we are just going to continue to keep limping along, fighting with the property management department for some assets to sell? Do you really think Sam will take this fight to Atwater and Paulsen?" Shannon asked.

"Don't give up, kid," Hastings answered her. "Just keep up the good work."

"This is like adding more shattered glass to an already deep pool of blood. The fraud and waste just keeps getting thicker."

Shannon entered the joint departmental meeting later that week and noticed that the same men from the property management department were present, with one addition. This time there was one new woman, in her fifties, with short, gray curly hair. Shannon wondered who she was.

As Mark Beneteau sat down his considerable bulk at the head of the table, he answered her question. "I would like to introduce our newest department Head, Rhonda Freeman, to our meeting. She is oversight for the Wellington SAMDA contractor and will be heading up the sales of single-family properties." Rhonda barely looked up or looked at any of the three sales center department heads; instead, she kept her eyes down on a report in front of her or on Beneteau.

Mark continued. "I think we should review the list of assets Shannon sent over with her wish list of assets for various auctions or sealed bids."

Shannon didn't miss the sarcastic 'wish list' comment.

"We all received the same Directive from Washington, DC, Mark, that gave clear instructions to place all assets valued at under $500,000 into immediate sales initiatives. I went through the entire list of available properties, and noted the ones that were already in signed SAMDA contracts from those that were just earmarked for a SAMDA contract."

With this last comment, she noticed several of the property management men exchange surprised looks, as if she had broken some secret code of theirs by discovering their system for designating SAMDA assets.

Mark Beneteau surprised Shannon with his comment,

"Well, now, Rhonda has some information for us on some of those properties."

Rhonda cleared her throat and began,

"Yes, well, I need to let you know, Shannon, that almost all the properties you have selected for California auctions or sealed bids were all put into new SAMDA contracts this week. The SAMDAs will be responsible for selling those properties now."

Shannon tensed and answered, "You know that those properties were identified for sales center sales initiatives as a response to the Washington, DC directive. That was the purpose of my memo, so the new properties would not be put under contract to incur the SAMDA fees. Why did you put them into SAMDA contracts after they had been reserved for the sales events? Why was this done deliberately?"

Rhonda smirked, and Mark stifled a chuckle. "It was a mistake on our part, Shannon. We were just doing our usual job in putting properties into SAMDA contracts, and your assets were put into their contracts too. You'll just have to cancel your sales events."

Ian saw what was going on and spoke up.

"You know that we are supposed to put those properties into sales events, and you have obstructed the sales center's efforts to be responsive to the DC directive."

Den Tang countered Ian's complaint with, "Oh, well, Ian, the properties are in the SAMDA contract now, and you can't pull them out. So let's just get over it."

Ian wouldn't give in to the younger smart aleck. "Isn't it true that the SAMDA contractor gets up to sixty days to even open the boxes with the property files in them? And then they get a couple more months to order appraisals and to prepare budgets on the properties before they even begin the market them for sale?"

"Yeah, something like that," Den smirked.

"So why would the property management department purposely take assets that Shannon had reserved for California auctions and other sales events and put them under a SAMDA contract that would purposefully delay the sale of the assets five to six months? Do you have any idea what the carrying cost and holding time is on those properties?" Ian was getting wound up now. "It's probably another half a million dollars. Did you even consider that?"

Mark Beneteau spoke up to defend Den Tang.

"Now just a minute, Ian. We said we were sorry, and we admitted we may have made a mistake by putting your assets for your sales events into a SAMDA contract. We'll try to be more careful in the future."

Shannon then said, "For the minutes of this meeting, I would like it recorded that we need to have our Directors, Sam Franklin and Gary Thomas, present at our next meeting to resolve these issues of putting properties into SAMDA contracts or being reserved for sales center initiatives. I would also like to discuss the lack of use by the property management department of the broker listing modification directive, to reduce broker listing commissions in the event the property is pulled for a sales event, as Washington, DC has directed. And I would also like to enter into the minutes of the meeting the lack of environmental reports ordered by the SAMDAs, thus preventing the marketing and sale of the commercial properties." Her heart was beating too fast again, but she wanted those important items in the minutes to the meeting.

Dem Tang smirked, "It don't matter anyway, because the SAMDAs will be selling the properties, they won't be goin' into any sales center initiatives."

"Just put my requests into the minutes, please," Shannon retorted.

"Is there any other business?" Mark Beneteau smirked.

With no one else bringing anything more to the table, the short meeting was adjourned.

When Shannon arrived back in her office, she was surprised to see Alan Donovan and another large man waiting outside her door. Alan smiled at Shannon as she approached.

"There she is!" he greeted her jovially. He turned toward the other large man and introduced him to Shannon, "This is my sidekick, Francisco," he chuckled. "We are the new seller financing division, the two of us," he explained.

"Hello, Francisco. And what are you financing?" She played along.

"Oh, you know, anything that the sales center might need financed, if the buyers don't have their own financing arranged," Alan informed her.

Shannon thought this was a bit strange since all the assets she had sold thus far had been purchased with the buyer obtaining their own financing through their own sources. The sales center's intent was to convert real estate and other failed bank assets into cash, although a seller financing note or loan could also be considered an asset, and then be later sold.

"Can we come in for a minute?" Alan asked.

"Of course," Shannon answered, indicating that they should all sit around the small conference table and chairs in her office. She put her files down on her desk from the earlier meeting and slipped into a chair while Alan and Francisco managed to place a portion of their generous selves onto the remaining chairs.

"So when did this new seller financing initiative come about?" Shannon politely inquired.

"Well, you know there's been rumors of a RIF, Reduction In Force, layoffs, because savings and loan closings have slowed down, and because asset inventory is declining because of your auctions. We wanted to make ourselves valuable."

"Oh?" she responded neutrally.

"A couple of weeks ago," Alan answered proudly. "Francisco and I were talking about what we could do to help RTC sell assets more quickly, and we thought that by offering seller financing we could do that. I wrote a memo to Headquarters, and they agreed to let us try it."

"So will you be developing protocols for your programs?" she asked, continuing the conversation politely.

"Ah, well, it's still really new," Francisco began. "You were our first stop to tell about it."

She paused for a minute, and then changed directions, "Do you have your financing terms or rate sheet developed?" she asked quietly.

"Ah, no, we'll be working on that next," answered Francisco again.

"And then how about the actual seller financing contract and details?" she inquired. "I'm guessing you'll need to go through our legal department and work with them on the contracts."

"See, I told you she was smart," Alan chuckled.

"I can see that," Francisco concurred.

Shannon didn't respond.

"Um, Shannon," Alan began again. "There's something else I wanted to talk to you about."

"All right," Shannon responded with a puzzled expression on her face.

"Well, you see, it's like this," Alan continued, now a little uncomfortable, Shannon could see. "You've really been selling a lot of the real estate assets and the loan pools around here for assets that aren't with SAMDAs, everybody calls you the Auction Queen."

Shannon eyed Alan carefully and said, "I'm sure I've been called other things as well."

Alan looked embarrassed and peered out the window, "That's been unfortunate with the property management group, I'll admit."

She redirected the conversation with, "Yes, the auctions have been quite successful, and they are a tremendous amount of work. My staff has done an outstanding job selling so much of the inventory in such a short amount of time," she agreed.

"You see, well, it's like this," he began and then trailed off, looking at the floor again.

"Yes, Alan, and what else?"

"Well, it's what you said, selling a lot of real estate in a short time."

"And what's your issue with that?" She inclined her head.

Francisco finally took over the conversation. "You see, Shannon, because you're selling so much of the inventory, there's just nothing left for anyone else to do here. RTC is supposed to sunset in 1997, and most of us were thinking that date would be extended because that's what usually happens with government agencies; they get extended several more years. If you had left the SAMDA contractors alone, we would all be just fine. But now you've gone and sold or designated most everything for auctions and other sales initiatives, and we don't have anything to do."

Shannon was extremely surprised at this message from Alan and Francisco. Alan finally looked up.

"Look, the economy still isn't very strong. The savings and loans are still failing, although at a slower rate, and RTC has been doing more whole bank sales to an assuming lender so we don't ever get the failed bank branches or foreclosures anymore. Some of the SAMDA contractors are talking about quitting the RTC since there isn't enough profit in their contracts anymore."

Shannon was again taken aback with this new information.

"We're not asking you to stop with your auctions, but leave something for the rest of us to do. We're afraid there's going to be a RIF—you know, a reduction in force, with us in the property management division. We'll be looking at layoffs. If you had just left everything alone with the SAMDA contractors, we wouldn't be in this position. Maybe you could have smaller auctions, or stretch them out, and don't have them so often. Or maybe just sell the out-of-state properties…"

With his last comment, Shannon stiffened. "You know, Alan, sometimes you have to step back and look at the big picture. The federal government is due an honest job by its' employees, not a slow down or delayed program performance…"

"But we have good paying jobs now, Shannon," Francisco tried again. "We're not going to find these salaries anywhere else outside the government."

Shannon just looked at Alan and Francisco, sadly knowing that neither of them had contributed much to the RTC in the last several years. Now they had summoned up a new plan to hang on a little longer with their seller financing plan. She didn't wish anyone to lose their job, but she did expect an employee to honestly earn the pay they received each week, instead of just coasting along day after day. Most of the property management staff was being paid six figures, although it was to stall the sale of the assets, not liquidate them efficiently. If the seller financing could help sell an asset, then that would be a justifiable action to take.

"Look, Alan, I can't slow down the pace of auctions we are doing here at the sales center; you and I both know it's the ethical thing to continue with an efficient auction program." She took a breath. "But if your seller financing program could make is easier to sell some of the larger commercial assets, then I think we can consider that and include the information in our marketing outreach materials."

Alan looked both hopeful and rejected at the same time. "So you won't release some of the assets from the auctions?"

he asked. "But you will consider offering our seller financing in your auctions?"

"Correct on both," she answered. "When you get your terms and contracts worked out with legal, let me know. I can put some information in the next commercial auction catalogue and talk about the seller financing in the auction seminars we do for the public before each auction event. Does that work for you?"

Alan and Francisco were quiet while pondering her response. "I guess it will have to do." Alan looked at Francisco.

"We're hearing rumbles from Washington, DC that RTC could close sooner than the sunset date," Francisco complained.

"We'll all have to see how it turns out," she said and stood to indicate that their meeting was over.

As Alan and Francisco stood to leave, Alan looked at Shannon, "Did you hear? Gary Thomas was fired this morning."

Shannon couldn't hide her surprise. "No, I hadn't heard that."

"It seems that Gary embarrassed Cinco in front of most of the property management staff. He yelled out at her when she was walking by, 'Hey, Cinco, I almost didn't recognize you with your clothes on.' That was when Cinco filed another sexual harassment suit against Thomas."

"I can see why she was upset."

"Yeah, it seems that a few other women had filed sexual harassment claims against him, and he was finally asked to leave."

Later that afternoon, two of Shannon's staff swung quickly into her office.

"What did you do to the property management staff this morning?" Barbara asked excitedly.

"Nothing unusual," Shannon answered, confused. "Why, what's up?"

"Well, the police just left with Craig Endive in handcuffs..."

"Why, what happened?"

"It seems that Craig was feeling a little pressured and anxious, and went home at noon to bring his gun into the office."

"A gun!! What!!" Shannon was incredulous.

"Yep, he carried it into the office in his sports jacket, and took it out, saying he was being followed and wasn't safe. The other people in his department are saying he was acting more paranoid than usual the last few weeks, but that the meeting this morning just really set him off."

"He was only in the meetings this morning for a few minutes," Shannon was trying to remember. "And he got up and left."

"That must have been when he went home to get his gun," Barbara said with wide eyes.

"Yeah, and he was going off about how he was being followed and had to protect himself," Jay, her other employee added.

"Is everyone OK over there?" Shannon asked, very concerned about everyone's safety.

"He's been escorted out by the police now," Barbara filled her in. "I guess two of the employees in Craig's department called 911 on their cell phones, and the police arrived immediately when they were told he had brought a gun into the office and was waving it around."

"I've heard that he was a little unstable," Jay informed Shannon. "He's been a little different, off, for a while now. Kind of paranoid about everything."

Shannon didn't want to talk about Craig with her staff, but had her own additional concerns about his behavior lately.

"Thanks for filling me in," she told her staff. "Let's hope this is all over now, and I'm relieved no one was hurt."

Shannon was called by the Washington, DC sales center and asked to make a trip down to HomeFed in San Diego for a special task force meeting. She was advised that HomeFed had a portfolio of new foreclosures that Washington wanted Shannon to analyze, have appraised, order environmental reports and then put into auctions or sealed bids. Washington did not want the properties placed into SAMDA contracts, and put forth this information in a memorandum for the entire California RTC office to abide by.

When Shannon arrived in San Diego, she met several new people from RTC Washington, DC, including Sandra Smelling, the new Washington, DC sales center auction department head.

"Glad to meet you, Shannon," Sandra said. "I've heard a lot about you. You come from the FDIC, don't you?" she asked.

"Yes, I was with the FDIC for about four years before I was transferred to the RTC."

"I understand you wrote the first FDIC REO training guide for all new real estate employees and new hires, is that right?"

"Yes, I did. I did all the initial training of new real estate employees. I enjoyed the experience."

"Well, I would like to ask you to work on the task force that is gathering information to put together a new RTC auction sales guide and accelerated marketing manual."

Shannon was pleased to be asked to be on the task force. "I would like that very much Sandra, thanks for asking me." Shannon sat down for the meeting.

She learned that a very large financial management company on Wall Street had been awarded a very lucrative, large contract by Washington, DC to be an advisor for the failed HomeFed institution. They had been assigned the task of performing an analysis on all properties to determine their market values and to determine marketing strategies to sell the asset inventory, including loans pools and real estate assets.

Shannon was assigned all the available HomeFed properties by the Washington DC sales center to prepare them and place them into sales initiatives. She also traveled back and forth to Washington, DC and Denver to work on the accelerated marketing and auction manuals. She was extremely pleased when the manuals were completed in draft form, listing all the necessary steps to conduct an RTC auction event. The manuals went into extreme detail and provided checklists of information to be gathered prior to any sales event, discussed the quality of marketing materials, and required postsale event reports. It was very satisfying to have a manual that was developed based upon her and her colleagues' actual experience and knowledge conducting government auctions. She was anxious to see it in final print. Sandra Smelling advised her it would be released soon.

After about three months of waiting for the final Auction manuals to be printed, Shannon e-mailed Sandra and asked when they would be released. Sandra said that she had been instructed to have an outside contractor come in and "polish up the materials and print them."

"Oh, well that seems odd. We formatted the material and indexed the samples. It seems unnecessary to have a contractor now go over the material that they are not familiar with."

"I thought the same thing," she responded. "I was completely satisfied with the manual we submitted in its current form. It was thorough and well presented. But it seems that the powers that be want to push money around to outside contractors, and our manual has been caught up in that effort."

Shannon asked if this was done yet, and Sandra said there had been some delays. Shannon later was informed that a contractor had indeed been paid over a quarter of a million dollars to put together the marketing and auction manuals that the RTC staff, including Shannon, had already developed and written. Another quarter of a million dollars of waste, fraud, and taxpayer abuse.

About five months after the HomeFed assets were sold, she received a surprise call from John Martin, one of the program directors at RTC in Washington, DC.

"Shannon, what do you know about the HomeFed properties that the Wall Street financial group evaluated?"

She thought back to the first meeting in San Diego and replied,

"Well, I remember that I was told that they would be a fee contractor, an advisor selected by Washington, DC for the HomeFed assets. I took that to mean they were supposed to analyze the loan pools and develop loan sales for that institution, as well as establish fair market values for the REO, the real estate properties, and bank branches."

John paused for a moment. "Well, let me tell you what I've got here in front of me right now. It's a bill, an invoice, from the Wall Street group, that needs someone's approval before I can process it for payment. They are billing the RTC for real estate sales commissions for the properties you sold at auction. Mostly the big commercial properties. They want about $ 1.3 million."

Shannon was completely taken by surprise. "You can't sign that invoice!" she exclaimed. "They didn't do anything to earn the commissions. They are asking for payment for something they simply didn't do."

"Did they perform any of the appraisals you used to sell the properties?" he asked.

"No."

"Did they do any of the due diligence preparation?"

"No."

"Did they do any of the marketing or advertising?"

"No, they didn't work on the properties or sale at all."

"I guess their contract said that they were supposed to analyze the assets from HomFed, determine the best marketing and sales programs, and then dispose of the properties. Even though your group was assigned the sales of the properties by the Washington, DC sales center, some other Washington DC group issued the Wall Street group a contract to do the same work, and they are now asking for compensation under their contract. I will send you a copy of the bill to review."

"I don't agree with their requesting payment for work they didn't perform," she answered strongly.

"Well, someof these firms are represented by lobbyist, and they have a lot of support behind them. Let me send it to you, and then we can discuss it."

Shannon then answered her ringing phone on her desk and was advised by her boss, Hastings, that he had just been told that there was going to be an Inspector General audit performed on her auction program, including every asset that had been sold through auction within California and out of state.

"How much time do you need to prepare for the audit?" he asked. "I'm in Sam's office, and I need to give them a date."

"Is there some kind a problem, Hastings?" she asked.

"It seems that someone, probably the property management department, has alleged that the auctions are wasting large amounts of money and are not recovering sufficient sales prices. I just need to know how much time you need to prepare for this audit."

"I have everything ready now. All my reports are in order. I always organize them after each auction or sale event. The Inspector General can come in at any time."

"I knew you would be ready, O'Toole. I'll let you know the date when I come back down to the sales center."

The Inspector General auditors sat directly across from Shannon as she sat behind her desk. They had been discussing the RTC sales center and sales efforts, including auctions, for over an hour. Shannon had explained the sales processes in detail to the auditors. She opened up the auction sales manual she had helped to write. She had it in draft form, since the new version prepared by the fee contractor had still not arrived. She was explaining the steps in preparing for an auction, and then pulled out her auction financial reports.

"What you are telling us is quite different from what the parties who filed this allegation against the sales center and auction program told us." The one male auditor frowned.

"What are the major points of difference?" Shannon asked quietly.

"We were told that your cost of sales was more than double what you have proved here, and that your prices received at auction and throughout the sales center were about 12-15% lower than you have proved here. Your holding time and holding costs are also about 30% lower than what we were told."

Shannon seethed at the apparent lies that had been spread about her sales programs.

"We don't understand why these allegations were even made," the female auditor wearing glasses and her hair back in a bun began to say. "Usually, when an allegation of this nature is filed with the inspector general's office, there is some truth to the allegation. Even if the figures are not exactly correct, there is some correlation between the actual and alleged figures and we find some element of mistake, fraud, breach, or misdeed. But I just don't see any of that here."

Shannon's heart began to race, and it felt like there was a butterfly loose in her chest again.

She had been accused of fraud! Her seven-year career had just been in jeopardy, not because of her conduct, but because of someone intending to do her career harm.

"Do you need anything else from me?" Shannon asked politely. "Can I give you any other reports, or figures, or copies of what we have just looked at? I want you to feel completely comfortable."

"I think we have looked at everything we can think of. We see that the sales center averages sales prices at 94.5% of appraised value, which is excellent. Your auctions have even higher recoveries, with a 3-5% cost of sales, which is the lowest in the nation. You provided us with some directives and memos from Washington, DC we had never seen before. We've traced the sale of the properties and the receipts clear through the accounting department. Everything is in perfect order."

Shannon waited to hear that they were satisfied with the extent of their audit and wanted to hear that their findings were perfectly clear with the sales center, Auctions and with her personally.

What the male auditor said next took Shannon by surprise.

"Why do you think this investigation and allegation was filed against you?" he asked.

Shannon shook her head. It was not corporate policy, nor was it politically correct to open up any grievances against other departments to the Inspector General's Office unless it was fraud. Any such problems were to be handled internally, and discreetly.

The male auditor continued. "I probably shouldn't tell you this, but the report against you came in from someone here at the California RTC office. Do you know why anyone here would want to do this to you or your program?"

Shannon considered her several options in responding to the inspector general auditor. *the entire property management department for starters*, she thought to herself but she did not say out loud. She could just ignore them, and consider the matter closed. She could plead ignorance. She could make excuses for some of the other departments.

The female auditor then spoke up. "You know, we didn't mention it until now, but the second portion of this allegation is saying that the SAMDA contractors are the most efficient means of managing and disposing of real estate assets. The figures that we were sent clearly show that the sales center has interfered with the SAMDAs' performance."

Shannon blinked hard. This was false information that had been provided to the IG.

"We are satisfied that your figures are accurate," the male auditor began. "In fact, this whole allegation almost looks like someone was just playing a joke on us and you."

At that Shannon retorted, "A joke! I don't take being implicated for fraud and waste a very funny joke!"

"Neither do we," the male auditor agreed. They all sat there quietly for a few minutes. The male auditor then leaned over to his female counterpart and said something quietly that Shannon could not hear. She nodded, and then he said to Shannon,

"I think we had better approach this from a different angle. The allegation that brought us here sort of dragged on with additional allegations that the sale center was interfering with the SAMDA contract process. For instance, it was stated that you demanded the SAMDAs perform work that was not a requirement of their contract. What do you think they meant? What do you know about the costs associated with the SAMDA contracts and the SAMDA contractor performance?"

"I see," Shannon said under her breath. She couldn't directly put these auditors off anymore or deny them information she had in her files. That in itself would amount to withholding information from the auditors.

The auditor only paused for a moment. "There was something about appraisals and environmental reports mentioned. Does that make any sense to you?"

Shannon wanted to be clear and honest with the auditors, and still not be airing any 'dirty laundry' or ill will between the departments. "There have been occasions when the sales center has requested copies of required appraisals and environmental reports from the SAMDA contractors," she began.

"And these reports are required pursuant to the directives and memos you have shown us from Washington, DC, correct?"

"Yes," she answered honestly and directly.

"So, were these reports always available?"

"No."

"Was it unreasonable of you to request these reports?"

"No."

"What effect did these reports have on the marketing and sales of the properties?"

She considered how to phrase her answer. "The marketing of the properties could not take place immediately without those sources of due diligence, and the marketing campaigns had to be modified."

The male inspector jumped in, "Do you mean delayed?"

"Yes," she replied. "Rescheduled."

"And did the SAMDAs ever credit the RTC for their monthly management fees for the period of time they did not order the appraisal or environmental reports, or did they bill for their management fees while they delayed the sale of the properties?" the female auditor asked.

"I don't have that information," Shannon replied honestly. "We don't see the SAMDA billings; you will have to see the property management and contractor oversight department for that information."

The auditors paused, and then the male auditor started again,

"We have a report here showing when the SAMDA contractors received boxes of files, and then billed for their setup and management fees. We see that sometimes the SAMDA contractor didn't bill for the appraisals and environmental reports until six and eight months after they received the files. Are you aware of this?"

Shannon answered honestly, "I really don't have access to the SAMDA billing system."

"Well, then, if I show you the date of the files were received by the SAMDA contractor, let's just say March first, and then I see the appraisals in the file dated August fifteenth, would it be reasonable to conclude that the SAMDA didn't order the appraisals when they received the files, that they delayed in ordering the appraisals, while they were billing for their management fees?"

"The SAMDA could have ordered the appraisals but they were delayed, or their billing was delayed..."

The auditor interrupted Shannon, "1325 times? And while the appraisals were delayed, the SAMDA billed for their full management fees, although they weren't preparing the properties for sale. This would increase both the holding time and fees for these assets, wouldn't it?"

Shannon answered honestly, "Correct. The properties couldn't be sold without a current appraisal. However, without looking at the management reports, I can't tell you what the SAMDA was doing with the case files and properties..."

"You don't have to," the auditor said quietly. "I think I get the picture."

The second auditor started a new line of questioning. "Shannon, can you give us some summary reports on the length of time it took your staff to prepare the properties for sale in the RTC auctions you ran and the total amount spent on the sales event?"

"Of course," Shannon replied, and turned behind her desk to pull out a file with the reports and figures the auditors had requested. They spent another hour discussing the RTC auctions and looked over several of Shannon's auction catalogues, familiarizing themselves with the terms of the auction sales event.

"These reports provide sufficient documentation that the auction method is an efficient method of quickly disposing of large numbers of real estate from the failed banks," the auditors concluded.

"We can see that the cost of sales for performing an auction here at the California sales center is significantly less than the cost of a SAMDA contractor cost of sales. You have demonstrated that the prices received at the auction are equal to or better than the SAMDA sales prices, and the holding time and cost to the RTC is about four or five months less than the SAMDA's holding time and costs. Is there also a tangible liability risk to holding the properties off the market?" the female auditor asked.

"Yes, there is a real tangible liability risk while the properties are sitting vacant. The properties deteriorate, need additional maintenance and upkeep, and are an attractive nuisance to local people. They often break in and have parties in the properties, sometimes homeless people move in, and then there are the meth labs."

"Seriously, meth labs?"

"Yes, often the police or FBI ask if they can use one of our REO for surveillance purposes to watch drug deals or meth lab activity. Sometimes the meth is made in our vacant REO, sometimes we are the surveillance property."

"All good reasons to sell the properties as quickly as possible."

"Yes, and I think there was an analysis done in headquarters that stated if all the assets from the failed savings and loans were sold one at a time it would take over 100 years to sell them all, but the auction method sells the properties in about 90 days."

The auditors nodded their heads.

"Is there anything else I can show you or you would like to know?" Shannon asked.

One of the auditors leaned forward. "We thank you for your honesty and integrity. We know this wasn't easy for you."

♋

The head of RTC and other Executive Managers from Washington, DC were coming out to California for meetings pertaining to the work being done on the recently failed savings and loans, and to meet with other weak and failing thrifts. They had scheduled several meetings with the California staff. Shannon had received an invitation to attend a meeting with LaMar Kelly, the RTC Deputy Executive Director from HQ.

Bennett Kemper, one of the real estate salesmen who had been slipped into his RTC position by one of the midlevel managers in HQ, sauntered by Shannon's office and leaned against the doorjamb,

"Hey there, blondie," he began. Bennett was in his early forties with balding blond hair and a perpetual suntan. He had been living in Hawaii for the last six years and teaching swimming and surfing. It was rumored that when the banks started failing and the real estate market began to shut down, he had moved to Hawaii to start a new real estate business, and when that had failed, he went into the local sports arena. When Bennett wasn't wasting time walking around the office, he was sitting with his feet up on his desk, talking and laughing on the phone with his friends.

"Gee, hi, Ben. Don't you have anything to do, again, today?"

"Now, Shannon," he clucked, "Tsk, tsk, that isn't nice."

"Really? Would you like to come in, and I'll show you what work looks like?"

"No, thanks, I have some calls to make. I just dropped by to see if you had received any invitations from Headquarters."

"Now why would you want to know that, Ben?"

"Well, because I hear they are coming here to present some awards, along with looking at some more banks that are failing."

Shannon raised an eyebrow, "I hadn't heard about the awards," she answered curiously. "But I knew they were coming out to meet with some weak banks and savings and loans."

"That's because I have friends in high places…" he didn't finish his sentence as he turned and left her doorjamb.

The day of the meeting with LaMar Kelly arrived, and Shannon was looking forward to seeing the Executive Manager again. He was a large man with a big smile and friendly manner. He could negotiate a hard deal but still make the other side feel valued. He never seemed to need to strip his opponent and usually left some skin on the table. He had managed some of the largest bank failures in history, including Sun Trust Bank. She had enjoyed working with him on other bank failures, and in senior credit committee meetings when he was visiting and she presented cases.

Today, he was moderating the meeting, sitting at a table on the small stage in the training room with four other Washington, DC managers. There were about 150 invited staff in the audience. Shannon was listening to LaMar's opening remarks and settled into a comfortable ambiance.

LaMar was repeating familiar statistics,

"As you know, if the RTC sold each asset individually, including the real estate from the current failed savings and loans, it is estimated that it would take over 100 years to complete all the transactions. And so, we have been in the forefront of offering properties through real estate auctions, to accelerate the pace of liquidation of these assets."

Shannon perked up. She was also the head of the real estate auction division, and had even expanded into auctioning off pools of real estate backed mortgage loans and what was called furniture, fixtures, and equipment (FF&E) from the failed thrifts. She had even auctioned off credit card loan balances, personal loans, other secured loans, and charge offs, each group recovering revenue according to how delinquent the loans were. It had certainly been a challenge, though, with the standard asset management disposition—SAMDA, for short—delaying the ordering of appraisals and preliminary title reports, holding on to the properties to get their monthly and setup fees for as long as possible before giving up the properties to Shannon for auction.

LaMar was continuing,

"The California office has been outperforming the rest of the nation in terms of the number of properties sold through the real estate auctions. The pace of auction events and closings has set a new bar for the rest of the offices to try and meet. The auction marketing is unique here and very effective, by looking at the results. This office has offered residential properties, condos, high-rise commercial properties, land, loans, and FF&E through auctions. But I am especially pleased with the dollar recovery values. The California office has brought in the highest recovery values, greater than anyplace else in the nation. The auction catalogues are very professional, and the entire process is extremely smooth. The planning for each event is impeccable."

Shannon sat up straighter. He was talking about one of her divisions. It had been a tremendous amount of work, developing the auction program and participating in writing the first government auction manual for staff. The entire contracting process to hire auction companies and due diligence companies had been a struggle, but worth the results in the end.

LaMar continued to address the audience, "By now, you have probably recognized that I am talking about the manager who has guided the California office into and through the auction process. And that would be, Ms. Shannon O'Toole. Please come up here, Ms. O'Toole," LaMar began to applaud as Shannon stood up. He continued to talk as she made her way along a row of chairs and approached the aisle. "She has been the heartbeat of the sales center, and she has demonstrated outstanding excellence in developing both the California and National auction process. She has recovered several billion dollars in real estate, loans and FFE assets sales," and he continued to list her accomplishments.

Shannon had not anticipated anything like this, and was a little stunned at the generous accolades the executive manager had given her. As Shannon stepped into the aisle to approach the stage, LaMar was saying,

"I have to tell you all, it gives me much pleasure, from one Irishman to another, to present this award." The audience laughed.

At about that moment, Bennett Kemper leaned across the aisle from Shannon and said,

"What are you going to do with the diamond tie tack award, Shannon? You can give it to me, at least I could get some use out of it."

In a low and steady voice, she replied, "If you ever manage to earn one, Ben, you can give me yours, and I'll make them into matching earrings." And she strode confidently up to meet LaMar, who was still grinning at her from ear to ear.

After Shannon had returned to her seat after going up to the stage and receiving a hug and her diamond tie tack from LaMar, one more unexpected announcement was made by Mr. Kelly.

"There is a new directive coming out of Headquarters, that I am sharing with you today." He reached over to one of the other headquarters staff sharing the lead table and picked up a letter.

"Commencing immediately upon the date of this Directive, all real estate assets from failed thrifts and loans will be sold through the RTC sales center through planned initiatives, sealed bids, auctions, or other appropriate methods of sale. Henceforth, the property management division and SAMDA contractors will provide support for the sales center in maintaining the properties until sold."

Shannon couldn't believe what she was hearing. She didn't hear the remainder of LaMar's comments, she was so stunned at the turn around in policy and these events. It was music to her ears.

10

Developing the Government Lien/IRS Program and Politics

The office was quiet now that the RTC staff had all gone home for the day. Shannon put her hand on top of the large stack of real estate title reports she had gathered over the past six months. The stack was over twelve inches high, and each one had a title defect or government lien against the title. She had been tracking these government liens and had watched the foreclosures to see if any of the government agencies had claimed their secured interest by purchasing the asset or by redeeming the property to recover their agency money. Just as she had discovered at the FDIC, by law, the government agencies had to be served with notice that the property against which they had filed a lien was about to be foreclosed, giving the government agency sufficient and legal notice and time to take the necessary action to bid the foreclosure sale to recover the government lien/loan amount. Once the foreclosure notice was filed, it became public notice, and once the government lien was filed, it also became public notice.

The twelve-inch stack of title policies from RTC properties that were either going into foreclosure or had already been
foreclosed upon were only a very small sample of all the foreclosures she had watched go through the RTC from the failed
savings and loans where a government agency, including the
IRS, Small Business Administration, Justice Department, and
the California Franchise Tax Board, had placed a lien against
a piece of real property, and then when the property went into
foreclosure, the agencies did not exercise their legal rights or
take legal action to recover their lien money. Instead, the private party that bought the property at foreclosure gained all
the equity, if any, in the property that should have gone to pay
the government agency lien.

By Shannon's estimation from the small sample, *over half
a billion dollars of unclaimed government liens had gone uncollected*
just from the FDIC and RTC controlled loans and real estate
sample she had monitored. And she knew there were a lot
more uncollected government liens from other bank and private foreclosures.

She pulled the stack closer to her and arranged a yellow
legal pad horizontally on her desk. She began making columns
across the page and writing in the names of the government
agencies she had seen with liens in the title policies that had
gone uncollected. Then she began listing each lien under the
government agency's name that should have collected and redeemed their lien from the property to recover their government funds. *The national debt could be reduced if all this money was
collected and put back into the Treasury*, she mused.

When she had finished this task, she turned to her computer and began formulating a letter to her local government

representatives, Barbara Boxer and Diane Feinstein. *Maybe if these two female politicians can listen to me for just a minute, it would be a real coup to create a woman's forum and platform for their next political platforms. I would just love to see these two women identify, understand, and then implement the reforms that are needed to go forward and collect these government agency liens. I would love to be a part of such a change, such an important program.* She went on to think more about being a part of a political machine that could make a difference. She also had a list of names of the members of the US congressional committees that had jurisdiction, power, and authority to act on Shannon's plan recommending collection of the government liens. Most of these politicians were Democrats, and the pertinent committees were presently democratically controlled. *No problem*, Shannon mused to herself. *The Democrats, Barbara Boxer, and Diane Feinstein would all greatly benefit from my Government Lien Collection proposal. It will make a great political platform for their upcoming reelections, and it will demonstrate that they are collectively progressive and responsible leaders, recognizing when there are problems within the several government agencies for lien collections that they are going to correct.*

Shannon penned the letters to the congressional committee leaders that could take action and implement the government lien collection program and felt a certain sense of satisfaction and accomplishment when the letters were completed.

After three months of following up with phone calls to Barbara Boxer, Diane Feinstein, and the several US congressional committee members Shannon had written to and sent a copy of her research and findings, she received a letter with the official government insignia from the Honorable Barbara Boxer. Shannon looked at the return address and felt her heart quicken. Finally, a response to her program, hopefully acknowledging the billions of dollars it would bring back into the Treasury, acknowledging the program had merit and would implemented. At least the letter would be requesting a meeting to further investigate the magnitude of the potential recoveries and the steps to start the program into action. Shannon slowly opened the envelope and withdrew the short, one-page letter. Instead of the anticipated and much-hoped-for acknowledgement and acceptance of her program or at least a request for more information, she received a short political response from Barbara Boxer stating that there was no interest in her program.

Shannon took a deep breath and slowly shook her head. Once again, Shannon realized that she was an apolitical woman, not understanding the political slant of elected officials and congressional committees that could not or would not recognize a billion-dollar revenue collection program when it was dropped into their laps.

Shannon prepared letters introducing her Government Lien/ IRS collection program to several Republican members and to some reelected officials. She received a call from Congressman Christopher Cox's office in Irvine, California.

"Hello, Shannon, this is Andy, assistant to Congressman Christopher Cox. How are you?"

Shannon was completely taken by surprise and answered, "Just fine, thank you. And you?"

"Just great, just great," the friendly young man answered. "Listen, Congressman Cox has asked me to get in touch with you about this Government Lien/ IRS collection program you've written about. He thinks it has merit and is going to contact Steve Horn, Congressman for Long Beach, about your program. Congressman Horn is the chairman overseeing the subcommittee on Government Technology and Improvement. Mr. Cox thinks that Congressman Horn will have an interest in hearing more about this program of yours."

Shannon sat straight upright in her chair, her eyes unblinking. "That's great," she managed to speak out. "I'm glad Congressman Cox saw the potential in my program."

"Well, yes, but he felt that Steve Horn's committee would have the jurisdiction over this sort of thing, and that he would be the best one to start with," the young man continued. "So, I am going to forward your program materials over to Congressman Horn, and you can follow up in a couple of days to see if he's had a chance to read over it. How does that sound?"

Shannon was becoming excited. "It sounds great, and I thank you for getting in contact with me regarding my program. I look forward to discussing it with Mr. Horn."

"You're welcome and good luck."

Shannon sat back in her chair and stared out the window. Maybe now someone will listen to this program. At least this seemed to be a real start. Finally.

At the office the next day, Shannon lost no time in calling Congressman Steve Horn's office to follow up on Congressman Cox's letter of introduction. Steve Horn had been the very successful top administrator and President of the California State University at Long Beach and was now the US Congressman from Long Beach, California. She was advised that Congressman Horn wanted to set an appointment to meet with her that week. He was interested in her project.

Shannon walked into Congressman Horn's office, confident that her program was an important one, but somewhat unsure of herself as an Apolitical woman, not fond of politics or of the political system that had so far stalled her government lien recovery ideas.

"Hello," Shannon said politely to the receptionist in the congressman's office.

"I'm Shannon O'Toole, and I have an appointment with Congressman Horn this afternoon."

The young receptionist smiled up at Shannon from her desk. "Yes, I have been waiting to meet you. Your program has a few heads spinning around here."

Shannon was surprised at the young woman's remarks but didn't have a chance to respond.

"Let me take you into Mr. Horn's office. He has been looking forward to talking with you." The young woman led Shannon to a large private office with a large desk, a conference table, and pictures of Congressman Horn with other political leaders decorating the walls.

As she was shown into the congressman's office, he was talking on the phone, setting some appointments into his appointment planner.

"No, that week I'm in Washington DC," he said calmly into the phone, and looked up at Shannon to smile and motion that she sit down at the conference table.

The receptionist smiled and said, "Why don't you have a seat at the conference table? He'll be off the phone in just a moment."

Shannon took a seat at the table, and removed a manila file from her briefcase containing the government lien recovery program.

"I want to see the agenda for the subcommittee meeting before we publish it," the congressman was saying into the phone. "And I want to schedule meetings with the new members right away. It's important that we be ready to respond to this matter immediately, and I don't want to waste any time." He went on to quietly finish his phone conversation. He hung up the phone, and then smiled again at Shannon and stood up. He came around the side of his desk, picked up a file, and extended his open hand to Shannon saying,

"This is a pleasure to finally meet you. Christopher Cox and I have had some lengthy conversations about your plan here, and I would like to hear more about it."

"I'm very pleased to be here, and that you would find time in your very busy schedule to meet with me."

He sat down at the conference table in the chair next to Shannon and put a finger on the file he had brought over from his desk.

"I've been reading the materials you sent over to me and to Christopher Cox. We would like to know more about your findings, and your recommendations. How did you come to discover that these government liens were not being collected?"

"I have been working for the FDIC and RTC handling the real estate from the failed banks', savings and loans for over ten years now. In reviewing the title for the real estate, I began to notice government liens that should have been collected, or redeemed. Especially in the case of the IRS. It is my experience that the Internal Revenue Service never collected on any of their liens against the properties foreclosed on by the FDIC, or RTC, or the failed institutions."

"I have had my staff do a little preliminary research in this area," the congressman said quietly. Shannon was impressed with his quiet and confident manner. "Please tell me what you know about the IRS laws as they relate to recoveries."

"By law, the IRS, and other government agencies, are served notice when a property is about to be foreclosed on, usually telling the agency the amount of the lien they are about to forfeit, the agency's lien document number and the location of the property."

"And what are you finding that agencies do with this legal notice?" he quietly asked.

"I'm sorry to tell you that they either ignore the notice, or simply disregard it. In any event, they are clearly not acting upon the notice that their opportunity to collect on their government liens is being forfeited."

"What do you mean forfeited?"

"When a property goes to foreclosure, and a new private party or an institution that holds the mortgage buys the property at the foreclosure sale, the government liens are 'wiped out', and removed from the title against the property. That way, the new owner gets the property free and clear of any government liens. The new owner keeps the value or equity in the property that could have paid the government lien. It's a windfall profit for the new owner, and a loss to the government."

"So, let's say that Mr. Jones owes the IRS ten thousand in taxes, and Mr. Jones doesn't pay his taxes. So then the IRS places a lien against his real estate. Is that right?"

"That's correct."

"And then Mr. Jones doesn't pay his house payments, so the bank starts foreclosure proceedings against the property, correct?"

She nodded her head.

"By law, any government agencies with liens against the property then receive some kind of legal notice that the property is going into foreclosure."

"That's right. And this is where the system is breaking down. The government agencies don't take any action when they receive the foreclosure information."

"What should they be doing?"

"At the time they receive a foreclosure notice, they should obtain a copy of their lien notice they recorded against the debtor and the debtor's property. The government agency's recorded lien document should tell the agency how much their lien is for, the debt or loan number, and other government debt information. The agency should also take action to determine if there is sufficient equity or value in the foreclosing property to recover all or a portion of their lien."

"And how would they do that?" the congressman asked.

"A simple report from a local title company listing recent comparable sales in the same neighborhood is a good place to start. And a quick desktop appraisal would further identify the value of the property. Then the government agency would need to determine what mortgage is foreclosing and the amount of the unpaid mortgage and property taxes. If the difference between the unpaid mortgage and property taxes and the comparable sales is sufficient to pay off some of the government lien, then the government agency should take action to buy the property at foreclosure and resell it to recover their lien and put the money back into the Treasury."

"And what happens when these government agencies don't take the properties at the foreclosure sales?"

"The government liens are erased from the title against the property. Keep in mind, the debt doesn't go away, the government agency must continue to try to collect from the debtor from any future earnings the debtor may make by wage garnishment, or seizing bank accounts or other assets. But it's just wrong for an agency to walk away from the money available from the real estate, and then pursue the debtor for his future earnings. It's walking away from a 'bird in the hand' pool of money, to keep beating the bushes to collect from the debtor's future dollars. It's unfair to the debtor as well. He's lost his home, and now he's losing his future paycheck."

"OK, I understand. Let's take the IRS for example. What can they do to get their money from a foreclosure with a government lien against it?"

"The IRS has an additional advantage, or chance to get their money out of a foreclosure. It's called *redemption rights*. Not only does the IRS have the opportunity to take the property at the time of the foreclosure sale to recover their lien against the taxpayer, but they have one hundred and twenty days after the foreclosure sale to come back and take the property from whoever bought it at the foreclosure sale. This one-hundred-and-twenty-day period is known as the redemption period. The IRS has to pay the party that bought the property at foreclosure sale the same amount they paid for it."

"And this isn't being done, I take it?" he asked in his quiet demeanor.

"That's right. First, the IRS is not responding to the notices that a property against which they have placed a lien is being foreclosed on. They are not picking up or buying the properties at foreclosure. And, second, they are not taking action to buy back the properties with IRS liens against them during their hundred-twenty-day redemption period. So the title company removes the IRS and all other government liens from the title to the property. And the new owner gets to keep the property, and the equity in the property that could have paid off the government liens."

"And what do you estimate to be the dollar amount of government liens that are going uncollected from foreclosure sales?"

"It's easily billions and possibly trillions of dollars. I've only been tracking the foreclosure properties from the FDIC and RTC. If we compound those numbers then we are talking in the mega billions and trillions."

"Trillions of uncollected government debts."

"Just think of the time/money factor, Congressman Horn. Think of what the lost interest income is on these uncollected billions and trillions of dollars."

The congressman shook his head. "You say in your program materials here that we have all the laws in effect now that are needed to implement your government lien collection program?"

"That's right. Each agency, including the IRS, has the power and laws to do the collections as we just discussed. They are simply not exercising their rights to do so or do not have programs or processes in place."

The congressman took a moment to ponder what she had just said. "Do you think another agency should be put in charge of collecting these government liens, and, if so, what agency?"

Shannon was a little surprised at his question. It indicated that he already felt that the IRS and other government agencies she had written about in her program were incapable or unwilling to do their own collections. "You know," she said, thinking out loud. "The RTC is going to be collapsed into the FDIC at the end of the year. The RTC and FDIC have the trained staff, legal department, and computer reporting systems to do collections, that's what they've been doing for the failed banks."

"Do you think the FDIC would be interested in taking on this Program?" he asked quietly.

"I really don't know," she answered honestly. "But since they have all the operations, equipment, and staffing available, it might interest them. I can certainly begin to find out."

"I tell you what," Congressman Horn began. "I am going to talk this over with my top administrative assistant, Mark Brasher, in Washington DC. He can finish up my research on this, and then we'll talk again. I want you to feel free to contact him next week. I will be getting in contact with you then too."

"I'll be looking forward to our next meeting," Shannon answered with a smile.

"This is quite a lot of information you have put together," the congressman answered with his own sincere smile. "It's a rare government employee who goes above and beyond her own duties and responsibilities to research and try to make right something as vast as this."

"It needs to happen," she answered simply.

They shook hands, she walked out of the office with the congressman, and then out to her car. The wheels were finally in motion.

The next two weeks were chaotic at the RTC as the agency prepared to unwind and be transferred into the FDIC. Meetings were held almost daily, and the FDIC advised they were sending over a 'Transition Team' to assist with preparing the remaining operations and assets to be transferred into the FDIC.

During this time Shannon had several conversations with Congressman Horn's chief assistant, Mark Brasher, discussing her government lien collection plan, how it could be implemented, and the dollars that needed to be collected.

Shannon was sitting at her desk with when Hastings Kemper called her into his office.

"What's up?" she asked

"The FDIC has just advised us of the staff they are sending over to make up their FDIC transition team."

"I should know most of the people they selected. Probably Sara Hanson will be on the transition team, she's good. She joined the FDIC straight out of college. Who else?"

"Yes, Sara is on the team. And so is your old friend Farley Tripp. I think he's a first level supervisor now."

Shannon closed her eyes. Not Farley, not now, when things were so frantic and so much had to be done. Why were they sending over someone who didn't perform at such a crucial time? Her opinion of Farley had not changed over the years since they had worked in Alaska together.

"Great. Hastings, I'm going to ask you to please assign someone else to work with him. I'll be happy to team up with Sara, but not Farley, please."

"Hey, you know I'll do whatever I can to try to make things work out."

11

Still Singles Dating

Shannon had been dating a new fellow, John, for several months. John was a big southern Tennessee man, about six-foot-four and two hundred pounds, with broad shoulders and a dark moustache. He bore an uncanny resemblance to Tom Seleck. People had actually asked him for his autograph! John was actually a very gentle man, who even loved cats.

It was a hot, ninety-degree summer day in Southern California. John, Shannon, and Jennifer were going boating in Mission Bay, San Diego.

They arrived at the marina, and John checked out the boat, tried out the engine, and added a few water toys, including water skis and a large inflated inner tube and tow rope to the boat. Shannon and Jenny jumped into the boat, ready for a fun day's adventure on the water.

Jenny went first. John stopped the boat out in the middle of the lake. Jenny jumped out of the boat, ready to water ski. "Throw me the skis, Mom!" she called to Shannon.

"Single or doubles?" Shannon asked her daughter, and Jenny answered, "Singles, of course!"

Shannon tossed the single ski to Jenny, who slipped her front foot into the ski boot, and then used her back foot to paddle and stay upright until the boat took off. Shannon tossed Jenny the ski rope, which Jenny caught neatly. Shannon picked up the red flag and held it up in the air, which every boater knew meant that someone was in the water nearby.

John started the boat and revved the engine, looking over his shoulder at Jennifer. Jenny yelled, "Hit it,!" and John floored the accelerator, providing the initial surge of speed necessary to pull a skier up out of the water quickly. Jenny popped up out of the water, tucked her back foot into the ski boot, and was jumping the wake back and forth to everyone's delight. She was nearly as graceful on the water as she was in her dance.

After a while, John announced that it was his turn behind the boat. "But I thought you didn't ski?" Shannon asked.

"Well, Ah don't," he drawled in his southern accent. "And that's wha' I brought this ol' rubber inner tube with us," he smiled. "This here ol' thing will float me around just fine," and he began to buckle on an orange inflatable safety vest.

"How fast would you like to go?" Shannon asked, as she handed Jennifer the red safety flag and moved toward the front of the boat.

"Ah'll let ya'll know," and John carefully pushed the inner tube into the water behind the boat, took the ski rope in one hand, and slowly lowered himself into the water, grabbing the inner tube and pushing away from the boat.

The humor began with John trying to lift and settle his long body into the bobbing inner tube. Every time he threw a leg over the tube, it sank, he would sink, and then the tube would flip over and bounce up from the water several feet away. John would dog paddle over to the inner tube in his orange safety vest, and try again, each time dunking himself thoroughly. He tried lifting his upper body into the tub, but then it would flip over him and push him under. Jennifer and Shannon were doubled over laughing, and were encouraging John to try different maneuvers to help him get into the inner tube.

Somehow, he finally managed to get himself situated with his big shoulders and long legs hanging over the edge and his bottom securely wedged in the middle of the tube. John arranged the ski rope in one hand, smiled at Shannon and Jenny, and gave them the thumbs-up sign.

Jenny shouted "He said to hit it, Mom!"

Shannon hit the accelerator hard. John was a big man, and she knew it would require all the power the boat had to give John a good ride. She floored the accelerator and felt the boat tug from his weight, and she kept the peddle to the floor. Behind the boat, John was jerking from left to right then right to left with so much splashing that he was almost invisible. The bottom of his inner tube was slapping the water while he skipped and bounced along the boat's wake. He was screaming. Then Shannon turned the boat in a large arc, and John did the most amazing pinwheel when he let go of the rope. At first his bottom stayed in the inner tube, so he spun across the top of the water with his head, arms and legs waving wildly. Then he began to slip from the inner tube, still clutching it with one arm. He finally came to rest, lying on his back, floating in his orange safety vest, one arm over the tube.

Shannon circled around him in the boat, Jenny holding the red flag high in the air. "Are you all right?" she shouted while still laughing. John was shaking the water from his eyes and said, "What were you two trying to do to me?"

Shannon leaned over the side of the boat and said, "You put your thumb up. You told us to Hit It!"

"What do you mean, Hit It?" he yelled back.

Shannon cut the motor on the boat. She leaned back over the boat's side. "You gave us the Hit It signal, to go fast, to floor it!" she told him.

"I did what? Ah put up my thumb, and you thought Ah wanted you to terrorize me? Ah only was telling you Ah was OK, settled in, comfortable after all that effort just to climb into this silly thing."

Shannon and Jenny looked at each other. "I thought he wanted to Hit It," Jenny said dubiously.

"I know," Shannon said to Jenny. "That's exactly what I thought too."

"John," Shannon called, "When you're water skiing or towing behind a boat, the thumbs-up motion means go faster, floor it, increase the speed. Thumbs down means go slower. I thought you knew that."

John responded rather sourly, "I *did not* know that. Ah can't even swim."

Despite Shannon's apparent attempt on John's life, they enjoyed several years of fun and laughs, and continued to grow in their respective careers, until John was transferred to the East Coast, and Shannon decided to stay on the West Coast.

12

Transferring back to FDIC and "Friends in Low Places"

Whispers in Her Ear

The RTC was going to 'sunset', a nice, political term for close down, one year earlier than Congress had first projected when the RTC was created to work on the failing savings and loan crisis in 1989. The FDIC closed failed banks, the RTC closed failed savings and loans and thrifts.

Congress had projected a December 1997 closing date for the RTC. All the speculation that the RTC would be extended for additional years was proving to be in error. All of the jockeying by the RTC property management department to hold assets in SAMDA contracts instead of making them available to the RTC Sales Center for a swift sale was proving to be unsuccessful.

The final list of names of the RTC real estate sales department staff that were to be transferred over to the FDIC effective December 30, 1996, was completed. Shannon sat in Hastings office, feeling pretty low after having to choose between great employees and very great employees to make the final cut.

"Stop looking so glum, O'Toole," Hastings said to Shannon. "This is hard on all of us, and I know exactly how you are feeling. I don't want to turn any of our people loose either. It sucks. But that's just the way it is. We can't do anything to change it. We just have to do the best we can and grin and bear it."

"I know, Hastings, you're right, but crud, it is just so hard to say good-bye to these hardworking people. It just makes me so mad that so many of the property management people get to transfer over when they don't do a thing except watch over their inept SAMDA contractors. Our people really work."

"I know, I know what you mean, but this is a political thing, Shannon, and there's just nothing that you can do about it. You are an apolitical woman. You want to improve programs and streamline systems. But there are political egos in the way. You don't want to get involved in the politics, but want to change the political systems.

"At least we have the satisfaction that this office was able to prove that the RTC real estate Sales Center was more efficient and saved the government millions of dollars when we proved the SAMDA contractors were wasting federal dollars. That in itself is a historical achievement."

"I suppose you're right about that.," she smiled weakly. "I am an apolitical woman, Hastings, I don't like the politics. I keep trying to make the government an efficient and cost effective entity and run it more like a business rather than a broken, old, lazy, political machine. I just wish we could reward our staff with being able to transfer them over to the FDIC, where they could continue to save the government more money."

"But you know that politically a certain number of property management staff has to be transferred to the FDIC, just to support the fact that RTC has been carrying them along for such a long time. If they were to terminate the property management RTC staff now, how could they substantiate that they shouldn't have been terminated a long time ago? And don't forget, it's not just what we are seeing here at the local California level, it's also about the powers that be in Washington DC, that sponsored the property management and contractor oversight programs. Those are big boys, Shannon, and they cannot be embarrassed."

"You know, Hastings, I don't want to understand it, I don't want to accept it. It's just plain wrong! You and I both know it's just empire building."

"Yep, it is, but stop beating yourself up over it." He paused and then continued, "Look, you were able to hang on to most of your staff, including Pao, after you were able to bring him over from the property management group...."

"Right, he was one of the only staff over there who had a handle on his failed institutions and pushed his Samda contractor to immediately order appraisals and environmental reports, he's very good..."

"And you have Kammy, Dani, Bailey and Barb. You were able to carry over more staff than anyone else."

"That's because my staff out performs everyone else, they are the hardest workers, most productive, and are recognized as being the best."

"OK, OK, tell me something I don't know. Tell me what's going on with your Government Lien/ IRS collection program. What's new?"

Shannon let her head roll to the back of her neck and then to one side. She shook her head slowly and answered,

"Well, it's kind of just like this RTC and FDIC thing. I know what's right and what's wrong, but the political answer is never what I expect. Instead, the political answer is always to satisfy some unknown constituency, or some politician's personal agenda."

"You mean it's dead in the water?"

"I'll never let it drown, Hastings," she chuckled. "In fact, I'm working with Congressman Steve Horn from Long Beach right now. He has his executive aid in Washington DC analyzing my proposal. I can't just quit, Hastings. I can't just give up, although sometimes I would like to."

"You're one of kind, kid," Hastings responded with a quiet smile.

The day Shannon had dreaded soon arrived, with Farley Tripp walking into her office. She had thought she would never have to work with Farley again, after transferring from the FDIC to the RTC, but here he was again. Farley looked around Shannon's office and began,

"Well, this is a pretty nice office, Shannon. A little on the large side, with room for a conference table AND a desk, but I guess you'll be getting used to a cubicle again soon when you move back to the FDIC," he sneered.

Shannon had hoped that Farley would have mellowed and would be tolerable, however, all hope vanished as he continued,

"I sure hope you've got the RTC files in good order, or I'll have to designate you for a special file cleanup project. In fact, I have set aside a couple of real special cases for you when you get back to FDIC," and his eyes narrowed.

Before Shannon could respond, Sara Hanson came into Shannon's office. Shannon had always enjoyed Sara when she had first met her at the FDIC offices in Irvine, on the rare occasion when Sara wasn't stationed somewhere in the Midwest, closing banks.

"Farley, there you are! We were supposed to meet in the lobby! And Shannon, it's great to see you again. It looks like you've been very successful here, and I love your office, it's so big and bright with all the windows! I wish we had offices this nice and big at the FDIC." Shannon could have hugged Sara for that. "I hear you have everything organized and ready for the transition, and all your reports were reviewed by Headquarters and were excellent. Thanks for the memo on the computer data systems and your analysis on where the RTC and FDIC systems are compatible and where there will be differences. You've made the whole real estate transfer seem effortless."

Farley didn't want to hear any more, and began giving orders as usual. He looked at Shannon, "I want you to sign as many of the escrow documents as you can in the next two weeks, so I don't have to step into these real estate transactions that I'm not familiar with," he complained.

"Oh, Farley," Sara answered. "You're going to have to come up to speed on the deals sooner or later. Why don't you just start learning about them now, so it's easier for you later?"

"I don't know anything about the affordable housing program, and I've never seen or read the documents before. Look at them, each transaction is over two inches thick in paperwork. I'm not going to go through all that stuff if Shannon can do it now."

Shannon just looked over at the lazy little man, whose hairline had continued to recede. Yes, she thought, that was a small justice, seeing his bald forehead shine under the florescent lights.

"If you'll excuse me for just a moment, I need to see if Barb has an updated list of open escrows for us. I'll be right back," and Shannon got up from behind her desk and left her office.

To her surprise, Farley followed her out of her office, with Sara trailing behind.

"Shannon, wait," Farley called. "I want you to explain this form," and he followed Shannon over to Barb's desk.

Barb was not in her cubicle, but the phone was ringing, and Shannon reached over her secretary's chair to answer it.

"Hello, Shannon?" the male voice asked.

"Yes," she answered briskly.

"Shannon," Farley interrupted. "Don't stay on the phone now, I need to ask you some questions about the RTC sales contract. Let your secretary answer her own damn phone," he said in an irritated voice since she was clearly not giving him the attention and response to his needs he wanted.

"I'm really glad I caught you just now. I have some really great news for you," the voice on the phone was telling her.

She didn't recognize the voice through the din of Farley's complaining and nagging voice continuing on behind her.

"I'm sorry, I can hardly hear you. Who am I talking to?" she asked.

"This is Mark. I am excited to tell you that all the analysis is done, and the recommendations have gone through. It looks like we'll be working together now."

Shannon ran through the list of Marks that she knew, with two real estate brokers coming to mind.

Farley Tripp was clearly becoming agitated with Shannon, and he pushed the contract he held in his hand under her face, glaring at her. "Tell them to call back," he hissed.

Shannon turned away from Farley, trying to hear the man on the phone. "I have some FDIC people here right now. Could I call you back later?" she offered politely.

The man on the phone sounded disappointed. "All right, then," he said. "But I thought you would want to know that Congressman Horn wants you to come to Washington DC to present your Government Lien/ IRS collection and redemption program before his congressional subcommittee. Call me back when you can talk," and with that the phone went dead.

Shannon stood, stunned, with her back still turned to Farley, who continued to shake the papers in the air, angry that she would not respond to his demands for attention. Sheri was trying to sooth Farley, and calm him down, telling him to just wait a minute. Shannon stared down at her secretary's desk, and silently reviewed the conversation she had just had. *Possibly the most important call of my career, and I have Farley Tripp complaining behind me so that I can't even hear Mark Brasher, Congressman Horn's executive aid, inviting me to Washington, DC to appear before Congress,* she thought. *My program, my plan, it's finally being recognized! And I am being invited to Washington DC to present my Proposal!* She was still in awe of the invitation. She was going to Washington DC! To appear before Congress! To present her collection plan and proposal! Yes! How exciting!

A slow smile spread across her face, and she slowly turned around to face Farley's red, angry face. He noticed the difference in her behavior and her smile, and said snidely, "Was that an important call, a date from a boyfriend?"

This time he couldn't rattle her. "No," she smiled brightly. "It is much more than that." She walked back into her office, letting Farley trail behind her, still holding the contract in his hand.

After finishing up with Farley and Sara, Shannon was walking back to her office, when Hastings came down from the tenth floor with an angry look on his face. Shannon was standing in the hallway when he flew by her and barked at her to follow him into his office.

They had all been under a lot of pressure, packing boxes and updating reports for impending transfer of assets and staff from the RTC over to the FDIC. However, she had a sense of satisfaction knowing that the staff that had outperformed the rest of the RTC personnel in terms of outstanding output, her staff, was going to be transferred over to the FDIC as a kind of acknowledgement and reward for their superior performance, and to ensure that the real estate properties continued to be managed and sold efficiently.

"Sit down," Hastings growled, "Close the door."

Shannon had seen Hastings angry, tired and upset. But seldom had she seen this very tense behavior in her favored boss.

"What's going on to have you so upset?" she started.

Hastings' eyebrows were knitted together in a severe frown, and he was obviously very unhappy about something.

"Hastings, what's wrong?" she asked again.

"You're not going to believe what's just happened," he started. "I just came down from a meeting on the tenth floor, where we were discussing the transfer of inventory and staffing. Then old Atwater passes out a new list of names of those people who are transferring over from RTC to FDIC. Remember

I told you some of us might have our grades and pay changed? Remember I showed you the potential staffing chart that FDIC was allowing for the transferred staff?"

"Yes, I know," she answered quietly, now frowning herself. "I saw the lower grades, but at least it allowed our staff to transfer over for another year of work. They've earned it, they deserve to be transferred over. They know the grades are going to be lower, they..."

Hastings interrupted her curtly. "They won't be going over. You won't believe what Atwater has done now."

"What are you talking about?"

Hastings finally looked up from the report he held in his tight hand. "Atwater has taken all of the highest grades in our department, the Real Estate Sales department, and put his own staff into those slots."

"Explain more," she gulped, fearing she knew exactly what was coming next.

"Atwater saw that the Sales Center had been given the highest grade positions by FDIC to reflect the responsibility and size of the portfolio of real estate property assets, so he bumped some of our best people out and put his own special assistants and favorite friends into our slots. He bumped Kammy Crawford. Then he bumped Dani Stefford and Barbara so his friends could bring their own favorite secretaries along." Hastings was clearly distressed.

"Oh, no! Not Kammy!" Shannon exclaimed. "She's our top performer. And Barb and Dani, there's no one else who works as hard as they do. They do the job of two or three people each. This is completely unfair and very wrong, Hastings. Who the hell is Atwater putting into Kammy's slot?"

"I'm not sure if it's Robert or Benner or—"

"Oh, no. They couldn't even help Atwater to understand the difference between property management and sales. They don't know the first thing about negotiating our real estate transactions or procedures. Not one of them could ever handle the waste and abuse from the SAMDA contractors, even after we demonstrated the waste over and again. They just rode along for the ride. They are typical government bureaucrats. This is crappy, Hastings. The FDIC is going to get a bunch of lazy do-nothings instead of the real estate specialists they think they are getting to handle the RTC-transferred assets." They sat in silence for a moment, each in their own thoughts. "Does FDIC know yet?"

"I don't think it matters."

"So, good ol' Atwater is putting his best friends in low places, into our jobs, that they've never done before. They are falling from their comfy, lofty positions into our positions, and Atwater is getting away with it. He's bumping excellent, hardworking staff, just to keep his old cronies around. What a crock!" She was angry at the injustice of one more action by the sloppy management. It was another lesson for an apolitical woman to learn.

And so five of Frank Atwater's buddies were transferred over to the FDIC, bringing with them their secretaries, each one bumping hardworking, successful RTC real estate Sales Center staff. Their new assignments were very simple and their responsibilities a fraction of what the position called for and a small fraction of the volume of work the other RTC Sales Center staff had been capable of doing. Again, the FDIC and RTC wasted taxpayer money to shield the old friends of an old administrator who doled out favors to his friends, who sat for the next year with their feet up on their desks while they burned the telephone lines searching for new jobs, while real estate files sat in boxes, untouched, at the FDIC.

Congress had created the Resolution Trust Corporation in 1989 to take over $125 Billion in assets owned by 296 failed savings and loan associations. Over the next six years, it added $394 billion in assets belonging to an additional 747 insolvent thrifts. The RTC's main job had been to sell those assets, mostly real estate and loans, at the best price it could get.

In the end, the S&L cleanup cost American taxpayers an estimated $123 Billion dollars. The RTC ceased operation at the end of 1996, a year earlier than planned, and the remaining RTC workload was transferred to FDIC. Despite the price tag of the thrift bailout, many believe the RTC successfully averted even worse (economic) consequences and higher costs.

⚭

The following week, the transition to FDIC took place, and Shannon settled into her new job. It was actually less work than her previous position with the RTC because she had managed multiple departments there, including the residential division, affordable housing, commercial, residential and multifamily auctions, sealed bids, customer service, and seller financing for Sales Center transactions. Wearing that many hats had prepared her to shift gears quickly, and to handle many tasks at one time, while providing guidance and decisions for her staff. Now she was handling the files from some of her staff that were so unfairly bumped off by Atwater's favorite friends.

Her first week was proving to be fairly smooth, when a large, round man with cowboy boots walked out of Farley's office and directly over to where Shannon was sitting in her cubicle by a window. He leaned on the cubicle doorway and said,

"Well, howdy there, little lady. And just who are you? Ah didn't see you here the last time Ah was in town."

Shannon turned around to see the red-faced cowboy peering at her through his squinty little eyes. Before she answered, he continued,

"Ah am Tommy Kinkaid, at your service," and he did a mock little bow.

Shannon just looked at the man, not enjoying his performance.

"What's your name?" he asked.

Unable to ignore the man completely, she answered shortly, "I'm Shannon O'Toole."

"And a pretty little lassie you are too." He did his best impression of an Irish accent.

Shannon didn't want to encourage the man and didn't respond.

"Ah'm from the FDIC Texas office," he continued without encouragement. "Do ya' like country western music?"

She didn't want to carry on a conversation with him, and tried to discourage him by simply shaking her head.

"Well, now, it can be kinda fun, you know, and I hear there's a good country western place not too far from here."

Shannon still didn't answer the man and just wished he would go away, but instead he took a step closer to her and grinned. "You're either a little shy or not sure about a big ol' Texan like me," and he laughed.

Shannon realized that silence wasn't going to discourage this man and said,

"Neither, actually."

"Well, now, back in my hometown, we would call you a little bit sassy." He continued to stand uncomfortably close to where Shannon was sitting.

She didn't like the way he was leaning toward her, and she stood up, taking several files off her desk, and turned to leave her cubicle, saying,

"If you'll excuse me, I have a meeting to attend," and she stepped past the big man and walked away, not knowing where she was headed, just away from him.

In the next few weeks, it became clear that Tommy Kinkaid was a good friend of Farley Tripp. Tommy visited Farley's office frequently and made a habit of stopping by Shannon's work area every time. Sometimes he would ask her out to lunch or to go for a drink after work, always complimenting her on her hair, clothes, and, even once, her tan. Each time she declined, and made it clear she had no intentions of taking him up on his offers.

It was around midnight, and the phone rang next to Shannon's bed. She rolled over, picked up the receiver, and said sleepily,

"Hello."

In a very thick Texas drawl, Tommy Kinkaid said,

"Hi there, doll. Don't hang up, I just wanna talk to you for a while."

Shannon recognized the slow Texas accent, and was fully awake then. She said very softly,

"Oh, Tommy, hello. Would you please put your wife on the phone. There's something I would like to tell her…"

The phone went dead. Tommy went back to Texas the next week and never contacted Shannon again.

13

The Congressional Presentation

After several attempts and messages left and received from Mark Brasher, they finally connected.

"I've been meaning to ask you, what was going on when I called you at the RTC office last week?" he asked her.

"I had FDIC people here needing help with the RTC transition program, and they can be a little demanding," she responded politely.

"A little demanding? Whoever it was sounded like a lost sheep bellowing for its mother," he said disapprovingly.

She laughed, still excited to hear more about Mark's invitation to Washington, DC.

"So tell me about this presentation. When is the Congressional hearing going to be?" she asked.

"I don't have the exact date, but we think it will be scheduled for February or March next year. Will that be OK with you?"

"I'll probably have to get all the appropriate ethics clearances from FDIC and all that, but I see no problem with it. In fact, I'm looking forward to it." It was now December 1995, and that would give her two or three months to prepare.

"That's great. Now let me tell you what Congressman Horn wants from you. Your proposal is great; it outlines the problems with government lien collections and gives a lot of great information. Now Congressman Horn would like to see a sort of step-by-step recommendation by you as to what needs to take place to put your program into action. Does that make sense?" he asked her.

"Sure," she replied happily, still elated about the prospect of finally getting the opportunity to present the program she had worked on for so many years.

"If you could prepare your materials and then fax them to me for review, that would be great," he continued.

"No problem, Mark," she smiled into the phone.

"And just one more thing. Congressman Horn mentioned that he had asked you about another government agency stepping up to handle these lien recoveries. Would you hold off on that just now? He wants to gather some more information on that."

"All right. Just let me know when he is ready to go forward," she answered.

"Shannon, I'm delighted to be working on this program with you. It has real merit," he said, complimenting her. "Now give me just a couple more minutes, and I want to give you some more information about the staff here in Washington DC that will be assisting you with your plans and scheduling..."

Shannon had received her formal letter in February from US Congressman Stephen Horn inviting her to speak to the subcommittee on government information and technology on March 6, 1996.

While she was working on her new job tasks, she wrote the appropriate letters to the FDIC ethics department and public affairs department to obtain the required approvals for her appearance before Congress. Because she was employed by the government, she had to clearly state that she was appearing before Congress as an individual, and expressing her own individual findings and opinions, and was not representing the FDIC or RTC.

After a few conversations with both the ethics and public affairs departments, she received the clearances she needed and prepared to send them on to Congressman Horn's aides in Washington DC.

Mark Brasher called. "Are you all set for your testimony?" he asked.

"Yes, I am," she answered enthusiastically.

"Your materials are great," he complimented her.

"Thanks, I'm pleased with them."

"You know, I was thinking, that while you are here, I would like to introduce you to some other people that can assist in moving your program from paper into reality."

She was impressed with his invitations. "I would like that," she answered positively.

"I want you to plan on meeting with Vicki McDowell with the US Treasury. She's the director of agency collections, and I will set up a meeting with her. I am also going to have you talk with another friend of mine, Tom Stack. He's a program director with the US Office of Management and Budget, the OMB. Tom's a great guy, and he knows a lot of people in DC. I'll see when I can get you all together."

She hung up the phone with a large smile on her face. She was going to Washington DC, and now she was going to meet the people who would help her make the program come to life.

Shannon was staying with friends in Bethesda, Maryland, while she was in Washington DC for her Congressional presentation. Kelly, her friend back at the FDIC, one of the few women that had escaped the lecherous department head, Bradley Donner. They were sitting at the kitchen table just finishing breakfast.

"We're so excited for you, Shannon," Kelly was saying, "We can't wait to hear all about the presentation tonight when you get home. Oh, I wish I didn't have to go to work today so I could come and hear you in person."

Shannon smiled at her old friend. "It's just as well, Kelly, I would probably just get nervous if I knew anyone was watching me that I knew."

"Won't there be anyone there you know?" Kelly said sadly.

Shannon laughed at her voice. "Just Congressman Horn and Mark Brasher. That's enough, and that's just fine with me. And thank you again for letting me use your home phone as my local contact and helping me fax all those last-minute reports over to Congressman Horn's Washington DC office last night."

"I'm thrilled to help! We have our fingers crossed for you, and we can't wait to hear how it went for you tonight." She hugged her friend good-bye and left for work.

Shannon was gathering her coat and briefcase when the phone began to ring. She had left Kelly's phone number as her local contact number with Congressman Horn's office. She almost didn't answer it, but thought that it could be the congressman's office with some last-minute instructions, so she picked up the phone.

"Hello, is this Shannon?" the anxious voice said.

"Yes, this is she," Shannon answered.

"Shannon, this is Annie with Congressman's Horn's office, and we have a serious problem. I thought you told us you had received all the clearances you needed from the FDIC to make this presentation today?"

"That's right, I have the ethics clearance and the clearances from the public affairs office. They know I'm appearing as an individual, not representing the FDIC."

"Well, we just received a call from your FDIC public affairs office in Washington DC. They said they had just learned about your testimony and that you were not allowed to speak today because you didn't have a clearance! The agenda is already published, your appearance has been published in the papers, and the committee members are expecting you to present your pilot plan. The media is even expecting you. This is awful!" she wailed into the phone.

Shannon went stone cold. How could this be happening? She had taken all the careful steps to obtain the two clearances. She had met with the respective ethics and public affairs department heads, had given them excerpts of her testimony, answered dozens of their questions, and had received a letter from each of the departments granting her clearance. The letters! She had the letters with her in her briefcase.

"Just a minute, Annie." She tried to sound calm. "I have two letters with me now, and I do have both of my clearances from both the ethics department and the public affairs department. Let me get them out of my briefcase, and I'll fax them to you."

Annie hesitated. "Are you sure?" she asked, not yet convinced.

"Annie," Shannon began patiently. "I would never have come this far if I hadn't taken all the appropriate steps to get my approvals. I may not be a political person, but I know how the political system works."

She walked over to her briefcase and purse by the door and pulled the clearance letters out. She felt around in her purse and found her reading glasses and said, "Let me give you the names of the signators on these letters."

Annie seemed to relax a little. "OK, just fax me the letters, but then call this man from your FDIC public affairs department and tell him you have the letters. I need him to call me right back and tell me everything is OK, or I'll have to go and tell Congressman Horn about this matter."

"I'll take care of it, Annie," Shannon answered, and quickly redialed the number Annie had given her for the local FDIC Washington DC public affairs office. After a few transfers, Shannon finally located the man that had called Annie.

"Well, Shannon, it's a surprise to hear from you so soon," he began, in a cheerful manner.

Shannon was in no mood for this man's twisted humor. "What seems to be the problem?" she asked curtly.

"Well, now, you see, we had no idea or information here in the Washington DC public affairs office that you were coming here, and that you would be speaking in front of Congress. That's very serious stuff, you know," he responded.

"Look," she replied quickly and looked at the clock on the wall. She had to get to the metro or she would be late for her testimony. "I have already spent three months obtaining the necessary clearances from both the FDIC ethics department and the public affairs department. I am appearing as an individual, not as an FDIC official. I have the authorization letters if you need to see them. But your timing here is really poor."

She was getting upset with his attitude, and she didn't care if it showed. She looked down at her briefcase and purse, once again sitting by the front door, and began to worry about missing the shuttle and metro train that would take her from Bethesda into Washington DC.

"This whole thing is really kinda funny, don't you think?" he laughed.

"Not one bit," she bit off at him.

"Well, it kinda is. After I got a call from your California office, from your boss, um, Farley Tripp, telling me you were here unauthorized, without his approval and without approval or clearance, I talked to Annie and told her we had a big problem..."

But Shannon had stopped hearing him. Farley Tripp! Interfering with her opportunity to appear before Congress. It couldn't be! She had not spoken to anyone except Hastings and Tanya Glasser about her testimony. She didn't have time to think any more about why they would have told Farley anything about her pilot plan and congressional appearance, at least not now...

"I called up the California ethics and public relations departments at FDIC, and they told me you had filed all the required requests and everything, and that they had given you the necessary clearances. They had sent all their paperwork here, but," and he thought this was particularly funny as he chuckled to himself, "I guess we just kinda misfiled your letters here, and we couldn't find them."

She tried to just focus on the content of the conversation and ignore the man's ignorant humor at her situation. She was still stunned that somehow Farley Tripp had managed to nearly destroy her opportunity. "So, then, do I understand that you have everything that you need now? Everything is in order?"

"Um, yes, it looks that way now," he still laughed nervously.

"Then you will call Annie back at Congressman Horn's office and advise her of your error?" She gritted her teeth.

"Uh, well, I guess I can call her back for you, now that I found copies of your letters..."

Shannon cut him off abruptly. "Just call her back *now!*" she ordered. "I have to catch the shuttle now, and I don't have any more time to talk with you on the phone."

But he wasn't quite done yet, and quickly inserted,

"I will have to come and listen to your testimony, you know, just in case you say something about FDIC that isn't approved..."

She hung up the phone, and put the copies of her clearance letters back into her briefcase. What's next? she thought. *FDIC spies?*

She turned around and slipped into her coat. She picked up her briefcase with the annotated version of her speech ready in its special folder, and picked up her purse. She went out the front door, and left her reading glasses, which she had used to read the signatures on the clearance letters, by the phone.

When Shannon arrived for the congressional hearing, she noticed there was an additional name on the agenda she was handed by a congressional aide, a Margaret Richardson, the then Commissioner of the IRS. "Well, this should be interesting," she mused, and signed in for her Government Lien IRS collection and recovery program presentation.

She entered the large room and took a seat in the "witness" section. She removed her wool coat, looked around, and observed the elevated area where the presiding official, congressmen, or senators would sit, with several additional adjacent elevated seating areas. She looked up at the high ceilings. She looked at the microphones at the witness podiums, and began to feel excited at the opportunity that was about to unfold. Then she felt a tap on her shoulder.

"Uh, hello. You're Shannon O'Toole, aren't you?" said a tall, thin man in his late thirties, standing in a rumpled suit. Next to him stood a shorter man with thinning hair. "I'm Jim, and this is Ken from the FDIC ethics office."

"Yes, I'm Shannon O'Toole," she responded with a tight smile. "Have you been able to resolve all your documentation problems?" she questioned the two men.

"Um, yeah. You know, sometimes things just get a little complicated."

"Well, I'm so glad they are uncomplicated now," she answered.

"Yeah, well, we just wanted you to know that we will be sitting here listening to everything you say and writing it down."

"You do know that I will be appearing and speaking as a private citizen, not in my position with the FDIC or former RTC, correct?"

"Well, yeah, that's what your papers all say. But just the same, we have some, um, other people who are interested in what you're going to say."

Before Shannon could respond, Congressman Horn entered the room, and the Congressional hearing began.

"We are here today to hear testimony pertaining to certain government lien recovery efforts, and to examine the lack of recovery by the Internal Revenue Service on liens they have placed against real property. We will hear from witnesses, including Shannon O'Toole, who will explain the government lien recovery program she has developed, and from Margaret Richardson, current IRS Commissioner," Congressman Steve Horn said, opening the congressional hearing. After a few other opening remarks, Congressman Horn invited Shannon and the IRS commissioner to approach the witness podiums and tables across from each other.

Shannon assembled her presentation notes in front of her on the table and quickly looked over at the IRS Commissioner. She was a fairly small woman with short brown hair, in a conservative business suit. She had with her two other IRS staff, both tall men carrying briefcases. Shannon assumed they were attorneys for the IRS.

Shannon tried to relax, and remember that her research was solid and extensive. It would make a huge difference to the American taxpayer if her program could be launched and reduce the federal deficit. She also had the support of the OMB with Tom Stacks, the United States Treasury, with Vicky McDowell, and others on their staff to whom she had been introduced. Though she sat alone, she felt confident that her professional knowledge and experience working in the federal government had prepared her for this presentation today. She fully understood the processes to be discussed, and the proven lack of IRS action to accept payment from a lien, or 'bird in the hand', by redeeming foreclosed properties with sufficient equity to pay off the tax liens. Instead, they pursued a taxpayer for ten and sometimes twenty years and garnished their wages because they had not put in place necessary procedures to redeem their liens on foreclosed properties.

She looked up again at Congressman Horn, and saw him smiling encouragement at her.

She scanned the other faces of the other Congress members and their respective staffs, and reached into her purse to pull out her reading glasses in preparation for her testimony. Her hand quickly ran around the inside of her bag and then onto the bottom, searching for the familiar glasses. Nothing. She slipped her hand into the outside pocket of the purse. Again, nothing. She quickly felt around her briefcase. Still no glasses.

Congressman Horn asked Shannon to approach the witness podium, and she stood and gathered up her notes, walked around her table, and laid her reports on the top of the lectern. As she did so, she looked on the floor to see if her glasses had fallen on the floor while she was assembling her presentation materials. She patted the podium table top to see if they might have slipped into one of the folders. She casually moved her name card on the testimony podium to see if they could have slipped from one of the files to under the name card. She slipped her hand into her suit jacket pocket, just in case she had put her glasses there for convenient access. Still nothing.

She looked up at the expectant faces of the Congressional committee members. She could see them, but she could not see up close, not without the reading glasses. She could not read her reports. Everything on the podium top was blurry and impossible to read.

"Miss O'Toole, are you ready to be sworn in?" came Congressman Horn's voice as he looked down at her from his elevated platform.

She knew at that moment that she would have to deliver her testimony from memory, and try and make it just as professional and thorough as if she could read it or refer to her notes. She tried to calm the rising nervousness she was beginning to feel. She knew her material inside and out, and had worked on the presentation for months, working and reworking it. She had even highlighted certain portions in different colors so she would be sure and make each point clearly and not lose her place during her testimony. Now she was about to learn just how well she had memorized the material.

"Yes, Congressman Horn, I am," she responded with what she hoped was a clear and firm voice.

"Then let us begin," he said. "Repeat after me....."

"I, Shannon O'Toole, swear to tell the truth, before this United States Congress, and the Subcommittee for Government Reform and Oversight, so help me, God," she promised as she held up her right hand.

"Thank you for coming here today, Ms. O'Toole, and appearing before this Subcommittee, to put forth your findings and recommendations concerning certain government debt collections, namely by the Internal Revenue Service. I thank you, and the committee thanks you for testifying today. I think we are ready, and rather anxious, to hear your expert recommendations in this matter," Steven Horn, the serious Republican committee chairman from Long Beach, California, said to open the meeting. He leaned back in his high-backed black leather chair, while his colleagues did the same. There were about ten other congressmen sitting along the raised platform.

She was excited to have finally been invited to present her government lien program to Congress, and Congressman

Horn had been excited as well to finally share the plan with his committee about IRS inefficiencies including their inability to know where they had placed billions of dollars' worth of liens.

Shannon stood at the lectern, feeling confident, with her hands folded across the lengthy report she had been working on for over a year, which she was finally about to present.

"Thank you, Congressman Horn. It is an honor to be invited here today, to speak to you and your distinguished colleagues on this most important issue of the inefficiency of the Internal Revenue Service, or rather, their lack of lien and redemption collections that is cheating the American public and the Treasury out of billions and trillions of dollars each year that could be put into the national budget. This is not a new finding; unfortunately, these gross mistakes and mismanagement have been occurring year after year, with billions of dollars being lost each and every year, while taxes are being raised because the IRS and other government agencies do not manage and collect their debts efficiently. I will present a plan for improving revenue collections by the IRS, which I will explain now."

No reading glasses meant no reading the reports. Her confidence quickly turned to near panic. She quickly squinted down at the now seemingly very blurry, very small print and could see the circles she had drawn around the most important points, and the color- coded paragraphs so she wouldn't lose her place when reading the paper to the congressional committee. But she could not see the print. She could not read a word. Pretty colors, though.

She felt butterflies in her stomach and found that she was holding her breath. The Congressmen were waiting. Suddenly, it became very, very warm on this rainy spring day of March, 1996, in Washington DC as she was standing at the witness table before the United States Congress.

Congressman Horn cleared his throat, signaling Shannon to begin. *I can do this*, Shannon told herself to try and calm down. *I know the material; I researched it, and I wrote it. So what if I can't see it? I can recite the reports with my eyes closed.* Shannon lifted her head and gently tossed her shoulder-length blond hair, smiled through her Lancome cherry-red lips, and stared through her blue eyes at the congressmen, noting that there were two or three additional people seated behind each of the congressmen, whom she assumed were various aides, consultants and clerks. It was three people deep all around the raised platforms where the congressional committee sat, with additional people to the side and below the platforms to handle documents and exhibits for the congressmen.

She ran her damp hands across her black-and-white houndstooth wool suit skirt, smoothing the black collar and cuffs.

She stood as tall as her five-foot, three-inch, 125-pound figure would stretch, squared her shoulders, straightened her back and firm, full bosom, and said,

"I'm sure you would be bored if I merely read my report to you, so, instead, I'm going to tell you a story about how a very broken government program requires immediate triage, to stop billions and soon trillions of dollars in IRS and other government agency ongoing collection losses each and every year. Some of these government liens are against our elected leaders in Congress. These are losses that the American people deserve to have recovered and paid into the Treasury to reduce our national budget deficit, and how we wouldn't even need to cut many of the present programs if you will listen to my plan."

She leveled her blurry eyes at the center of the dais where Congressman Horn sat, moistened her lips, and took a very deep breath. "That is, if the IRS and other agencies could find where they put the liens. Unfortunately, the IRS and other agencies can't report to you about these liens, because they've lost them."

And so began the ad-libbed testimony of Shannon O'Toole, on the most important day in her career, before the United States Congress.

"What do you mean, lost them?" Congressman Horn queried. "Please explain."

"Our current laws provide for the IRS and other government agencies to place a lien against a taxpayer's assets, including real estate, for unpaid debts or income taxes. The purpose of these liens is to encumber or cloud the title so that the government agency is notified if the property is transferring to a new owner. By law, the IRS and other government agencies are served notice when a property is about to be foreclosed on, telling the agency the amount of the lien they are about to forfeit, the agency's lien document number, the amount of the lien and location of the property. This notice provides the necessary information for the agency to take appropriate action to collect or redeem their lien."

"And are the IRS and other agencies doing this, collecting and redeeming their lien monies at the time of foreclosure?" Congressman Horn asked.

"Unfortunately, no. I'm sorry to tell you that they either ignore the notice or simply disregard it. Or they don't have the processes in place to act on the notice to collect their lien amount. In any event, they are clearly not acting upon the notice that their opportunity to collect on their government liens is being forfeited. I have watched tens of thousands of foreclosures proceed with IRS liens against their title, but never once has the IRS collected or redeemed their lien revenue. The properties then go through foreclosure, and the equity in the property goes into the pockets of the new owner.

"As a case in point, I have asked the IRS for a list of liens they have placed during the last year throughout the nation by state. They could not provide that information. I then asked for a list of liens placed against properties in just California. They could not provide that list either."

Congressman Horn looked at the IRS Commissioner and asked, "Is that correct, Commissioner?"

The Commissioner looked down at her podium, shuffled uncomfortably, and then answered, "At this time we are unable to provide such a listing. Additionally, the IRS protects the taxpayer's confidentiality."

Shannon spoke up. "I didn't ask for any taxpayers' names or identifying information, simply the number of liens placed in each state. There's no confidentiality conflict in that."

The Commissioner leaned over to one of her attorneys for a quick consultation before answering, "We don't have that information available."

Congressman Horn then interrupted. "Why can't you provide that information?"

"As I said, the IRS has the duty to protect the taxpayer's privacy...."

"And as Ms. O'Toole stated, she hasn't asked for any specific taxpayer identity information, simply a lump-sum figure. Can you or can you not provide such a figure?"

The Commissioner turned again to her attorneys, who put their heads together.

Congressman Horn said again, this time louder,

"Can you answer my question?"

The Commissioner paused, clearly distressed, and responded,

"We are not required to provide information or data in a format that we do not have on hand or readily available…"

The congressmen around the large desk on the raised platform began to talk among themselves, clearly displeased with the Commissioner's unacceptable responses.

Congressman Horn then leveled his gaze upon the Commissioner and asked,

"Do you know how many liens IRS has placed against properties in California, or any state, for that matter?"

The Commissioner hesitated.

"Ms. Richardson, please answer the committee," he repeated.

She looked at her two attorneys, and down at her notes. She looked briefly over at Shannon and then at the congressmen on the raised platform. She took in a small, deep breath and then answered the congressional committee,

"No, not at this time."

Then Congressman Horn shifted his gaze to Shannon and said,

"And this is why you say that IRS has lost their liens?"

Shannon paused for a moment to wait for the buzz in the room to die down, as the several congressmen sitting with Congressman Horn finished their conversations.

"Yes, because the IRS has no method for reporting the number of liens they have placed against real property. They cannot track their liens. And because they can't track or report their liens, they cannot match up any foreclosure lien notices they may receive with the liens they have placed. And we are losing billions of dollars every year in uncollected liens because of this."

Again the congressmen and others in the hearing room sitting behind Shannon began to murmur and discuss the new information and its ramifications.

Congressman Horn allowed the conversations to continue for a few minutes and then redirected his attention back to Shannon.

"You have said that the liens are forfeited. What do you mean by that?"

"The IRS actually has two opportunities to collect their lien at the time of foreclosure. The first opportunity is when they receive the notice of the pending foreclosure. At that time, IRS can elect to purchase the property at the foreclosure sale and then resell the property to pay off the lien. Assuming the IRS does not purchase the property at the foreclosure sale, they have up to one hundred and twenty days after the foreclosure to redeem their lien, or set aside the sale, by paying the new purchaser their purchase price, and then the IRS takes the property and resells it to collect their lien amount. If they do neither of these two things, the law provides that the IRS liens are wiped out; they are forfeited, removed, and erased from the title to the property. And the new owner then has clear title free of liens and keeps the equity in the property, that could have paid some or all of the IRS lien. It's a windfall profit for the new owner, and a loss for the US Treasury."

"And what happens to the previous owner, the taxpayer who didn't pay his taxes and was issued the lien?"

"IRS continues to pursue the taxpayer, garnish his future wages, attach the same lien to any other assets, seize his bank accounts, possibly ruin his credit, and receives a judgment for the lien amount to continue collecting the lien amount for ten and up to twenty years. It's a double whammy for the taxpayer. First, he loses his house to foreclosure; then he loses his future paycheck."

The conversation continued as Shannon explained more about the foreclosure process. She explained her government lien redemption plan proposal, and answered the many questions for the panel of congressmen. The IRS Commissioner was silent.

Overall, the presentation had gone extremely well, considering she had to do it nearly blind.

14

The United States Treasury and Jealous Little FDIC Puppies

The rest of the week in Washington DC was a flurry of introductions to Vicky McDowell with the US Treasury and Tom Stacks with the Office of Management and Budget. Congressman Horn and Mark Brasher had ushered Shannon around to the meetings. It had been decided that they wanted to move Shannon, or do an interagency detail transfer as it was known in federal government speak, from FDIC over to the U.S Treasury to start Shannon's government lien collection and redemption program planning, the Pilot plan, for short. They also concluded that a formal memorandum of understanding, or MOU, would be prepared and issued by the Treasury to the FDIC requesting additional FDIC staff also be detailed to the Treasury to support Shannon with this work. The program Pilot was being renamed the 'Inter-Agency Debt Collection Plan'.

They discussed pending legislation HR 2234, which would provide additional funding for developing the machine to conduct collections of government debts, which would be Shannon's portion of the work. Shannon's program was the machine that would do the work and report their progress to the Treasury and Congress.

With these last decisions made, Shannon advised that she could not make any commitments for the FDIC. Vicky McDowell stated she would complete the MOU and get a copy to Shannon, so she could start it up the chain of command.

Returning to the California FDIC office on Monday morning from Washington DC, Shannon anticipated receiving messages and faxes with the promised MOU, timelines for the pilot plan, and interagency detail from the Treasury waiting. She was still sorting out all that had transpired the previous week as well as organizing her desk after having been out of the California office.

Instead, Farley Tripp walked up to her desk and said abruptly, "Shannon, I want to see you in my office, NOW."

Oh, boy, welcome back, she thought to herself. *Here it goes.* She gave Farley a minute to get back to his office before she went to his door.

"What the hell is all this about you being in Washington DC last week? Why didn't you tell me? Why didn't you think you could confide in me?"

Shannon just about broke out laughing, and although she could barely speak through her suppressed giggles, said, "It doesn't concern you, Farley. It's a program I developed on my own time, not the FDIC's or RTC's time."

"Like hell it doesn't concern me or the FDIC," he bellowed. "You work for ME!"

At about that moment, Mark Long appeared, and walked into the office, slamming the door.

"What did she tell you?" he growled and looked over at Farley.

"Nothing," Farley complained.

Mark Long glared at Shannon. "I don't know what the hell you think you're up to, but you're not gonna make me or Farley look stupid because we don't know what you're doing. I don't like getting phone calls from public affairs telling me that I have someone testifying before Congress that I don't know about !!" he roared. "Tell us what this is all about."

Ahhh, so that's how they found out, Shannon thought. Public Affairs must have called to inform them as a CYA maneuver. "Public Affairs must have told you the subject matter of my presentation, and also that it was done as an individual, not as an FDIC or RTC Director or staff person, and that I had ethics approval."

"I don't give a shit what public affairs said, I want to hear it from you what this was all about," Mark continued to yell.

Shannon wasn't even fazed by all the blustering and bellowing from Mark or Tripp. She smiled slightly and calmly said,

"I hope it will be the beginning of a new Program supported by Congress that will soon prove to provide overdue relief to the Treasury."

"What the hell does THAT mean?" Farley snarled.

She wasn't interested in giving them much more information, and answered,

"It's a program to increase the Treasury's balance sheet."

"What the hell, the Treasury's *balance sheet*?"

"That's correct."

"How do you plan to do that?"

She paused and then answered,

"I'm still working on the details."

Mark and Tripp weren't happy with her answers, so Mark took a different approach.

"And WHO's gonna run it?" taunted Mark.

Shannon was surprised at their aggressive stance and obvious power grab, but answered,

"I wrote it, and I expect to run it," she answered, and turned and left the office.

As she walked away, she could still hear Farley and Mark talking to each other.

"You know we could run the program, it can't be that hard. We have to find out what she's got going, and talk with the boys in Washington DC to get set up for this new thing..."

"Yeah, she'll be going out the door in just a couple of months with the downsizing; we just have to wait for her to go, and then we can step in..."

"Let's get a copy of her testimony from your friend in public affairs, and we'll see what her 'Program' is all about..."

She walked on, now feeling increased pressure to get her new Program launched and funded with the Treasury to move forward.

Shannon also knew that Vicky McDowell was buried with presidential demands on her time and Treasury projects. She hadn't received the letters yet from Vicky that she needed, and time was running short now because the government moved so slowly, with only about 180 days to the end of the year. FDIC had decided to close the California office at the end of the year, and that meant that most of the staff would be released, with only a few moving to Texas or Washington DC. Moving her transfer detail from the FDIC to the Treasury would have to go through several channels and levels of approval that would take time. It needed to start now, and she needed the MOU being prepared by the US Treasury to start the paperwork.

She would share the Inter-Agency Lien Collection and Redemption program, the Pilot plan, with her FDIC management as soon as she received the MOU. The legal contract work would need to begin immediately.

Shannon began to draft a letter to Vicky McDowell to encourage her to complete the MOU, making an effort to sound cordial and conversational… *I'll tell her how much I've enjoyed working with her and let her know I've also been working with the GSA, Government Services Agency, in providing them with auction documents. She should take a second look at the letter when I mention Laura Yeager's name, her old friend from the Treasury who has recently gone over to run the G.O.R.E. auctions for GSA. At least it should gain her attention.*

Shannon began creating her letter.

And then I'll bring up the subject of time escaping, that there are only one hundred eighty days left in the year before FDIC lays off about seventeen hundred people, some that could be transferred to the Treasury to perform the much-needed collection work.

She finished the letter and reread it for the third time, each time trying to make it sound more collegiate than demanding.

The letter was faxed to the Treasury, and now the waiting game began again. She needed the memorandum of understanding to begin involving FDIC into the equation.

On April 19, 1996, she received a fax from the Executive Office of the President of the United States, Office of Management and Budget, stating…

"Vicky McDowell requests that FDIC detail Shannon O'Toole to the United States Treasury for the purpose of developing the Inter Agency Government Lien and Collection program. The Treasury proposes that FDIC, OMB and Treasury discuss FDIC's participation in providing initial staffing and resources to this project, to be reimbursed upon upcoming 1997 budget approval..."

There! She had what she needed to start the process of involving the FDIC into the new Pilot plan if she could reach the right decision makers in Washington DC. It seemed like a natural flow to move FDIC staff over to the Treasury to begin to operate the lien recovery program.

And then she picked up her ringing telephone, surprised to hear Tom Stacks' voice,

"Good morning, Shannon. Did you receive a special fax this morning?" She could hear the smile in his voice.

"If you mean the letter from the Executive Office..."

"The letter from the Executive Office of the President of the United States, compliments of the Office of Management and Budget..."

"Well, yes, I did, as a matter of fact," She grinned into the phone.

"This program is so important and high profile too," he informed her. "President Clinton is looking for something new and big for his political campaign, and this just may be it !"

Shannon was stunned. "Seriously?"

"Seriously," he answered, still enthusiastic about the possibility. "We are jumping through hoops getting data and reports ready on a multitude of programs and recommendations for him. It's a madhouse around here. Everyone's working overtime, and there's still more to do than the staff can keep up with. That's how it is during an election cycle back here."

"Hectic, yes, but it also sounds exciting," she answered.

"It always is," he chuckled. "So go ahead and submit your transfer detail to your powers-that-be. We want you here as soon as possible. Let me know if you need me to talk to someone from FDIC on this end," then he said good-bye.

Shannon had done some research on the process and divisions she would need to navigate with the request from the United States Treasury for her detail transfer. Initially, she would speak with personnel but would simultaneously have to seek release from her own FDIC office in Irvine, California, which meant Farley Tripp and Atwater.

She prepared her notes and made an appointment with Mr. Atwater. He was receptive and welcomed her into his large, cavernous office, with the same old dark wood, oversized bankers' desks and chairs that Shannon had to sit on the edge of or fall back into and disappear.

"Shannon, do come in. I hear you've been visiting up in Washington DC," and he leaned forward in his chair, placing his elbows on his desk. "I hear you even have some congressmen who are interested in some new plan you have," and he smiled at her encouragingly.

This was a surprise to Shannon that there had been conversations proceeding her appointment or the request she was about to make. She selected one of the oversized chairs and sat neatly on the edge, crossing her legs, resting one elbow on the arm of the chair.

"Well, yes, I have been developing a new plan that has interested the US Treasury. It ties into other plans they are working on to increase Treasury recoveries and revenue, which always interests our congressmen and senators," she tried to be level and straight with Atwater.

"So I hear," he answered. "Tell me more about your plan."

She didn't want to go into all the details of the proposed pilot plan but had anticipated discussing it in general terms. She took a deep breath,

"I developed my plan as an individual, not as an FDIC or RTC manager or representing either agency. I wanted to introduce the plan based upon some independent research I have done regarding foreclosures and liens placed against those properties in foreclosure by government entities."

At that moment, Alan Lawrence leaned against the open doorway and said,

"I'm interested in hearing about your recent time in Washington DC. Mind if I sit in?"

Lawrence was the executive managing director for FDIC at the office, while Atwater remained the executive managing officer for RTC. Lawrence was a tall, blond man with broad shoulders, while Atwater was much older and smaller. The two had somewhat parallel roles, with Lawrence having the top billing, and larger office. She was again surprised in the apparent knowledge of her recent activities in Washington DC.

"Come on in," Atwater answered.

Lawrence took a chair adjacent to Atwater's desk, sat, placed his heel on his knee, and addressed Shannon,

"I heard part of what you just said to Atwater. Something about government liens placed against real estate?"

She smiled slightly, thinking that he had heard everything she had said, but she repeated it for his benefit anyway,

"That's correct. Government agencies place liens against real property, for instance, when income taxes or Franchise Tax Board taxes are not paid…"

Atwater interjected, "And some of these government agencies are…"

"The IRS, the California State Treasury, SBA, liens for unpaid student loans. Really any federal or state agency can place a lien against a person's property for unpaid debts…"

"And they do this because they think the taxes or loans have not been paid?" he queried.

"Yes. The liens are placed to secure payment from the property equity."

"But don't they place the liens in the regular course of business?" Atwater continued.

"No, not usually until the taxes or loan become delinquent," she explained. "For instance, you and I pay our income taxes annually. However, if we should not pay or arrange a payment plan with the federal or state treasuries to make payments for back taxes, the government agencies can then place a lien on our assets, including any real property we own. They can also attach bank accounts, or garnish wages."

"I see," Atwater said.

"But why is this a big deal? If there's a lien on the property, doesn't it have to be paid off before the owner can sell their house?" Alan Lawrence asked.

She turned from Atwater to Lawrence,

"For a regular sale, yes, the lien has to be paid off to clear the title. The property cannot be sold by the owner without paying off the liens. But I'm talking about properties that go through foreclosure in my plan."

"How is that different?"

"When a real estate property goes through foreclosure, all of the liens are 'wiped out', or removed, so the title is cleared, and the property can be purchased by a new owner."

"Really? Why is that?"

"Actually, the laws are such that when the homeowner or debtor stop making their contractural payments, they default on their loan, and the lender or holder of the loan against the property can take back the property, through the foreclosure process, where the liens are removed or wiped out. The title to the property is then clean and marketable. Otherwise, the title to the property would never be clear, and could never be sold with a clean title again. It's a way of making the foreclosed property sellable, or marketable again."

"But, you say that these liens are not being paid off. Why?" Lawrence continued to ask questions.

She paused. She hadn't planned on discussing all of the details of her plan. Her purpose had been to begin the process of being detailed or transferred over to the US Treasury to implement this Pilot plan. Now she was being asked for the particulars of her discovery.

"Let's just say that the collection system is broken, and I hope my plan will repair it," she answered, hoping that it would satisfy Atwater and Lawrence.

It seemed to work, and, instead, Lawrence redirected his questioning with,

"Did you really speak before Congress?" he asked her directly.

She barely answered, "I did…" when he interrupted her.

"Even I haven't done that, or Atwater here. Weren't you scared?"

Shannon wanted to answer them honestly and wanted to gain their support for the request she was about to deliver. She was trying to adjust to having the two top executive directors interview her about her recent activities.

"I suppose I was nervous, but also excited. I really believe in this program I have developed. It was well received by Congressman Steve Horn and others I was introduced to, so I was very hopeful that it would be viewed as having merit."

"Sounds like it has more than just a little merit," he answered, a little under his breath.

"I hope so." She smiled at the two executives. "So now the US Treasury has asked if I may be detailed over to the Treasury to work on this program. I'm hoping I can have your support," she finished, glad she had finally been able to put her request in front of them.

Lawrence looked over at Atwater and then back at Shannon.

"I can forward your request up the chain," he offered. "I suggest you contact Jay Keller in FDIC headquarters in Washington DC. He will need to be involved."

Shannon left the executive's office, feeling that she had made it past the immediate hurdle of gaining her local office's concurrence, and making a note of the contact information Lawrence had provided for her regarding the person in Washington DC who needed to be brought into the transaction.

She later informed Farley Tripp of her potential detail transfer to the US Treasury. For the most part, his mouth just hung open, and he didn't have much to say when she told him she had already spoken with Atwater and Lawrence.

Shannon returned to her computer, and pulled up Jay Keller's name in the FDIC staff index, and saw that he was the assistant chief of staff for the FDIC Chairwoman, Ricki Helfer. She was surprised that Lawrence had directed her to contact someone so high up in the chain-of-command at FDIC. She had contacted the human resources division earlier, and they had indicated that they would process the paperwork after she had approval and concurrence from FDIC management.

She decided it would be more appropriate to first e-mail Jay Keller, introducing herself and the subject she wished to briefly discuss with him. She felt that the e-mail would make him more comfortable than receiving a call out of left field. She was careful to continue to emphasize that she had developed the Pilot plan on an individual basis, and had appeared before Congress as just that, an individual, not as an RTC or FDIC manager or employee. She gave a very brief outline of the Pilot plan and closed the e-mail with a request for a convenient time to call him and discuss her request.

Keller had responded with a date and time for an initial call the following week, and Shannon had prepared her notes and files in front of her in preparation for the call. Her phone rang, and she answered it pleasantly.

"Hello, Shannon O'Toole, FDIC."

"Hello, Shannon, this is Jay Keller, assistant chief of staff for Chairwoman Ricki Helfer."

"Thank you for calling, Mr. Keller, I appreciate it."

"I've been looking over the information you sent me. You don't have to go into the details of your proposed plan or of your ethics and public relations clearances. I've been advised about it. And I've been in contact with the public relations and ethics people here in Washington DC. So I understand you actually spoke before Congress regarding this plan of yours?"

His initial comments weren't very friendly, and she wasn't sure if he was being provocative or merely stating the facts.

"Yes, I did. It's a great program that has garnered support from certain congressmen, the United States Treasury and the Office of Management and Budget."

"And you say this is a private matter—that is, you have done all this on your own time?"

"That's also correct."

"And now the Treasury wants to transfer you over to their offices to work on this program?"

"Also correct. I sent you a copy of the letter I have received from the Executive Office of the President through OMB."

Keller paused.

"You know that most of the RTC and FDIC staff in California are going to be released at the end of the year, don't you? That's just a little less than six months from now. And a lot more staff here in Washington DC will also be going out the door. It's a tough situation. Everyone is looking around for another job now. How many people does the Treasury want to work on this new Pilot plan?"

Wow. Cut to the chase, she thought.

"They have asked for me to select ten to twelve additional staff from FDIC who have knowledge and experience with real estate title and database management as well as collections. I will do most of the program writing since I have developed it."

"Have you written much of the operating details for this program?"

Where is he going with this? she wondered.

"I delivered a detailed outline on how the government lien recovery plan would work to Congress, the Treasury, and OMB...."

He interrupted with, "Does any new legislation need to be passed, or new rules or laws established to make this plan work?"

That is an interesting question, she mused.

"Actually, no. The rules and laws are all in place, but the process is not. I have detailed the process necessary to make the government lien recovery plan a reality and recover billions of dollars for the Treasury."

Keller was quiet again for a moment. Then, he startled her with, "You know, there's a lot of highly qualified people back her in headquarters that could work on the project. Why do you want to bring people over from FDIC California?"

She was not prepared for that question. She was stunned at his boldness. Was he trying to shift the work or trying to find jobs for his friends?

"At this time, Mr. Keller, I need the skills and experience that many of the real estate staff here in the California FDIC have demonstrated for the last several years. The initial work will be very hands on, with a lot of brainstorming and trial and error. It will be a start-up operation."

"I suppose you are right about that. But it will still need an oversight group and advisory board. Who are you working with at the Treasury?"

"I sent you the letter from the Executive Office and from the Office of Management and Budget. I am working with Vicky McDowell from the Treasury. She has been my primary contact."

"How did you get introduced to her?"

"Through Congressmen Steve Horn and his Washington DC manager, Mark Brasher."

He paused again.

"How did the OMB get involved?"

She was surprised at his question, and offered him,

"Because the Office of Management and Budget is focused on revenues, Mr. Keller. And they work hand in hand with the Treasury when evaluating program funding and budgeting."

"This is all very interesting," he answered. "I want you to send me the contact information for McDowell and the OMB person, Stack. I may have some questions for them after I get a chance to look at this more."

She knew she would have to comply with his request if she wanted to further her efforts to commence her new program and to gain his agreement for her detail transfer to the Treasury, but she felt like she was giving away some very confidential proprietary information just the same.

She didn't answer him immediately, and he said,

"Shannon? I'll look for the contact information by the end of this week. I'll get back to you after I have a chance to look over more of the substance of this request."

The call was over. She didn't feel very encouraged by Keller's remarks. She didn't know why she felt uncomfortable, but she did.

Shannon cleaned up her desk and zoomed along to finish her normal work before she left for a business trip to Northern California to deal with a failed bank the following week. She knew she wouldn't receive a quick answer from Jay Keller with such a highly visible, far-reaching request for her detail transfer to start up the Inter-Agency Debt collection project, and she refocused on the tasks at hand and on the loan portfolio from the Northern California bank.

Several weeks after she returned from Northern California, she still hadn't received the approval she needed from Jay Keller, although she had left two messages. The recent return message had said he was out of the office for two weeks, so she didn't expect any movement until he returned.

She had promised her daughter, Jennifer, a couple of days on the beach after she came back home from Northern California.

It was midsummer, Jennifer was out of school, and Shannon was feeling guilty for working long hours and bringing work home, including the inter-agency government collection program pilot work.

As Shannon packed bathing suits, lots of sunscreen and a sundress, she debated bringing along the laptop computer. *This is supposed to be a mini-vacation,* she said to herself. *And Jennifer deserves all my attention. She has been a real sweetheart and has not complained when I'm so tired I can barely find my way to bed."* Shannon was a pro at creating self-guilt. *On the other hand, she is seventeen years old and has a very busy schedule herself with her Ruby's job, school, ballet, cheerleading and church, maybe I'm just company when there's nothing else to do?* Shannon contemplated starting their vacation the next morning, when she would try to wake up Jennifer, which was always so much fun, and listen to her daughter's assorted grunts and vague mutterings about it being too early. Jennifer simply was not a morning person.

So the laptop was also packed into the convertible for the trip down to San Diego. There would be time in the early mornings to work a little more on the policies and procedures, scope, and report formats for the government lien recovery program.

Back in the office, Shannon had been working on a complicated file for a multiuse property located in the Embarcadero area in San Francisco that was encumbered with environmental issues. The local high tides brought debris and other chemical deposits that rendered the property unusable without environmental remediation, cleanup, and required mitigation. It was a valuable property, it had sufficient parking, which was a plus, and great views of the ocean. She was preparing a spreadsheet on the bids she had received for the environmental phase-three cleanup actions when the phone on her desk rang,

"Hello?" she answered.

"Hello to you," she heard the familiar deep voice of Tom Stack and she smiled.

"Hi there, nice to hear your voice."

"And yours' as well," he answered her. "How have you been?"

"Working, trying to move some of the complicated environmental properties through and into a marketing status, which is always a challenge. But never boring."

"Have you heard anything on your detail transfer over to Treasury yet? It's been several weeks since you were here."

"I've been pestering Washington DC regularly to get their signoff. It would be a lot easier if my contact person was in the office more than not."

"Hmmm, sounds like you could use some help from this end. Who is your contact person, and what's their title?"

His question bothered her. If he was asking her this, that meant that Keller hadn't contacted him yet.

"Jay Keller; he's assistant chief of staff to the chairwoman. He had already heard that I had delivered my Pilot plan presentation to Congress before I ever contacted him. Seems he had also been contacted by ethics and public relations, so I didn't have to brief him on much."

"I haven't met him before. I know a few of the staffers in the Chairwoman's office, but not him. What's his contact info?" Tom asked, and Shannon gave him Keller's phone number and e-mail information.

"Listen, I have more to tell you," Tom continued. "Vicky and I have been in endless meetings regarding the upcoming elections and the possibility of using the Inter- Agency Debt collection plan in President Clinton's platform. We talked more about the Pilot. She wants you to be detailed and transferred to the Treasury here in Washington DC immediately to start the ball rolling and help her define the program, but then return to California and have you operate from FDIC office space and equipment with the additional staff to be detailed to the Treasury to support your build up for the program. Office space is too tight here now, and with the upcoming elections all the extra office space is occupied with every conceivable staffer and program consultant. And she had some Treasury staff refuse to relocate and that has jammed up her plan for your programs office space here."

Shannon paused. This was a significant change. She couldn't commit for FDIC. She was thinking fast as to who she would need to contact in FDIC Washington DC to open the conversation for the Pilot program and these changes and requests. She had only approached Keller with her request for the detail transfer to the Treasury, not all this.

"I'll see what I can do," she finally answered. "I can probably start with Keller and add this new information to my pending request. I'll have to talk with the local management team here, too, since it includes office space here in California. But this is a big request."

"I know this is a big change, but I think it can work. Let us know who you are talking with, and we'll work on it from this end. I think we can all meet in the middle and make this come together. I'll get on Vicky to get the Memorandum of Understand, the MOU to you. For now, you can at least introduce the ideas and start explaining our intent."

Shannon spent some time thinking about the new requests from Treasury to work the Inter-Agency Debt Collection Pilot Plan from the FDIC California office. She knew that most of the employees would be released on December 31, 1996, but that some would be retained, and the office space would be primarily empty. She had to contact both Jay Keller and the local executive managers, Atwater and Lawrence, again with these new requests. And to make it more difficult, she didn't have the formal memorandum of understanding from the Treasury that would undoubtedly give the requests more validation.

She e-mailed Atwater and Alan Lawrence requesting a brief meeting to update them on the interagency pilot and, to her surprise, received a nearly immediate response and meeting acceptance invitation.

When she arrived at Atwater's office, he waved her in again, and was very cordial.

"Lawrence was just here but has a meeting out of the office, so I will convey to him your updated information.," he smiled at Shannon. "Listen," he continued. "I think it is great if you can help some of our good employees find a job after this place closes down. More power to you. I'll do whatever I can do to help."

Shannon was a little taken aback at his well wishes and positive reinforcement for her pilot plan, but then quickly understood his attitude when he said,

"And, you know, there are some fine people up here in the executive management office area who could lend you their experience and knowledge. You'll probably need some high-grade oversight and a guidance board of some kind, and they would love to help you. I would, too, but I plan on retiring, but they would love to join your program."

When Shannon couldn't hide her surprise, he quickly added,

"Oh, you'll run the pilot program, of course, Shannon, because you know it and have shaped it. But usually in these situations there are also slots of higher-ranking executives, and, well, since you already know everyone here, it might make sense to recommend some of them to the Treasury to, you know, work alongside your group, to be on your governing Board." He seemed pleased with himself for offering her his subordinate managers who had replaced her hardworking staff when they were transferred over from the RTC to the FDIC.

She pulled herself together and answered,

"Thank you for the offer, Mr. Atwater. I'll remember that. But I have some important information to share with you that was just conveyed to me by the Treasury and OMB. Do you have a few more minutes?"

"Of course, of course." Atwater was at her disposal, and very interested.

"The United States Treasury had office space and slots for employees to start up the Inter-Agency Debt Collection Pilot plan in Washington DC, however, the pending elections and contractors have filled the available space and certain staff have elected not to move into new divisions. Thus, the Treasury and OMB are asking if they can still detail transfer staff from FDIC to work for them but from space here at the California FDIC office. Since much of the staff will be leaving on December thirty-first, there will be abundant vacant space, desks, computers and other office equipment idle."

He hadn't said no yet, so she kept going, "I know this is a big change. I understand that it is unusual. However, it is also very doable."

Atwater didn't answer immediately as he thought about Shannon's information and request.

He finally answered, "Do you have anything in writing from the U.S. Treasury or OMB?"

"I gave you their earlier letter requesting my detail transfer and the same for additional staff I would select to start the Inter-Agency Pilot."

"And has Washington DC approved that yet? Wasn't it Jay Keller that was advancing the request?"

"Not yet. He's talking with the Treasury at length about this program," she answered reluctantly.

"Yes, but now they are asking for FDIC office space here in California," he answered slowly.

"Is there a Memorandum of Understanding for this?" he asked.

Darn! He was asking for something she knew he needed and she had been trying to procure before talking with him or Washington DC.

"It's being written by counsel," she answered, stretching what she knew to be the truth. Tom had said he would push Vicky to write the MOU, hadn't he? So, she wasn't too far off base.

"Good, that's good," he answered, nodding his balding head. "That will be helpful when we talk with Headquarters."

They talked more about how the office space issue could be handled, however, Shannon knew that the MOU was the key to moving the request forward.

"Is there anyone else in Headquarters you think I might talk to about this request from Treasury in addition to Keller?" she asked.

Atwater thought for a moment and then answered slowly,

"No, I don't think so. Keller is the assistant chief of staff, so *everything* goes past him before it gets to the chairwoman. Anyone else would be subordinate to him, and be reporting to him, so I think you're with the right person."

Labor Day came quickly, ending the summer, and marking the rapidly approaching end of the calendar year, when FDIC would release most of the staff in California.

Shannon awoke Tuesday morning at 6:00 a.m. and padded into the kitchen to place the call to the Treasury from home before going into the office, hoping to reach the Treasury early before the day's meetings and conferences began. Surprisingly, the Treasury director answered immediately, and Shannon said,

"Good morning, Vicky," trying to hide her surprise. "I don't know if I should apologize for being so persistent or just tell you what's been going on around the FDIC," Shannon began.

"Well, let me tell you what's been going on *here*," Vicky interrupted. "For the last ten and a half weeks, I have been working 10 hours a day personally writing material for President Clinton's convention re-election nomination speech. I have had my staff doing nothing but preparing material for the President. Every time his staff asked for something different, we turned on a dime and researched the request and prepared a response the President could use at the convention."

"It certainly sounds as if you have been under some heavy orders," Shannon sympathized. However, she knew that all this work for the President meant that Vicky's staff would have been too busy to touch the inter-agency debt collection plan now, and the memorandum of understanding, that was so important to Shannon. She had to know if the program was going to fly, because they were simply running out of time if she was going to be transferred to the Treasury to work on the project. If the transfer did not happen before the end of the year, her work for FDIC would come to an end, and she would no longer be eligible for a transfer. Nearly all the RTC staff that was transferred back to the FDIC would be at the end of their tenures at the end of the year. She had been able to talk with Jay Keller in Washington DC, however, he was refusing to go forward with her detail transfer or discussions on having her and selected staff work on the Treasury Pilot plan from the California office without the MOU.

She would at least ask, and give Vicky the opportunity to bow out and say that she just wasn't interested in getting Shannon's program off the ground. So she offered Vicky an out.

"Vicky, do you still want to pursue the inter-agency debt collection program, the Pilot plan, and go forward? I would understand if you and your staff are just too busy and swamped with other—"

"Oh, no! Let me tell you. Yes, I want very much to go forward with the Pilot plan. In fact, I wrote part of President Clinton's conference speech about the new program! It was going to be part of his platform, however, he didn't use it at the conference. But I think he may use it now with his reelection platform efforts. Oh, yes, I certainly do want to go forward with the plan." She had sounded quite excited with this news, and then she sighed. "I've found that I just can't do any staff work anymore, and my staff's assignments are exceedingly increasing. What I've done is to transfer a new attorney in for the Pilot project, and her first task is to get your MOU program/detail proposal completed to get FDIC to loan you and another ten or twelve people you choose to me at the Treasury to work out of the FDIC California office. I have given her all my files for the program, and your proposal, and other materials. She should be able to focus on it and get it done right away now."

Shannon, ears perking up and heart beating faster with this unexpected great news, tried to sound casual and asked, "Oh, what's the new attorney's name?" She poised her pen to capture this magic information.

"Mindy Quan."

Shannon again tried to think of the politically correct way to approach her next question, so as to open another door, without closing the previous one. "OK, then, would you like me to contact her regarding this plan?"

"Yes, that'll be fine. And I've told her to contact you." Vicky gave Shannon the attorneys' phone number.

"Vicky, let me review the terms of the proposal to be drafted for the FDIC, so I am sure to have your thoughts in front of me when I talk to Mindy Quan. I want to be sure and give her your feelings and how you want the draft structured. We will define the Inter-Agency Government Debt Collection Program and discuss the lost IRS liens..."

Vicky jumped in, "There may be an issue with the IRS portion right now; they are making noise and hiding behind their so-called privacy rules, so we will focus on all agency lien collections. That's why we changed the name and are now calling it the Inter-Agency Lien Collection program. You and I and our attorneys know that once an IRS lien is placed against a property and the lien information is recorded in the local county records, that it is public notice."

Then Shannon remembered the aggressive e-mail she had received from Jay Keller, the FDIC puppy, as Vicki called him, who demanded he be included in any telephone conversation Shannon had with Vicky. "Um, Vicky, Jay Keller had asked that we conference him in when we talked today. Shall we try and get him on the line so we can go over some of these details?"

"Oh, no, I don't want to deal with that little yappy puppy right now," Vicky responded quickly.

"He's been around here with his co-puppy, Inca Stevens, the last month trying to throw his weight around, giving talks to anyone he can lasso, and touting the Inter- Agency Lien Collection program as his own! And recommending himself and his friends to run it! He's been shoving his résumé and the résumés of some of his friends at us."

Shannon blanched, she could barely hear Vicky talking. She was stunned at what she had just been told about Jay Keller's actions and intentions.

When Vicky had told Shannon that she was considering asking FDIC to detail staff to the Treasury to commence the Inter-Agency Government Debt Recovery Program, and to possibly house the startup operation in a small area at

Shannon's FDIC office, she had no choice but to go through the appropriate political channels to further the Treasury's intentions and request. Shannon had done everything right. She had explained the request from Treasury to each level of approval she was compelled to talk with, and had finally ended up with Jay Keller, again, the chief of staff to Ricki Helfer, the FDIC Chairwoman. Shannon was aware that Keller was self-important and egotistical. She was also aware that with the downsizing of staffing at the end of the year, even staff in Washington DC, were concerned with their longevity, and now it seemed that Keller was looking for his next step up, if what Vicky said about him was true That he was espousing that he was the right choice to set up and run the new Inter-Agency Lien Collection Program, along with his friends. Shannon was shocked, and could feel her heart pounding too hard.

"I told you I have asked Mindy Quan to prepare the MOU proposal for you and about ten or twelve others from the California office to be detailed or loaned to the Treasury, and work out of the California office. It will not include Jay Keller or his friends."

Shannon was stunned at Vicky's disclosure about Jay Keller and Inca Stevens's attempts to take over the debt collection plans, all behind Shannon's back and with Vicky's obvious disinterest in bringing Jay Keller into the teleconference. No wonder Jay had been working very hard to keep Shannon out of Washington DC. He had made excuses, delays, and wouldn't approve any travel plans she had tried to discuss. He had never mentioned that he had been over at the Treasury, beating down doors. Jay had been persistent in requesting Shannon's contacts at the Treasury and OMB, all to be used for his own selfish purposes. She had gone stone cold at this news as her stomach lurched.

Every FDIC employee knew that the FDIC was downsizing in all their locations, with some offices to be closed completely, including the California office. Even Washington DC was going to have to let some staff go, and now she knew why Jay Keller and Inca Stevens had been trying so hard to get to Vicky McDowell.

They had never been supporting Shannon's efforts, but instead, had been trying to sell their own programs, plans, and staffing plans, along with their own egos.

But she had no other avenue or choice but to work through Keller, since she couldn't access the FDIC Chairwoman directly. She had to plug forward to understand the terms to be presented to Keller, whether or not he was included in this phone conversation. And it appeared she would have to offer to assist Keller in his efforts to join the Treasury at a later time.

Shannon tried to refocus on her conversation with Vicky, "Now I understand that we have a budget of around six million dollars that you were able to carve out of the 1997 remaining budget funds for this work..." Shannon began, in an effort to define the scope and available funds to run the program.

"Well, yes I did, and now I don't. You know how easy it is for Congress to giveth and taketh away, and they took the money away to finish other project work for the year. So we don't have any money to run the project until the 1997–1998 budget is approved."

Shannon was trying to quickly comprehend that fact that the six million that was set aside for her Inter-Agency Debt Collection Pilot program was now gone, and her stomach started to lurch again; yet she heard that funding was planned for 1997–1998.

Shannon interrupted with, "So you have included the Inter-Agency Debt Collection program in with the 1997–1998 Treasury budget, but how do we get started now in 1996?"

"Well," Vicky said slowly, "that's where it becomes very important that I will be negotiating with the FDIC in proposing that FDIC will run the Pilot work, and I think we should propose that you are detailed for, say, nine months just in case the budget is not approved by the end of the year or early next year. We don't know how the new line-item veto is going to work out."

Nine-month detail? Shannon thought. *But the FDIC is downsizing at the end of this year, in about three months.*

"That way, if the FDIC will agree to carry the program for, say, up to nine months, it will be reimbursed by the Treasury as soon as the 1997 to 1998 budget is approved. It may be only four months; it could be nine months, and, of course, it is contingent on the budget being approved. But that way, you and the program won't be falling off the edge at the end of 1996 in case the 1997 to 1998 budget isn't approved yet."

Shannon was feeling a bit skeptical about the FDIC agreeing to extend any staff beyond the end of the year or to pick up expenses, and she thought again about Jay Keller's e-mail arguing with her about not making any promises for the FDIC, and about conferencing him into this call.

"You know, this is going to take some serious negotiations," Shannon began carefully. "I can't commit for the FDIC. I think we should bring Jay Keller in on this now. How about we call him, and he can hear the new terms now so we can get this feedback?"

"No," Vicky said strongly. "I'll call Keller later, and I will negotiate my proposal with him later. I don't have time for all his pompous proliferations right now."

Shannon just didn't see any alternative to the situation at this moment, except her next question, "Why don't we just have my group start working directly for the Treasury now and not be concerned with transfer details to get the program going? Just hire them directly into the Treasury?" she asked, anticipating not only Jay Keller's wrath at not having been included in this phone call but also with the change in terms Vicky was proposing.

"Because we have a hiring freeze on," Vicky responded quickly. "One of the Treasury sections has been moved out of state, and the employees in that section that were expected to have now decided not to. They have involved the federal employees union to protect them. They have raised a huge union action. Those were the available slots for you and some other people from FDIC and RTC and the space I had set aside for you. There are rules that state these employees have to be given other spots here, so these people will need to be factored into any future hiring and program staffing and office space.....I don't think I'll be using the people that Jay Keller had been pushing at me, and I don't want to just take a bunch of stale wood when I don't know how they perform," Vicky trailed off. "Keller has given me boxes full of FDIC job descriptions and a stratification of grade levels and numbers of FDIC staff being laid off at the end of 1996 and 1997. He thinks I should take people from his group in Washington DC."

Shannon was unaware that Jay Keller had been pushing Vicky with applications, and her head was spinning with this news.

"I won't take his word for the quality of these employees. I won't just fill the slots. We may have to start your work program with liens other than the IRS liens. As I said before, IRS is fighting hard to maintain their turf, and are hiding behind privacy laws again, that I don't think apply. We just need to get you here and then we will work on getting the privacy and lien situation organized."

After hanging up the phone with Vicky McDowell, Shannon thought about calling the puppies in Washington DC. Since Jay Keller had sent such a strongly worded e-mail regarding being included in the phone conversation, Shannon tried to think about the various scenarios. She could not call him, and just let Vicky call him in the morning, if she would. Or, she could call him herself and bring him up to date. She was trying to calm herself down, after learning about Keller's duplicity and self-dealing actions.

After deliberating a few minutes, she decided to do the 'politically correct thing' and call Jay herself. She had the advantage of knowing what he was up to now.

"Hello, Jay, this is Shannon. I had a short talk with Vicky just now; she's not on the line, though. She had to catch her carpool. I just wanted to let you know what she said, though it was really fast."

Shannon could hear Jay typing as she talked.

"I can hear you typing. I tried to do the same with Vicky, but she went too fast. I could barely take a few notes."

"Yeah, well, tell me what went on."

"Well, she said that she did not have the timelines done or the proposal memorandum of understanding written for us. She said she had transferred in a new staff person, an attorney, for the purpose of working solely on the interagency collection program and writing the MOU."

"Oh, yeah? What's the attorney's name and contact number?" Jay said in a quiet voice and continued typing what she was saying.

Sure, Jay, more contacts for you at the Treasury, she thought. She ignored his request for the moment.

"Vicky also said she had been very busy working on priorities given to her section by Congress." *Now should I go into the part about the program being written into the President's convention speech, or not? Probably not*, she concluded quickly. *It would be a political error to raise this flag and sound like I'm bragging.* She was being very careful now with Keller. Shannon decided to change the subject a little.

"What do you think the FDIC chairwoman is really going to do when she gets this proposal on her desk soon? Is she completely briefed as to how this has been going along?"

With Jay's next answer, Shannon's blood turned to ice.

"I haven't really discussed it with her, Shannon," he answered in a rather thinly veiled, condescendingly manner. "There's really been nothing to report or brief her on. It's all just been talk, and without something tangible or a written proposal from the Treasury, I'm not going in there and start talking about nothing. I'm not going to be embarrassed."

Nothing, Shannon thought. *Nothing? I have been planning this new program for four years; this will be my next career, and the work of many other folks is nothing to Jay.* She was reeling with this selfish, cavalier attitude of his. *Just hold on*, she reminded herself. *You don't want to burn this bridge; you need to cross over it many times.* His lying about the insignificance or tangible status of the Inter-Agency Collection Program when he was over at the Treasury pitching it himself was nearly more than she could handle.

"Really, Jay? We're talking some major news and changes here. I would just think that you would want to brief the chairwoman so you would know early on what her thoughts on this were, especially if we are going to be negotiating a pilot plan and more with the Treasury soon. Then you would know the chairwoman's position before the Treasury asked the questions and could steer the negotiations along the FDIC chairwoman's path of most likely concurrence. Wouldn't that be the way to do it?"

"Listen, Shannon. I'm not doing nothin' until Vicky calls *me*, and I can talk with her myself. And I'm not going to the chairwoman until I'm satisfied and think we've got something real." Keller sounded indignant.

I've apparently ruffled his feathers, she thought.

"Well, Jay, I'm sure she will call you next, especially since she has assigned legal now to work on the program. There will be a lot to be negotiated, and she knows you are the one she needs to talk to for this." *And she thinks that you are keeping the chairwoman briefed; won't this be a surprise?* Shannon thought.

"Yeah, well, let's see if she calls this time," muttered Jay. "You know the time is really getting short here," he reminded Shannon.

"Yes, I know," she responded. "I'm acutely aware."

They ended the call.

Sure that Vicky had called Jay on Friday as she had promised to do, Shannon sent a quick e-mail to him in Washington, DC, making sure it sounded unthreatening and chatty.

"Have you heard from Vicky today?" was the message Shannon left on Jay's voicemail as he didn't answer his phone.

On Friday, the director of the Treasury called Jay Keller, only Jay had gone home early, and missed his call.

It was Monday again, and Shannon needed to find out where the memorandum of understanding for her program was with the new attorney for the Treasury. She needed to show support, not criticism, if it wasn't completed as expected. So she called and had an early-morning wake-up chat with Vicky's secretary, Pam.

"Good morning, Pam. Did you stay dry over the weekend?"

"Oh, good morning, Shannon. It is pretty early for you in California now."

"Oh I kind of like watching the sun come up. I'm in the office so much that it's nice to see the day start. Did you catch much wet weather from the Caribbean hurricanes over the weekend?"

"You know it really rained a lot, and we couldn't get a basket of male crabs like we enjoy, only a basketful of female crabs."

"I don't understand why male crabs or female crabs are better or harder to get, Pam."

"Well, I don't really know that either except that when the weather is all rough and the ocean is torn up, for some reason we can only get female crabs, and the male crabs are protected or something like that."

"Sounds to me like the male crabs just go into hiding when the weather gets rough, and no one can catch them!" Shannon laughed, and Pam joined her in the observation.

"You know, Vicky told me she had assigned my proposal to a new attorney, Mindy Quan. Do you happen to know if she's in? Then I won't have to bother Vicky."

"Oh, sure, I just saw her. I'll transfer you to her."

"That would be great, and I'll be talking to you again soon. Bye."

In the next moment, Shannon was connected to what she hoped would be the new heartbeat to her revenue recovery plan.

"Hello, you've reached the desk of Mindy Quan. I'm not available to take your call right now. If you'll leave your name and a message, I'll return your call as soon as possible."

OK, Shannon thought. *This is going to be the woman's first introduction to the living me, my voice and attitude. I need to make this upbeat, friendly, and encouraging, not as if I'm checking up on her, which I am doing.*

"Hello, Mindy. This is Shannon O'Toole from FDIC California. I understand that Vicky McDowell has given you my project and her files for the new Pilot program. I'd like to see what I can do to assist you with this. Please feel free to call me."

About two hours later, Shannon received a call,

"I'm glad to hear from you, Mindy. I'm here to assist you in any way I can," responded Shannon, wanting to impress upon this new person how willing she was to help.

"Yes, that'll be great. I've read over the files, and I know the pertinent legislation HR2234 back to front. I'm a specialist with that public law bill."

"Oh, good," Shannon said to encourage her new attorney. "I worked with Mark Brasher, Congressman Steve Horn's administrative assistant on parts of that bill. Do you know how

Vicky wants to format this program and the Pilot proposal to go to FDIC?"

"Not completely. Why don't you tell me how it is supposed to go?"

"Well, I'll tell you what I think Vicky intended, and then Vicky can review your draft and make corrections as she feels is necessary. I think Vicky wants to first get a small group of people from the California FDIC office to work on a Pilot Program, to get the reporting systems set up, programs defined, policies and procedures worked out. The Pilot is supposed to be for an Inter-Agency Debt Collection effort. Vicky has mentioned about five agencies and a contact person for each one. For the Justice Department the contact person is Kathleen Haggarty. I don't remember the contact names for the SBA and HUD, and Vicky asked me if I had a contact with the IRS. To get this going, we have to prepare a proposal to borrow me and another ten people or so from the FDIC, to work out of the California FDIC office on the Pilot Plan."

"Uh-huh," Mindy said slowly. "I don't think the legislation allows any collections for tax debts, or IRS liens for sure. It clearly says that this legislation is for collection efforts for non-tax debts because they have been using a privacy dodge, alleging privacy issues pertaining to the taxpayer.

"There is no separate legislation to collect on the IRS debts, yet. I don't see how anything can be done there now. IRS is hiding behind their privacy rules, although we all know that's just a ploy to retain their agency's control, reach, and power. We will be working on this going forward."

"Well, Mindy, I'm talking for Vicky now, and I'll try and tell you how I think she envisioned this program being set up. I know about the lack of funding until the 1997 budget is approved. So Vicky was proposing that I be detailed from the FDIC with another ten or so employees with the FDIC carrying the expense until the '97 budget is approved; then FDIC will be reimbursed. If that's not possible, we would just be detailed to the Treasury and work on formatting the new program until funding comes through the budget.

"Secondly, we would begin with other agency debt collections, and I think Vicky was going to or had already approached the IRS with the lien redemption idea. I'm saying this because she asked me if I had a contact at the IRS, and I offered her the staff person who responded to the questions I propounded when I testified before Congress this last March. In the IRS's responses to the Government Oversight and Reform Committee, IRS admitted they had never tracked or could not account for real estate that was subject to IRS liens, and that this was an area that could be improved, and that my plan had 'merit' to correct this weak area within the IRS. Vicky and Tom Stack both had some pretty strong ideas on this; maybe we should have a conference call with Tom and see what he knows," offered Shannon.

"That's a good idea, conferencing with Tom. I think I'll give him a call and see what he can tell me."

"Good," added Shannon. "Then you can prepare the draft proposal to go to the FDIC for Vicky to review when she gets back from her travels."

Wednesday began with the two Government Grade permanent FDIC employees, Kay and Charlotte, pushing for reports, asking for updates and generally panicking over trying to get the soon to be departing RTC staff transferred over to the FDIC to do as much work as possible so they wouldn't have to when the departing staff was gone at the end of the year.

Shannon had been working on keeping her other cases going forward, including the Squaw Tahoe case where she was selling 1,332 timeshares in the Olympic Village that had been housing for previous Olympic games. She was feeling the day was almost over and that the Treasury revenue recovery program was hopefully going forward with the new Treasury attorneys assigned to complete the MOU. She finished the case for the timeshares, printed it, and placed it into a folder on her desk, put two other case files into her briefcase that she wanted to look over more at home, picked up her purse, and headed for the parking garage.

As she approached her car on the fourth level of the adjacent parking tower, she stopped and stared at her little LeBaron convertible. Someone has taken a sharp object and ran it the length of the front of the car across the hood on the driver's side, across the front windshield, and across the driver's-side window and made gouges along the entire length of the side of the car. The gouges were deep, and she could see where the paint had rolled up along the scratches from the pressure applied when gouging the car.

My gosh, she thought in surprise. *This is really awful. Vandalism like this right here in the parking structure.* And then she thought, *Wait a minute. My car is parked nose in, right up against the wall. Somebody really had to go out of their way to get up in front of my car and scratch it at the grill and then along the driver's side so I would be sure and see it. I can't believe somebody really hates me so much or is really pissed at me.*

With the Thanksgiving holiday approaching, Shannon was disappointed that the completed memorandum of understanding had not yet been issued by the Treasury for the FDIC.

Shannon knew that the next five weeks would fly by with the downsizing of the FDIC. Jay Keller had continued to hold up her detail transfer without the MOU.

She swiveled around in her office chair, looked out the large plate-glass window of her cubicle, picked up the phone, and dialed Tom Stack, OMB, Washington, DC.

"Hi, Tom," she said, starting her message in a sincere voice on Tom's voicemail. "I thought I would catch you now and tell you how much I've enjoyed working with you this last year. I will always remember your voice and, of course, you.

"I'm very concerned that the Inter-Agency Debt Collection Program is not going to happen. It looks like I'm not going to be able to work on the Pilot project as we discussed. Unfortunately, there hasn't been any new communication between FDIC and Vicky McDowell about the MOU, and you know how busy she has been on official travel. It looks like it's just too late, and I'm really disappointed. I appreciate all you've done and won't forget you. Bye now," she said to Tom's voicemail, and crossed her fingers that he would pick up the phone and call Vicky after he received Shannon's message.

Shannon was home the next day when Tom Stack called her.

"Hi, Shannon," Tom said in a positive voice. "How are you doing?"

"I'm fine, Tom," Shannon answered a little carefully, trying to evaluate his tone of voice and wondering how he would tell her that the interagency program was all but dead.

"Well, tell me what you know about the Programs and how things are going."

Shannon took a slow breath and responded carefully,

"Well, Tom, I wish I could tell you, but I just really don't know. I understand that Vicky has been on the road announcing HR2234 and the Inter-Agency Debt Collection Plan and how she envisions it coming into reality. I attended a meeting in Los Angeles, where her team was presenting the scope of the program to a few agencies, but I don't see that any of the actual *machine* for collections has been developed because that was to be my piece. And the IRS is still resisting their portion of the redemption plan; it has not moved. Vicky has been very busy, and the materials that have been developed and distributed show that there has been terrific effort put forth to bring the program to the level it is at today. However, the Treasury has not sent over the MOU yet to FDIC."

"Well, we know that *you* are the machine she is talking about to get the plan rolling and in force. And how about you? What's happening with you? Is your detail transfer in the works? The detail transfer and the MOU matters are separate."

"I'm afraid not, Tom. FDIC Headquarters has been waiting for the MOU from Vicky regarding the detail we discussed and the computer software and programs that would be needed."

Tom interrupted. "Nothing has been done to pick up the FDIC computers and staff?"

"That's right, Tom," Shannon responded.

"Who's that person on the Chairwoman's staff who is supposed to be moving your detail transfer to the Treasury... Keller something? Hasn't he engaged the chairwoman in this yet?"

No, because Jay Keller *was a backstabbing jerk.*

"Not yet. He's been talking with the Treasury at length about this and other programs." *Because he's a lying, sneaking cheat*, she wanted to add. "It seems that Keller may also have an interest in participating in this program."

Tom thought for a minute and then said, "I don't think Vicky wants that. OK, I'm going to make some very careful inquiries about Vicky's program, and then I'll get back to you."

"I know she is traveling and won't be back in the office until Monday after Thanksgiving."

"OK, then, I'll make some real friendly calls to her and see what's happening, and then I'll let you know, OK?"

With that, Shannon said good-bye to Tom again.

Two weeks later, Shannon came back to her desk to find the message button blinking. There were two calls, one from Tom Stack, and one from Vicky McDowell.

Tom's voice announced, "The letters have been sent to Jay Keller, and it says....."

Dear Mr. Keller,

As you know, with the passage of the Debt Collection Improvement Act of 1996, my staff and I have been extremely busy with various implementation plans and hosting of the government-wide debt collection conferences. However, I do remain interested in exploring a partnership with FDIC, specifically, the assistance of Ms. Shannon O'Toole. As we continue to formulate the plans for this organization/ – Debt Management Services (pending final approval by main Treasury), I see the growing need for your support. The delays in our organizational establishment have also limited my ability to fully staff and hire personnel.

Therefore, what I would like to propose is an option. That we consider a one-year extension for Ms. O'Toole…I would like to have her work here in the Washington DC office.

> Sincerely,
> Victoria I. McDowell
> Director
> Debt Management Services"

Vicky's message simply said, "I sent the letter to Keller. You should be on board soon."

Shannon called to speak with Jay Keller on December 23 to get his feedback and hopefully final approval of the Treasury letter requesting her extension with the FDIC and detail to the Treasury. She was trying to keep herself from being excited at the slight possibility that this would work.

"Jay, have you received the letter from Vicky yet? I know she just faxed it over to you."

There was nothing unfamiliar in Jay's voice, filled with lack of interest in the now-very-much-discussed program. "No, I haven't seen it yet, and, you know, I'm still really very unhappy about Vicky's lack of professional conduct in never returning my calls or letters. Frankly, I've never seen anything like this, ever, in my professional experience. She is just down right rude, unprofessional, and just plain unbelievable. She can't even have the courtesy to pick up the phone and call me."

Shannon could plainly hear the slowly boiling anger in Jay's voice, and she tried to placate him carefully.

"Well, Jay, you know how much she's been traveling, and the pressure she is under to push her new program through and then report back to Congress next March."

"Sure, Shannon," Jay responded in a surly voice. "But we at the FDIC in Washington could have made it so much easier for her, by providing her with the resources she needed to have experienced staff with incredible training to make the program a success."

"I know, Jay," Shannon stroked him. "I am concerned about the collection mechanics too." Shannon then tried to redirect Jay's attention to the letter. "But you know, when I am detailed over to the Treasury, I will be able to walk into Vicky's office and just sit down and get things done. I'll be able to put organizational charts and programs right down in front of her, and present her with complete plans including FDIC collection programs. We won't have to wait for phone calls anymore, or wonder what's happening over there. Do you think the letter from the Treasury is OK? We can still talk with Vicky today if you want to discuss any terms or need anything reworded."

"It sounds like the letter is on the right track, but I haven't seen it yet."

"Well I know it has been sent," Shannon tried to get Jay's support. "Do you want to have a conference call now with Vicky?"

"No, no, I'll wait until I see the letter. Maybe I'll go over and see her too."

"Well, from what I've explained to you, does it sound do-able? Does it sound OK?"

"Yeah, it sounds like it's OK. You're doing everything right. Just keep pushing for FDIC staff."

"I can get a copy of the letter and fax it to you if that will help."

"OK, I just need to see it, that's all."

With that, Shannon said good-bye to Jay and placed a call to Debra Smith, Treasury personnel, requesting a copy of the letter; she reached another voicemail.

December 24 provided no opportunity to talk with Vicky McDowell, Debra Smith or Jay Keller. But Shannon still enjoyed the holiday knowing that the long-awaited letter requesting her participation in the new Treasury debt collection and IRS Redemptions would soon become a reality.

The Christmas holiday was an unusual one. For the last twenty-something years, Shannon had cooked Christmas dinner for dozens of relatives and friends and had enjoyed Christmas eve at the candlelight service of her Lutheran Church. This year, however, was one of change.

Christmas Eve was one of attending the Nutcracker ballet with Jennifer instead of attending a family Christmas Eve party and the usual candlelight service at her church.

Christmas morning dawned with only Shannon, Jenny and her mother together at the Irvine house. They laughed and shared memories of Christmases past, and decided to have Jenny go into her Christmas stocking first. They would wait until they were at Toby and Lisa's house for brunch later. Toby had been dating a young woman he was very serious about and very much in love with. It was a quieter-than-normal Christmas, a very different holiday. But, then, Shannon thought, everything was about to change.

Back at the office on Friday, December 27, 1996, to complete transferring files on her remaining portfolio, Shannon tried to reach Jay Keller again in Washington DC. She was able to reach Pam Carr, Vicky McDowell's secretary, and receive a faxed copy of the very important Treasury letter requesting that her entire life be changed. Shannon practically danced back to her desk and cubicle after quickly scanning the letter from the Treasury, thrilled to hope that her dream was finally becoming a reality.

Friends stopped by Shannon's desk, and could not miss her high excitement and large grin. Manny, her IT guru friend, sitting across from Shannon, asked,

"What's got you all bright and happy?"

"I finally received a copy of the Treasury's letter for my detail !"

"Oh, that's really great, Shannon, you've worked so hard for it. What does it say?"

Shannon handed Manny a copy of the letter and said, "That they want me to come to Washington DC to work on the Debt Collection Project and to engage FDIC in performing some of the work on a pilot basis until the 2007 federal budget is approved !"

"This is great, Shannon!" Manny exclaimed, sharing her excitement and reading the letter at the same time.

Pao walked by her desk and said, "Hey, you look awfully happy. What's going on?"

"It looks like the inter-agency debt collection program is a go!" she grinned at Pao.

"Oh, Shannon, that is so great. Do you know what you'll be doing yet?"

She laughed at Pao and said, "I only know that this country is going to stop missing out on billions of dollars of liens, and maybe we won't have to pay so many taxes!"

"I like that part about not paying so many taxes" and Pao laughed with her.

Tanya Glasser walked over and said, "Hey, what's all the noise all about?"

Manny passed the Treasury letter over to Pao and informed Tanya,

"It looks like our Ms. Shannon has finally gotten the Treasury's attention and will now be going to Washington to set up the Debt Collection program."

"It really happened?" Tanya squealed! "You're going ! Now those jealous little FDIC puppies in Washington can't keep throwing up road blocks and Farley won't be able to harass you anymore!"

Sara Hanson walked over to see what all the commotion was about.

"What are you all celebrating over here?" she smiled.

"I just received a letter from the United States Treasury", Shannon bubbling.

"They want me to work with them to develop the IRS lien recovery program."

"That sounds like great news." Sara grinned.

"Well, that is the good news," Shannon agreed. "But it will present a little challenge in deciding what I can do for Jennifer. She's in college now, and I know she can stay alone or maybe have a roommate move in."

Sara interrupted with, "Wait a minute, Shannon. If you are really going to Washington DC, then maybe we can talk about me renting half your house while you are gone, since I'm commuting back and forth to Arizona to take care of my mother."

Shannon was surprised, and liked the idea. She wasn't too keen on leaving Jenny without someone she knew and trusted to share the house.

"I think that could work out," Shannon smiled.

Later, Shannon tried calling Jay Keller in Washington DC to review the terms of the Treasury letter, however, he was not available. On his voicemail, he gave his assistant's name in his absence. However, when Shannon spoke with the assistant and briefly summarized the detail assignment and Treasury projects, he wasn't knowledgeable about the project, and he suggested,

"Maybe we can discuss this with Inca Stevens. He is a special assistant to the Chairwoman."

Inca's name sounded familiar, and she tried to remember where she had heard it or if she had ever met him, when she used to travel frequently to Washington DC before Jay Keller had made a concentrated effort to keep her away.

Then she froze. Hadn't Inca Stevens been the sidekick that Vicky McDowell had said was running around the Treasury with Jay Keller, trying to sell themselves and their friends to Vicky?

Shannon took a copy of the Treasury letter up to the RTC regional manager, Frank Atwater, who had transferred over from RTC with his friends, to advise him that she was hoping to be staying on and finally working on the Treasury programs.

"I'm really happy for you, Shannon, I'm glad to see that this thing has finally worked out for you. Ride this as far as you can."

"Thank you, Frank, I appreciate your support, and all the help you provided me before in setting aside the office space, computer systems and all earlier this year when the Treasury indicated they wanted to run the Pilot from this California office."

"I'm happy to help if it will make jobs, Shannon. I have a few people here who would have liked to join your new team."

Shannon sidestepped his obvious comments about his staff also wanting to join her effort.

"I'm also very pleased that this Treasury program is going forward. And, Frank, I'm waiting for Jay Keller or Inca Stevens in DC to get back with me with the details as to how this will be working."

"I know Stevens pretty well, I'll give him a call."

"Well thank you, I appreciate that very much."

"No problem, I'm glad to help with this, and I'm happy for you."

About two hours later, Keller's assistant in Washington DC called back.

"Well, Inca doesn't feel he can OK the Treasury letter. He says he doesn't know anything about it, and it can wait until Monday when Jay Keller comes back."

"Well, you know, the powers that be at the Treasury are available today if there are any questions the FDIC wants answered, or any questions on the terms of their request. Unfortunately, no one will be available at the Treasury next week, they will all be on holiday. Do you think we should have a quick conference call to confirm the terms in the letter?"

"No, I think we'll have to wait until Monday."

About twenty minutes later Frank Atwater called.

"Shannon, I tried to talk with Inca Stevens about getting everything settled for you and all that, but he said that, he ah, didn't know anything about it, and ah, he just couldn't make any decision, so ah, he's going to wait until Monday for Jay Keller to get back since he's the one who's been working on this. I'm sorry I couldn't help."

"Well, Mr. Atwater, I appreciate your trying and calling Mr. Stevens for me."

"Yeah, well, I'm sorry anyway."

"That's OK, Mr. Atwater. Thanks."

Shannon stared down at the phone, and felt a twinge of a sting from having tried so hard, having worked endless hours, and coped with endless political maneuvers as an Apolitical woman, who only wanted to fix a very broken government system.

She made long lists of things she needed to accomplish and organize prior to her pending move to Washington DC the first of the new year, if that were to happen, and to begin the long-awaited new work with the Treasury. She called and got tentative airline schedules and ticket prices, and organized the names and phone numbers of about three or four friends that she would be able to stay with until she found an apartment. But she had a heavy feeling that her idea and program were being stolen away from her.

On Monday December 30, with only two days remaining for most of the FDIC staff prior to the reduction in force (RIF) final day of December 31, Shannon placed calls to Jay Keller in Washington DC to finalize the details of her transfer detail to the Treasury. After leaving early-morning voicemails and follow-up e-mails, she set about finalizing reports for the incoming FDIC employee who would hopefully pick up her work in progress. She updated her reports showing she had somehow closed four additional transactions during the last two weeks. She wondered quietly how she had really done it with all the Treasury negotiations and planning taking place while preparing for Christmas and the normal family holidays, not to mention making arrangements to rent out half of the house to a girlfriend who traveled to Arizona on the weekends to be with her own long-distance family. By renting out half of the house, Jennifer still could finish up the college term at home, while Shannon could feel Jenny was safe with a friend Shannon trusted.

At about 10:30 a.m., the phone rang on Shannon's desk. She reached across two boxes of closed files she had been packing to send to the storage department and answered,

"Hello, Shannon O'Toole, FDIC."

"Uh, hi there, Shannon, this is Jay Keller and Inca Stevens."

"Hi there. Did you two have a nice Christmas holidays?"Keller was the first to answer, "Oh, yes, it was nice."

Stevens echoed, "Yes, very good, thank you."

"Well, great, I'm glad you found some time to relax and enjoy your families."

"Uh, yes, we did," stalled Keller.

Shannon heard the tentative stall in his voice, and it felt like a cold hand squeezed her heart.

"Well, listen, Shannon, I don't see how I can recommend the Treasury letter be accepted by the FDIC."

Shannon felt the cold hand grip her heart tighter. "What do you mean?"

Jay continued, "Well, I just don't see why the FDIC should cooperate with the Treasury after the way they have treated the FDIC so shabbily. I have *never, ever,* seen any organization so poorly run, or so unprofessional in my life. I mean, they *never, ever,* return **my** calls. I have had to brief my superiors a few times, and it's really embarrassing to tell them about, well, you see, I put on three really A-plus firstclass presentations for the Treasury for Vicky McDowell's department and other departments. I mean these were really *professional, outstanding presentations* to demonstrate how I, uh, the FDIC, could provide them with the skilled and experienced staff to perform collections. And then when my superiors asked how things were going with the Treasury, it's just unbelievable that I have to tell them that the Treasury hasn't responded or asked for my, um, more help."

Shannon's blood went cold at this admission from Jay that he had tried to go behind her back and use her contacts to further his career and hide the presentations from her, intentionally not inviting Shannon to participate. And then obviously setting himself up with his bosses and the Chairwoman as the originator of the FDIC cooperation with the Treasury collection efforts, never mentioning that Shannon had first brought them all to the table in April.

"You mean they haven't been interested in your recommendations?" Shannon asked in an even tone, trying to keep all emotion from her voice.

"Yes!" Jay nearly yelled.

"Well, you see, Shannon," Inca Stevens began quietly, as was his style. "The FDIC has so much to offer the Treasury, and they just don't respond to our offers, and Jay has tried really hard to meet with them, and, well, Jay and I have met with them to give them everything they could possibly need to do the new work set out for them. We gave them staffing charts—"

"And I can't believe how unprofessional they are, especially Vicky McDowell!" Jay Keller exploded. "I've called her *dozens* of times, and she never calls me back. How can I brief my superiors when it's one-way communications?"

Shannon wanted to pull Jay through the phone. Her brain reeled at the thought of the backstabbing that Jay had been doing to her, and now his selfish insistence that he was consumed with protecting his career and himself from embarrassment over signing off Shannon's successful attainment of a Treasury career.

Shannon quietly said,

"I can appreciate your frustration with Vicky and the other Treasury people. I, too, have had to wait for their responses as you know, and I've kept you in the loop all along, Jay."

"Oh, yes, I know," Jay squeaked. "And then you would call me and tell me you had talked with Vicky and that she would call me next, and she never did!"

Shannon could tell that Jay was becoming very agitated, and that his ego was very badly bruised by his embarrassment with his superiors.

"Listen, Jay, I opened the initial doors to the Treasury and made the initial contacts. I developed the government lien program and got the Treasury interested. I gave the congressional testimony that started this ball rolling. And I introduced you to the Treasury. It only makes good sense that I now go and work directly at the Treasury because then I am inside, where I can sit face to face with Vicky and discuss all the potential and up-side of implementing FDIC proven collection programs with her. She is going to need a collection machine like the FDIC to report back to Congress that her plan is fully developed and is ready to commence collection activity."

"Oh, yeah, Shannon, you think you can get time with Vicky, sure—" Jay started, and then Stevens interrupted,

"I don't think that you will have any more opportunity to help us by getting inside to Vicky, if she won't see us, she isn't going to listen to you."

There it was, it was so clear. Jay and Inca had been toying with Shannon and keeping her away from Washington DC in order to use her contacts with the Treasury and Office of Management and Budget for their own career advancement. And if they couldn't play, they certainly weren't going to let Shannon play.

"Accept it, Shannon," Inca Stevens said. "You're not going over to the Treasury; we're not going to approve it. You might as well get used to the idea, starting now."

And then Jay Keller said, "And if it does go forward, Inca and I can run the Government Lien Collection program."

Shannon placed the telephone down on its receiver, and stood staring out the window, completely stunned at this turn of events. Maybe she should have seen it coming, she should have seen the lack of cooperation, the unreturned letter of de-tail to the Treasury. But she didn't, she had thought that be-cause she had presented the Program and it had been endorsed by the US Congress and Congressman Horn's office, and with Tom Stacks at OMB and Vicky McDowell at the Treasury, the new Program would become a reality, and she would be part of that reality.

She turned slowly, still numb, and the thought that she should start packing up her office began to seep into her mind. She just looked around her cubicle office, reviewing in her mind what files and projects were contained in each drawer. She shook her head in disbelief. She had a letter, an invitation from the United States Treasury, to come to Washington DC to start up the program she had written, and convinced Congressman Horn of its value and, that she had presented to Congress—the program she had brought to the table with the OMB, Treasury, and FDIC, with the proposal to have the FDIC pick up the program and run with it. When the puppies said FDIC declined to run with the Program, she should have known that the politics were bigger than she was, and that the puppies would never let her succeed where they couldn't.

When the personal invitation for her to go into the Treasury was offered that didn't include the FDIC jealous little puppies, Jay Keller and Inca Stevens had shut that down, too.

She turned her computer to its menu index and began to scroll over its contents, trying to make some sense of what programs and documents she should copy onto disk.

Instead, she picked up the phone, and called Tom Stack, and by some miracle, he answered.

"Tom Stack here."

"Hello, Tom," she began quietly and slowly. "This is Shannon."

"I know this is Shannon, how the heck are you?"

"Well, I'm really not too well this very moment, Tom."

"Why, what's wrong? You got Vicky's letter, didn't you?"

"Yes, I did. But I just got off the phone with Jay Keller and Inca Stevens."

"Yes, and?"

She was trying hard to hold back the tears and not let Tom hear it in her voice.

"And they just informed me, just now, that they are not going to accept or honor the Treasury's request to have me detailed over in January. I have about eight hours to pack up twelve years of my work from the FDIC and RTC."

"They what?" Tom exclaimed. "They aren't going to approve your detail? Why not? What's the deal?" he thundered.

"I guess I'm kind of stunned, Tom. It seems that they are still somewhat bent out of shape because the Treasury didn't want to pick up any of their proposals or them, and so they weren't about to let me go without them. I just can't believe this is happening."

"Have you talked to Vicky yet?" he quickly interrupted.

"No, I haven't, she's on vacation until next week. There's no one at the Treasury this week, between the holidays, that can help."

"Just hold on a minute," Tom tried to reassure her. "I'm gonna call over there and see who's in this week. Give me Jay Keller's phone number, and who's the other guy? Ink something?"

"Yes, it's Inca Stevens." She turned her glazed eyes onto her telephone listings book and read off the telephone numbers of the sneaky FDIC puppies to Tom. She was moving slowly as if in a fog now.

"I'm just stunned," she responded slowly and quietly. "By next week, I will have been 'downsized', and no longer a Federal employee, so the detail employment from the FDIC to the Treasury will be impossible."

"Don't say that," Tom insisted. "I'm not going to let those little snips get away with this. Can't you be on vacation or something next week, and then we can get this whole thing cleared up?"

"I would like to think so, Tom," she was talking very slowly now, the reality of what was happening beginning to really sink in. "Maybe it would be possible to retroactively reinstate me. Oh, gee, I don't really know..."

"With the government, there's always a way to put people on vacation, whether they want to or not," he chuckled. "I'm gonna call FDIC right now. And give me your home number again too."

"Hey, Tom," Shannon began slowly. "You know, you're one of the good guys, one of the very few who really care about fixing a very broken system."

"Oh, come on," Tom resisted.

"No, I mean it. You've really been a shining knight among a lot of very dirty, dark players, and I am so fortunate to have met you. I've enjoyed every minute of working with you, and I'm only sorry that we won't get to work together to see this project through."

"Don't say that!" he insisted again. "I'm gonna see what I can do right now, and I'll get ahold of Vicky and Virginia first thing when they come in and fix all this."

"Alright, then, that sounds good to me," she whispered into the phone. "Thanks for all you've done, Tom, good-bye..." he hung up the phone, with tears in her eyes, feeling her heart fill with sadness for a future program that should have been and now would never be, and with anger, for the political tricks played by the FDIC puppies. She had danced on delicate glass trying to launch her program, and it had shattered.

FDIC downsized further that year and moved staff to either Texas or Washington DC, closing the California office. In their efforts to save funds, they continued to sell failed banks to other strong banks or conglomerates, so the FDIC didn't have to retain staff to sell off the assets of the failed bank. They developed an 'Asset Sharing' contract where FDIC went into a sort of partnership with a larger, healthy bank. FDIC actually gave the new stronger entity millions of dollars to offset any losses they may experience when they finally sold the bad loans and foreclosed properties from the failed institution. These asset-sharing deals cost the FDIC, and the American taxpayer, millions of dollars. Once again, a strong lobby prevailed that pushed its influence upon the FDIC to handle the failed banks, instead of staff.

15

California State Treasury and California State Bond Issues for Operating Funds

*U*nexpectedly unemployed, Shannon knew she should begin looking for a new job. It was pouring rain outside, and she realized she had used all her time developing the government lien recovery program and in preparing for the transfer to Washington DC, not in preparing for a job search in California.

After about two weeks and Tom's reluctant information advising Shannon that the FDIC was still holding firm on their lack of cooperation in transferring her on detail to the Treasury, and that the Treasury didn't want Jay Keller or Inca Stevens or their programs, Shannon finally seemed to wake up with enough anger at the FDIC puppies to propel her into action again.

"Tom, what if I was able to do a study for the Treasury and identify specific transactions where the IRS had passed on picking up their lien money from a foreclosed property. Do you think the Treasury would pay for such a study?"

"I think that's a great idea, Shannon," Tom answered slowly. "But I think you should look for other government liens in addition to the IRS," he advised. "Because we want to get as much support as possible for locating government liens, and as long as you are going through foreclosure files, you might as well record all the liens you find."

"That sounds good to me," she replied with increasing enthusiasm, her mind beginning to spin again after its numbing fall from the FDIC to Treasury detail. She was envisioning how the report might be formatted. "I'm sure I can capture all that information in one report, and then let the Treasury see just what additional agencies are missing out on collecting their debts from foreclosures in California."

"I bet the Treasury would even pay you for the research," Tom added. "Let me talk to Vicky. I think she can put it on a purchase order for you. Why don't you e-mail her or fax her the proposal tomorrow, and ask her to issue the purchase order for the research? Then call her and work out the details. I'll call her too, so she knows we've talked and I support the project."

"Gee, thanks, Tom," Shannon smiled appreciatively.

"Maybe this will get you a little money in the meantime while we're trying to get everything else organized."

"Sounds really good to me," she answered.

"I should also tell you what the IRS has done to Vicky. They have issued a statement saying that the information contained in their liens is protected under the Privacy Act, so they can't be required or compelled to share the information or list of liens."

"Well, that's not exactly correct. Once a lien is placed against a piece of real property, it becomes public notice. In fact, there is usually a lien notice placed on the property's front door, mailed to the debtor, and then filed with the local county recorder's office for the purpose of making it 'Public Notice'."

"Is that true?"

"Absolutely. The purpose of recording the IRS lien with the local recorder's office is to give any prospective buyer notice that there is a lien against the property and that title to the property is not clear. That's why it's called 'Public Notice'."

"Why am I not surprised the IRS is trying to hide behind their Privacy rules?"

"Because they can't produce a list of their liens?"

"Exactly."

Shannon placed the call to the largest foreclosure servicer in California, and held her breath while she waited for the vice president, Mr. Hammon, to answer. She was prepared to offer a description of the Treasury research she planned to do after talking with Tom Stacks, and she wasn't completely sure of what authority she had to actually go into the servicer's files. She wasn't an employee of the FDIC any longer, and she wasn't an employee of the Treasury yet.

"Hello, Mr. Hammon, this is Shannon O'Toole. I'm working on a special project, to try to document what government liens are being lost through California foreclosures."

The gentleman listened politely.

Shannon continued. "I would like to see if I could make arrangements to come into your office and go through some old closed files to see if I can determine the number of government liens that should have been collected or redeemed by government agencies including the IRS, SBA, Justice Department, and Franchise Tax Board. This is all public information. Do you happen to know off the top of your head if you have seen many of these types of government liens collected?" she asked.

He chuckled. "No. In fact, I think I can say that one hundred percent of all the government liens against the properties we process for foreclosure go uncollected by the various government agencies."

This was a stronger statement than Shannon had expected to hear. "One hundred percent?" she echoed. "I knew it would be a high number, but that's more than I had anticipated."

She seemed to have found another ally, and he went on to explain. "Watermark services handles about ten percent of all the foreclosures in the state of California. If you want to come in and go through our closed files, you can get a pretty good picture of the uncollected government liens here. You will see that even though the notices are sent out to the various agencies, they don't respond, or I have even been told by one agency that they just throw away the notices."

Shannon was taken aback at this information. "I would like to come down and discuss this project with you sometime this week at your convenience," she continued.

"That would be fine with me," Mr. Hammon replied.

Later in the week, a meeting was set up to begin the enormous but very important project Shannon was undertaking to further support her Government Lien/ IRS Collection recovery program.

Shannon had been working on the research for about a week when Mark Brasher, Congressman Steve Long's assistant in Washington DC, called asking how the government lien program was working out.

"What does it feel like to have developed and launched such an impactful program?" Mark asked Shannon, and she could hear the smile in his voice.

"Well, Mark, I guess I don't know, because it hasn't gotten off the ground."

"What do you mean? I'm calling because Congressman Long wants an update on the program."

"Well, I'm sorry to tell you that the FDIC decided that they wouldn't detail me to the Treasury for the project, and others at FDIC wouldn't cooperate with Vicky McDowell because their programs were not picked up by Treasury with mine. And with the federal budget still not passed, Vicky doesn't have the funding and needs the FDIC to operate the program until the budget is passed."

Mark paused to consider what Shannon had just said.

"So you have not had a chance to implement the government lien program then?" he repeated.

"Unfortunately, that is correct," Shannon answered slowly. "And I understand IRS is putting up a valiant fight to protect their liens, and not provide the requested list of liens or other information."

"What are you working on now?"

"I'm researching foreclosure files for government liens that could have been redeemed within the last two years but were not, and how much money the various agencies have missed."

"That's great. I want to see your report as soon as it is done. What are you finding preliminarily?"

"That the IRS has NEVER redeemed any of their liens they have placed against California properties that have gone through foreclosure."

"I'm putting in a call to Vicky right now. If the Treasury can't pick up the program at this time due to budget issues, there's always the Government Services Administration (GSA)."

"That would be interesting," Shannon responded.

"This is too important, Shannon, for it not to get launched..."

The foreclosure servicer Shannon had chosen was the largest foreclosure servicer in California, responsible for processing approximately 8–10 percent of all the foreclosures throughout the state. In California alone, there were about sixteen to seventeen thousand foreclosures *per month*, of which two-thirds were in the seven Southern California counties.

Shannon was becoming bleary eyed after working for about two weeks, every day, by herself. She called her friend, Pao Helo, to come in and help her. Together, they spent another three weeks going through 10 percent of the closed foreclosure files at the servicer's office during the past two years.

They had examined eight hundred California foreclosure cases, and found that 17.75 percent of the California foreclosures had one or more government liens against the property. A total of 270 government liens were filed against these eight hundred properties, including IRS, Small Business Administration, U.S. Justice Department, FHA, California Employment Development Department, California State Income/Franchise Tax Board, and the Board of Equalization Sales Tax, and the combined amount of these uncollected liens totaled $7,731,611, over $7.7 million dollars! About half were State of California liens and half Federal liens. And that was the amount of uncollected liens on just 10 percent of the California foreclosures. Assuming the remaining 90 percent California foreclosures had similar uncollected liens, that meant that *the state and federal governments had lost a staggering $70 million* DOLLARS over the previous two-year period just in the state of California. All the other states would have tax lien losses as well. And these losses would continue because the liens were not tracked, collected or redeemed by the government agencies. Without a lien collection and redemption plan in place, the state and federal governments would continue to lose a vast amount of revenue that could be used to reduce budget deficits, pay for much-needed operations and programs, and reduce the burdens placed upon the taxpayers.

With this newly researched information, Shannon prepared a new report for Vicky McDowell at the US Treasury and Tom Stacks with the Office of Management and Budget and sent a copy to Mark Brasher. She mailed off the report and then followed up on the phone. Because she had discovered millions of dollars in Franchise Tax Board liens that had gone uncollected, she also decide to call her old boss, Sam Franklin, from the RTC, who had been recently appointed assistant state treasurer for the State of California.

Sam Franklin called back and told Shannon he had set up a meeting with Shannon, Pao Helo, Manny, and Jack Chipman with Sam and Steve Spears, the deputy state treasurer who reported to Matt Fong, the current California state treasurer.

The presentation went well, and at the end of the presentation, Steve Spears said, "I will prepare a summary of our meeting here today, and forward a copy to Matt and to our corporate counsel, recommending that we appropriate about ten million dollars to initiate this program. That way, you will have enough seed money to act on the foreclosures that will benefit the state Treasury and provide the largest recoveries. I think this is a great program."

Shannon and her colleagues exchanged satisfied glances, silently congratulating each other for a job well done and for the future work they were about to begin.

Two weeks later, when Shannon had not received the promised contract from Sam Franklin, she finally reached him on the phone.

"Uh, hello, Shannon", Sam greeted her. "I'm afraid we've run into a little political problem here that was earlier unforeseen."

Shannon's stomach sank. Another political problem? What would it be this time?

"Oh, what is it Sam?" She tried to sound relaxed and unconcerned.

"Well, as we were preparing to implement your collection program, we started receiving the most unexpected resistance from the Franchise Tax Board."

"Oh, in what way?" she asked slowly.

"It seems that the Franchise Tax Board doesn't want your group to come in and do any collections because it would complicate their bookkeeping or something stupid like that," and he gave an embarrassed chuckle.

"What do you mean?"

"It seems that the California State Franchise Tax Board is creating their own 'Super Collection Agency', and they feel it will be ready to operate in, oh, maybe two years or so." Again Sam gave one of his embarrassed chuckles. "And so it seems, that what they are doing right now is bundling up all their receivables, their uncollected tax liens, and then borrowing against these receivables from the banks for operating cash."

Shannon was once again stunned at the unprofessional workings of yet another government agency. "So you are telling me that instead of doing collections now and recovering taxpayer money, they are borrowing money and paying interest on the money to operate their agency?"

"Well, yes," he laughed nervously. "It seems that if we were to sign the contract with you and your group performed collections, it would interfere with the Franchise Tax Board's receivables and their ability to borrow operating funds. They would have to continually go into their receivables pledged and assigned to the banks as collateral, and update or change the receivable information, and they just don't want to do that."

"Sam," she began earnestly, "do you hear yourself? You are agreeing to let this agency take two more years to start collecting on their liens, when we are ready to start tomorrow. Just the interest alone on a billion dollars is enough to run the Franchise Tax Board for a year. And the rationalization that it is too much of a bother to update their collateral receivables is just plan unacceptable and irresponsible."

Sam's voice became more reserved. "I know how it sounds, Shannon, but the California State Treasurer's office does not have jurisdiction over the Franchise Tax Board. It is run independently from the Treasurer's office. And we can't make them go along with your collection program, although we wish we could."

She couldn't believe that another agency was going to be allowed to sidestep their responsibilities to collect on government debts, and additionally, was going to be able to prevent Shannon's group from collecting on the liens also.

"So, not only is the Franchise Tax Board NOT collecting their debts and putting that money back into the State Treasury to provide the much-needed money for state-funded programs, but they are incurring interest liabilities because they haven't done their job in collecting on judgments and debts. In essence, the California Franchise Tax Board is creating more debt for the taxpayers because they aren't doing their job."

"Look, Shannon," Sam began defensively. "You know I wanted your program to work. I took it as far as I could with Steve Spears. You know that we thought it was a great program and that we could use it as part of Matt Fong's political platform when he ran for the US Senate. But we just can't make the Franchise Tax Board agree to your plan. And there's more to it than that. Kathleen O'Conner heads up the Franchise Tax Board, she's a democrat, and she's opposing Matt Fong."

Well, there it was, finally, the political agenda once again that had precedence over an ethical, well intentioned program to put the taxpayers' money back into the Treasury.

"Sam, I know you went to bat for us, and we appreciate it," she attempted to deliver a politically correct response to the man that was once her boss.

Sam softened. "I really wish we could have made it happen," he offered. "We were so close. But politics are politics, and they are strange bedfellows sometimes."

The next week, Shannon was scanning the newspapers and stopped cold as she found something she couldn't quite believe she was reading. There, in the *Los Angeles Times*, was a headline, **"State Kills $99 Million Computer"**, with a byline reading. ...

"The State of California scrapped a failed computer system...after spending $99 million on it, a decision that could...delay a new statewide system...considered the most costly failed computer project in state government history, surpassing a $50 million project canceled by the Department of Motor Vehicles... the cost of the project, funded mostly with federal tax dollars for a State Automated Child Support system had ballooned from $140 million to the latest estimate of $356 million... it is already more than two years behind schedule ... and is risking the loss of a $3.7 billion federal grant..."

Ahhh, Shannon thought. That was the 'fast track' program that Tom Stacks with OMB had mentioned about the the US Treasury California child-support collections that hadn't even been launched after seven years of planning.

Additional California failed or delayed computer systems included:

Child welfare services case management system

- Initial cost: $90 million
- Revised cost: $204 million
- Officials believed it would take two years to work out all the bugs
- Additional statewide automated welfare system- Unknown initial cost
- Revised cost: $ 382 million

The most expensive computer project in state history. After state officials realized the system would never work statewide, the project was broken into four separate contracts; the state auditor warned that the final price tag could exceed $1 Billion.

California department of corrections management system

- Initial cost: $54.2 million
- Revised cost: $136 million

Initial contract canceled because it was behind schedule, and the contract price had more than doubled.California Motor Vehicles database

- Initial cost: $28.5 million
- Revised cost: $49.5 million

Initial contract canceled after company delivered nothing usable

"In the private sector, if you failed in project management, they take you out back and shoot you," one state official said. "Here, that doesn't happen. No one really cares. What are the consequences? The head of the DMV at the time got promoted."

The waste in taxpayer dollars appalled Shannon, but the next headline stunned her:

"An initial bond offering by the California State Franchise Tax Board to raise money for their operating expenses!"

*Not only had the California Franchise Tax Board been successful in quashing Shannon's collection proposal, but they were **now borrowing additional funds** from the public to continue operating the inefficient agency, incurring still more debt for the taxpayers.*

Ten years later, California State Treasurer, Bill Lockyer, would advise the Sacramento politicians and public that payments on bond borrowing were becoming uncomfortably high, crowding out funds for universities, healthcare, and parks – with all the other government services being slashed.

California Assembly Budget Chairwoman, Noreen Evans, would tell a committee hearing that bond payments are like "Pac-Man eating up the general fund" and that the state's main checking account was again running a deficit. The latest projection was a $21-billion hole for the next eighteen months.

And California still had a crumbling infrastructure. A Washington-based transportation think tank called TRIP reported that annual spending on major roads, bridges, and transit in California was running $11 billion short of what was needed. California has the second-worst roads in the nation, falling only behind New Jersey, the study said, as reported in the *Los Angeles Times*.

According to the same *Los Angeles Times* article... "'California has the lowest bond rating of any state, requiring it to pay relatively high interest...paying substantially more than Third World countries, er, emerging markets,' Lockyer told the California Assembly Budget Committee."

By 2009, California would be the largest issuer of long-term bond debt of any municipality, state, or corporation in the nation.

It seemed to Shannon there was a contagious fiscal insanity spreading in the California and U.S. Treasury Departments.

And at the national level, there was more bad news about the IRS. *USA Today* reported, "IRS official testified superiors ignore the bad, punish the good...The IRS ignores evidence of misconduct by its top officials and punishes employees who try to point out wrongdoings...and those senior officials who engaged in the misconduct are not only protected, but often rewarded, a personnel official in the IRS chief counsel's office told the Senate Finance Committee."

Newsweek reported an exclusive story, "Inside the IRS, Lawless, Abusive and Out of Control," with a second article entitled the "Infernal Revenue Disservice."

USA Today reported, "IRS veteran agents testified before a Senate finance subcommittee about how a Pennsylvania horse breeder saw $247,000 of her assets snared (by the IRS) without any written notice because the IRS was trying to get to her boyfriend. A Texas taxpayer was hit with $400 in penalties for a 2 cent mistake, and the agency even seized $70 from a nine-year-old's account because her grandfather allegedly owed money."

A GAO, Government Accounting Office report stated… "the IRS is unable to keep track of unpaid taxes properly, which means it cannot concentrate on collection efforts…The upshot is that only about $26 billion out of the $222 billion in unpaid taxes…is likely to be collected, with $119 billion—a whopping 54 percent—to be written off."

Ann Landers, the famous newspaper advice columnist, published a letter from the acting commissioner of the Internal Revenue Service:

"Commissioner Steps Up in Defense of the IRS…
Dear Ann,
…I would like to address some of the concerns that have recently arisen in Senate hearings…our Code of Conduct requires all IRS employees to work with taxpayers in a courteous and professional manner…and they almost always do…. as I told the senators, I deeply apologize to the taxpayers who were not well treated by the IRS. I promised and am taking

immediate actions to prevent this from happening in the future...1"

Then the *Los Angeles Times* ran an article with the headline: "Unpaid Tax Total Put at $195 Billion a Year by IRS,"... Charles O. Rossotti, IRS commissioner in May 1998, disclosed during Senate hearings that "'the $195 billion annual gap is enough to pay for all of Medicare, the program that provides medical and disability assistance for 38 million older Americans. It is more than 75 percent of the entire defense budget. And if the IRS were able to capture that money, the federal government could cut taxes by $1600 for every American family or individual filing an honest tax return.'"

Shannon's reaction was mixed with disbelief at such a broken system and the far-reaching vastness of the inefficiencies, waste, and illegal actions now exposed by IRS employees and Senate hearings. The apparent and continuing cover-ups, excuses, poor business practices, and outright illegal actions by the IRS appalled her.

A sense of frustration began to grow again at having her proposal quashed to act on government liens placed against properties going through foreclosure and ignored by the IRS, the California Franchise Tax Board, and other government agencies.

She had just learned that the IRS had succeeded in its' efforts to hold off her program for collections working inside the government, as well as other proposals by private companies to continue with IRS unpaid tax efforts by citing Privacy codes. The IRS had fought hard to keep Shannon's *internal* program and other private *external* companies out of the IRS collection process by convincing Congress that the taxpayer's personal information could be at risk if private companies had access to IRS files. The private companies had fought back, citing the multitudes of collection companies that handled collections for nationwide vendors, creditors, and companies without personal information leaks, and demonstrated layers upon layers of risk protections in their systems to protect private information. The far-reaching power of the IRS had also been sufficient to stop Shannon's program from being activated through HR 2234.

The General Accounting Office (GAO) had looked at a pilot program for IRS tax collections by five private collection agencies and noted that the IRS believed that collecting taxes was an "inherently government function" that could not be performed by private companies. This further caused a major obstacle and limited the success of these private companies. The private collection companies could only locate and contact taxpayers to remind them of their outstanding tax liability and to suggest various payment methods. Additionally, the IRS refused to allow private agencies access to its data system to prevent sensitive taxpayer information from being divulged.

The IRS had prevailed in their efforts to protect their kingdom of unpaid taxes, preventing Shannon or any other private company from efficiently and effectively collecting on the billions and trillions of dollars annually in unpaid tax revenue. It would take an act of Congress, literally, to change this.

Tom Stack soon retired from the Office of Management and Budget, and Vicky McDowell transferred into another division at the Treasury, saying, "I've never been so utterly and sorely disappointed in the lack of action by the FDIC and Treasury in my entire career." It was time to finally accept that the system had blocked the forward motion of the government lien and debt recovery program due to special interests and power-grab positioning, allowing the hundreds of billions of dollars to go uncollected and allowing those who did the blocking of the program to retain their perceived positions of power and authority.

16

FEMA: Who Is Watching the Watchers?

Federal Emergency Management Agency

Still feeling let down by the power brokers at FDIC, the California State Treasury, and the IRS, and with her hopes for ever seeing her government lien recovery program becoming a reality rapidly fading, Shannon accepted a position with the Federal Emergency Management Agency, FEMA, as a project auditor for the Office of the Inspector General.

FEMA emergency money was granted after the United States president announced a national disaster in a given area, usually due to hurricanes, earthquakes, fires, floods and other natural disasters. In this position, she was responsible for reviewing the emergency funds given to various cities and local governments for assistance by FEMA, after a national disaster in a given area was declared.

Gabe Bowen, the FEMA office manager and chief auditor in Los Angeles, greeted Shannon on her first day.

"Well, hello there. I'm glad to finally get to meet you. The FEMA Washington DC office told me you would be joining us today. I guess our little audits here will seem quite puny after all the national government lien and recovery work you've been presenting to Congress."

Shannon wasn't quite sure if he was being sincere or sarcastic, either way, she wanted to assure him she would focus on his areas of responsibility and support his office efforts.

"Nice to meet you too, Gabe. I understand you handle a broad reach of audits and disaster funding projects. It sounds like you have a heavy load, and I'm pleased to have the opportunity to contribute toward your commitments and goals." OK, so maybe it was a little stuffy, but it still conveyed her focus on his priorities.

Gabe seemed to like her response. He was a small man of about five feet, four inches and very fit.

"Yes, we do have a full load of audits on the boards," he said and led Shannon over to a large chalkboard on one of the office walls. "See, here I have listed the FEMA disasters, the approximate amount of FEMA emergency funds that were expended, and the target dates for our audits."

Shannon was looking at the board with multimillion-dollar government programs listed to be audited. She was familiar with some of the California disasters, and was about to ask about the extent and composition of the damages, when a young, slender, attractive brunette came into the office and brushed against Gabe as she reached over his desk for a file.

She smiled and flirted with Gabe. "Don't forget to practice your dips!" she said demurely, as she turned and sashayed out of the room.

Gabe chuckled and explained to Shannon,

"When a man is of a stature similar to mine, he has two choices: he can lift weights to attract women or learn to dance.

I chose to learn to dance, and I compete. She's been offering to be my partner for an upcoming competition."

Shannon smiled and imagined the partnership the young woman and Gabe had in mind.

Shannon resumed scanning the board and long list of FEMA disasters, but noticed that some of the disaster dates were five to ten years old. She was curious about the dated events and asked,

"How are the assignments made for the audits?"

Before she could ask about the dates, Gabe offered, "We have been directed to start working on the Loma Prieta disaster next. Headquarters has advised that the funds are unreconciled, and the disaster took place over ten years ago."

Ten years seemed like a long time to wait to do an audit to Shannon.

"So will all of us work on Loma Prieta individually or on teams?" she asked.

"I have to talk to my boss, Warren DiAngelo in San Francisco, about that," Gabe replied. "He typically lets the auditors select their own work assignments, and he is going to have to change that now to try to get Loma Prieta done to satisfy headquarters and Congress."

"Did no one want to work on Loma Prieta?" Shannon asked.

Gabe laughed and, then said, "Well, it's like this. The auditors choose to go to, well, let's just say, more desirable locations, like Hawaii, Florida or Guam to conduct their audits. Loma Prieta is a local audit. So they would rather go where they can enjoy the sights, maybe make a little vacation out of their several weekends and free time, so they chose assignments where they can enjoy the scenery and local activities, away from home."

"How long do they stay out on these assignments?"

"Oh, it can be for four to six months at a time, sometimes longer."

"That seems like a long time to be away from home," she pondered.

"Oh, well, the auditors are on full per diem, and of course their hotels are paid for by the government, so they actually end up saving a lot of money when they are out on an audit. We have auditors that save most of their per diem of say, oh, fifty to seventy-five dollars per day, and cook most of their own meals, and come home with several thousand dollars saved. They have their spouses come along sometimes, too."

Shannon was taken aback by Gabe's candid comments. She had heard that the auditors saved much of their daily allowance for food but knew how much a tab like that costs the government. A government employee staying at a hotel for an average cost of one hundred dollars per night would run up a tab of three thousand a month in hotel bills and another eighteen hundred to two thousand dollars in per diem. That amounted to almost five thousand a month in addition to their salaries, and the auditors stayed out for several months. Additional expenses included air fare and transportation while they were on the audit.

Gabe continued, "Some of the auditors don't even have a house or apartment locally, because they can just save that money they would have spent on personal housing costs, too. They just take a low cost motel when they come back here for their next assignment." He seemed to think that it made perfect sense. Shannon wasn't convinced.

"So, how many auditors are there?" she questioned.

"In San Francisco and here in Southern California about fifteen auditors altogether."

Shannon did the math, and calculated that that would add up to about one million dollars a year in auditor travel expenses, hotels, and per diem, just for the California auditors, not counting the other forty-nine states.

"Who approves the budget for that?" she asked.

"Our San Francisco FEMA office prepares the request, and it goes through channels in Washington DC. FEMA's inspector general's office is mandated, so we almost always get our full budget requests approved. After all, we are the watchers, and we have to perform the audit of FEMA funds," he added smugly.

"So, have the auditors been advised that they will be staying home and working on the local Loma Prieta audits soon?"

"No, I haven't told them yet. They're not going to be very happy, and I will probably get some serious resistance."

"But the Loma Prieta earthquake disaster took place some time ago, didn't it?"

"Yeah, and it was a huge emergency bailout too. We're getting a lot of pressure from headquarters to get it reconciled now because it has just sat there for over ten years."

Ten years ago, she thought! She was shocked that such a significant disaster had been left untouched from an audit for ten years because staff preferred to travel to warm and tropical climates.

"I have a summary of that disaster here someplace," Gabe said, as he shuffled through his desk file drawer, moving reports around in his drawer. "Here it is," he announced triumphantly when he located the file he was looking for. "You may find this interesting," and he handed Shannon the Loma Prieta disaster notes to review. The report was a detailed synopsis of the Loma Prieta earthquake in California.

Introduction from USGS (United States Geological Survey)

On October 17, 1989, at 5:04:15 p.m. (PDT), a magnitude 6.9 (moment magnitude; surface-wave magnitude, 7.1) earthquake severely shook the San Francisco and Monterey Bay regions. The epicenter was located at 37.04° N. latitude, 121.88° W. longitude near Loma Prieta peak in the Santa Cruz Mountains, approximately 14 km (9 mi) northeast of Santa Cruz and 96 km (60 mi) south-southeast of San Francisco. The earthquake occurred when the crustal rocks comprising the Pacific and North American Plates abruptly slipped as much as 2 meters (7 ft) along their common boundary-the San Andreas fault system. The rupture initiated at a depth of 18 km (11 mi) and extended 35 km (22 mi) along the fault, but it did not break the surface of the Earth.

This major earthquake caused 63 deaths, 3,757 injuries, and an estimated $6 billion in property damage. It was the largest earthquake to occur on the San Andreas fault since the great San Francisco earthquake in April 1906.

The most severe property damage occurred in Oakland and San Francisco, about 100 kilometer north of the fault segment that slipped on the San Andreas. MM intensity IX was assigned to San Francisco's Marina District, where several houses collapsed, and to four areas in Oakland and San Francisco, where reinforced-concrete viaducts collapsed: Nimitz Freeway (Interstate 880) in Oakland, and Embarcadero Freeway, Highway 101, and Interstate 280 in San Francisco. Communities sustaining heavy damage in the epicentral area included Los Gatos, Santa Cruz, and Watsonville.

Liquefaction, as evidenced by sand boils, lateral spreading, settling, and slumping, occurred as far as 110 kilometers from the epicenter. It caused severe damage to buildings in San Francisco's Marina district as well as along the coastal areas of Oakland and Alameda in the east San Francisco Bay shore area. Liquefaction also contributed significantly to the property damage in the Santa Cruz and Monterey Bay areas, which lie near the epicentral zone. Structures damaged by liquefaction include buildings, bridges, highways, pipelines, port facilities, airport runways, and levees. Subsurface soil conditions, which amplified accelerations in the San Francisco Bay area, strongly influenced structural damage patterns and probably contributed to liquefaction problems in loose, sandy fills underlain by deep, cohesive soil deposits.

Engineered buildings, including those near the epicenter, performed well during the earthquake. Hospital buildings in the region sustained only minor system and cosmetic damage, and operational interruptions did not *occur. Only five schools sustained severe damage, estimated at $81 million.*

Most of the spectacular damage to buildings was sustained by unreinforced masonry buildings constructed of wood-frame roof and floor systems supported by unreinforced brick walls. These structures failed in areas near the epicenter as well as in areas far from the epicenter, at San Francisco and Monterey. The severe shaking near Santa Cruz caused heavy damage to the unreinforced masonry buildings in that area, particularly in the Santa Cruz Pacific Garden Mall, which consisted of several blocks of unreinforced masonry store buildings.

More than 80 of the 1,500 bridges in the area sustained minor damage, 10 required temporary supports, and 10 were closed owing to major structural damage. One or more spans collapsed on three bridges. The most severe damage occurred to older structures on poor ground, such as the Cypress Street Viaduct (41 deaths) and the San Francisco–Oakland Bay Bridge (one death). Damage to the transportation system was estimated at $1.8 billion.

Most of the more than 1,000 landslides and rockfalls occurred in the epicentral zone in the Santa Cruz Mountains. One slide, on State Highway 17, disrupted traffic for about 1 month.

The earthquake produced a pattern of northwest-trending extensional fractures in the north end of the aftershock zone northwest of the epicenter, but through-going right-lateral surface faulting was not found above the rupture defined by the main shock and its aftershocks. Six feet of right-lateral strike-slip and 4 feet of reverse-slip was inferred from geodetic data. The only surface fracturing that might be attributed to primary tectonic faulting occurred along a trace of the San Andreas near Mount Madonna Road in the Corralitos area, where echelon cracks showed 2 centimeters of right-lateral displacement.

Extensional fractures (maximum net displacement of 92 centimeters) were observed about 12 kilometers northwest of the epicenter, in the Summit Road-Skyland Ridge area, east of State Highway 17, whereas zones of compressional deformation were found along the northeast foot of the Santa Cruz Mountains between Blossom Hill and Palo Alto. In Los Altos and Los Gatos, ground deformation appeared to be associated closely with zones of heavy structural damage and broken underground utility lines.

Other towns in the area that also experienced severe property damage include Boulder Creek, Corralitos, Hollister, Moss Landing, and several smaller communities in the Santa Cruz Mountains.

This earthquake was felt over most of central California and in part of western Nevada. The rate of aftershock activity decreased rapidly with time, but the total number of aftershocks was less than that expected from a generic California earthquake of similar magnitude. Fifty-one aftershocks of magnitude 3.0 and larger occurred during the first day after the main shock, and 16 occurred during the second day. After 3 weeks, 87 magnitude 3.0 and larger aftershocks had occurred

She had known that the 1989 Loma Prieta earthquake occurred in northern California on October 17 in the early evening near

Santa Cruz, San Francisco, and Oakland and had been rated a Mercalli Intensity of IX (*violent*), with a moment magnitude of 6.9. Damage was heavy in Santa Cruz County and less so to the south in Monterey County, but effects extended well to the north (and farther from the epicenter) into the San Francisco Bay Area, both on the San Francisco Peninsula and across the bay in Oakland.

She had read that the Loma Prieta (or southern Santa Cruz Mountains) segment of the San Andreas Fault System had been undergoing a long period of quiescence until several moderate foreshocks occurred in June 1988 and again in August 1989. The foreshocks were of significance because that segment of the San Andreas Fault System had been so quiet that it had been labeled a seismic gap. No large earthquake had occurred in that region since the 1906 San Francisco earthquake. No surface faulting occurred, though a large number of other ground failures and landslides occurred, especially in the summit area of the Santa Cruz Mountains. Liquefaction was also a significant issue, especially in the heavily damaged Marina District of San Francisco, but its effects were also seen in the East Bay, and near the shore of Monterey Bay, where a nondestructive tsunami was also observed. Abundant strong motion records were captured due to a large number of seismometers that were operating in the region.

She remembered that there had been extensive sports coverage of the 1989 World Series that included the first major earthquake in the United States that was broadcast live on national television. Rush-hour traffic on the Bay Area freeways was lighter than normal due to nearly sixty-two thousand people present at the game at Candlestick Park in San Francisco, and this may have prevented a larger loss of life as several of the Bay Area's major transportation structures suffered catastrophic failures. The collapse of a section of the double-deck Nimitz Freeway in Oakland was the site of the single largest number of casualties for the event, but the collapse of manmade structures and other related accidents contributed to casualties occurring in San Francisco, Los Altos, and Santa Cruz

She had read stories about the streets undulating and power lines swinging in the air, hitting the ground, and making electrical sparks and popping noises. Broken water mains flooded the streets. People were caught or buried underneath rubble and collapsed brick and stone buildings. It had collapsed second and third floors onto first floors, emptied home and store shelves onto the floor, shattered glass everywhere and caused fires. Phone service was cut off.

The city's marina district suffered great damage. Built before 1972, on an area of the city where there was no underlying bedrock, the liquefaction of the ground resulted in the collapse of many homes. Burst gas mains and pipes also sparked fires that burned out of control for nearly two days. Also hard hit by the quake were two area roads, the Nimitz Expressway and the San Francisco-Oakland Bay Bridge. Both roads featured double-decker construction and, on each, the upper level collapsed during the earthquake. Forty-one of the sixty-seven victims of this disaster were motorists on the lower level of the Nimitz who were killed when the upper level of the road collapsed and crushed them in their cars. Only one person was killed on the Bay Bridge, which had been scheduled for a retrofitting the following week, because there were no cars under the section that collapsed.

Other heavily damaged communities included Watsonville, Daly City, and Palo Alto. More than 10 percent of the homes in Watsonville were completely demolished. The residents, most of whom were Latino, faced additional hardship because relief workers and the Red Cross did not have enough Spanish-speaking aides or translators to assist them.

The earthquake caused billions of dollars in damages and contributed in part to the deep recession that California suffered in the early 1990s. And this audit had been left untouched for over ten years?

As she observed the other staff come and go, mostly go, from the office, she began to understand that the FEMA auditors were given free rein to pick and choose their audit assignments, without concern for audits closer to home that would reduce travel costs or hotel costs, or for the size or scope of disasters, not to mention how long ago the disaster occurred.

Instead, the FEMA auditors chose audit assignments in tropical or exotic locations, where there had been natural disasters such as beach-area hurricanes and floods, where they would stay for three to six months in a comfortable hotel, getting paid a per diem for their meals and other incidentals.

Office management brought up the need to conduct the local audits because they were becoming very dated; however, the staff continued to arrange for assignments away from the FEMA office and to collect their travel expenses. Often FEMA auditors would save their per diem, usually around fifty to seventy-five dollars a day, and live off of TV dinners for a fraction of the cost of eating meals in restaurants. The auditors would save the per diem for up to six months, returning home with close to ten thousand dollars in their pocket in addition to their salary and more savings from not maintaining a permanent residence. They might work eight to five, five days a week, but it appeared to Shannon that they enjoyed their chosen environments freely on the weekend, on the government's dime. It was cheaper to have auditors stay at their assigned locations through the weekends than to fly them home and back again, so the government picked up their hotel costs for the weekends. Shannon was shocked when she learned that several auditors didn't even own their own home or have a local apartment because they arranged their audits so that they could save their income and live off the government lodging and per diem expenses paid by the taxpayers.

Shannon quickly determined that her skills were in the program audit area, not finagling to stay out of the office for up to six months at a time. She ascertained that FEMA was not in her long-term career plans, and left FEMA for the US Department of Housing and Urban Development in 2000.

She later learned that FEMA and HUD cooperated with executive orders to assist with FEMA disasters with HUD providing temporary housing to victims of natural disasters. During the Katrina disaster, HUD identified over two thousand pieces of real estate foreclosed on and owned by HUD that could be used for housing for the Katrina victims. FEMA and HUD entered into an agreement whereby FEMA would pay the Katrina victims' rent to HUD, and reimburse HUD for any repairs needed for the properties. HUD authorized their real estate contractors to spend up to $10,500 on each house to repair the HUD properties to make them habitable to be used for FEMA housing, including installing new roofs, heating and air conditioning, floor covering, and appliances. Three years after the initial Katrinia disaster and placement of victims into HUD properties, FEMA still had not paid HUD $52 million for use of HUD homes for Katrina Hurricane victims.

Shannon wondered, who was watching the watchers?

17

Fraud at the Environmental Protection Agency (EPA), the IRS, and Medicare

S hannon settled at her kitchen table and took the current *Fiscal Times* periodical from her briefcase she had been wanting to read. She took a sip from her orange juice and focused on another case of government waste and fraud. This time it was the Environmental Protection Agency, the EPA, making the headline.

The *Fiscal Times* headline read: "How John Beale Swindled the EPA Out of $1 Million."

The EPA's highest paid former employee, John Beale, will be sentenced in a federal court after spending more than ten years taking months off work to do "intelligence work for the CIA in Pakistan" when he was actually kicking back, reading, riding his bike and relaxing at his vacation home in Cape Cod, NBC News first reported...(Beale) plead guilty in September to defrauding the federal *government…and retired from his post after learning he was the subject of a federal investigation for defrauding the government by ditching work for months at a time, while still collecting his $200,000 salary…Another time, EPA Assistant Inspector General Patrick Sullivan said Beale emailed his supervisor to tell her he was urgently needed to leave for Pakistan because the Taliban was torturing another CIA operative. His email said 'Due to recent events that you have probably read about, I am in Pakistan…got the call Thurs and left Fri. Hope to be back for Christmas…'*

"*However, after a bit of investigating, Inspector General Sullivan concluded that Beale didn't have so much as a security clearance. He hadn't ever been to Langley. And probably hadn't thought about how a CIA operative would likely not be so open about dispensing information on a top secret mission in an email.*

"*But Beale's CIA cover wasn't his only creative excuse. According to NBC, he didn't show up for work at the EPA for six consecutive months in 2008 because he told his boss he was part of a multi-agency election year project regarding 'candidate security'. During that stint, he billed the government $57,000 for five trips to California that were "for personal reasons."*

"*He also told EPA officials that he needed to have a special handicap parking spot at EPA headquarters because he suffered from malaria, which he had contracted while serving in Vietnam. And no, he had never served in Vietnam.*"

Shannon shook her head in disbelief. But the next case left her speechless. The next *Fiscal Times* headline read ...:

"Environmental Protection Agency: In one case, Allan Williams, deputy assistant inspector general for investigations, said that an EPA manager allowed an employee to stay home and not report to work for *20 years. The auditor said it started as an accommodation to work at home due to a medical condition, but then apparently escalated into full-blown fraud.*

"For years, the manager allegedly entered fraudulent time and attendance records for the employee as well as approved them. "The senior executive, who was the absent employee's prior supervisor, remained aware that the employee had been teleworking for more than 20 years with very little substantive work product to show for this time," Williams said.

"Still, the senior executive took no action even though, the auditor noted, "He knew the EPA was being defrauded." The IG estimates the fraudulent records cost taxpayers about $500,000.

"Upon receiving a target letter from the U.S. Department of Justice, the senior executive retired and was not prosecuted," Williams said. "The DOJ declined to prosecute either the absent employee or the current supervisor."

"Similarly, the EPA's IG is conducting an ongoing investigation of an agency employee who hasn't been able to physically complete any work for at least a year due to a debilitating disease, yet continues to receive a full salary and benefits as an active employee. In fact, according to the auditors, the employee has been living in an assisted living facility for more than a year, and the supervisor was aware of the situation.

"Misconduct at the EPA isn't limited to just fraudulent time and attendance records. The auditors also cited an investigation about an employee who allegedly stored pornographic materials on an agency-wide server. Williams said when the investigators arrived at the employee's office space they found him viewing the pornography on his work EPA-issued computer.

"The employee confessed to spending two to six hours per day viewing pornography while at work," Sullivan said. He noted that the EPA worker had viewed more than 7,000 files during working hours.

"Of course, these are just a few examples of bad apples at the EPA. The agency employs at least 15,000 workers across the country. Still, the auditor recommends that EPA managers and executives establish a culture of accountability in order to curb misconduct.

"The Environmental Protection Agency, EPA, later also came under fire for a lack of oversight over its government charge cards. An Inspector General report said that some of the agency's employees had used their federal charge cards to buy personal items like gym memberships for themselves and their family members, lavish dinners and DVDs."

Additional Top Reads from The Fiscal Times: IRS Probe

"This has been a busy year for auditors at the Internal Revenue Service ...delving into lavish, multi-million-dollar agency conferences and conventions.

"Now J. Russell George, the Treasury Inspector General for Tax Administration, reports that some IRS credit cards were used to buy pornography, copious amounts of wine and

food, and personal items like smart phones, romance novels, baby clothes and diet pills. In one case, $2,500 worth of personal items was charged to an agency credit card.

"Auditors stressed that the vast majority of IRS credit cards have been used appropriately, and that two cards that were used to purchase online pornography had been reported stolen. But the audit turned up numerous examples of misuse of IRS credit cards and the agency's surprisingly lose control over credit cards it issues to employees.

"The auditors also found employees had used agency credit cards to treat foreign guests to expensive meals—at $100 per head. At an international executive conference in Washington, an IRS credit card was used to purchase 28 bottles of wine...quite a bit of wine for the 41 guests in attendance.

"The inspector general, not surprisingly, concluded that the IRS "lacks oversight to identify inappropriate purchases" with agency credit cards and recommended that it "develop an oversight process to identify IRS employee personal use of purchase cards and other inappropriate purchase card transactions."

"The report also found that the IRS doesn't have a policy in place to cancel credit cards when employees leave the agency. The inspector general found that 98 percent of the 387 cards that had been assigned to former employees were not canceled prior to the employees' departure—leaving the credit cards "vulnerable to misuse." The auditors recommend that the IRS require that credit card accounts be closed before the cardholders leave the agency.

"This isn't the first time IRS employees have come under fire for misusing agency credit cards. In May, the Treasury IG reported that at least 1,000 IRS employees had "misused" their travel credit cards between 2010 and 2012. The report provided few details, but noted that IRS employees spent a total of $121 million on travel in 2011.

"As its mission includes requiring taxpayers to pay taxes owed on time and voluntarily, the IRS should take further steps to address employees who do not voluntarily pay their travel card bills on time," George, the inspector general, said. "Identified misuse should be met with appropriate disciplinary action."

"There's a presumption in the private sector that anyone with a corporate or government credit card must fill out a monthly expense report, detail the expenses with receipts and submit that report to his or her direct supervisor for approval.

Once again, the competence of government IT systems as well as the competence of managers in charge of spending taxpayer dollars are in question."

Shannon put down the *Fiscal Times* and shivered. She had looked through the lens of government waste and abuse with her IRS lien recovery program. The extent of the ongoing waste was increasing and was mindboggling.

Medicare

Shannon then reached for the *Los Angeles Times* newspaper, one of her favorite reading periodicals, and came across an article on waste and fraud in Medicare. The article's headline grabbed her, "Why Medicare Is Struggling Financially." The article's first line intrigued her:

Medicare has a zombie problem. An investigation by the U.S. Department of Health and Human Services found that the federal insurance program paid nearly $300,000 to cover HIV drugs for about 160 people, however, all those people were dead. And these payments "have implications for all drugs," the investigators said. The report was a reminder that Medicare struggles with fraud, waste and abuse that remains a drain on the more than $580 billion insurance program. The Medicare Hospital Insurance trust fund, which finances about half of the federal program, is projected to be fully depleted by 2030 unless Medicare is restructured.

With tongue in cheek, Shannon read further: "Drugs for deceased beneficiaries are clearly not medically indicated," the report said. "In response to the report, the Centers for Medicare and Medicaid Services said it would tighten its claims processing procedure to make it more difficult for dead people to fill prescriptions." She blinked to make sure she had read it right and then thought, *Really? Wow, I'm awfully glad to hear that*, and she shook her head.

She read on. "Medicare and Medicaid shelled out more than $62 billion in 'improper payments' in one year alone, according to the Government Accountability Office. These are payments that should not have been made or were for an incorrect amount. Losses to fraud are estimated to run an additional $60 billion a year. Medicare's Inspector General managed to secure refunds in some cases. But tens of billions of dollars are still lost annually to fraud and waste, according to the officials."

Shannon folded the *LA Times* and placed it on top of the *Fiscal Times* she had just read, got up slowly, and poured her unfinished juice in the kitchen sink. She couldn't wrap her mind around so much fraud and abuse.

How does the government even continue to operate? she wondered. *I need a run to shake off the shock of all the fraud,* she thought., *and then a shower to wash off the willful cheating and dirt in all the federal agencies.*

18

U.S. Department of Housing and Urban Development (HUD)

HUD Homes–Marketing & Management (M&M), Real Estate Sales, Intentional Fraud, Waste and Abuse

As a Director for the Federal Housing Administration (FHA) Quality Assurance Division for the U.S. Department of Housing and Urban Development (HUD) and as a Housing Program Officer, Shannon entered the world of politics once again. Her job was to monitor FHA Lenders to ensure their compliance with laws, rules, FHA handbooks, and to stop fraud, waste nd abuse in the mortgage lending arena.

She was immediately impressed with the genuine concern most of the HUD staff felt and demonstrated in their work to help primarily low-income customers and buyers of single-family homes. It seemed to her that it was an agency with a real heart. She noted many employees working overtime and on weekends, and volunteering for community outreach events, to let the public know about HUD services. She found it interesting that HUD had the most long-term staff of any federal agency; the employees believed in the public service they were administering and felt a sense of pride and accomplishment in their work.

HUD operated the Federal Housing Administration (FHA), as an insurance company, often for low- and moderate-income buyers due to its more lenient lending terms and programs.

Throughout the United States and its territories, local banks and lenders originated the purchase and refinance loans for real estate according to the rules and regulations of the FHA, and then submitted the home loans for FHA insurance. Simply stated, the FHA insurance would pay back the bank or lender in whole if the loan defaulted and went into foreclosure. In exchange, FHA received the property to resell and regain all or part of their insurance payments they had made to the banks and other lenders.

However, in 2000, when Shannon was invited to HUD headquarters in Washington DC, she began to realize that HUD was once again, another government agency that was often inefficient and wasteful with taxpayer money and unaccountable to Congress. Shannon listened to then-HUD Secretary, Andrew Cuomo, speak to the audience of newly hired HUD staff, and learned that HUD offices had been located in eighty-nine different locations throughout the country, with eighty-nine different data and accounting systems, that didn't talk to each other or share data. These eighty-nine accounting systems couldn't provide Congress with concrete or reliable figures or data, such as to how many public housing units HUD controlled, the costs associated with those projects, or how many foreclosed HUD homes the agency held, although HUD continued to request more appropriated funds from Congress.

Contest for Experimental Low-Cost Housing

HUD's mission was to provide safe, affordable housing to moderate- to low-income borrowers, and it announced a program to evaluate new methods for building low-cost housing. In Sacramento, California, building codes and permits were made more lenient to encourage experimental housing build outs, to cut costs, to use new materials, and to provide more affordable housing.

Shannon was visiting her staff in Sacramento and was being taken on a tour of the experimental project, "Greenfair", to determine the cause of the recent increase in complaints from the residents, claims that the properties were inferior, and thus the residents were declining to make their mortgage payments. The defaults were significantly mounting.

Shannon arrived at one of the Greenfair projects, and noted they had flat roofs and a square foundation footprint, all conducive to a very affordable, low-cost housing model. They had grape-stake wooden patio fences, looking as if they were going to fall down at any moment.

"These are the Greenfair condos," Max, the HUD property inspector explained to her. "They are part of the experimental housing program that HUD initiated to try to build very low-cost housing."

"They are very unusual," Shannon commented, as she looked around at the dry lawns and noted that several of the windows were boarded up. "Is there a lot of vandalism around here?" she questioned.

"Not more than usual, except the vacant units attract the kids and gangs, so we try to board up any units that are vacant as soon as we find out about them."

"Are there any vacant units that we can go into?" she asked.

"Sure, I have two more vacant units that haven't been boarded up," Max answered. "I haven't been inside yet, so I'm not sure what we'll find."

Max took Shannon up to the front door of a unit with peeling paint, a badly dented door, and a sagging fence and suggested, "Why don't you stay downstairs until I can go upstairs and make sure no one is in the house and you're safe?"

Shannon agreed that was a good plan and stood inside the door while Max climbed the stairs. She looked around and observed filthy tan carpeting that looked as if a car or motorcycle had changed its oil on the living room carpet, torn curtains hanging in the front windows, graffiti on the walls in the living room, eating area, and stairway walls, and cracks in the back sliding-glass door. Several of the kitchen cabinet doors were missing; the linoleum was curling up along the walls and covered with stains.

Max came back downstairs and said, "It's all clear upstairs, but it looks about like it does down here."

"Is this condition typical of what you find here?" Shannon inquired with a frown.

"Pretty much," Max offered. "The residents complain for a while, and then they strip their units, don't make any house payments, usually sell the appliances, and move out."

"I've noticed that the defaults and foreclosures for this group of houses have really increased recently over the last two years. Do you have any idea what is going on or why that might be happening?"

Max looked over at Shannon with a grim look and said sarcastically, "Well, let's see, it could be because these houses were built with glue and cardboard, to save costs."

Shannon's eyebrows shot up. "What do you mean?"

"Well, as part of the experimental building project HUD ran, these houses have their walls glued to the ceilings and have insulation made out of rip-rap cardboard; that's cardboard just bent back and forth and then used behind the walls."

"As insulation?" Shannon was unbelieving.

"If you can call it that," Max was obviously disgusted.

"How do these units stand up at all?" she continued.

"Oh, they added some nails to the glue along the way, but when you use flat roofs like these units, the rain just slips right down the walls and causes the structures to deteriorate," he answered, looking around the room. "You can just about punch the walls and find your hand clear through into the next person's unit."

Shannon was taken aback. "And HUD made loans on these units?" she queried.

"Yep, all in the name of experimental, low-cost housing units. Maybe somebody even won a prize for these little gems," he growled.

"An award!" she exclaimed. "These units should be condemned!"

And that's exactly what happened. Enough of the units went into foreclosure, HUD hired consultants to examine the project and determine that the units were unsafe and unfit, and men in environmental moon suits took down the remaining structures and removed the materials from the site. HUD then sold the vacant land to the city of Sacramento to start over, with a better affordable project.

To Redact or Not Redact—FOIAs

The Freedom of Information Act, commonly known as FOIA, was often used by the public, public officials or any other entity that wanted to gain knowledge, information, facts or data not readily available. To request such information from government sources required the filing of a FOIA.

The law required that the government agency release data not deemed as sensitive or private, but the government did not have to prepare a special report, it only had to release information in the form that it already had on hand.

Shannon had been with HUD as Quality Assurance Director for six months when she received her first FOIA requesting information on recent FHA lender activity and lender monitoring reports. It was from a company that intended to sell its expertise and services to lenders in the quality assurance area of FHA compliance, and they wanted copies of lender audits prepared by Shannon's staff so they could see what violations of FHA handbooks and rules had been discovered. If the company could see what Shannon's staff had found they could assure their new clients that could protect them against similar discoveries and potential penalties.

As was protocol in her office, she forwarded the FOIA request to the designated group and pulled the requested reports from her systems. She redacted the name of the lender, individual loan customer personal names and social security numbers in the reports by lining out the names and numbers with a heavy black marker, but left the general and requested information and sent the reports to the FOIA group.

Within an hour, the Deputy Director and FOIA staff person knocked on her door.

"I can't use this report for the FOIA," the pretty blonde FOIA employee challenged. "It's all marked up with black all over, and I can't see any of the names."

Shannon looked from the FOIA employee to the Deputy Director and responded slowly,

"Yes, that's the whole idea with redacting, so we don't give out private or sensitive information."

"Well, I can't tell what lender you audited," the pretty blond complained.

Shannon paused again, not sure that the FOIA employee fully understood the rules engaged in FOIA reporting.

"That's right, it could be construed liable if we released a lender's internal audit to the public. The report could be published, shared, or distributed and used to hurt the lender's standing in the industry and community, harming the lender. The lender has the opportunity to respond, counter or mitigate the discovered violations. Do you understand that?" Shannon asked.

"We've never done this before," the ultra-thin Deputy Director scolded.

"Well, then, we haven't been doing it correctly," Shannon answered, leveling her gaze at the two women.

"I always give the reports to the FOIA requester, clean, and legible," the blonde answered.

Shannon considered the lack of knowledge about FOIAs the Deputy Director and FOIA employee were operating with, and decided a bit of an explanation would be helpful.

"You see, when we receive a FOIA, we are only required to offer reports we already have on hand, we are not required to create a new report. And we do not ever release our FHA customer's credit, employment, or social security number information. That could easily lead to identify theft and harmful disclosure as well as lawsuits. Nor do we release the name of the lender, only the findings or violations without naming who or where they occurred. Are you telling me we have been releasing this sensitive information in the past?"

The FOIA employee and Deputy Director looked at each other, and then the slim director answered,

"I'll get back to you on that," and they turned and left.

FHA Foreclosures—HUD Homes

Shannon's Executive Director, Bentley Johnson, asked her to attend hearings pertaining to FHA HUD Homes.

In 1998 and 1999, the United States Department of Housing and Urban Development, HUD, had embarked on unchartered waters for the agency.

They had been piloting a test case for a new method for managing and marketing their foreclosed real estate. They were changing from having HUD employees market and manage the foreclosed HUD homes, to having contractors do the work. In 1999, the Southern California HUD office had over 18,000 properties that they have received as a result of failed loans insured by the Federal Housing Administration (FHA). Other areas of the country had even more foreclosed properties. Because of the heavy increase in the foreclosed real estate owned (REO) by HUD, a decision had to be made to increase HUD staffing to handle the management and marketing of the increasing number of REO, or have a contractor manage and market the real estate. HUD made the decision to use contractors, and they became known as the 'M&M' contractors.

A Government Accounting Office (GAO) report dated May 2000 stated,

......"The M&M contractors are responsible for:

- *inspecting*
- *appraising*
- *securing*
- *maintaining*
- *and selling the REO.*

"For these services HUD pays the contractors a fee based on a percentage of the property price. HUD pays the contractors 30 percent of their fee when they list the properties for sale and the remainder of the fee when they are sold."

The M&Ms usually were paid 2–4 percent of the sales price for each property, although some contracts were for more. The M&Ms utilized an online electronic bidding system for marketing available REO to the public and to accept offers on a competitive bidding basis. Buyers were given the opportunity to inspect the homes prior to making a bid. But before offering the properties to the public for purchase, the M&M had certain responsibilities and tasks to perform."

The M&M's government contract with HUD called for the contractor to inspect each property, immediately repair certain health and safety items, change the locks, issue an initial property inspection report, clean the foreclosed houses, and clear out the debris from the properties. They also had to order an appraisal to set the current market value. The early M&M contracts also called for a broad listing broker to prepare a market evaluation, to also inspect the property and determine the marketability of each property. For these services, the broad listing broker (BLB) was often paid half a percent of the sales price for each property, a very lucrative fee paid by HUD. This was in addition to the fees charged by the M&Ms.

It immediately became apparent that the M&M contractors were taking shortcuts, ignoring contract requirements and were in breach of their government contracts. An Office of the Inspector General (OIG) report dated September 1, 2000, stated...

...“FHA did not accomplish other core elements of its program mission. It did not maximize the return to the mortgage insurance fund or maintain properties in a manner that strengthened neighborhoods and communities. FHA has had numerous other problems with the contractors, including bankruptcy by one, inability to meet contract performance deadlines, countless complaints from homebuyers and real estate professionals, and billings for ineligible costs. Employees of two contractors were arrested for taking kickbacks.” However, HUD continued to appear before Congress and the State Committee on Banking, Housing and Urban Affairs, and Subcommittee on Housing and Transportation touting the success of the M&M program.

“Our audit results indicate such optimism is premature and misleading,” the OIG report rebutted. “Our audit confirmed that outsourcing of program operations resulted in reduced returns to the mortgage insurance fund of about $204 million.”

The OIG report continued.... “None of the contractors we audited managed properties according to contract requirements. Contractors did not perform timely initial inspections, perform adequate inspections, correct hazardous conditions, make repairs, or perform routine maintenance to preserve and protect properties. The poor property conditions decreased marketability, increased FHA's holding costs, negatively affected surrounding communities, reflected poorly on the Department, and in some cases, threatened the health and safety of the public."

The OIG report had criticized HUD for not performing a cost analysis, commonly known as an A-76 report prior to awarding the M&M contracts. An A-76 study compares the cost of having HUD staff perform work as compared to a contractor performing the work. "M&M contractor's sales produced lower returns than FHA staff historically obtained prior to outsourcing operations. Outsourcing also resulted in substantially increased program costs. FHA's decision not to perform a cost benefit analysis in accordance with -76 may prove to be a costly mistake. We recommend FHA perform a detailed cost analysis to use in making informed decisions on how best to accomplish its program mission."

Additionally, the OIG report focused on HUD management's reports to Congress: "(FHA) boasted that the net recovery rate…as a percent of the mortgage insurance claim increased by nearly 10 percent. This is misleading as an indicator of property disposition operations. Property disposition…should be evaluated based on the percentage of current appraised value returned on sales less program operating expenses."

A GAO Draft Study dated May 2000 reported:
"Every year, thousands of borrowers default on their single family mortgage loans insured by the Department of Housing and Urban Development's (HUD) Federal housing Administration (FHA). When borrowers default,

lenders may foreclose on the properties for which the loans were secured, file claims against the FHA insurance program, and convey the properties to HUD. In fiscal year 1999, HUD acquired over 70,000 properties through these foreclosures. If HUD's acquired properties are not properly secured, maintained and resold, they can become eyesores and may contribute to a neighborhood's decay...

"HUD estimated that it will spend $927 million over a 5 year period for these (M&M) contracts...Six of the seven contractors have had significant problems with securing and maintain the properties assigned to them...after trying unsuccessfully to secure better performance from this contractor, HUD terminated all of its contracts. HUD transferred the properties to three of the six remaining contractors, even though two of these replacement contractors were also having performance problems...

"HUD's management and marketing contractors experienced startup problems after being awarded their contracts...their contractor's performance under 11 of the 13 contracts reviewed was high risk in at least one of the performance dimensions, the performance under five of the contracts was high risk in three or more performance dimensions...

"One of the areas in which most of the contractors have had particular performance problems is that of property maintenance and security. Contractor's failure to properly secure and maintain the properties assigned to them may cause a decline in property values and have a negative impact on surrounding neighborhoods...HUD staff's assessments depict high risk performance in terms of property maintenance

*for over half of the contracts reviewed…staff noted that over
60 percent of the properties reviewed in some contract areas
were in less than satisfactory condition."*

Further GAO reports stated:

…"Contractors did not correct health and safety hazards
within 24 hours as required…

…"Thirty-five percent of the properties sampled had a
hazardous condition, *such as missing stair and balcony railings, a
porch held up by a broken tree limb, improperly covered swimming
pools, rotted porch steps, fire damage, electrical hazards, drug para-
phernalia and dead animals/rodents were present…*

…"During visits to 16 properties, several were not properly secured or maintained. For example, in Washington DC,
homes were poorly maintained and had open front windows
and doors, beer bottles inside, and although the grass in the
front yards had been trimmed, the backyards had overgrown
brush and weeds waist high. A property in Philadelphia that
was listed for sale by the contractor still had the previous maintenance contractor's sign on the front door, unrepaired vandalism along the side of the house, trash in the rear courtyard,
and an unsecured opening into the house. A number of the
properties visited in California had trash left in the yard, had
been vandalized or had unlocked doors or windows. HUD officials said that because of these two contractors performance
as recently as December 1999 over half of the properties reviewed for each of these contractors were in less than satisfactory condition. Aside from pointing out deficiencies in the
monthly assessment reports, issuing letter of concerns or de-
ficiency letters, or taking steps toward contract termination,

HUD staff did not have other tools available to address performance deficiencies…

For instance, the contracts did not provide for penalties to enforce compliance with the contract terms. As a part of its audit of FHA's fiscal year 1999 financial statements, KPMG LLP, in a report on FHA's internal controls, recommended that FHA devise a method of penalizing management and marketing contractors that routinely do not comply with performance requirements. The report noted that penalties would effectively communicate the importance of strictly adhering to HUD's guidelines."

Some M&Ms issued notice to their employees that they were not allowed to spend more than five hundred dollars on any property, and that included a $175 appraisal, because the M&M contracts were written such that the M&M had to pay for all maintenance and repair out of their own pockets, and earned their fees when the property was listed and sold. That left very little money to remove debris, clean up the yards, maintain the yards, shampoo carpet, paint or otherwise clean the property. Sadly, the public was being cheated, as these properties were often purchased by low-, moderate-, and very-low-income people who could not afford to replace broken windows, doors, appliances, carpeting, and paint or haul away tons of garbage. HUD contractors were abusing the poor, and HUD couldn't stop them.

HUD's revitalization and asset control area programs required the M&Ms to identify properties in certain designated "down town revitalization" areas. HUD would instruct the M&Ms to pull any foreclosed homes in those areas and to discount them up to 30 percent and offer them to the local government entity who in theory would make the properties available to low income buyers through their own local government programs. However, the M&Ms delayed, ignored, or otherwise hindered several cities' efforts to create new revitalization zones by not sending advice of available properties to the cities, including the City of Moreno Valley, City of Paramount, City of Santa Fe Springs, City of Compton, and others. The M&Ms' contract stated they would only be paid 30 percent of their customary fee when a property was sold to a city agency or nonprofit in a revitalization zone. The M&Ms did not cooperate with these cities and others to approve and designate them as new revitalization zones because they would lose too much commission money.

When the M&M contractors did sell properties to nonprofits and government entities, they failed to utilize land use restriction agreements, or "LURAs". The LURA controlled the amount of increase in sales price for subsequent sales of the property, thereby retaining the affordability of the property in future.

However, ... "Because the land use restrictions were not executed or recorded, several nonprofit organizations resold properties to trusts and investors that then resold the properties for amounts ranging between 177 percent and 597 percent greater than the HUD discounted sales amount. Some properties were resold on the same day the nonprofit organization purchased the property from HUD, and multiple properties were sold to the same buyer," reported the OIG in the Semiannual Report to Congress in September of 2000.

The same OIG report to Congress stated that delays in performing inspections, obtaining appraisals, approving disposition programs, and reviewing sales contracts... "caused these properties to remain in HUD's REO property inventory longer than necessary. The delays could also increase property holding costs and expose to deterioration or damage due to vandalism."

Real estate brokers reported to the M&Ms that the properties were not maintained, had broken windows, kicked in doors, graffiti, missing appliances, sinks, plumbing and electrical. Still, the M&Ms did nothing because it would cost them out of pocket. Local cities began filing liens against HUD properties and criminal charges for lack of maintenance and providing public nuisances. San Bernardino reports wrote columns about "HUDs DUDs," referring to the lack of maintenance and repairs by the M&Ms and the declining values in neighborhoods due to the poor condition of the HUD homes.

HUD also contracted with various closing agents and title companies to close each transaction and account for the distribution of funds affecting the sale. In a routine audit, it was discovered that one closing agent was following their contract deliverables and tasks, except for one item. And that one item was wiring the proceeds of the sale to HUD. The closing agent was performing all of its functions and closing the residential transaction, but never forwarded the funds to HUD. It was discovered that one M&M contractor did not review the final HUD-1 settlement closing statements, they didn't think that was part of their job.

HUD has a "Cash for Keys" program whereby residents in a home that was being foreclosed, were offered five thousand dollars to move out and leave the property in clean and un-damaged condition. Shannon knew that FDIC and RTC had operated similar programs. HUD and other lenders argued that this was an efficient program because the properties were generally left in decent condition, when holdover owners were offered the cash for keys incentive. However, it could be argued that the previous owners lived in the property for free for up to six months or longer while not making any mortgage payments during the foreclosure process and then were paid five thousand dollars to vacate. Additionally, the holdover owners often illegally occupied the property after the foreclosure, which then required an eviction; the eviction process, taking up to four months, allowed them to stay in the property for another four months free. This type of cash incentive contributed to the current 2008–2009 mortgage housing crisis and reward for not making housing loan payments and living for extended periods in the house for free while waiting for a five-thousand-dollar reward for finally moving out.

The M&M contracts required the M&M to obtain an appraisal prior to marketing or listing the property for sale. M&M staff later reported that they instructed appraisers to "gain access anyway you can, if that means kicking in a door, breaking a lock or breaking a window, just do it. HUD will have to pay for the repairs and damage or the buyer will pay when the purchase the property." Because of the large volume of properties assigned to the M&M contractors, some did not have the time, staff, or systems in place to change the locks on the foreclosed homes, though their contracts had a provision requiring that the M&M change the locks.

The M&Ms were supposed to remove hazardous waste from any REO, however, that would cost them money out of their pocket, so they often did not remove hazardous waste, they simply ignored it. The environmental industry advised HUD that they would remove paint cans from the foreclosed properties for seventy-five dollars per can. These hazardous waste companies also followed the M&Ms to see where they were disposing of their environmental waste, and reported it was being thrown into dumpsters or vacant lots.

The worst part of the OIG report dealt with recommendations made by oversight staff to withhold payment from the M&M contractors for lack of performance and breach of contract. Washington DC managers refused to support the recommendations, and released the payments. HUD committed staff to responding to "congressional correspondence" from senators and congressmen from their constituents about the poor condition of the HUD homes; however, HUD Headquarters would not approve corrective or punitive action or sanctions against the M&Ms, and the poor performance continued. …"the M&Ms willfully and knowingly listed uncleaned, unmaintained properties for sale in order to collect 30 percent% of their fees, rather than hold them off the market and prepare them pursuant to the terms of their government contract. They collected the remaining 70 percent after the sale closed. The faster they put the properties on the market for sale and sold them, the faster they received their money. They had information identifying broken windows, graffiti, lack of floor covering, holes in floors and porches, and staircases without handrails from the field inspectors' reports and from the appraisals as well. However, one M&M contractor issued the

"Abacus Blessicus," an attempt at Latin humor perhaps, for blessing the uncleaned and unprepared properties for marketing. The manager informed staff that "HUD won't remember we sold uncleaned properties with broken windows in six months; they will only remember that we were able to put hundreds of REO on the market for sale so quickly. And HUD headquarters will like that very much."

Special Property Inspection (SPI) contracts were awarded by HUD, to inspect the property management and maintenance required of the M&Ms. The inspector general stated that…. "SPI reports indicated that property conditions were getting worse instead of improving, with unsatisfactory property inspection results of 65%–80% for one M&M and 38% to 83% for another." The results were similar across the nation.

In a quality control analysis of appraisals ordered by the M&Ms, the Inspector General stated that their "…analyses revealed that over 23,000 (12%) of the appraisals varied by 30% or more of the sales price…"

The Inspector General also discovered that potential duplicate payments and ineligible payments were made to the M&Ms in the amount of $1,797,750, looking at only a small sample of payments.

As HUD struggled to improve the performance of the marketing and management contractors, the option years for the contracts were signed to continue the program with annual draws of $7,356,172 to $28,796,000 depending on the geographical area for the real estate. Other draws were even more. The total contract amounts varied from $83,820,000 to

$393,180,000, with additional extra compensation for work deemed outside the scope of the contract.

The marketing and management contractors then filed a contract lawsuit against HUD, charging that if a property was assigned on the very last day of the month to the contractors, they should be paid for the whole month for managing the property. They alleged that HUD's contract was silent as to what day the fees were to commence.

HUD countered, saying that in the post-award meeting, HUD contracting staff advised the M&M contractor that for such end-of-month assignments the billing would start the next month since the contractor would not have performed any services such as rekeying, inspecting, appraising, securing, or cleaning the property.

The M&M contractors responded that at the meeting they heard that HUD had not yet made a determination as to how the billing would be handled for end-of-month assignments and that since no direction or decision was issued by HUD in writing, that a reasonable man would say that when the assignment for a new property was made by HUD to the contractor, and the billing commenced.

The M&Ms were now suing HUD for millions of dollars for properties awarded at end of the month even though services were not provided because the contract was silent and no further written information regarding this matter had been provided by HUD. If the lawsuit prevailed on behalf of the plaintiff M&Ms, HUD would lose on all other M&M contracts across the nation, which would likely make a class act, and HUD would owe hundreds of millions of dollars.

HUD real estate staff had prepared extensive reports and memorandums sent to Washington, DC that detailed many of the same breaches of contract that the Inspector General reports had called out. The lack of maintenance by the marketing and management contractors was detailed, the excessive billings were spelled out, failed property inspections by the HUD staff were listed, and recommendations to suspend some of the M&M contracts and withhold unearned fees were made to reel in the M&M contractors and force them to perform according to their contract terms or be terminated for cause. HUD staff prepared extensive supporting documentation and evidence to support their breach of contract actions.

However, instead of supporting local staff who were charged with overseeing the M&M contracts, top management in headquarters roared back to staff that the staff would make the M&M program work and that no more negative reports were to be sent up the chain. Literally, one Assistant Secretary in Washington DC called, yelled and cursed at staff,

"I don't give a shit what you are seeing out in the field. I want this program to work., do you understand me? I don't want to read any more of your fucking negative reports. If you can't figure out how to write a positive report, I will find someone else who can. Do I make myself clear?" He further threatened staff to stop sending recommendations to decline payment to the contractors, and he didn't want to ever see a negative report again. Staff was stunned, especially in light of the Inspector General's report. However, the lobbying by the M&M contractors was no match for the HUD staff, and there were no consequences imposed upon the contractors for their documented breaches.

With the departure of the fuming Assistant Secretary and the dates approaching for the expiration of the M&M contracts and due to all of the early issues with the M&M contractors, HUD formed several task forces and working groups to address the weaknesses of the existing M&M contract, and to rewrite the program, examining each element and service to be performed. HUD began a new effort to redefine the tasks and duties of the M&Ms and determined it would mitigate loss if the contracts were broken down into smaller areas, that could be more efficiently monitored. HUD also worked on developing new data systems to provide more early detection of poor performing contractors. The M&M concept would remain, with more stringent oversight by HUD staff and sanctions for ill performing contractors. HUD anticipated that the new M&Ms would maintain the value of the REO properties better and increase recoveries through the selling of better maintained properties for the FHA fund.

The fees to the M&Ms were generous, 'making mega-millionaires out of ordinary millionaires, and making millionaires out of ordinary men,' many HUD real estate staff said. A property management contract for a large Southern California area amounted to nearly $394 million.

A contract for marketing real estate properties in Southern California and portions of Denver was awarded at just under $1.2 Billion dollars.

Shannon was now initiated into the political world of HUD.

HUD FHA Lender Activity
Shannon walked into her office and sat down, opened a file that had been placed in the middle of her desk. She took a moment

to appreciate her new corner office, with the light blond wood cabinets and desk she had selected when her group had been moved into the Federal Building in Santa Ana, California.

She looked at her name plaque on the open door: Shannon O'Toole, Director of FHA Quality Assurance Division, U.S. Department of Housing and Urban Development (HUD).

She was still responsible for FHA lender oversight and compliance, to ensure the lenders were originating FHA loans according to the rules and regulations, manuals, handbooks, codes of federal regulations and other guidance materials distributed to the lenders. She had been the Quality Assurance Director for five years now, ensuring that fraud, waste and abuse of FHA programs did not occur. She continued to be impressed by the professionalism and high level of knowledge the quality assurance staff possessed. Her division was comprised of thirty-two staff members, some of the highest-grade employees in HUD, due to the complexity and nature of their work. Shannon especially enjoyed directing her staff in discovering fraud against these lower-income homeowners and stopping the lenders who violated FHA rules. Shannon and her staff worked with the district attorneys, United States Attorneys, Inspector General's Office and FBI in developing cases that would eventually pay restitution to HUD and FHA.

Her program assistant, Buena Bonita, stepped into her office with a stack of files and placed them on the corner of Shannon's desk. Buena Bonita was a delightful young woman with long, shiny brown hair who kept the department organized and running smoothly. She teased anyone who wasn't in a good mood, and she could make anyone smile, even if they didn't want to. She was a bright light in a very serious division.

"Here you go, Boss," she smiled at Shannon. "I don't want you to be bored today."

Shannon smiled at her assistant, and answered,

"Thank you, Buena Bonita, you keep me focused."

"I do my best," she said. "But to save you more time, you could call me Bee, that is only one syllable instead of five, so you could get back to work faster."

Shannon stifled a laugh, then asked, "But Buena Bonita is so pretty. It means both 'good' and 'pretty,' doesn't it?"

"Si, it does," Bee answered. "My parents said they couldn't decide if I was a good baby or pretty baby, so they named me both."

"I understand. But if you like to be called Bee better, I can do that. And save time," she teased Bee.

"Bueno. Now I have to go fix more files for you in case you finish those files I gave you before. Let me know when you have signed all the letters, and I will come and get them."

Shannon smiled at Bee. "All right, I'll let you know with my progress."

Again, Shannon appreciated the quality assurance staff for their skills and knowledge, as well as the hope that they were making a difference in a risky industry.

Federal Housing Administration (FHA) was an insurance company, with more lenient lending terms and programs intended to provide financing for an underserved market, which was often lower-income buyers. As an insurance company, FHA would not insure a loan that did not follow FHA rules and guidelines, thus the lenders would not have insurance to cover their loss in the event the loan failed and went into foreclosure.

Shannon continued to be intrigued by the various fraud schemes she and her staff discovered. From 2000 to 2004, the Riverside, San Bernardino, and Los Angeles areas had the highest fraud activity in the nation. Shannon was asked to attend a mitigation conference in Los Angeles following the sentencing of a real estate broker who was found guilty of fraud after her staff had exposed the false employment and income records used by the broker.

"Shannon, we need you to attend this mitigation meeting to see if what the broker says matches what you and your staff discovered during your fraud investigations," the inspector general agent advised her. "The FBI will be here too."

"I will be there," Shannon assured the agent. "I would like to hear what the broker thinks can mitigate her sentence."

"Well, the purpose of this mitigation meeting is for her to offer anything that will reduce her sentence, help, mitigate or repair her actions of fraud. This is her one chance to spend less time in jail."

Shannon arrived at the mitigation conference, and was discussing the details of the case with the agent from the Inspector General's Office and the FBI when a small, dark-haired woman entered the room. Shannon recognized her as the broker that had been arrested for providing false employment documents to the banks that made the FHA loans.

The woman began her story, "I made loans to people that really deserved to own homes," she said. "They worked hard."

"Did they report their income to the IRS?" the FBI agent asked.

"Well, no, they didn't," she answered quietly. "But they made enough to make the house payments, so the bank wasn't going to get hurt."

The FBI agent shook his head. "So how did you get involved in this fraud?"

"Well, when I was showing property, the buyers told me how much they made. I asked for pay stubs, but then they told me they didn't have any because they worked for cash. So I calculated how much money they would need to satisfy the bank they could make the payments, and I made up the pay stubs."

"You made the pay stubs?" the FBI asked.

"Not exactly. I paid to have the pay stubs made up. I paid two hundred and fifty dollars out of my own pocket to have them made."

"But the banks usually had to also do a verification of employment," Shannon said.

"Yes, I paid for that too. I would set up a phone bank, maybe five phones on a desk, and have someone answer the phones and say a made-up employer's name that matched the pay stubs. I would give them copies of the payroll documents and pay stubs I had made, and then they would say they were the employer and give the bank the numbers I had given them. The phone bank cost me extra money."

"And did this always work?" the Inspector General agent asked.

"Sometimes that was enough," the convicted broker answered. "But then there were times when the bank insisted on more proof of income, so I had to get tax returns prepared."

"And how did you do that?" Shannon asked.

"I paid over one thousand dollars for the tax returns," she answered. "They were expensive, and I paid for those out of my own pocket too. No one was going to get hurt because the buyers made enough cash to make the house payments."

"Except that all the documents were fraudulent," the FBI said to her.

Shannon continued to listen to the woman describe how she had filled out false loan applications for her buyers along with the fraudulent income documents and listened to how she had altered bank statements or had false bank statements prepared as well. As Shannon was leaving the conference, the convicted broker was discussing the skills of the forger she had used with the FBI who had helped her with all her fraud. The FBI would be paying a visit to the forger next, and Shannon or her staff would appear as expert witnesses at the trial against the forger to testify and identify his fraudulent work and describe the losses to HUD and FHA attributed to his handiwork.

After this meeting with the convicted loan officer and soon-to-be convicted forger, Shannon began an in-depth evaluation of FHA's more lenient lending policies. FHA had offered a program called the 'Alternate Credit program', whereby if buyers did not have a credit report or FICO score, they could submit other documentation such cell phone bills, utility bills, or insurance payment information, showing that they made timely payments for these services.

This program was intended to expand the universe of buyers who had not built up a credit score or who were not experienced with using customary credit sources, although it was a risker loan program. It was also heavily encouraged and protected by the FHEO section (Fair Housing and Equal Employment Opportunity) at HUD to expand homeownership for underserved and lower-income buyers.

In addition to the alternative credit program, a down payment assistance program was also available. Most banks and lenders require that a buyer have a suitable down payment to purchase a home to reduce the risk of default. They want the buyers to have a 'vested interest' in the property, so they will have an incentive to maintain the property and make timely house payments. But FHA implemented the "Gift Down Payment", or donor program, to assist with down payments to expand homeownership opportunities to those without savings or down payment funds.

A six-month Pilot Program was commenced to allow nonprofit groups to offer down payment 'gifts' to borrowers with no assets or money for a down payment. Several nonprofit groups were approved by HUD to offer down payment assistance. In theory, these nonprofits had a 'pot of money' for the purpose of giving buyers the needed down payment to purchase a home. However, this 'pot of money' was actually cash given by the sellers to the nonprofit, that was funneled to the purchasers to provide the down payment funds. And the nonprofit kept a portion of the seller's contribution for their fee. The nonprofits were earning hundreds and millions of dollars in transaction fees, the sellers were often raising their selling prices to cover their contribution of the down payment to the buyers, and the buyers didn't have to put any of their own money into the purchase. Shannon ordered several data reports to take a deeper look into the performance of the loans made with these programs.

There was also an epidemic occurring in the lending arena where officers from a failing lending company would simply walk across the street or next door and open up a new shop to make FHA and other conventional loans. There were real estate attorneys actually advising lenders to obtain not one but two licenses and FHA lender-approval identification number, so that in the event the lenders experienced numerous loan defaults and became bogged down in FHA violation issues and administrative actions by HUD, they could walk away from their failing business and start up shop in their alternative location. Thus some bad actors were showing up in multiple companies and locations.

Shannon was examining the FHA lender application and was writing another memo to headquarters, recommending that the language in the application be changed from…

'Have you (the new entity) ever been charged with a violation of Federal laws…' to … 'Have any of your officers, employees or contractors or any company in which they owned an interest' ever been charged with a violation of Federal laws… She had discussed this proposed language change with the Washington, DC HUD attorneys, stating the obvious—that the new entity was obviously clean, it was new, it hadn't conducted any business yet, and would not have incurred any federal or HUD administrative actions for violations of HUD/ FHA rules. Whereas, the previous company would have been named in HUD Mortgagee Review Board actions, lawsuits or other administrative actions.

She continued to bring up this application change recommendation often in headquarters, since the attorneys were not expedient in their efforts to modify the old application format. And it would stop the bad actors, who were causing significant losses to the FHA fund, from expanding their poor practices to other businesses.

Shannon had been running 2004 reports for selecting lenders to assign her staff to visit for compliance with FHA rules and regulations, and she began to see a serious pattern emerging for the loans with down payment assistance. She noted that there was an increasing percentage of defaults, foreclosures and insurance claims for the loans with down payment assistance. She calculated that over 22 percent of the defaulted loans had been originated with the seller-funded down payment assistance program that was making a deep dent into the FHA insurance fund. She prepared a detailed report of her findings and submitted the report to HUD in Washington, DC. However, she was taken aback when the response came back to her that HUD did not intend to take any action at that time pertaining to the down payment assistance program because it was vital to expanding homeownership, one of the President's mandates, and was supported by the Equal Opportunity divisions to make housing available to those who otherwise could not purchase a home due to lack of down payments and credit. The down payment assistance program was also a program that no other lender at the time was offering, and it gave FHA an important market share, and also a political chip.

"I'm thinking like an apolitical woman again, a business-person again," Shannon chastised herself, and thought that stopping loan losses was good business. But, it seemed that the program was a political one, and that HUD could anticipate and accept the losses continuing to mount up from the failing loans to satisfy the current Washington, DC administration. She disagreed strongly with continuing a loan program that had known losses of approximately 22–25 percent and was fraught with fraud in the form of inflated appraisals and sales prices, which increased the FHA loan amount that would ultimately fail. She struggled with the political powers that kept the program going even after the six-month pilot period demonstrated that a high percentage of the loans failed and went into foreclosure. When HUD resold the homes after the foreclosures, they only recovered a portion of their insurance money since the houses were overappraised. She continued to discuss the mounting losses from the seller-funded/non-profit down payment program; however, she was directed by Washington, DC to stop her recommendations to discontinue the program. Politics, not business sense, prevailed.

Shannon's division continued to uncover false social security number fraud, false and inflated appraisal fraud, and false identity fraud. The Quality Assurance division often made recommendations to headquarters for new legislation, policies, and procedures to better control risk to the FHA program and protect against fraud, waste, and abuse.

Shannon had assigned five of her quality assurance staff to go into FHA approved lenders in Nevada since that state was experiencing some of the highest default and foreclosure rates in the nation. She had watched the fraud spread from Southern California into Nevada and Arizona from 2003 to 2006 and was reallocating staff to monitor the FHA lending activities in those two states to quash the growing fraud in the FHA programs. Shannon's staff in Nevada called with an update on their review of a prominent Las Vegas lender.

"We have a serious pattern of fraud here," Mary Simms, her Nevada lead monitor, informed her. Mary was about forty-five years old and very thorough with her lender-monitoring reviews. She often received tips from unhappy buyers or employees from lenders' offices reporting unethical and illegal lending practices. "We have thirty files now, all with the same false employer and false paystubs. We've verified that there is no such employer at the address on the payroll statements, and found an entirely different business at that address."

"Did you check the internet for the employer at another address, and our other databases for additional reports on the false employment?" Shannon queried.

"Yes, and there were no other locations for the employer."

"Did you get an interview or signed statement from the business operating at the address on the paystubs, and their years of operation at that location?"

"No, but I will. I plan on going out to pay them another visit tomorrow."

"Good," Shannon responded. "Let's try and get them to sign a statement of facts if you can."

"I will. I am also going to pay a visit to two gift donors that provided down payment gifts on about twelve of the loans."

FHA continued to be the rare real estate loan program that allowed a 'gift donor' through the 'down payment assistance' program to give the required down payment to the buyers. The gift donor had to be a government entity, nonprofit entity, an employer, a family member, or a close friend. The seller-funded down payments, funneled through the nonprofits, continued to plague the FHA fund. Shannon had been trending a higher default rate with this type of loan product for several years, watching it increase from 22 to over 30 percent failure, and had reported the higher risk with this type of FHA loan product to Washington DC. But headquarters had continued to tolerate the losses because it supported the agency's efforts to assist first-time homebuyers and was a political hot potato.

"I'm sure you will follow the money through the respective bank statements to see where the money really came from," Shannon asked the rhetorical question.

"Yes. In these cases, I believe the money for the down payment actually came from the real estate agents that sold the properties to the buyers."

"And that usually means that there was an incentive for the real estate agents other than just their sales commissions. Watch out for the 'flipping' or increased sales amounts from the previous sale to the present sale, see if there is a significant increase in the sales amount. Maybe the real estate agents owned the property and were flipping it for undue profit." Shannon pondered the extent of work that had to be done. "I'm going to assign Mark and Casey to help on this one," she advised Mary. "It's getting pretty deep now, and I want someone with you when you conduct any more interviews."

"Thanks, that'll really help. We know where to look, and we'll pull a chain of title too to see who has owned the property in the past and when they sold it, to whom, and for how much."

"That's good," Shannon replied. "And you'll take a close look at all the appraisals, too, to see if they are inflated and if the comparable sales are acceptable? I don't want to see our little $ 175,000 FHA home being compared to larger $ 250,000- $ 300,000 homes in other tracts or far from the subject homes in order to increase their appraised value."

"We will get right on it," Mary answered.

By the time the three Quality Assurance monitors had finished examining the lender's files and conducting their interviews, they had compiled five banker boxes filled with fraudulent documents. When Shannon had finished reviewing the documents, she talked with her colleagues with the Office of the Inspector General. Together, her department and the OIG expanded the investigation and developed three hundred cases of fraud with the lender, and Shannon's staff testified in court that the same techniques had been used in all three hundred cases and the same fraud had been perpetrated. The fraud had been organized by a ring of real estate agents, appraisers, accountants, and loan officers. The court ruling provided restitution to the FHA insurance fund and provided additional penalties and sanctions, including prison time.

The fraud discoveries continued as Shannon's division expanded their work. They discovered online websites selling fake social security cards and numbers, often associated with recently deceased person's social security numbers, and highly creative driver's licenses from any state the purchaser requested at any address. False paystubs could also be generated online, with a worksheet provided to make the deductions look legitimate according to in what state the fraud was being committed.

The Social Security Administration had created a type of 'code' in the social security numbers, that reflected the state in which the card had been originated and approximate date, which should match the borrower's date of birth and place of birth. However, this didn't seem to concern the fraud perpetrators.

Shannon's staff investigated a Southern California lender and interviewed several purchasers who had recently lost their homes to foreclosure. One man told her staff that he had been standing in a soup line, when two men from the lender's office approached him and asked if he would like a house to live in for six months, where it would be dry and warm and comfortable. All he had to do was give them his name and social security number and, sign some documents, and he could live in the house for free for six months. The soup line man agreed, and said he enjoyed living in the house, but that it had no utilities and sometimes was a little cold. But then there were notices placed on the property after a few months and he was told he had to leave. Shannon's staff discovered that this unscrupulous lender had tapped on several homeless people with the same scam, where the loan officers bought a property and 'flipped' it to the homeless people, making a significant profit on their initial purchase, sharing a small portion of their profits with the appraisers that helped them with the flip. They ran the homeless person's social security numbers through their lender credit checking systems until they found the 'clean' social security numbers for their property flips so that no credit red flags would show up in the files. And they created all the employment documents to qualify the homeless people for the home loan. Everything in the lender files was fictitious.

Shannon investigated a lender and its escrow company subsidiary, and found that the same cashier's check for a thirty-thousand-dollar down payment was used multiple times by different buyers to purchase different homes. Again, the loan officers handled the transactions, faxing over a copy of the same cashier's check to the escrow company where an employee at the escrow company involved in the scam entered it on the several HUD-1 statements as down payments to make it look like the buyers were making a sizeable down payments so the lender's management would approve the loans. The properties had all been purchased by the loan officers and "flipped" to the new buyers, who were told they didn't have to put any money down. The loan officers made a significant profit of $75,000 to $ 100,000 or more on each property they flipped. This type of fraud may have gone undiscovered if the buyers hadn't started defaulting on their loans. Shannon had noted the increase in delinquent and defaulted loans with the lender and sent her staff in to investigate.

Appraisal fraud had increased, and Shannon discovered seven files that used the same picture of the same house on seven different property purchases located in seven different cities. She called the FHA appraiser in to discuss these files. He was an elderly gentleman in his midseventies and had had no previous complaints against his license. When Shannon laid out the seven identical home pictures each for a different address, the gentlemen exclaimed,

"This is not my work. I haven't even done any appraisals for the last few years, I'm retired."

Shannon was somewhat surprised at his response, but continued, "If you didn't perform these appraisals, who did?"

"I have no idea," the elderly man stated.

"And you are sure you never inspected these properties or took these pictures?" she inquired gently.

"I'm positive!" He insisted.

She leaned back in her chair for a moment and then discussed a plan with the appraiser.

"I am going to instruct the lender that is using this appraiser to give him another few assignments, but to hold his payment for the appraisal. I will have them tell this person that he or she has to come into the lender's office to pick up their check. I want to find out who is impersonating you. Do you agree?"

"Yes, I do, absolutely!" he forcefully answered.

Shannon called the lender and explained the situation. The lender agreed to make the additional assignments and have the appraiser come in to pick up his fees. Three weeks later when the appraiser went into the lender's office to pick up their money, Shannon's staff was there with the local district attorney's staff. A young man approached the appointed lender manager, who quietly led the appraiser into an office. Shannon's staff and the district attorney office staff followed and asked the younger man for identification. He was startled, and looked quickly at the door of the office, but the district attorney had blocked it. The younger man appeared to be high, on what drug they couldn't tell, and became very agitated.

"The license number you have written on these new appraisals and seven others is not your license number," the district attorney's staff stated to the younger man, watching his reaction.

"Yes it is," he argued, "Look at the name."

The district attorney did not pause, "Do you have identification?" he asked.

"Yeah, sure," the appraiser mumbled, and produced his driver's license.

The district attorney and lender manager examined the driver's license, and the manager said, "The names are the same."

But the district attorney had done some background investigating and explained, "Yes, but the license number on these appraisals and the other seven was issued about forty years ago, before this young man was born. This young man's appraisal license has been revoked for cause."

The young man stepped toward the door, but the district attorney stopped him.

"It appears you have been using your father's appraisal license, son, and you have committed identity fraud and lender fraud."

Shannon had been watching certain lenders in the Pacific Northwest and the rapidly, extensive delinquencies appearing in her reports. She had noted that the common pattern with the increasing delinquencies was due to bankruptcies. She sent a team up to Seattle to interview some of the delinquent borrowers and determine the endemic cause of the spreading delinquencies. When her team called her to report in, she was impressed with her team's findings.

"So it seems that the suspects were gleaning the notices of default published in the local newspapers," Kane Harringer, one of her more seasoned lender monitors, was explaining to her, "so that when a lender published their intent to foreclose, the suspects went to the homeowner and promised to help them modify and reinstate their loan with the lender. Then the suspects told the homeowner that in order for the lender to talk to the suspects, they had to hold an interest in the property and be on title to the real estate."

"Oh, no," Shannon groaned, guessing at what came next.

"Oh, yes," Kane continued. "So the homeowners agreed to put the suspects on joint title to their house since they were about to lose their home anyway. And then when the lender moved to foreclose, the suspects would file a bankruptcy action in the name of the homeowner, which stalled the foreclosure. And when that bankruptcy action was lifted in about two months, the suspects filed another bankruptcy action in the name of one of their phony companies, which they had also put on title to the property, which again further stalled the foreclosure for a few more months."

"And during all these foreclosure filings, the homeowner wasn't making any payments to the lender, correct?"

"Again, correct. The homeowners were paying the suspects each month, who said they were paying the bank, but of course they were not."

"And where are the suspects now?" Shannon asked wearily.

"We have traced them to France at the moment," Kane chuckled. "But they are due to return in about ten days, according to their itinerary. I think we'll have a greeting party meet them when they arrive home."

"Speaking of a greeting party, have you spoken to the local district attorney yet?"

"No, not yet. That will be tomorrow. I want to finish my report and attach a few more statements from the delinquent homeowners to the report."

"Nice work," she praised Kane. "I knew you could find the scam if it was there."

"Are you sitting down?" he then asked.

She hadn't anticipated any more news but answered, "I am. What else is there?"

"I think I've discovered another scam when I talked to a few of the homeowners. It seems that they also received a letter supposedly from their lender, saying that their loan had been sold, and to start sending their payments to a new, different address."

"But the new assuming lender needs to also send notice if that is true," Shannon offered.

"The scammers did that, too, and sent the second notice letter pretending to be the new lender who had bought the loan, also instructing the homeowners to send their payments to a new PO. Box."

"Ughhh," Shannon groaned. "How extensive is this scam?"

"Well, this seems to be a different set of scammers, and I'm still working on defining the extent and scope of this one, so I'll let you know as soon as I can define it better."

"What else did these homeowners tell you?"

"Well, they were part of the group of delinquent homeowners we came up here to talk with, but they either were not contacted by the first scammers or turned them down. Then came the second scammers with these letters about their loan being sold. Several of them sent some money to the new payment address because they were told it would postpone their foreclosure. And then they received letters from their real lender who insisted they had not received any funds and were proceeding with the foreclosure. I'm picking up canceled checks tomorrow from a few of the victims and will see where the house payment money was deposited and who is on that account. I could use some more help up here if anyone is available. This all just keeps expanding..."

"I'll have two more monitors get up there late tomorrow to help you," Shannon promised.

"Kane, thanks for all your hard work. I'm impressed. I think I've seen all the scams, and then you surprise me."

"It never gets dull in this industry, does it?"

She could hear the smile in his voice.

19

Hello and Good-bye

A personal day—a day to enjoy the warm sunshine and ocean breeze, to taste the salt air, and to enjoy looking across the Newport Beach Golf Course in Newport Beach, California. A rare day to be out of the office, volunteering for the Toshiba Golf Classic. She had volunteered for three days over the weekend, and was looking forward to seeing some exceptional golf, maybe even help her own golf game while contemplating retirement.

Shannon had been taking care of her mother, as she appeared to be declining in health. At seventy-five her mother had been diagnosed with ovarian cancer, and had been given about nine weeks to live. But she beat the odds, and at seventy-eight, was still active and reading books voraciously, although slowing down. It was a treat to sit out in the sun, before Shannon would take dinner to her mother that evening, and enjoy some of her mother's great sense of humor.

She sat in the spectator stands, listening to instruction from the tournament supervisors about their responsibilities as volunteers that day. She was wearing her official Toshiba Classic red polo shirt, her khaki slacks, black windbreaker and visor. Her blond hair danced lightly around her face and shoulders in the beach breeze. The first fellow, Dean, thanked the volunteers for coming, and described the various areas they would work in. Next came a rather tall and large man, Bob, who talked about the tournament and the senior golfers that would be on the course that weekend. He talked about keeping the public away from the golfers. Then came a tall, slender fellow with a big grin and brown curly hair. His name was Dave.

Dave seemed excited to get the volunteers moving to their assigned positions, and told them he would be making the rounds to assist them with any problems. His enthusiasm was contagious, and the volunteers perked up with his energy and humor.

Shannon was assigned a "Hospitality Tent", where companies had purchased a large tented area and provided drinks and food to their customers and guests. Shannon's responsibility was to check the credentials of the folks coming to the hospitality tent and verify that they were invited guests.

She soon found that the woman assigned to the adjacent guest area was a lot of fun to talk with, and they began working on a dance routine behind their umbrellas as it had started to rain. They were becoming very proficient in twirling their umbrellas both above their heads and in front of themselves. Then they added a few jazz square steps and grapevines to their routine. The dance began to attract some attention, and about then Dave pulled up in his golf cart and observed the entertainment.

"Very nice," he said, greeting Shannon.

"Glad you like it," she countered.

He grinned, "I see you have many hidden talents."

"Dancing is near the top of my list," she laughed.

He struck up a conversation with Shannon as they moved under a tent for cover from the rain, and they discussed their appreciation and enjoyment for golf, the ocean and anything water—scuba diving, snorkeling, kayaking, swimming, boating, and more.

The rain stopped and Dave left to continue his rounds to check on his other volunteers, as Shannon and her new friend alternated watching the golf game and performing the credential checks.

"Oh, here comes Fuzzy, I would love to see him finish this round," Shannon exclaimed.

"Then go ahead, I'll watch the hospitality tents," her partner answered.

"OK, but I'll be quick. He's such a great golfer, I don't want to miss him," and Shannon darted between the two hospitality tents to the 18th hole to watch the famous master golfer.

Dave returned to find Shannon not at her assigned post, but instead, watching the 18th hole as the professional golfers finished out their final shots. He waited until she returned, teased her about her negligence, and while she laughed and promised not to do it again, he shook his head, knowing better. They talked a little more and Dave asked,

"What do you do when you're not shirking your responsibilities and sneaking around watching golf?" he said with a big grin.

She giggled and answered, "Walking on the beach. Reading a book at the beach. Kayaking. Golf. Enjoying the sunsets."

He seemed to like that, and asked more seriously, "And where do you work when you're not playing?"

She continued to smile. "I work for the Department of Housing and Urban Development, HUD, in Santa Ana. But it's really not work, I very much enjoy what I do."

"And what do you do?" he joked.

"We perform lender oversight, making sure that the FHA loans are insurable, and made according to our rules and handbook guidelines."

"Lender oversight?" he repeated.

She laughed and shook her head little, as if to indicate she hadn't been clear with her previous explanation, and said, "And we investigate fraud. We find the phony telephone banks where a bad lender or broker hires someone to answer several different phones, each one with a different phone number, answering with a different fake employer's name."

"Then what?" He seemed intrigued.

"We might drive by the employers address, and find a vacant lot, where an office building should be."

"That's probably against your rules, with the false employment and missing office buildings and such," he joked and his blue eyes twinkled.

She laughed again and said, "It's highly discouraged as a business plan."

They continued to talk and laugh and learn a little more about each other. She thoroughly enjoyed his intelligent banter, quick comprehension, and his descriptions of scuba adventures and misadventures. When Dave finally said he had to leave and check on his other volunteers, she thought, *What a great guy. He seems to be so funny and smart. Handsome too.*

Shannon went home after the golf match, and took dinner to her mother, who had not been feeling well. When Shannon walked in, she knew something was wrong. Her mother was leaning against the kitchen wall, and was having trouble talking. Shannon put her purse down and ran to her mother,

"Mom, what's happening? What's wrong?"

Her mom didn't respond immediately and finally said, "I've been feeling a little dizzy, but this time it's different."

"Different how?" Shannon asked, concerned that she hadn't known about this.

"It doesn't seem to want to go away this time," she said slowly, while still leaning against the wall.

"Let me help you sit down, Mom," Shannon said, as she slipped her arm around her mother's back and shoulders. Shannon noticed how thin her mother had become and helped her mom navigate to the sage-green sofa.

"Have you eaten anything today?" Shannon asked, thinking that maybe her mother was weak if she hadn't eaten.

"I think so, but I'm really not hungry. I don't want anything. I can't really taste anything."

Shannon frowned. "How long has that been going on? How about a cup of tea, Mom?" she asked.

"That would be fine," her mother answered weakly.

Shannon busied herself in the kitchen preparing a cup of tea for her mom while watching her from the kitchen. She noticed that her mom was very disoriented, moving extremely slowly and putting her hands out to reach for support on the wall or chair, and she seemed to be unable to coordinate her limbs to do what she wanted. Her mother reached for the television remote, and changed a couple of channels, but had no facial expression when she spoke to Shannon,

"I think I could use some help getting to the bathroom."

Shannon was alarmed, as her mother was one of the most independent and physically strongest women she had ever known at five-foot-ten; she was also strong emotionally and intellectually. To ask for any kind of help was unlike her.

Shannon went to the couch, and reached down for her mother, who barely raised her arm. Shannon bent down and put her arm around her mother's waist and lifted. Her mother barely helped by pushing up weakly with her legs. Shakily, Shannon navigated her mother to the bathroom, where her mother again leaned against the wall and said,

"I'll manage myself," and closed the bathroom door.

By now, Shannon was becoming more alarmed, and wondering if this was no ordinary dizzy spell, because her mother had experienced vertigo in the past, but if she may have suffered a stroke. When her mother opened the door, leaning heavily upon the door frame, Shannon said softly,

"Mom, I think we need to go to the emergency hospital. I think you may have had a slight stroke, and the sooner we find out the details the sooner you can start therapy and get well."

Unexpectedly, her mom resisted, although now Shannon noticed that her voice was very weak and her words somewhat slurred. Again, her mother didn't show any emotion.

"No, not yet," her mother said.

"But Mom, obviously something is not right, and we need to know what it is to help you get better."

Her mother hesitated again. Shannon thought maybe she hadn't heard her, and started again, "Mom, I'm worried. This isn't like you…"

"I'm not ready yet," her mother answered quietly, although with finality.

Shannon helped her mother get comfortable on the couch again and sat down next to her, and took her mother's hand, but her mother didn't respond. Her mother had enjoyed working on her computer and e-mailed constantly with her friends, acquaintances and family, and loved to play games. She also always had two or three books going at one time. Shannon looked around the room and didn't see any books open, but the computer desk did look actively used.

"Do you have any good books you are reading now?" Shannon tried to engage her mother, but she didn't respond. "Mom, did you hear me?" Shannon asked, concerned.

Still her mother did not respond, look over at Shannon, or so much as nod her head. There was simply no reaction. Shannon was becoming alarmed. This was completely unlike her intelligent mother. As Shannon began another attempt to communicate, her mother spoke, very, very slowly, and with difficulty,

"I loose words," she said. "I start to talk, but the words float away."

Shannon was startled by her mother's comments. Her mother didn't say anything more for a few minutes, and Shannon tried to fill in with quiet conversation. "I need to understand more," Shannon whispered.

After about twenty minutes, her mother added painfully, slowly, and very quietly, "I try to read, but there are blank spots all over the pages, no words." She didn't look at Shannon when she spoke.

Now Shannon was sure her mother had had a stroke, and said sweetly, lovingly, and quietly to her, "Mom, I love you. I am so worried about you. I believe you have had a stroke that is giving you those symptoms. I would like to take you to the hospital now."

Initially, her mother did not respond, or look at Shannon. They sat in silence except for the low voices on the television in the background. Shannon continued to hold her mother's cool hand.

Then her mother spoke in barely a whisper, "Not yet."

They sat in silence for another hour, with no conversation, while her mother dozed. Shannon wanted to call someone to share what she was seeing, but it was getting too late, it was after 10:00 p.m. now. Her aunts and uncles were older and would all be asleep. She could call her children, Toby or Jenny, but she didn't really know enough to tell them what was occurring.

Finally, her mother stirred and whispered very slowly, "I need…help…to go to the bathroom."

Shannon stood up, leaned down, and put her hands around her mother's waist, but her mother fell backward onto the couch, not able to straighten up.

Shannon became very alarmed. "Mom, I'm sorry. I will go get your computer chair, and we can move you onto it and then work on getting to the bathroom."

Her mother didn't agree or disagree, but sat leaning back on the sofa. When Shannon had the computer chair in place, she once again leaned down and put her arms around her mother's waist and pulled up. Although her mother barely could assist or push herself up, together they managed to get her mother seated on the chair. Shannon wished the chair had wheels, but it didn't, so she told her mom,

"I'm going to try to push you on the chair and sort of weeble-walk it if I can to the bathroom."

She started pushing. It was slow going, but since her mother didn't seem to be able to stand up now, there were no other alternatives. This time Shannon had to push the chair into the bathroom, pick her mother up by the waist, and move her to the toilet. Shannon stepped out of the bathroom, gave her mother a few minutes alone, and then moved her mother slowly back onto the computer chair while pulling up her jeans for her as she was unable to do it for herself. When Shannon had pushed and pulled the computer chair back to the living room, she began to cry softly. She could see that there was a very serious problem.

She asked her mother, "Can we please go to the hospital now, Mom?"

Surprisingly, her mother was not silent long, and answered, "Yes, just give me a minute."

A minute lasted about twenty or thirty minutes of quiet silence as they continued to sit together on the couch. Shannon thought that if she didn't get her mother moving, they would probably stay as they were on the living room sofa the rest of the night.

"Mom, I'm going to pack a few things for you to take to the hospital," Shannon said quietly.

She walked slowly to her mother's bedroom, pulled an overnight case out of the closet, and placed nightgowns and underwear into the bag, along with a pair of slippers. She added her mother's toothbrush and hairbrush, and came back out into the living room.

To her surprise, her mother was standing up, although shaking and swaying, holding on to the kitchen counter with both hands. She said without emotion,

"OK, let's go." And then as an afterthought she said, "Bring... my purse."

Shannon was amazed at her mother's efforts, and exclaimed, "OK, but do you want to sit down? I can push you in the chair."

Her mother answered carefully, quietly, and slowly, "No.... I want to walk in."

Shannon slipped under her mother's shoulder to support her as best she could, put an arm around her waist, and her mother put her free hand on the wall for more support. Shannon carried the overnight bag and purses in her other hand, and they painfully, slowly, inched their way out of the senior apartment out to Shannon's car. When they reached the car, Shannon leaned her mother up against the red Jaguar and said, "Hold on, Mom. Lean against the car, I'm unlocking it for us."

She put the bags down and kept on arm on her mother while unlocking the passenger door. Her mother was slipping downward as Shannon opened the door. She released the door and turned to use two hands to hold her mother up, and managed to lift her into the seat and then lean down and move her legs in. Shannon was crying harder now, as she felt the increasing weakness in her mother's body. She put the purses and overnight bag in the backseat, reached over, fastened her mother's seatbelt and closed the door. As Shannon walked around the car to get into the driver's side, she paused, and said a silent prayer, because her throat was too constricted with tears to even whisper,

"Please, Lord, be with us as we now go to the hospital to learn about my mother's condition. Let there be some treatment, some rehabilitation that will help her and correct her condition. She's my mom, Lord, and I love her so much. She means everything to me."

When they arrived at the hospital a few minutes later, Shannon pulled into the emergency entrance and parked. She came around the front of the car and reached for a wheelchair at the entrance, opened her mother's door, unfastened her seatbelt, and reached in to help her mother out of the car and into the wheelchair.

"No wheelchair," her mother said softly, startling Shannon.

"But Mom..."

"No...I'm walking...in," her mother insisted, still without emotion or even looking up at Shannon.

So Shannon pushed the wheelchair back, reached into the car, and swung her mother's legs out. With both arms, she lifted her mother, who shuffled and swayed. Her mother held on to the open car door for a moment, took a few shuffling steps, and held on to Shannon heavily for the few steps to the wall of the emergency entrance, which she leaned against, then continued her very slow shuffle into the hospital, leaning on Shannon and using one hand on the wall. As they entered, a nurse and orderly ran to them, and Shannon said,

"I think my mother has had a stroke."

The nurse and intern didn't ask any more questions at that moment, but helped Shannon's mother back to the doctor's emergency area, and then directed Shannon to an intake information area.

With her mother whisked away for tests, Shannon sat down stiffly at the intake desk and began answering a litany of questions about her. She took the various cards from her mother's purse and gave them to the hospital staff. She was going through the necessary motions, but her heart and mind were on her mother. She was remembering the last several years she had shared with her mother, because they could talk about anything, everything, absurd things, political issues, cultural events, and literature since her mother was so knowledgeable in all things such as literature, plays, novels, and historical chronologies. Shannon still called her mom when she was stuck, looking for just the right word for a report, because her mother's command of the English language was superior, and it was fun, for both of them. The computer games were a fill-in until Shannon could come over or would call to talk and catch up on each other's days. Shannon would share her day at the office with her mother or tell her about her golf games, talk about financial controls and political events in the world of HUD, and her mother would discuss world events. There was no end to their conversations, laughs, and shared love.

Her mother had sold her house and moved closer to Shannon, and had delighted in decorating her new apartment in the senior property she had chosen. She was engaged in and enjoying all the local activities with new friends. Shannon blinked back heavy tears as her concern for her mother's condition loomed on her mind.

It was around midnight when the emergency room staff brought Shannon back to a room to talk to the doctors. One solemn middle-aged doctor stood by her mother's bedside. Her mother's eyes were closed.

"Is she asleep?" Shannon asked in a hushed voice.

"She has been sedated for the tests we just ran," the doctor answered. "We ran extensive blood tests and full body scans."

He paused, and Shannon asked sadly, quietly,

"Has she had a stroke?" expecting the doctor to confirm her thoughts.

"No, I'm afraid it's not that," he said in a very low voice that Shannon could barely hear, which caught her unprepared for what he said next. "I understand she had advanced ovarian cancer but that she has somehow managed to keep going for the last three and a half years."

Shannon couldn't move. She was hearing the word "cancer" again, not "stroke."! Not just "tired," "aging," or "dizzy." It was the dreaded 'c' word she had hoped she would never hear again. She had thought her mother had beaten the cancer, had been in remission, had survived, and was even more full of life than before.

"I'm afraid that the cancer has spread to her brain; there's a tumor about the size of an egg in her brain. The tumor can roll around or swell up and then decrease, and affect different parts of her brain, sometimes affecting her motor skills, other times her speech, smell, vision, and so on. She is an amazing woman to have managed this for so long."

Shannon still couldn't move and didn't want to move; she just looked down at her mother through her tears.

"Can you remove it?" she asked.

"No, it's gone too far, the damage would be far greater and she might only survive a few weeks or months if we did. I suspect that the cancer has spread throughout her body, and the brain tumor is the one affecting her the most right now. We will be getting the rest of the blood tests back later tonight or tomorrow, and we'll see where else the cancer may have spread."

"Treatment?" Shannon managed to breathe out, but couldn't say any more.

"We will keep her comfortable, but that's about it. A hospice person will come and see you here tomorrow, and she will be able to help you decide what your next steps are."

Shannon couldn't comprehend any next steps, or decisions, or understand how the course of the day had changed so severely. Again, she wanted to simply share this with someone, anyone, but she didn't have any siblings to share it with, and didn't want to burden her children, yet, until she knew more. She would then tell her uncles the dreaded news. But two of her mother's brothers had already passed away, with two now remaining. Shannon would call her own close friends eventually, but not until she understood more. Her mother's ovarian cancer had spread to her brain, but it had taken three and a half years. For that extra time, Shannon was eternally thankful. She settled into the visitor's chair in her mother's room, and tried to get a little sleep, but the night was long and heartbreaking.

In the morning, Shannon called the golf tournament and explained that her mother was very ill, and she wouldn't be able to work the next two days as scheduled. Shannon hung up the phone, she had much more important problems to worry about, and she knew she would have some hard decisions to make.

Dave came around the golf course the next day, expecting to find Shannon at her post, but assumed she was sneaking off to watch the golfers again, so he walked toward the golf green, still expecting to see her blond hair blowing in the Newport Beach breeze, but he couldn't find her anywhere. He walked up to the woman Shannon had conspired with to watch the golfers finish their round on the eighteenth hole, but Gloria informed him that Shannon had called in early that morning saying her mother was ill, and that a new volunteer was going to be assigned to the hospitality tent shortly.

Dave walked back to his golf cart, and was surprised at how disappointed he felt in not seeing Shannon that morning. He barely knew her, but he had enjoyed the friendly banter and her laughter so much that he realized he really wanted to see her again. He had been going through a difficult divorce for about three years, and had focused on maintaining equilibrium with his children rather than being concerned with dating or being set up with acquaintances. He had avoided the obvious female colleagues at the office, and had not been interested in or impressed with anyone else he had met.

He finished his early round of supervision and drove the golf cart to the parking area for the managers' lounge at the Newport Beach Golf Club for lunch. As he entered, he was still mulling over his disappointment at Shannon's nonappearance that morning. He realized he found her very pretty and could visualize her blond hair breezing around her face and her easy, ready laugh. She was smart, he thought, and very knowledge-able about areas much different from his computer technol-ogy work. She was banking, finance, real estate and law. He was gigabytes and terabits and cloud technology. But they both were ocean, water, kayaking and golf. And what had she said about music, was it country, pop and classical? That was quite a far reach in preferences. He hadn't met a woman as athletic as Shannon and also as pretty. It was easy to look into her gor-geous blue eyes and see her intelligence. Darn! He wasn't will-ing to just give up and walk away from this opportunity. He paused for a moment and wondered if she was deeply involved with her mother's condition and situation, and decided that might provide him with a purpose to call her and express his concerns.

Or maybe he could just man up and call her for coffee! He acknowledged to himself that he wasn't the hipster smooth guy who cruised around asking women out, but he reassured himself that he was still someone who could carry on an intelligent conversation with a beautiful woman. Dave startled himself as he admitted that he had never found anyone attractive like he had found Shannon. He acknowledged that he had had a long marriage, but still, this was very different. He turned around into the hallway that housed the tournament staffing office.

He pushed open the door that read "Course Officials Only", and walked over to the interior office marked "Volunteer Director". He rapped his knuckles lightly on the semi open door and stuck his head in.

"Hey, Doug," he said in an upbeat voice. Dave had known Doug for over ten years as they had worked the Toshiba Golf Classic together before for eight years. Doug had brought Dave in as a supervisor official.

Doug looked away from his computer screen and greeted Dave,

"Hi there, I'm glad you stopped by. I need to give you a new volunteer to replace the one that called in this morning," and he shuffled through some papers on his desk. He handed Dave a note and said, "I've already called this volunteer, and he will be here later this afternoon. He can finish the rest of the tournament this weekend so we won't be short on the course."

"That's great," Dave responded.

"It's a great tournament this year, don't you think?"

"It does seem like there's a good fan turn out."

"I've spoken with a few of the concessionaires, and they said they're selling more food and drinks this year than before."

"I thought I had noticed more spectators walking the holes than last year," Dave answered a little vaguely.

"I sure hope it doesn't rain tomorrow. You know there's a chance we'll get some drizzle."

"That could put a damper on the tournament."

Doug noticed that Dave was a little quieter than normal and asked, "Is everything OK? You seem a little quiet?"

Dave wasn't quite sure how to approach Doug with the question he had on his mind. The Tournament kept their contact information for the volunteers very confidential, and didn't circulate a list with names and phones numbers to the supervisor staff. It had never been an issue before for Dave, because he hadn't been interested in reaching any of the tournament volunteers before.

"Well, uh, Doug, I know the golf course keeps the volunteer information to themselves and that you don't publish the names and lists with contact information for circulation, but here's the thing..." And he drifted off with a slight frown on his face.

"Yeah?" Doug queried his old friend.

"Well, you see, I kind of would like to contact one of the volunteers. You know me and know I'm not an axe murderer or anything, so I was hoping that maybe you could give me her number, or even call her and give her mine, and maybe she would contact me...."

Doug chuckled. "Let me guess. It's Shannon, right?"

Dave looked up, a little surprised at his friend's directness. "Yes, it is."

"Yeah, I can understand that," he smiled. "She is quite exceptional, and I'm not talking about her golf skills."

Dave finally smiled back, "I know. She is really smart."

Doug laughed out loud, "I meant she is beautiful! That blonde hair and blue eyes and all. She even looked good in the polo shirt and khakis we had all the volunteers wear this year."

Dave laughed back, "You can sure say that again."

Doug continued to laugh, "You know, Dave, I've assigned you the majority of female volunteers since your divorce, but you've never said a word. I don't think you even noticed."

"You did?" Dave asked, surprised.

"Yes, I did. Thought I'd give you a little help. But this is the first time you've ever expressed any interest in meeting any of them off the course."

Dave felt a little embarrassed, but put his head back and said, "Yeah, I guess it's about time."

"You can say that again!" Doug answered and turned back to his computer. He wrote down some information on a yellow sticky pad and handed it to Dave. "Here, this is her contact information. It does say she plays golf. You'd better go practice your own golf swing before you ask her out. I saw you the other day, and it needs work!"

The two men talked for a little more, and Dave got up from his friend's office and went back to his rounds. Planning to definitely go and hit a few balls at the practice range before he called Shannon.

20

Inside HUD

*H*UD Section 232 is an FHA-insured loan product that covers housing for the frail, elderly, and those in need of supportive services. Nursing homes, assisted-living facilities, and board and care are all examples of this type of housing. Section 232 may be used to finance the purchase, refinancing, new construction, or substantial rehabilitation of a project. A combination of these uses is acceptable, such as to refinance a nursing home coupled with new construction of an assisted-living facility. It's a good program; however, HUD 232 was traditionally a 'paper process' and wanted to come into the 'electronic age' and convert the process to an electronic one where all documents were scanned and kept in the computers. A notice to the public was issued that HUD was streamlining the 232 process and would now process and approve these projects only electronically.

However, the HUD Health care 232 program was taking a beating over the new, fangle-dangle, state-of-the-art, electronic system they had implemented for processing applications for senior housing and long-term-care projects. Those that had developed the new system and had taken credit for it, and their bonuses, were in hiding, and HQ management was looking for heads to roll.

Previously, HUD staff had processed all the applications manually, and all the required forms and documents were on paper. It had taken about one month to process each file. However, it was now taking in excess of seven months' origination lead time using the new super-duper electronic system.

Builders, nonprofits, senior housing and long term-care operators, the "Industry", were irate and went to Congress for legislation to compel HUD to drop their new electronic system that was taking over seven months longer to process new applications and instead go back to a manual process that only took one month to process. Fifty-seven steps had been reduced to sixteen steps. An inefficient program that took an act of Congress to change and improve.

HUD HECM—Home Equity Conversion Mortgage

This was a good product to allow cash-strapped seniors to stay in their homes. However, early on, the rules stated that the amount of money seniors could pull out of their home equity was based on an algorithm and the age of the youngest senior legally on title and living in the property. The algorithm calculated the senior's actuarial statistics with each senior's anticipated life span; thus it allowed a greater amount of money to older seniors as their expected life time was shorter, and they had less time to use up the equity in their home than a younger senior with expected longevity. So seniors took the younger spouse off title in order to receive a larger lump sum or larger monthly installments. This is all fine until the elder senior passed away. The younger senior was no longer on title, and the foreclosures and evictions began.

Shannon was reading over the legislation and handbook guidelines for the HECM program and continued to be concerned about the removal of a spouse from a title, knowing that it left the removed senior without an interest or in a legal position to claim title to the property.

She turned to her computer and began a memo to HUD headquarters, detailing the apparent risks associated with advising a senior to be removed from title to a property. She opined that removing seniors from a property left them without a vested interest in the property, and potentially no way to remain in the property upon the death of the other senior, usually a spouse, who took out the HECM loan. She felt deeply convicted that removing a spouse from title was unethical, and left the spouse exposed to future displacement when the elder spouse passed away.

Shannon's staff prepared additional suggested language to clarify other HECM guidelines, which she included in her memo to HUD headquarters.

However, headquarters did not agree, and the program continued to operate without making the recommended modifications.

HUD Customer Service/Resource Center—Left Hand and Right Hand Ununited

HUD headquarters had determined that staff spent too much time on the telephones answering questions for the public and industry partners such as lenders, brokers, and buyers that were their customers. Where most businesses want to increase the amount of time staff spends with their customers to build relationships and transaction activity, HUD wanted less time spent.

A national service center was developed, intended to take the heavy call volume off the field offices. After much effort to start up the Center and more than two failed small contractors who couldn't handle the volume of calls or technical materials, a new, larger contractor was trained and put in place that operated well for two years.

HUD had been trying to increase FHA loan activity that had slipped significantly due to the SubPrime lending spree. In 2007, headquarters marketing division was very excited about a new direct marketing piece they had fashioned, touting the advantages of taking out an FHA loan instead of a subprime mortgage. They also sent out tens of thousands of fliers to homeowners about avoiding foreclosure, offering to assist struggling borrowers. The Marketing division was so excited about their piece that they overlooked notifying the national service center, who would be receiving all the calls. Over eighty thousand HUD mailings were sent out to promote FHA just as the national service center phone contract expired and the phones at the national service center were unplugged. The calls went into an 'FHA Abyss'. Another example of the left hand and right hand at HUD not knowing what the other was doing.

HUD had to contact each of the four homeownership centers (HOCs) across the nation and arrange to have the auto-answer system reroute and forward the marketing responses to the four centers until a new service center contractor was hired. It took four or more people at each of the four HOCs to take the massive increase in calls and e-mails and took those employees away from their regular jobs and duties, which, in turn, pushed their work onto others. The lack of coordination by the marketing group caused weeks of decreased production in the HOCs, slipped deadlines, frustrated staff, and, unfortunately, a very frustrated public.

Sub-Prime Begins

In 2005, FHA loan production continued to decrease, just as the conventional lending and real estate markets were heating up and growing rapidly. FHA's market share was free falling from about 15 percent of all new loan activity to about 3 percent.

While FHA had been able to offer its low down payment programs of 3.5 percent with their alternative credit program and down payment gift donor assistance programs, they were no match for the new Sub-Prime Programs beginning to be offered by conventional lenders, that would later lead to the entire global financial collapse. The conventional lenders were offering easy credit and what were often referred to as 'liar loans' or NINJA loans (no income verification, no job verification, no account verification) in the lending industry, because proof of income was not required. The conventional lenders were offering zero down, 100% financing, in the form of an 80% first trust deed loan with a 20% second trust deed loan, instead of requiring any down payment. Thus, the buyer did not have to put any money into the purchase, but did pay a higher interest rate and fees on the loan.

Sub-Prime loans also offered negative amortization where interest was deferred or interest-only loans where the principal was not paid down, and, in fact, often the principal balance on these loans increased. The lenders' and their investors' philosophy was that the value of the real estate was continuing to increase at such a pace that if the borrower defaulted on a loan, the investor could foreclose, take the property back, resell the property, and make a profit.

The fees on these loans were often exorbitant and highly profitable for the lender, and the yields were astronomical for the investors buying the loans. The fees for the Sub-Prime loans often carried eight-thousand-dollar prepayment penalties in the event the borrower later sold the home or tried to refinance, and the interest rates were 7 to 11% instead of the conventional or FHA 4.5% -5.5% interest rate. The Sub Prime borrowers were also charged points or origination fees of three to seven thousand dollars or more to make the loan, all of which was profit for the lender and was added to the loan balance. And the 'garbage fees' were endless, including processing fees of $1200 to $2500 or more, similar underwriting fees, escrow tie-in fees, audit fees, broker tie-in fees, loan document preparation fees, loan doc review fees, signature review fees, title review fees, wiring fees, funding fees, and appraisal review fees. Shannon was seeing conventional Sub-Prime appraisals in the same neighborhood for the same house increasing by $20,000-$30,000 in a month.

The Sub-Prime lenders were gouging the borrowers and making money hand over fist. All of the 'points and fees' went into the lenders' pockets as profit. The Sub-Prime loans were then bundled and sold to investors, so the originating banks wouldn't get caught with the foreclosures that would surely follow from these risky loans. The investors were willing to buy the bundled loans and thrilled with the higher-than-market interest rates and hefty prepayment penalties they would be paid as well as the perceived increases in the equity of the real estate assets. The Sub-Prime market, which typically made home loans to borrowers with less than stellar credit, didn't require any buyer down payment, and didn't require proof of income, was skyrocketing.

Shannon had seen this all before at the FDIC in the mid-1980s and RTC in the early 1990s, when the overvalued real estate loans caused broad failures of banks and savings and loans across the nation. She had seen the consequences of greed and easy credit turning a blind eye on customary underwriting. These loans would ultimately be the demise of the mortgage lending industry in 2008 through 2011. She believed the current real estate market crash would be epic and continue throughout 2012.

REBOP—Real Estate Brokers Outreach Program

Reduced FHA loan origination activity translated into reduced revenue and insurance premiums to FHA. FHA insured these mortgages, and the insurance fund was rapidly dwindling.

Washington DC asked staff for ideas and recommendations on how to get back some market share. Conventional lenders were offering 80/20 loans, where the lender would make both a first mortgage for 80% of the purchase price and 20% as a second mortgage, to equal 100% financing for new purchases. The conventional lenders were also offering 'no doc' loans, where no employment or asset verifications were required. Whatever the borrower said they made, the lender accepted without re-verifying the information with income tax returns, which would prove to be disastrous in about twenty-four months.

HUD continued to hold management conferences, summits, and meetings to brainstorm on how to get back into the market and increase market exposure and share. Shannon developed a real estate brokers outreach program, or REBOP, to go out into the real estate sales broker and agent industry and teach them about FHA loans. As it turned out, about 95% of the real estate agents in Southern California had never processed an FHA loan and didn't know anything about them, except a negative reputation from the lenders. Shannon developed a power-point presentation, handouts, and oral presentations which she distributed to Headquarters in Washington DC and the local Homeownership Centers.

Shannon reasoned that the first mortgage professional to have contact with a potential buyer was actually the licensed real estate broker, not a lender or lender agent. After all, the real estate agent showed the property to the buyer and developed a relationship with the buyer. Shannon developed a program to inform and interest the real estate agents and brokers in FHA programs; it would be a natural fit and have a substantial effect and increase in FHA loan production. If she could reach out to the real estate brokers and agents that were showing the prospective buyers a home, they could also tell the buyers about the advantages of FHA, including a low down payment, alternative credit programs, and gift donor programs.

She was told to put it away. Because, she was told, HUD had never had a relationship with the real estate brokers to educate them about FHA loans, and they weren't going to start. HUD had only reached out to lenders, and the idea of reaching out and educating licensed real estate brokers had never been done before. Shannon argued that the real estate broker is the first line entity to work with the buyers, and the most logical entity to tell the buyers about FHA programs and advantages. She was told she was off base, and because she came from outside the agency, HUD, she thought she could change HUD, but she couldn't. It was an old agency, and change didn't come easily.

She received strong resistance from other departments who had traditionally had the responsibility of marketing and outreach efforts to the lenders but who never approached the real estate brokers' community.

For eighteen months Shannon continued to recommend the REBOP program when HQ was mining for new ideas to increase market share, and HQ continued to decline to accept her ideas. She felt frustrated with HUD's inability to consider change, and her ideas because they were different.

Then, when the FHA market share dumped further in 2006 down to barely 3% because borrowers were flocking to the no-document conventional Sub Prime mortgages, her boss, Bentley Johnson, the Santa Ana Homeownership Center Director, reluctantly agreed to permit her to go out to the real estate brokers community to talk about FHA loans. She pulled out the power-point presentation and handouts she had developed over a year ago, and trained additional speakers. She trained staff to use her Power Points and speeches. In ninety days, they had covered ninety-five speaking engagements, and the FHA loans started to increase where they spoke.

Shannon continued to rework the REBOP presentations and schedule speaking engagements for her staff. HQ was taking notice, and the REBOP concept was spreading across the country. Requests for HUD speakers and FHA training were pouring in.

GAO—Government Account Office High-Risk Report

During this time, HUD was on the GAO high-risk list for its public housing and single-family programs. GAO and the Inspector General stated that HUD did not have sufficient management controls or training in place to prevent unacceptable losses. HUD's staffing had been reduced to about the lowest level and number of employees it had experienced. FHA Executive Management was being called to testify 'on the hill' almost daily regarding FHA programs and to answer questions from Congress about the stability and sufficiency of the FHA insurance fund. They felt the FHA Insurance Fund did not have the reserve funds to pay anticipated claims and losses from failed FHA loans. Congress asked about the adequacy of HUD's internal quality controls and its compliance and monitoring programs to ensure that FHA lenders were being monitored to control risk, that loans were being originated with management controls in place to ensure their quality, and that HUD's housing missions to ensure the public trust were being fulfilled. HUD's Office of the Inspector General had audited HUD and found it still to be lacking in training for compliance and monitoring efforts in its single-family programs, and GAO had put HUD on the High Risk list of agencies.

Shannon had been the Director for the Quality Assurance Division for HUD for over eight years now and had directed her staff in lender oversight and compliance with FHA regulations and fraud discovery and had written several internal memos pertaining to risk and loss mitigation, including the earlier recommendation to discontinue the seller-funded down payment program. She received a phone call from Washington DC asking her to develop and write the training material for a special project, Compliance and Monitoring Initiative Training, or CMIT for short, for the five Single Family divisions.

"HUD really needs this training to respond to the GAO and OIG's position that we are not adequately trained in program monitoring and compliance, especially with our volume increasing now thanks to the REBOB outreach. We're so pleased to have you on board for this training effort," the training officer said to Shannon. "We've read some of your other work and are excited that you will be developing the student and trainers manual."

"Is this just for the FHA/HUD Single Family division?" Shannon inquired.

"No, there will also be courses for the Multi-Family, Public Housing, Section 8 rental assistance, and other divisions. Because we are on the High Risk list and Congress is breathing hard on us to take action to provide training for our staff to prevent risk, fraud and loss, this effort is extremely important to the department."

Shannon listened to the training officer continue with her vision of how the class would be structured.

"A contractor had been hired to assist with the effort, who will take the draft materials you prepare and edit them, give them a consistent professional finish, and then print the training manuals for distribution. The contractor doesn't know the subject matter; they have been hired to polish up your submissions. And the contractor will also give 'train the trainer' classes for those persons who would be doing the actual training, using the manuals you develop. We plan on having five trainers for your FHA single-family course work. The training will be conducted all around the nation, including Washington, DC."

"So you want a separate student manual and trainer's manual, is that correct?" Shannon asked to clarify the requirements for the class.

"Yes, with detailed talking points for the trainers," the officer answered. "So that in the future, whoever picks up the trainers manual will know the key points to be emphasized."

"And this will be a three-day course covering all five single-family program areas?"

"That's correct. We want it to be comprehensive and for all the divisions to understand how they relate to each other. We want them to understand how to monitor and make sure that their respective program areas are reducing risk by ensuring that their contractors and program participants are in compliance with all HUD rules and regulations and how to recognize fraud and prevent it. And we need a Power Point too."

Shannon paused for a moment. "This is a pretty large project," she began.

"Yes, it is, and it's highly visible too," the training officer agreed. "We want the training presented all across the nation to all Single Family FHA HUD staff. The training will be closely reviewed by GAO and the Inspector General as well."

Shannon interviewed staff from each of the five single-family divisions, gathered pertinent program information, rules, regulations, and case examples, and drafted a lengthy training manual. She developed the visual aids materials for a three-day training class consisting of 180 power-point slides to demonstrate compliance and monitoring techniques. She compiled exhibits, case files, handouts, and sample fraudulent documents for the training classes. She included a cashier's check that had the same series number, but the convicted criminals had changed the dollar amount on the check from twenty dollars to twenty thousand dollars to close multiple real estate sales. They had faxed a copy of the altered cashier's check over to the escrow closing agent, who then reflected a false down payment amount to defraud the bank making the mortgage loan. Shannon used copies of falsified employment paystubs and showed how the convicted criminals had made mistakes in their tax withholdings and had misspelled several items on the paystubs. And she demonstrated how bank statement fraud was often caught, when the forward balances didn't match. She prepared slides demonstrating the re-verification process for assets, including driving by or using Google maps for real estate used as collateral, and discovering a vacant lot where a house should have been standing. She spent a great deal of time discussing appraisals, and how fraud was committed by using comparable sales from high end surrounding neighborhoods instead of similar properties in the same tract.

The training included a portion on loan servicing. She used the Seattle examples, where an unscrupulous couple had sent letters to a few thousand homeowners telling them that their loan had been sold, and that their mortgage payments should be sent to a new address. It was only after the unsuspecting homeowners started receiving late notices from their lender that the scam was discovered by her staff. And she detailed how another scam was committed by a group that gleaned local newspapers for foreclosure notices and then went to each home, telling the owners that were behind in their payments that the group would save the homeowner from foreclosure by negotiating a mortgage workout with the lender, but that the lender would require that someone from the group be on title to the property to make it successful, and of course, that the catch-up payments needed to be paid to the group who would give the money to the lender in exchange for the work-out. The group then filed multiple bankruptcies, in the name of the original owners, then in the name of the group which caused multiple delays in the foreclosure, and more money in the pocket of the group, which kept all the money and never paid any of it to the lender, while the original owners were evicted. She submitted her draft and felt confident it was a solid piece of training.

When she contacted Headquarters in Washington DC and inquired into the progress of the contractor who was hired to organize and produce the manual and the anticipated availability of the finished manual, she was informed that the funds for the contractor had been depleted for other divisions manuals and that Shannon's material was simply copied and bound as she had submitted it in draft form.

Her first response was, *I thought I had the contractor's support for editing and formatting,* and then *I wonder how much money I just saved the government—maybe $500,000?*

Shannon was asked to attend the 'train-the-trainer' courses, where HUD had selected five potential trainers to present her materials. When it came time to give the three-day training events, it was discovered that three of the potential trainers had retired two months after being trained, one was afraid of public speaking, and the other simply disappeared and was suddenly not available. Shannon presented all the three-day training across the nation.

"This has been a highly successful training effort," Jessie Reim said, beaming. "It has been recognized by the prestigious Graduate School, USDA, for the W. Edwards Deming Outstanding Training Award !" she exclaimed. Jessie Reim was the Director of Operations in Washington, DC.

"The award says that…HUD was singled out for the honor because the office completed a "Compliance and Monitoring training, CMIT, effort that resulted in the removal of HUD's programs from GAO's High Risk watch list. HUD used a multidisciplinary approach to develop the training program, resulting in revised and updated policies and procedures, and involved training more than twenty-seven hundred HUD staff members and eight hundred managers and supervisors nationwide."

Shannon listened to the exuberant Director and smiled at the enthusiasm she and other political staffers were exhibiting during the live teleconference.

"This is a good day for HUD and a great day to recognize and thank the subject-matter experts that developed the courses." Ms. Reim went on to recognize each of the course designers, including Shannon. "Your contribution is duly noted, and our appreciation is endless."

Shannon was contacted a few weeks later and learned that her course was also going to be applied to another Inspector General audit of HUD internal quality controls. Because the coursework had developed policies and procedures, checklists, and timelines for carefully planning, implementing, monitoring and auditing compliance procedures, risk of loss would be mitigated or reduced. The course would now also be applied as the framework for internal quality controls.

While Shannon had been working on the CMIT material and presentations, her staff had been conducting ongoing marketing and outreach of the REBOP program. They had also attended various political outreach and foreclosure prevention events, averaging three events a week. She had attended those with invitations from congressional leaders along with her staff, and was pleased to watch the FHA loan

origination numbers exponentially increase. It was personally satisfying to see the success of the REBOP program. She
had believed in it and had continued to recommend it until
it was not only approved but expanded on a national basis.
Her staff was doing about 70 percent of the REBOP outreach across the nation. The California, Arizona, Nevada,
and Washington state real estate sales brokers were leading
buyers into the real estate market and returning to the FHA
product as a source for first-time, low down payment, and
lower-income buyers.

She was completely surprised when she came to the office
and turned on her computer to see an e-mail from Bentley
Johnson directing her to meet with him and another program
director, Muesel Junovic, that morning to transfer the REBOP
program to him. Shannon walked down the hall immediately
to Bentley's office and tapped on the open door.

"Do you have a minute?" she asked Bentley.

He looked up from his desk, removed the reading glasses
he was wearing to read the report on his desk, and answered,
"Sure."

She settled into a chair, crossed her legs, and then began,
"Bentley, I just received your e-mail about the REBOP program. You want to transfer it to Muesel now?"

"Yes, Shannon, I think that would be best. Since you manage the Quality Assurance group and lender oversight, it could
be construed that there is a conflict of interest with your enforcement duties and the marketing and outreach efforts you
and your staff have been conducting."

"You do realize the significant increase in FHA loans that
have originated due to the REBOP efforts, don't you?"

"Yes, and headquarters had noticed too."

"I suppose that I see quality assurance that oversees FHA lender activity a pretty far distance from the real estate broker industry that sells the house to the buyer."

"That may be," Bentley countered, "but there could be an *appearance* of conflict, even if there really isn't one."

"You know that we've conducted over two hundred and fifty outreach and marketing events so far, and I worked on getting REBOP up and running for over two years now."

"Yes, I know all that. But I want REBOP moved over to Muesel's group and to send over Lars Cedrick as well. I think he is your primary speaker when you can't do it?"

"Lars is a great speaker; he is very well received by the brokerage community as well as congressional leaders. But he also does other important Quality Assurance work on the FHA lender reports. I will be short if I don't have him for that role."

"All of our divisions are short staffed, Shannon, you know that." Bentley frowned. "If I can find another employee to swap for Lars, will that help?"

"Yes, it would," she answered unhappily.

"All right, then, can you have the REBOP materials and Power Points to Muesel by the end of the week? And a list of any committed speaking engagements you have?"

She didn't like it, but she didn't have any choice. "I can," she said simply.

"Look, Shannon, Headquarters has decided to put the REBOP program in the admin and customer relations division in all the homeownership centers across the nation, and Muesel manages that group. I have to do this. You should be proud that you started this program, that it's seen as the reason we are experiencing a significant increase in new loan activity as a result, and that it's been so successful it's being expanded across the country."

"I know. I understand."

"Then I'll see you back in about an hour to meet with me and Muesel on this?"

"I'll see you at ten," she answered. Then she stood up and left the office.

HUD Secretary's Award

A few weeks later, Bentley caught Shannon as she walked past his office.

"Congratulations, Shannon, everyone in Washington headquarters is talking about your CMIT training piece. It's not just the material, which is outstanding, but the fact that you did the actual training, all three days, alone, without any other instructor. You presented it all across the nation, and HUD is now off the GAO high-risk list as a result. You should be planning a really big vacation for this one."

Shannon wasn't sure what he was alluding to and asked, "A big vacation? Do you think HQ will give me a time-off award for it?"

Bentley chuckled. "I'm talking about some real cash here, Shannon. I've seen awards for twenty-five to thirty-five thousand and up for something like this. I think it would be fair to say that's what you can expect."

"You really think they will do that?"

"Sure. I worked in headquarters for a long time. If a contractor had prepared the material and sold it to HUD, which they were considering doing, HUD would have paid hundreds of thousands of dollars for it. The contractor wouldn't know what the Single Family division does; they would have had to fly around the nation to learn the programs and interview people like you, and then ask you to prepare samples and exhibits. But instead HUD ran out of money and asked you to do the work, to develop the training. You can really expect a nice bonus for this."

"Well, I will let you know if that happens, and you'll see my vacation time slip on your desk," she said and smiled.

"Think about it, Shannon. You were part of the effort that resulted in HUD being removed from the GAO high-risk list. That is huge."

Shannon walked away thinking that although she hadn't expected a large bonus for her work, it would certainly be a nice acknowledgment for all the extra time and hours, travel, and lack of sleep.

Shannon returned to her office and turned on her computer. The first e-mail she read said, "Congratulations! You have been selected for the prestigious HUD Secretary's Award for your Outstanding efforts with the CMIT Fraud Prevention Training. You are invited to come to Washington, DC for an awards ceremony on your behalf " … and the e-mail continued to add the dates and arrangements for the ceremony. So Bentley must have known!

Washington DC released the news about the pending Secretary's Award event to all staff, and as the news spread through the office, staff and other supervisors stopped by Shannon's office to offer their congratulations.

Her program assistant, Bee, tapped on Shannon's door and popped her head in,

"Hola, Boss. It looks like you really are in the big lights now for the training program you made us all sit through." Bee was an expert at delivering a compliment with sarcasm.

"I didn't make you sit through the training, it was optional."

"Yes, but the option was to stay back at the office and answer the phones for all three floors! I optioned to not do that."

Shannon laughed at her program assistant's wit, and answered,

"And you know you learned a lot from the training."

"Si, I did, but I did not know how all the departments were working together, how did you say it, interdependent and supportive. But I know that you taught everybody how Quality Assurance does the best work, and how they can use the same skills to do similar work in their own departments."

"Well, I do think our Quality Assurance division is outstanding, and our techniques for discovering and preventing fraud are excellent."

"We will be happy for you when you get your reward."

"That's '*Award*', Bee."

"That's OK too," she said, and smiled good-bye to Shannon as she left.

As Shannon walked into the awards ceremony in Washington DC, she was surprised and taken aback to see Muesel there.

"Hey, Muesel, I'm surprised to see you here. Are you here to work on another project?" she asked pleasantly.

Muesel looked uncharacteristically sheepish, and actually looked down at his shoes. "No, not exactly," he answered.

Shannon waited to give him time to complete his answer, but Muesel wasn't continuing his thoughts. She asked,

"OK, then will you be attending the awards ceremony and banquet today?" Thinking that it might interest him.

He usually liked snacks that helped him maintain his 250-pound body.

"Uh, I will be there," he said lamely.

Just then the assistant secretary walked by and stopped.

"Congratulations, Shannon. I want to get a picture with you after the ceremony. I'm really happy to see you here, you deserve it!"

Shannon smiled and felt warmed by his kind words, I'll find you after the ceremony," she said and smiled.

"You know your work on the CMIT really contributed greatly to getting HUD FHA removed from the inspector general's high-risk list of agencies. Everyone here is really happy about that, and you."

She didn't have a response to that, and the assistant secretary squeezed her arm as he left to take his place in the awards ceremony.

Shannon turned to talk more with Muesel, but he had disappeared, and an aide came up to Shannon and told her it was time to take her place to receive her award. She followed the aide inside the auditorium, blinking at the bright lights set up for filming the event, and smoothed her plum-colored skirt suit.

It was a career highlight, to be presented with the Secretary's Award for Outstanding Program Performance. Other outstanding employees had also been invited back to HQ to be recognized from other divisions. As the aide brought Shannon to the steps leading up to the ecretary's stage and podium, she looked at the familiar faces of her Washington, DC colleagues on the stage.

The Secretary smiled at Shannon, standing just off stage, and began his announcement,

"I am pleased to announce my Secretary's Award for Outstanding Performance to Ms. Shannon O'Toole, also Quality Assurance Director in the California office. Under her direction, her staff has recovered more revenue for fraudulent actions than any other office in the nation.

"She also is instrumental in developing the format and beginning the audits for servicing lenders who were robo-signing and rubber stamping foreclosure documents without attempting to assist delinquent borrowers stay in their homes.

"She recognized early on the affects that would soon occur from the dangerous loan pools originated and serviced without regard for our FHA rules and regulations.

"And I understand that Ms. O'Toole also conducted the three day training sessions for the CMIT program herself across the nation, reaching about nine hundred HUD employees with fraud prevention training.

"Her attention and definition of risk and mitigating actions has resulted in FHA Single Family being removed from the inspector general's high risk list.

"We applaud Ms. O'Toole. And I am happy to present this award. She will also be receiving a large plaque for her wall commemorating her honor today," he said as he handed her a folder with an award certificate inserted inside. There were more complimentary words spoken and pictures taken as she crossed the stage and shook hands with other assistant secretaries and colleagues.

As she made her way down the stage steps, she heard another name called that she hadn't expected.

"And I would like to recognize Mr. Muesel Junovic, also from the California office, for his invaluable work on the new national REBOP program. For those of you who don't know what REBOP stands for, it is Real Estate Broker Outreach Program. It has substantially increased the number of new FHA loan originations wherever the REBOP has been presented, especially on the West Coast. It is an important program that reaches out to new partners in the lending space that HUD has not worked with in the past. This innovative, new program has educated the real estate broker in FHA home loan advantages and protects their buyers from the sub-prime market that has greatly disrupted the lending world. REBOP began in California, and has now been implemented throughout the nation," the Secretary boasted.

And Muesel walked up and shook the Secretary's hand, received his award folder and left the stage.

Shannon stopped walking, looked back at the stage, and pondered the strange twist of events that caused the REBOP program she had fought to launch and had developed, to now be moved into another group that was taking credit for it. The new group was making changes to it, and meeting on a national basis to discuss it and make it a consistent program across the nation. But she had birthed it, brought it to life, and had given it legs to run well. This was another Apolitical moment.

For developing this CMIT and internal quality control training, for helping remove HUD from the GAO government high-risk list, and for saving the government the contractor's

fee of hundreds of thousands of dollars for editing and preparing the training manuals for her work, Shannon received
the highest, prestigious HUD award for this training effort,
the Secretary's Award, from the HUD Secretary sitting on the
President's cabinet. It was a large plaque for her office wall.
She was recognized for her outstanding work and contribution
to HUD. But there was no cash, no bonus, because the federal
government had pulled back funds from all the federal agencies to help fund their extended entitlement programs, and
HUD had run out of money, again.

Loan Servicing—Robo Stamping

Shannon had been watching the new FHA loan production increase and fraud decrease in her jurisdiction, but she had noticed increasing delinquencies and defaults and began to look at
the servicing side of the FHA loan activity. That was where the
FHA lenders accepted the monthly mortgage payments from
the borrowers, set aside property tax and insurance impound
accounts, and allocated the payments to principal, interest, and
FHA mortgage insurance premiums that were sent to HUD
and to hazard insurance companies. She had been watching the
conventional and subprime lending industry closely, due to the
easier credit qualifying by the conventional lenders, while FHA
still continued to require proof of income, acceptable credit, and
appraisal valuations to support each purchase. She had become
concerned with the servicing lenders procedures and increasing
delinquencies. She had written initial reports of her findings
and recommendations to headquarters, in fact, the Secretary
had mentioned her work during the awards ceremony.

She had continued to refine her approach to examining
the servicing lenders, had her staff pull reports on the FHA

servicing lenders delinquency data, and analyzed the number of loans that were sixty, ninety, or 120 days delinquent or more. What she found interesting was the length of time many of the loans had been sitting delinquent without foreclosure, or any type of loss mitigation activity, often six months, and some a year, without an obvious reason such as bankruptcy, which would delay a foreclosure.

FHA had released new servicing guidelines and rules requiring FHA servicing lenders to offer several loss mitigation steps to assist the delinquent homeowners in bringing their loans current, including modifying their loans, restructuring, conducting short sales, or returning the property via a deed in lieu of foreclosure. These loss mitigation efforts were mandatory. HUD had determined that it was less costly to assist a borrower with saving his or her home than it was to foreclose and resell the home. HUD's mission was also to help low-income, first-time, and minority homeowners, and the loss mitigation program was a strong effort to provide an alternative to foreclosure.

She prepared a select staff to go into one of the nation's largest lending institutions, and FHA approved lenders to examine their servicing program and reports. What they found was staggering, and the beginning of the entire servicing area litigation meltdown that quickly spread across the nation. The banks had been reporting their loan delinquencies incorrectly into HUD data systems. Her staff discovered missing original loan documents, unauthorized management signatures, and unauthorized foreclosure actions. They discovered untrained servicing staff, unknowledgeable management, and a general lack of adherence to FHA loss mitigation requirements. The banks were unable to provide accurate reports on their loan servicing activity, and admitted they didn't have sufficient staff to handle the continually increasing default and foreclosure activity. As a result, the delinquent loans had sat untouched, and became further delinquent, sometimes for a year. Many of the fees charged by the lender against a borrower were later reversed, and a moratorium was placed on all pending foreclosures until the lender could provide an approved plan to provide correct and required documentation and loss mitigation on any delinquent FHA borrower and loan file.

Appraisal fraud was discovered, including comparable sales data from entirely different tracts that were more expensive to support an inflated appraisal for a smaller property. Often pictures showed the subject house, but omitted the factory or freeway or airport right next to it, which would affect the property's value. Other files had pictures of the house, but not the roof, which was partially missing or badly decomposed, which was discovered when her staff performed field visits of the properties. Other field visits discovered missing foundations and damaged or missing walls, all of which were not shown in the appraisal pictures or mentioned in the appraisals. Her staff discovered properties in the same neighborhood, one with an ocean view and another without a view, being valued the same. Shannon's staff prepared a quality assurance case that was sent to Washington, DC and was heard by the mortgagee review board (MRB), detailing all the violations to FHA rules the lender had committed. The fines assessed by the MRB were staggering, and thus began the long process of examining other servicing lenders for similar activity.

The *Los Angeles Times* would report,

"Bank of America halts foreclosures nationwide…with calls mounting for a national moratorium, Bank of America Corp said that it would halt the sale of foreclosed homes indefinitely in all 50 states as they nation's largest lender widens its investigation into how it seized homes from troubled borrowers. The freeze came after lawmakers, consumer groups and civil rights organizations called for a moratorium on bank seizures. State attorneys general across the country have also called on lenders to prove that they are complying with state laws as they process record numbers of repossessions…Bank of America reported that it had 420,000 properties in some stage of foreclosure through the first half of the year (2010). About 126,000 of those were in California, which has been among the states hit hardest by the foreclosure crisis. The freeze came as disclosures of alleged irregularities, including mishandling of records in the foreclosure process, have raised concerns that lenders have been evicting homeowners using flawed procedures…PNC Financial Services said that it was reviewing its foreclosure practices and Litton Loan Servicing, mortgage servicers owned by Goldman Sachs Group, said it had suspended foreclosure proceedings in certain cases while it completed a review."

Other major banks followed suit, and suspended their foreclosures while their collections, loss mitigation, and foreclosure processes were examined.

Shannon was asked to come back to Washington, DC again to present her findings and demonstrate the process for examining the FHA servicing lenders. HUD was about to expand its examination of servicing activities across the nation.

The conventional lenders did not fare as well. The subprime meltdown was beginning.

Then the Wall Street loan mortgage fraud began to emerge, and the entire lending industry paused.

21

Par for the Course

An Unexpected Call

Shannon came back to California to a desk piled high with letters to read from her staff pertaining to FHA lenders they had just examined. She stole a few minutes for lunch before tackling the next stack of letters. As she returned to her desk from lunch, she saw the message light blinking. She sat down and picked up the phone, listening to her messages and making notes. Then an unexpected call surprised her.,

"Hello, Shannon, this is Dave Haack, we met at the Toshiba Golf Classic a couple of weeks ago. I hope you don't mind me calling, but I wondered if you would like a have a cup of coffee with me? I'd like to know more about your golf game."

Shannon was very surprised, but pleasantly. She really liked his deep voice on the phone and remembered how much she had enjoyed talking with him. Because that weekend she had volunteered at the golf tournament had ended so sadly, she hadn't had much time to think about anything except arranging for the care of her mother. She reflected back on her meeting Dave on the golf course, his smile and obvious intelligence. And also how attractive she thought he was. But how would she find time with both her career and care of her mother?

As the day wore on, Shannon thought about the surprise call she had received from Dave and couldn't decide if she would call him back or not. She certainly liked what she knew about him, liked his deep voice and upbeat personality. But how could she carve out any time to get to know him? Was it even fair to meet with him at all if she was committed to caring for her mom after work and weekends? She had hired 24/7 nursing for her mother but still talked with hospice daily and picked up whatever prescriptions or items were needed for her mom on the way home each day. But she just couldn't ignore Dave, either. He was so cute! And so smart! Maybe she could just return his call, to be polite, and she dialed his number,

"Hello?" He answered.

Yikes! Now what do I say? she panicked. She had counted on just getting his answering service. "Oh, hi, Dave, this is Shannon, returning your call."

"Oh, hello there," he had a smile in his voice. "I hope you don't mind my calling. I was just so disappointed when you didn't come back." He bit his tongue, he didn't mean to criticize. He knew about her sick mother. "I mean—"

She smiled sadly on her end of the line. "Yes, I wanted to be there, but my mother was very ill when I saw her after the tournament that first day, and my world just kind of tilted..."

Nice work, Dave, he chastised himself. *Make her sad, why don't you?* "Oh, I am very sorry to hear about your mother. I wanted to call and express my concerns and ..."

She interrupted anxiously. "That's all right; it was unexpected, that's all, and it's a little hard right now." *Oh, great,* she thought to herself, *you're making this conversation depressing.*

Dave tried to think of something upbeat to say. "Well, I know you must have work to do, so would you like to have a cup of coffee some evening soon?"

"I don't drink coffee," she blurted, then kicked herself for being too fast to answer even though it was the truth. She couldn't handle caffeine, it made her heart beat too fast. She made an exception for chocolate, of course.

Dave was a little taken aback, and hoped he wasn't being put off, so he tried again, "Well, how about something else? Maybe a bowl of onion soup at Marie Callendars." *Very romantic*, Dave scolded himself.

"I don't eat onions, either." She just about choked on her words. *Oh, come on, Shannon, say something positive; you are sounding like an idiot.*

"I'm sure we can find something." He was not about to give up.

"Well, sure, that sounds great," she managed to answer without blurting out some other stupid comment.

"Good, so what night looks good? I'm pretty open. I play a little tennis but can work around that."

She looked at her calendar and decided that right after work might be best so she could still go by her mother's house on the way home. "Um, how about Wednesday next week?" she offered.

He smiled. Success! "OK, that sounds great. What time is best for you?"

"I would appreciate right after work, if you don't mind. That way I can still take dinner to my mom."

"OK, next Wednesday at six o'clock. Where do you work so we can find someplace close to your office?"

"Santa Ana," she answered, and Dave gave her the location and directions to the nearest Marie Callendars restaurant.

"See you then," he smiled into the phone.

She actually smiled, and said, "I'm looking forward to it."

Par for the Course

Several weeks later, on the way home from another trip to Washington, DC, Shannon laid her head back on the airline seat, and began to unwind. The meeting had been a good, productive one. She was pleased with the new goals for her division, and the recognition she had received for initiating some high risk lender reviews, which had resulted in identifying new fraud and risk operatives. Just when she thought she had seen it all, all methods of committing fraud, a new scheme would emerge. She was watching the lenders with the highest number of defaulted loans and claims against HUD's FHA insurance fund to identify those new schemes. However, she realized that there was no way of knowing how much *performing fraud* there was in the loan portfolios, loans that contained fraud in employment and income but that continued to perform with timely monthly payments. The loans with performing fraud would not show up in her reports.

Of late, lenders would make risky loans that went into default within two years and then close their business and move across the street with a new name. Much of what Shannon had hoped to accomplish in HQ this trip was to change the rules for allowing the same high risk people from reopening a new lending operation after they had caused losses to HUD in their previous business.

Shannon had also taken the opportunity to discuss her thoughts on the approaching real estate and lending tsunami starting to take shape in 2006 in the form of increased defaulting loans and unsustainable housing prices. She had given a presentation on the high risk subprime loans being made to unqualified buyers, and her expectation that FHA would be the last and only lender standing to make home loans when the dust settled. Her experience with FDIC and RTC with similar market activity was illustrated to support her projections.

Her mind finally released the day's conversations, and she drifted into pleasant thoughts of Dave, whom she would be seeing when she arrived home. She was pleasantly surprised that he had called to make the date since she had had to turn down his several offers because her mother had continued to decline and had finally passed away. She still keenly missed her mother, and missed sharing her days' activities with her.

Dave had made a date to meet her at a golf range in Irvine, to practice their chipping and putting the next day. Maybe not the most romantic of dates, but surely it would prove to be fun. This would be the first time they played golf together. Shannon always thought that the best way to get to know a man was to play golf with him. Their sense of humor, temper, patience, sense of fairness, and the conversation always soon revealed a man's real personality and character on the golf course.

Shannon laughed to herself as she remembered one golf date with a golf pro, Tom. It had been in the fall, as the leaves were changing color and dropping from the abundant fairway trees. The course was long and a difficult one for her. Her golf partner had watched her hit her orange, yellow and pink golf balls with disdain, telling her that she really needed to learn to take the game of golf seriously, and use *an official* tournament approved quality white ball. When she had said she liked the colored balls, he criticized her for not selecting a properly calibrated golf ball and explained that golf was a serious sport. She hit a few 'provisional' balls off the tee because she couldn't see where her ball had gone since, after all, she was keeping her head down. When she had commented that she couldn't find her golf balls in all the leaves and that she used colored balls because they were usually easier to find, the man couldn't contain himself any longer and had gruffly said,

"Well, you should try hitting your ball on the fairway where *there are no leaves*. Then you wouldn't lose them! You keep hitting into the rough, where all the colored leaves are!" No patience or sense of humor! That was the one and only date she had with him!

But now, she was meeting with Dave. Their first date at Mimi's had been a delightful surprise. He continued to impress her with his wonderful intelligence, and had a terrific sense of humor. He could make fun of himself before anyone else. He seemed responsible, for himself, his work, and especially his children. Not to mention how attractive she found him, with his easy smile and great laugh. His hair was a little short for her preference, but it could grow. And he loved watersports, as well as golf. Not too many other people enjoyed ocean kayaking but they both did and talked about taking out his double kayak in Dana Point. But what really made her laugh were their similar tastes for things not quite conventional, like brussel sprouts and pistachio ice cream. And he liked cats. Although their professional fields were far apart—his computer technology and hers political, legal, and banking—they could talk for hours on the phone and appreciate each other's fields of interest.

The Oak Creek golf course in Irvine had a perfect practice area for chipping onto the green and putting. Shannon and Dave met at the golf course after work since the days were long enough now to stay light until eight o'clock or later. She was just now ready to go out and try to smile again after losing her mother. She had worn brown slacks and a tweed jacket to the office that day, with a silky cream blouse. Dave spotted Shannon parking and jogged over to greet her and offered to carry her golf bag to the course.

"Hi, there", he greeted her with a smiled. He had changed into golf shorts and a polo shirt, and Shannon immediately felt overdressed. She hadn't thought to bring a change of clothes.

"Hi. It's good to see you again."

"How was your trip? Anything exciting happen in the sky?"

"No, thank goodness," she laughed. "Other than flying around a couple of thunder heads, it was relatively smooth."

"That's good. I'm glad you're home."

She looked up at him, and thought she could get used to hearing things like that.

"Shall we go get a couple of buckets of balls?" He asked, as he swung her golf bag up onto his shoulder.

"Sure, I just need to change into my golf shoes."

"That's an awfully pretty blouse to be playing golf in," he complimented her.

"Thank you," she smiled, feeling overdressed again. *Oh, relax*, she told herself.

She finished putting her golf shoes on and they walked over to the pro shop counter to get the golf balls. Dave was the first to pull three clubs out of his bag and drop several balls on the ground, aiming at a flag stick about twenty yards away. Shannon stood back as was golf courtesy to allow him a full swing and follow-through and to stay out of his line of vision. She took her bucket of balls and moved away several yards and dropped a handful of balls on the ground. She pulled her nine iron from her bag and took a few practice swings. She approached the ball, waggled her bottom, and set her feet into this grass, took another practice swing and sent her ball flying toward the flag stick, only to hit a sprinkler head and have it fly off forty-five degrees to the right.

"Nice crooked shot!" Dave called over to her.

"It wasn't crooked!", she called back, "I just hit a sprinkler."

"I don't see any sprinkler," he teased.

She approached another ball, waggled, pulled her club back slowly, and this time sent the ball flying way over the pin and down the other side. Now she was truly embarrassed.

"Hey, did you eat Wheaties today for breakfast?" He chuckled.

"It was so early, I don't remember," she laughed.

"Well, then, let's make this more interesting," he suggested. "How about a little bet before each shot?"

She wasn't really interested in betting, but decided to be a good sport and answered, "All right. How does this work?"

"It's easy. We each shoot ten balls, and the closest to the pin wins a dime."

They each placed ten balls on the ground, giving each other sufficient room to swing, and Dave began, landing his first pitch five feet from the pin.

"Not bad," she said.

"OK, your turn," he answered.

She approached her first ball, waggled, took a practice swing, and then sent the ball about four feet from the pin.

"OK that's a dime for you." Dave smiled, and he approached his second ball. He sent it a little high and over the top of the pin. It rolled a few feet away.

"Your turn," Dave turned to Shannon.

She squared her shoulders to the target, waggled, pulled her club back with a short swing, and landed the ball to the right of the pin, about four feet away again.

"Not bad," Dave called. "You win again."

She wondered if he was letting her win and questioned him.

"Hey, you don't have to let me win. I want to earn it, or pay up."

"That's what I hoped you say," and he sent one flying to the left of the pin. They continued to play until their buckets were empty and the sun began to fade.

"Looks like I owe you forty cents," Dave joked, walking over to Shannon.

"I can take a check."

"Even better," he continued joking and pulled a pink plastic shark out of his golf bag, "We can play for Sharkie. Whoever wins each game can keep him until the next game. But I'm warning you, be prepared to loose Sharkie the next time we play."

Shannon put her hand out with her golf glove still on and accepted the six-inch pink plastic toy shark. "Wow!" she exclaimed, "My first golf prize!"

"Just don't expect to keep it long," he laughed.

"We'll see about that," she laughed in return.

It had been a lot of fun, and she was thinking that he was a very attractive man, and athletic too. She had enjoyed watching him concentrate and then execute his shots. Nice shoulders, nice long back, handsome face. But his hair was too short. She'd have to encourage him to let it grow longer. It had been great to go and play after sitting behind a desk all day in the office, and the evening had been warm and balmy. The sun was getting ready to set.

He picked up her golf bag, put it back on his shoulder, and walked her back to her car.

"Nice car," he said, as they walked up to her cranberry red 'S' type Jaguar. It was a beautiful car, with extensive wood on the interior and a wood steering wheel. The leather upholstery was a soft tan color.

"I do enjoy it," she admitted honestly. "I bought it when my daughter finished college with one of my first paychecks that didn't have to go to tuition, food, or books."

"You're ahead of me," he responded. "I still have three to put through college."

"Well, save well then. And pray for scholarships!" She laughed.

"I hope we can do this again soon," he said softly as he put her bag into the trunk of her car.

He is really a lot of fun, she thought. And if that concept of hers about really getting to know a man when you played golf with him was true, then this man was exceptional.

"That would be fun. But next time, let's play on a real course."

"OK, I'll be prepared for a slaughter."

"Whose, yours or mine?" She laughed.

22

Deep Inside HUD

*H*UD was growing again in 2008, and would be growing more in 2009, hiring new staff to respond to the growing FHA market as a result of the subprime and conventional mortgage market meltdown and all the FHA marketing and REBOP activity.

Anyone who has applied for a federal job knows that the old 171 form, about six to ten pages of small print job application questions and a long history portion, is tedious, repetitive, and out of step with current job-seeking activities and methodologies. HUD finally came into the present and allowed the new, shorter version Optional Federal Application Form 612 or a résumé for prospective job seekers to submit, and then finally developed an online application system.

However, HUD's personnel division was sorely unqualified to do its own job. It took four to seven months to fill a vacant position.

Odd or Even?

The employees in the very broken, inefficient human resources division at HUD couldn't handle their workload, so they reduced it by conducting a sort of lottery by which they selected an odd or even number and then only processed the job applications with social security numbers that ended with the selected odd or even number. The others were simply not even opened or looked at. It was highly unfair to federal job applicants who applied for HUD jobs to not be given equal opportunity because their social security number was odd or even, depending on the lottery of that day. What other federal division was permitted to do only half its work, odd or even?

A False Application—a Federal Offense

Shannon had posted an open job position for a lender auditor over four months before to review the FHA loans files for newly originated mortgage loans, and to investigate the reason for increased delinquencies and growing foreclosures. The position required the candidates to have recent expert knowledge in all FHA handbooks, mortgagee letters, rules, and other guidance to determine if the selected lenders had abided by and applied all current rules.

She received the list of best candidates as determined by the HUD HR division, and noticed that a veteran was at the top of the list. She would not be able to look at any other candidates until she thoroughly considered the top vet. And if the top vet was not deemed acceptable, she would have to write a lengthy explanation as to why the vet was not acceptable in order to go down the list and look at other candidates. There was a serious push by the executive administration in the White House to place veterans into as many federal jobs as possible. She was reviewing the application and was quite impressed with the breadth of the applicant's experience, including writing the military base reuse plan and other financial documents. She had thought that that work was done primarily in Washington, DC. But as she continued to read the application, she began to notice that much of it appeared to be a cut-and-paste from her job announcement and that the supervisor contact information to verify the candidate's previous work history contained what appeared to be peer information, not supervisory information. Shannon had to either accept the top vet or have a good reason for not accepting the candidate. She knew that HR did not take the time to verify any of the information provided by the candidates, and she decided she would do it herself instead of asking her branch chiefs to do it to save time. She had been waiting over four months for the candidate roster, and was anxious to fill the position.

She turned to her telephone and called the first name and phone number under the 'Supervisor' heading, and reached a pleasant young man at a local military base.

"Hello, Martin Rotherberg here," he answered.

"Hello, Mr. Rotherberg, this is Shannon O'Toole, calling from the US Department of Housing and Urban Development in Santa Ana. How's your day going so far?" she asked pleasantly.

"Just fine, ma'am. What can I do for you?"

"I am looking at an application from one of your previous employees, and he listed you as his supervisor. I was hoping to verify his dates of employment and major duties and accomplishments."

"Yes, ma'am," he answered politely. "What's his name?"

"Kino Macman," Shannon answered.

There was a slight pause on the other end of the line. "Kino Macman?" he echoed.

"Yes, that's correct. He listed you as his supervisor with this number to call."

The young man on the phone hesitated, and then answered with a chuckle,

"Well, you see, I'm not his supervisor, Rich Holly is. I'm just a coworker, and sometimes I was a team leader in some of the projects we worked on."

Shannon's lips tightened. She didn't like untruths, and falsifying an application was high on her list.

"Can you tell me if Mr. Macman designed the military base reuse plan for your installation?"

Again, a chuckle. "No mam, he did not. But he was the typist."

Shannon bristled, and then went through the remainder of the accomplishments the candidate had listed and verified that none of them were accurate. She also procured the name and phone number of the candidate's actual supervisor, and had a similar conversation with him, further confirming that none of the experience or accomplishments on the application were valid, and in fact, were fictitious. Shannon called the next three supervisors on the application, and each turned out to be a friend or colleague, none supervisors. But the third call solidified Shannon's decision to report the application as fraud.

"So let me confirm with you, that you are not Mr. Macman's supervisor?"

"No, I certainly am not. He was the admin clerk here at the office. He supported all of us with arranging travel, ordering supplies, typing documents and reports. I'm a coworker. We all tried to help him and teach him more, you know, to help him advance."

"Can you please give me the name of his actual supervisor?" she asked.

"Sure, you can call Sheila Watts, our commander," and he gave Shannon the supervisor's phone number.

When Shannon finally had a chance to call the commander, it was a surprise when the commander said,

"We hope Mr. Macman finds a suitable job for himself. He always wanted to be promoted, but too often he was missing in action, that is, away from his desk for two or three hours. He always had an excuse, that his car broke when he was out to lunch, or he had a flat tire, or a medical appointment he forgot to report. He was warned about his use of unapproved leave on several occasions. That's when he left for his last job with another agency."

Shannon made a few notes in her file, thanked the commander for her help, and turned to her computer. She summarized her telephone conversations and findings, noting that the applicant had falsified the names and contact information for his supervisors, and had fabricated most of his work experience and accomplishments, as well as his job titles. She sent her memo back to HUD HR and requested a new list of applicants, hating to lose more time in filling the position but needing an honest and trustworthy new employee.

She was more than stunned when she received a phone call the next week from HR.

"Ms. O'Toole, this is HR calling, about the list of candidates and the memo you just sent back to us."

"Yes?" Shannon answered. "Do you have a new list of candidates for me?"

"Well, that is what I am calling you about. I would like to suggest that we send this application back to the candidate and ask him to correct it, you know, make changes that will be more reliable."

Shannon didn't answer immediately, she couldn't answer. She couldn't believe what she was hearing. "I don't think that is allowed," she finally said to the HR woman.

"Well, you see, we get audited on the number of veterans we place into open positions, and since this posting shows a qualified veteran as the top-ranking candidate, and he's also a minority. It would look bad for us to have to explain that he didn't get chosen for the job."

Shannon paused for a moment, trying to measure the HR woman's position of passing an audit over selecting an honest employee to go through lender loan files, and determine if she was really serious.

"Do you expect me to accept an employee who knowing and purposely falsified their federal application for employment? Do you expect me to put that person in a highly sensitive, highly confidential position that requires serious trust and handling of personal financial information?"

Apparently she did expect her to do just that, because she answered,

"Well, yes, I think we should give him another chance to clean up his application. We have goals to meet, about the number of veterans we place into jobs."

"No."

"What do you mean, no?"

"I mean just that, no. He falsified his application, and I won't accept him. I would like a new list of candidates. And if you won't verify their credentials, either I or my staff will."

"We don't have time to verify previous employment or talk to their supervisors."

"How many applications do you read, and review before you send out the best qualified candidates list?"

"Well, there are so many applications, you can't even imagine. So we read until we find three candidates for each job posting. First we look at the veteran applications, and then the public ones."

"And the rest of the applications?"

"Oh, we don't have to read those. We just have to put down their names on the applications received list so we can send back a 'sorry but you didn't make the Best Qualified, or BQ list'. But we don't have to rate or evaluate them because we already have enough qualified candidates."

"You mean three candidates?"

"Yes, that's right."

"I don't agree to return the falsified application to the candidate and consider him again for this position. I expect to receive a new, fully verified list of very qualified candidates for my division."

Shannon did receive a new list of qualified candidates, but it took another seven weeks.

Best Candidate–a Felon

Shannon had just received another roster of candidates selected and approved by the HUD Human Resources division. She had posted the job five months before and had been waiting for the HR group to process the applications and send her a list of candidates. She was reviewing the applications and saw that the top candidate ranked by HR had previously worked for HUD.

That should at least help with the initial orientation to federal, executive, and judicial rules that all government employees must work under and to the HUD policies and procedures that can take weeks, if not months, to learn, she was thinking, when her branch chief, Marc Spencer, came into her office. Marc was a smart, sharp young man with whom Shannon enjoyed working. He wore his curly hair long on his collar and worked out religiously to keep his body well toned. He had started his career with HUD earlier than Shannon and often offered intriguing historical perspectives into the origination of certain policies and processes. His computer skills were excellent, he knew the HUD/FHA loan origination and servicing policies inside and out, and he had a weakness for cupcakes, thus the regular workouts.

"Marc, I have a candidate here who HR has sent over as the 'Best Candidate' for our lender oversight and management position. It says here he has worked for HUD before, but it must have been before I started here. Is this person familiar to you?" And she handed him the application.

Marc's eyes widened, and he said, "Is this some kind of a joke?"

She didn't understand what was concerning him, and answered,

"Not that I know of. Why?"

"Oh, gee, nothing special, just that he was convicted by HUD and a criminal court for fraud and has been in prison for the last few years."

Shannon was stunned. "Maybe there's been a mistake."

"I hope so," Marc countered.

"What kind of fraud did he commit?" Shannon questioned her branch chief.

"It was for some kind of grant manipulation, something to do with selecting vendors for awards and pricing matters."

"Are you sure this is the same person?"

"Absolutely. And he even accepted gifts from some of the vendors, expensive gifts."

"Are you sure he's not a politician?"

Marc grinned. "Very funny. He had to go to trial, I think the Inspector General was involved with some of the investigation, and he landed behind bars for several years. Does his application say what he has been doing the last seven or so years?"

Shannon scanned the application and answered wearily, "No, in fact, his application just skips from his time at HUD to very recently, some contract/consultant work he says he's doing now. There's a big gap for about seven or eight years."

"Well, that answers the big mystery," Marc frowned.

"I will contact HR later, advise them of their error, and ask for a new roster. You know they will have to remove this name in order for us to look at anyone down further on the list."

"I think the HR rules suck," Marc growled.

"Ditto. I owe you a cupcake."

Shannon called the HR specialist assigned to her job posting and reached the HR woman after several tries. However, the HR woman was disinterested in Shannon's rendition of the felon-at-the-top-of-the list situation.

"He has the required experience," insisted the HR specialist.

"His experience is ten years old. All of the manuals and handbooks and rules have changed. But, more important, he has been convicted of a felony against HUD, and the job we are filling requires the highest degree of ethics and honesty while examining the internal documents of a lender."

"He's done with prison."

"He's not the best candidate," Shannon tried to rationalize with the obstinate HR woman. "I need someone with more current experience. Most of the FHA loan origination rules have changed and been modified in the last three years. Ten-year-old experience won't help me. And he's a felon."

"He can update his knowledge. His previous experience is strong, and he's served his time, his debt, in prison."

"Do you really think it is acceptable to bring a convicted felon into a high-security area? With social security numbers, credit reports, employment documentation, personal and business tax returns, and such? Do you really think that's wise?" Shannon was beginning to lose her patience with the stubborn woman.

"I don't think we can disqualify someone because they just came out of prison."

"Do you think it is wise to rate this person so highly with ten-year-old experience who doesn't know the current rules and regulations, and cheated on grants with HUD programs?"

"I can't change my rating, it's in the system now. He wrote a good application."

"Did you even notice the ten-year gap from when he last worked at HUD until just recently?" she tried to get the woman to see reason.

"No, I guess I missed that. But I saw the experience he had ten years ago was close to what you are looking for in your job description."

"No, it isn't!" Shannon said firmly, losing patience now. "The job description calls for *current* knowledge and experience with FHA lending practices, rules, and handbooks. The handbooks are all new, and several thousands of pages of rule making."

"Like I said, he can update his experience and learn the new...."

Shannon cut her off. "I want a new list of candidates. I am rejecting this list. How soon can I have a new list?"

"I have to have a good reason for issuing a new list."

Shannon was ready to hang up on the woman. "I need to talk to your supervisor."

"That won't help anything," the HR woman wined. "If you insist on a new list, I will look and see."

"Let's make this perfectly clear," Shannon said tersely. "A new list, with candidates with current and applicable experience, and *no felons* who have previously committed fraud against HUD."

The new list did not arrive in four weeks, and Shannon placed several calls to the stubborn HR woman, who did not return any of the calls. Shannon then called the woman's supervisor, also getting a voicemail instead of a live person, and left a summary of the problem and requested a new list of candidates.

Shannon never received a return call from the HR supervisor, but she did receive a new list of candidates in about seven weeks. She opened the interoffice envelope and pulled out the candidate list.

It still had the felon at the top! It had the same candidates as before, but in a different order. By then Shannon had had enough of the incapable HR woman assigned to this hiring effort. Instead of hiring one person from the list, Shannon had received funding to hire three. She called the HR woman and left a message, asking why she had not removed the felon from the top of the list as most qualified. The HR woman returned Shannon's call two days later,

"You are hiring three new employees now, instead of one, so you can take the best qualified from the list and choose two more."

"The felon you listed as best qualified isn't, don't you understand that?" Shannon said, fuming quietly.

"I told you, I put the scores into the system, and I can't change them."

"So because *you* made a mistake putting numbers into your scoring system, *I* am supposed to live with it?"

Shannon could see that this woman was being uncooperative, and she would have to appeal to a higher level manager to make any progress. The reputation of the human resources division was bad to grim, and she was certainly getting her turn with the grim. Her patience was just about spent, but, more than that, it was the lack of professionalism, consideration, or understanding by the stubborn HR woman, her unwillingness to understand she had made a mistake that needed to be corrected.

"I would like to take this up with your supervisor," Shannon advised the woman.

"Why do you want to do that?" the HR woman asked.

Shannon paused, could this woman really be so dense?

"Just put me through to your manager," Shannon instructed her. Of course, Shannon was put through to a voicemail, again.

It took five more weeks to get another list of acceptable candidates, but Shannon was finally able to make a selection of three excellent potential new employees with current knowledge and experience in FHA mortgage lending. However, she wrote a lengthy e-mail to the director of human resources, outlining the delays in filling the positions.

.... "It is a disservice to HUD to look at only a handful of applications, and when HR deems the candidates are qualified, they stop looking at additional applications that may be for even better qualified candidates. It is unethical and unfair to the candidates that they are at the mercy of HR as to what order in the pile they are tossed, and thus if not at the top, the likelihood of ever being reviewed or considered is moot. It took HR over eight months to send out an acceptable list of candidates in this hiring effort. Such an elongated timeframe is entirely inefficient and unacceptable. It is a disservice to HUD to not hire the most-qualified and capable staff because HR doesn't have the time or interest in reviewing all applications for open positions...."

The Office of the Inspector General had even recently audited the HUD human resources division and published its findings that it was inefficient and sorely needed immediate intervention and improvement in its systems, which was in part the cause for HUD contracting out their human resources/hiring process to the Treasury department in 2012, only to learn that the Treasury group handling the HUD job postings first looked only at the applications from veterans, since they had first priority now for federal jobs. And when the Treasury found three veterans who, according to the Treasury HR staff, qualified for the HUD job, they stopped looking at any further applications. None of the job applications from the public were ever looked at, reviewed, or considered unless the Treasury determined there were no veterans who qualified for the position. Shannon had argued that HUD program staff needed to see the applications since they were the program experts and knew the qualifications that would best be useful to accomplishing the program work. She had demonstrated that the veterans on the list produced by the Treasury were not always the best qualified and had significantly less experience than other applicants from the public, since several applicants had contacted her with their frustration in not even being considered for the jobs. There was many federal jobs that were good matches for the veterans; however, it was difficult to find many that had experience in bank audits, or that knew the contents in the six-inch government lending manuals.

HUD/REO $ | Sales Program

HUD continued to attempt to fulfill its stated presidential mission to provide housing for lower-income buyers; however, fraud, waste, and abuse in the mortgage industry persisted.

"Homes for the Needy Profit Others" was a news article written by William Heise in the *Los Angeles Times* on April 12, 2009:

> ... "HUD's $1 plan offers bargains for the poor. But in San Bernardino, California, builders and investors benefit, records show." The article cited an example:

> *"Jerry and Carol Ptacek bounced from one cramped apartment to another most of their adult lives, so they could hardly believe their luck when they were able to buy a San Bernardino (Southern California) house for the bargain price of $63,000. Both disabled, Mr. Ptacek with back injuries and Mrs. Ptacek with depression, they were getting by on Social Security checks totaling about $1600 a month.*

A real estate agent steered them to a two bedroom home in San Bernardino, priced at $63,000, with just $500 down payment. San Bernardino had acquired the house under the HUD Dollar Homes program and sold it for $2,000 to Schechtman Construction of Riverside, one of several companies that had applied with San Bernardino to buy and repair Dollar homes and other HUD owned properties...

"...The city required that these companies make repairs noted by the city inspector and that they sell the homes to low income families when they were finished. But San Bernardino did not screen the buyers to make sure they met any income requirements. Nor did HUD place any restrictions on the local governments after they bought the homes for $1. The Ptaceks moved into the home but it still needed substantial repairs. They say the home's electrical wiring was connected to one circuit breaker and that the plumbing leaked. The home's one bathroom didn't have a window; it had been covered up with stucco from the outside. 'It seemed like once we got through fixing one thing, we would have to turn around and fix something else,' Mr. Ptacek said. To cover the costs of repairs and other improvements, the Ptaceks said they refinanced their home several times with New Century Financial Corp, Ameriquest Mortgage Co, Washington Mutual Inc and Countrywide Financial Corp, all lenders which ultimately collapsed under the weight of the soured mortgage loans. By July 2006 they owed more than $220,000 on the home they had bought for $63,000. The Ptaceks acknowledged that they too made mistakes. One

was to get a negative amortization loan, which kept their monthly payments artificially low, but at the cost of adding to the principal they owned. They also gambled thousands of dollars from their home equity at Indian casinos, they acknowledge.

"Nine years later, they are renters again—a testament to the failure of the federal government's Dollar Homes program.

"Congress launched the program in 1998 to clear the Department of Housing and Urban Development's books of foreclosures and provide affordable housing. Local governments would buy the homes for $1, fix them up and resell them at a discount to poor families, who would get a chance to put down roots in the community.

"At least that's how it was supposed to work.

"A Times investigation has found that the Dollar Homes program has helped housing contractors and investors, but there is no evidence that it has provided any lasting benefit to people like the Ptaceks. **_The findings offer a cautionary tale as the Obama administration works to craft similar efforts to help communities ravaged by the housing slump._**

"This is bad for taxpayers on both sides of the transaction," said Dean Baker, co-director of the Center for Economic Policy Research in Washington. More than 2,300 homes have been sold by HUD for $1 each nationwide, with 326 in California. Nearly half of the homes in California were bought by companies or individuals who typically resold them at a much higher price. Only 15% were sold to nonprofit housing groups such as Habitat for Humanity, records show.

"The City of San Bernardino bought more Dollar Homes - 62 - than any other city of county in the state. But San Bernardino officials could not provide The Times with any account of what happened to the homes after they were sold. "They went back to the private market, and hopefully they were maintained and kept up," said Carey Jenkins, the housing director of San Bernardino's economic development agency, which oversees the city's Dollar Homes purchases. "And that was pretty much the end of our involvement." Using county property tax and assessor records, federal bankruptcy files and real estate listings, the Times tracked every property sale to San Bernardino under the program since 2000. Among the findings:

"At least 43 of the 62 homes were sold to housing contractors and investors. Within months after purchase, nearly all were resold, and for an average of three times the original sales price.

The homes continued to change hands frequently. Some homes have been bought and sold eight times in as many years, defeating the intent of the program to encourage buyers to put down roots and revive downtrodden neighborhoods. Instead of continuing to provide opportunities for low income buyers, these homes have become priced beyond their reach, shooting up more than 450% in value from 2000 to 2008. Moreover, there are no rules to ensure the homes remain affordable when they are resold."

Shannon knew from her earlier work at FDIC and RTC, that a simple deed restriction, called a LURA or land use restriction agreement, could have been developed and recorded against the title to the properties to preserve their intended afford-ability for future generations, making the program a success. Unfortunately, this was not done by HUD.

"Nearly half of the homes ended up with buyers who strug-gled with homeownership, missing property tax payments, defaulting on their loans, and in at least nine cases, falling into foreclosure.

The program goes unmonitored. Cities are by law re-quired to give HUD detailed accounts of who bought the homes and for how much. But in at least 31 cases, San Bernardino provided inaccurate information, incorrectly listing either the buyer or the sales price.

"HUD officials said that because the Dollar Homes pro-gram was mandated by Congress, it does not receive the same type of attention and follow up as programs created by HUD itself.

A few blocks from the Ptaceks' house, a Dollar Homes residence that was sold by the city for $27,000 to an investor was resold several times before being sold for $355,000 less than six years later.

"Housing advocates such as the Rev. David Kalke, ex-ecutive director for the Central City Lutheran Mission in San Bernardino thinks cities could better serve poor people if they used the homes for subsidized housing and tapped nonprofits for the rehabilitation work. The mission bought two of the Dollar homes for $2,000 in 2001 and turned them into low income rental housing for homeless people with HIV. Turns out that only three of the Dollar Homes were sold to nonprofits in San Bernardino. "Sometimes the

government doesn't do things very brightly, and the people who are supposed to be helped end up being hurt'," Kalke said."

FHA Loans—Seller-Funded Down Payment and Alternative Credit Programs

The default and claim rates on FHA seller-funded down payment loans continued to increase. In 2007, the defaults from seller-funded down payment loans were around 30 percent, and finally HUD Headquarters in Washington, DC determined that the down payment assistance program presented an intolerable risk to the decreasing FHA insurance fund. HUD issued notice via the Federal Register that the nonprofit seller-funded down payment assistance program would be discontinued.

But the nonprofits recognized that if this were to occur, their income stream of hundreds and millions of dollars would be cut off, and they resisted.

HUD tried to stop the program on several occasions, but each time the nonprofits resisted, again due to the great source of revenue this FHA program provided to them, at one point suing HUD for improper notice of the program's pending discontinuance. They filed injunctions blocking the termination of the seller-funded down payment program and challenged HUD's statistical data for loan losses.

The IRS joined in the action, issuing a statement that certain nonprofits were not truly nonprofits, but they were, in fact, earning a profit and owed taxes on these profits.

After much debate, discussion, and legal posturing back and forth, HUD reissued their notice of intent to discontinue with the seller-funded down payments, and restated statistical support for the unacceptable losses. The program ended. But only after the FHA insurance fund had suffered significant losses due to the ultimate 30 percent failure of all seller-funded down payment program transactions.

Shannon felt it was unfortunate that it had taken so long for headquarters to finally take the much-needed action to terminate the program and mounting losses. However, she understood the political pressure they had been dealing with and was relieved to see that it was finally over.

However, she questioned why a public agency, or entity, or insurance company, which is what FHA is, couldn't simply discontinue a program that causes significant losses?

The answer was, that the decision to discontinue a program that causes significant losses was a business decision, but the decision to continue and allow a program that causes significant losses was a Political one, paid for by the taxpayers.

The alternative credit program was allowed to continue, however. If borrowers applying for an FHA loan did not have a FICO credit score or other customary credit sources, they were allowed, under the alternative credit program, to provide utility bills, cell phone bills, or other sources of credit demonstrating that they paid these bills timely. Often these buyers did not provide bank statements because they said they paid their bills on a cash basis only. Pressure had been applied on FHA by the Presidential administration to develop a program to bring more first-time homebuyers into the FHA program, many of whom had not built up their credit yet but wanted to buy a house.

Federal Employee Unions–Unreasonable Accommodations

Shannon was called back to Washington, DC for another management forum. She groaned to herself, another week of long meetings and getting up at 3:00 a.m. Pacific Coast time to get to the East Coast meetings in the morning, with little sleep, not her favorite situation. She still couldn't drink coffee or Coke because the caffeine made her heart beat too fast, also not her favorite condition. However, she always made an exception for chocolate.

Shannon made her way through the HUD HQ building security stations on four hours' sleep and began to focus clearly enough to recognize the many faces of HQ colleagues and friends, saying sleepy hellos and "how are yous." Brenda McCune and Saquil Negil, two friends in HQ, fell into step with Shannon.

"Have you seen the agenda?" Brenda asked Shannon. Brenda was one of the brightest young women on the Assistant Secretary's staff, a pretty brunette with green eyes. Shannon envied her tall, slender, five-foot-eight stature.

"No. As usual, the agenda was finalized while I was in the air flying here, and I didn't pull it up this morning yet. It's a little hard to prepare for these meetings if you can't see the agenda before you get here. Anything interesting?"

"You might say that," said a chuckling Saquil, a strikingly handsome, tall young man with olive skin and curly brown hair.

"Want to give me a hint?" Shannon smiled.

"It's billed as 'Managing the Federal Budget,'" Brenda provided while shaking her pretty head.

"But that's code," Saquil said as he tossed a casual wave at a passing acquaintance.

"OK, I'll bite." Shannon perked up. "Code for what?"

"Oh, you're gonna love this," Brenda sighed.

"OK, I'm ready…" Shannon prompted with questioning look.

"It's really about all the federal labor union activity the agency has been experiencing lately. There are so many unfair labor practices and grievances going around that the Secretary and Assistant Secretary have brought us all here to discuss the effect it is having," Brenda said, filling her in.

"Is there really that much union activity that makes it necessary to pull us all back here to discuss it?" Shannon questioned as they continued walking toward the auditorium on the first floor, where the meeting would take place.

"Evidently, and we are about to learn more," Brenda answered.

"We have had an increased amount of grievances and unfair labor practices here in Washington, DC. Now the unions have been knocking on the Assistant Secretary's door constantly for the last couple of months to complain about operations in the field. Haven't you had any union grievances in your office?" Saquil queried Shannon.

Shannon thought a moment and shook her blond head. "Just some disagreements about cubicle space."

"Like what?" Brenda asked.

"Oh, some staff have asked their managers if they can move their work station to another floor in the office. Management has explained that the staff needs to stay in their department and teams since they share the case files and information, and to process the work product to maintain the work flow."

"I hear there have been some pretty serious discussions going on between the Secretary's office and the unions because of the President Obama memo," Saquil offered, lowering his voice.

They stopped just before they entered the auditorium as other managers meandered around them to get their coffee from the coffee station just outside the double doors.

"We just saw the memo," Brenda said quietly as she opened her tote bag and extracted a folder. "It looks like Obama is changing the rules so he can assure the union vote for his administration," and she handed the presidential executive memo to Shannon. "It says something like... 'Management will consult with the Union on any matters pertaining to staffing, assignments, changes, realignments, really just about anything, Pre-decisionally, which I think means before management takes any definitive actions or puts any new plans into effect. It sounds like the President wants to ensure the Unions' votes...'"

Before Shannon could respond to Brenda and Saquil, through the open double doors they saw the Assistant Secretary enter the meeting room and call out a general greeting to the managers to begin the conference.

"We had better take our seats," Saquil said, and he ushered Shannon and Brenda into the conference room. He spied three empty seats with conference folders on the chairs and directed his colleagues to the partially empty row. Shannon entered first, followed by Brenda and Saquil. A fiftysomething black man with white hair, Corey Anderson, nodded and smiled to Shannon as she sat down to his right. Shannon had known

Corey for over twelve years and knew him to be one of the best division managers in headquarters, often making intelligent and applicable recommendations for program and legislative improvements. She respected him for his straightforward but well-mannered and professional way of addressing difficult situations including public protests and media challenges regarding program deliveries.

"This is going to be very interesting," he whispered to Shannon.

The Assistant Secretary asked everyone to be seated and began his comments.

"I would like to thank you each for coming into Headquarters today, some of you look like you could use a little more sleep," and there was a tittering of soft laughter throughout the conference room. "But, I assure you that what we are about to discuss will wake you up!"

The assistant secretary was a pleasant person, of average height and a little rotund, but it was well disguised in his dark suit and starchy ivory shirt and tie. His black wavy hair was thinning. He crossed over to the speaker's podium and cued a power-point operator, who flashed an opening remarks slide on the large screen above the podium.

"Our jobs as leaders and managers are integral to the successful operation of HUD and in meeting the goals we set out each year, as well as to Congress, when we submit our performance metrics and our budget requests," he began. "Congress expects us to meet our mission of assisting low income and first time homebuyers with our FHA single family programs and providing safe, sanitary, and affordable rental housing, as well as providing financing for other apartment, Section 8, Public, Senior and Hospital projects."

"I think that covers just about everyone in the room," Corey leaned over and whispered.

"He forgot PIH, the American Indian program," Shannon teased.

"Oh, yeah, maybe he'll talk about that next."

The Assistant Secretary continued,

"I am confident that we have a fine management team on board, with extensive experience and skills as well as with the highest ideals and standards that are setting HUD apart as a sensitive as well as successful agency." He paused. "However, we are still near the bottom of the best federal agencies to work for on the employee satisfaction survey poll conducted last quarter. In fact, HUD came in about third from the bottom out of fifty agencies."

"Well, the compliments and accolades didn't last long," Corey whispered to Shannon.

There was a little quiet rumbling in the audience. The assistant secretary held up his hand. "Now, I already know that you will say that the employees who entered negative responses were encouraged to do so by their respective local unions, and that may be true. However, as leaders and managers, we will be discussing what we can do as leaders to change the misconception that HUD is not an employee-friendly agency." He queued up the next slide.

"Recent labor negotiations," he continued. "On this slide, you can see the more recent policy agreements HUD HQ has entered into with the various federal labor unions across the nation."

The low rumbling of managers' voices grew louder. "I see you have some thoughts and questions about our recent negotiations," he responded to the managers. "Headquarters staff has spent the better part of the last several months negotiating with the several labor unions and we have proposed the items on this slide as compromises. We think they will significantly improve our standing in the employee satisfaction survey. And I personally have had personal contact with all of the union's' leadership, because they camped outside my door so I couldn't come or go without talking with them." If this was his attempt at humor, it fell flat, and he seemed to turn red in embarrassment. "What I meant was, the unions have contacted me continuously for the last several months with phone calls, constant emails, memos and face-to-face meetings. They have approached the Secretary of HUD and have reached out to several Congressmen in their endeavors to negotiate certain employee rights and to modify the labor management contract agreement."

A male voice came from the back of the room,

"Why weren't we brought in sooner to discuss these negotiations? Why hasn't management been involved before now in these negotiations and issues for our input?" The volume of displeased voices increased throughout the room.

"There is a team," the Assistant Secretary started to explain uncomfortably, "a team made up from human resources, our internal labor management staff here in Headquarters…"

"But no one from the actual field offices, Program offices or management that will be required to implement these policy changes and deal with the impacts they will have on our operations," the voice in the back of the room continued.

"Let's try and focus on the items on this slide. It's clear you want to have some discussions on these matters," and the Assistant Secretary awkwardly stepped a few feet from the podium and indicated he would take comments from the floor.

A small woman with gray hair raised her hand, and the assistant secretary acknowledged her to speak.

"Mr. Assistant Secretary, with all due respect, I have been a manager here at HUD for nearly thirty years, and I have never seen the policies regarding employee requests and union demands as aggressive as they are now."

"Can you be more specific?" the Assistant Secretary queried with a frown.

"I will begin with the very liberal telework policy we now have," she offered. "In private practice and the conventional world, telework is very prevalent for higher-ranked and salaried employees, usually not administrative staff. However, in the conventional world, employees are generally paid on commission, and if they don't work, they don't get paid. Their administrative staff do not telework as a rule; they are needed in the office to answer phones, route the mail, respond to e-mails, greet customers and clients, and generally process the paperwork of that business. However, in the world of government, much of the work is administrative, and all staff is paid on salary, so there is no correlation of work production to pay."

"Well, you know HUD is looking at ways to save budget money, and teleworking is a way to reduce office space and rent," the assistant secretary countered.

"Saving on office space but needing to hire more staff because the work isn't being done sufficiently while teleworking will not save the agency money." She stopped, while the managers in the conference room spoke among themselves.

She then continued, "When we receive a congressional inquiry or request for information from HQ, we can't reach the teleworking staff for the data. The new labor management agreement even says a supervisor cannot IM, instant message, a teleworking staff for a quick answer. Because that is considered harassment by the unions. So as managers, we have to wait until that employee returns to the office or returns an e-mail several hours later. We hear children in the background when we do call and reach the teleworking employee because they are babysitting. There was an employee that even brought the children she was babysitting to an office meeting because she was babysitting that day! This employee even bragged how she was making great money babysitting while teleworking full time as an administrative person. Teleworking is taking its toll on field operations and I would have to imagine here in Headquarters too."

Another arm shot up, and a gray-haired gentleman in a blue shirt and tie stood up.

"In my office, I had an employee go to the union with a grievance because I wouldn't approve full-time telework for her to stay home to make sure her eighteen-year-old son, a senior in high school, took antibiotic medication after an illness. Needless to say, her work production for those several weeks was not acceptable; however, the union grieved that management was treating her differently in demanding her work assignments be documented. I offered her liberal sick leave or annual leave to go to his school or home when it was time to ensure he took his medication; however, the union again raised a grievance."

A woman near the front of the room stood up.

"I have a staff person who alleged they had hurt their back and couldn't sit. I offered a stand-sit desk, but they refused and said they needed full-time telework to stay home. I declined and offered to approve sick leave, so the employee went to the union and filed a grievance against me. This employee stayed home for three weeks and did not perform any work. When the employee returned to the office and the supervisor asked for the completed file work, the employee laughed and said they were on so much medication and painkillers they couldn't work at all. But the employee took their full salary and did not use sick time. When I contacted our HR people to start disciplinary action, HR said we couldn't. Three weeks wasn't enough time, or there wasn't enough documentation; there had been no previous warnings, and the union would prevail in any action we attempted to take. We, the government, paid them to stay home, and this is happening in all of our field offices."

The rumbling in the room increased, and the Assistant Secretary stepped forward to the podium. He was clearly uncomfortable with the reaction in the room, and he looked at the front row.

"Let me have the labor relations chief come up here to address your questions and concerns," and he motioned to a middle aged man to come up to the podium. "Craig, maybe you can talk more about these negotiations," the weary Assistant Secretary said.

As Craig stepped up to the podium, another manager stood up in the conference room, looked back at the woman who had just spoken, and reported,

"I sympathize with you regarding your employee who stayed home three weeks on telework and didn't produce any work product, but I have an employee who was in an accident and requested advanced leave for two months. This employee had been with HUD for about six months, and had not earned much sick leave because he used it as soon as it was accrued. He also asked for full-time telework for two months, which I declined. The union took his request to HQ reasonable accommodation, which did an override on my decision and approved the employee's two-month full-time telework from home. This employee also did not complete any work product. His excuses included computer problems and changing program rules he had to read up on. Basically, when I wrote him up for poor performance, the union charged me with a hostile work environment action. This employee stayed home for two months, did no work, did not complete any work assignments, took his full taxpayer-paid salary, and now is suing me and the agency because we expect him to do his work assignments."

Additional hands flew up in the air, and the labor relations chief raised his hands in defense. "Whoa, now, let's just slow down this train. I'm just hearing about those examples for the first time."

"That's because you haven't spoken with the program and field managers," more than one member of the audience responded.

A tall, slim, female manager near the front stood up and took aim squarely at the assistant secretary and labor relations chief,

"I have a *supervisor* who was out five months on full-pay, full-time telework supposedly working on a complicated technical evaluation panel, or TEP as we call them for short, reading over proposals from contractors. This *supervisor* decided to have a full face lift while she was teleworking from home," a general gasp came from the room of managers and supervisors. "The supervisor did not take any sick time or annual leave for the facelift, and I'm sure there were several pre- and postsurgery doctor's appoints in addition to the several days for the actual surgery and recuperation. You see, gentlemen, the union-sponsored and

HQ-supported telework and reasonable accommodation are being abused, and HQ has issued direction to HR to not challenge the union when we find abuses. We are getting no support from HQ when we try to take disciplinary actions, and the abuses are only accelerating. The money being wasted is staggering." The room full of managers began to rumble again.

The labor relations chief walked over to the assistant secretary, and they held a brief conversation away from the microphones and managers. The labor relations chief then turned back to the audience and said,

"We have several additional items to cover on the agenda today now. We could break into committees or concurrent sessions after lunch to address each of the power-point items and then report back tomorrow morning. Supervisors, we will assign you to a committee, and, managers, you can roam from one concurrent committee to the next this afternoon."

Unreasonable Accommodations

After lunch, Shannon and Corey walked toward the makeshift concurrent session for reasonable accommodations.

"HUD's reasonable accommodation program seems to be evolving," Shannon began. "I know that all reasonable accommodation requests are handled by Headquarters."

"I know a little about the law surrounding the program," Corey answered. "The purpose is to allow genuinely eligible employees the opportunity to work around a disability to enable them to continue with their work."

"And how is the genuinely eligible status determined?" Shannon asked.

"A medical doctor is supposed to write up the employees' medical condition that makes it impossible or very difficult for them to perform their work duties. The doctor can make recommendations that would assist his patient, our employee. Or the employee can request certain accommodations that would make it possible to complete their work assignments. Then the reasonable accommodation staff determines if the work could still be performed with certain modifications to the work environment or work schedule."

"OK, that all sounds reasonable," Shannon agreed.

"Yes, except what I understand is happening now is that the unions are going to the reasonable accommodation, or RA, staff in HQ and inserting their opinions and recommendations for an employee's reasonable accommodations, but the HUD managers are not contacted by the RA staff for their input, so the reasonable accommodation actions have been very one sided."

"So that's what you expect we are going to hear in this first committee breakout session?"

"I do," Corey said as they came around a corner and entered a door with a "Breakout Session—Reasonable Accommodation" sign on the door. Corey and Shannon stepped in quietly and took seats behind a row of supervisors facing each other.

"So, in my office, employees are told by the union to not submit their reasonable accommodation requests to their supervisors, including me, but to send it in directly to the HQ reasonable accommodation division," a supervisor was explaining to his committee. "I don't even know there is a pending request until the employee or the union comes and tells me his request was approved or, very occasionally, the RA staff sends me an e-mail saying they've made a decision in favor of the employee. I don't have any input, can't provide alternatives of my own, or have anything to say about the change in the employee's duties and work. When I disagree with the RA request or remedy, I am overruled by the HQ RA staff. I have to balance the workload for my department, the assignments and schedules, but I don't know that an employee is asking for changes until it's done."

A second supervisor spoke up. "In my office, I denied advanced sick time for an employee, and I denied full-time telework for three months when the employee was going to have a medical procedure. The employee had used up all accrued annual and sick leave, and it would have taken two years to earn back and pay back the advanced leave that was being requested. As a responsible manager, how could I approve that kind of advanced leave for an employee who constantly used their leave as soon as it was accrued? It was unlikely that I would see the advanced leave paid back to the agency. So the union had the employee file a hostile work environment against me and file for reasonable accommodation to work from home for three months. And although the doctor's note said nothing about not lifting files, the union added that language. I don't know of anything in the labor management agreement that allows the union to change a doctor's orders, but they are doing it to get additional benefits for the employees."

A third female supervisor added then, "I don't mean to make light of the seriousness of this reasonable accommodation process, but I had a female employee who was 'too hot' all the time. This employee's supervisor was working with her on improving her performance. Now keep in mind that she wore a sweater or jacket over her blouse all the time; she could have dressed cooler or removed layers like the rest of the staff does. She requested moving several times across the office, where she also could be away from her supervisor, who was also working with her on time and attendance, disruptive talking and visiting with other staff, wandering away from her work station, and lack of productivity But her supervisor had counseled her for constantly talking and roaming around the building, so she went to the union and told them she had a medical condition that required her to sit in a cooler area. The union filed a reasonable accommodation with HQ to allow the woman to move across the office, in the farthest corner away from her supervisor and team, with whom she shared files, because that was the coolest spot on the floor. She was moved two other times, but the other closer cubicles were not cool enough; additional close cubicles were offered by her supervisor, but the employee and the union rejected each one and even called the assistant secretary to complain that management wasn't cooperating with the reasonable accommodation request. But to top it off, there was a recommendation to provide this employee with a new twelve-hundred-dollar chair that the union demanded that would blow cold air up the employee's...well, ...bottom, if you follow me."

Shannon's eyebrows raised, and she couldn't quite believe what she was hearing. "And did the request for the chair get approved?" Shannon had to know.

The female supervisor chuckled and said, "No, one of the supervisors had considered it because he had spoken with the reasonable accommodation people in HQ and they said it would be a good way to resolve the union complaints. But we use the *Washington Post* test. If a headline should be posted saying, 'HUD employees given $1,200 chairs to blow cold air...' well, you get the idea. No, the request was not approved, and even though the union stalked the Assistant Secretary to report to him that field management was not cooperating with the union, we did not approve the chair."

"Well, that's a relief." Corey smiled.

"My office has one of the longest-running reasonable accommodation cases," a tanned, young, male supervisor offered. "It went on for over four years. I hired a new employee and paired him up with Al, let's call him, to take the new employee around and introduce him and take him into the field to train him. So Al took my new employee to a shopping mall his first week. The new employee asked why they were going to the mall, and Al told him, 'This is what we do. We go out in the field, stay away from the office, stay out of your supervisors' line of vision, and avoid all new work assignments. If we are asked for reports, we say we are working on them.'"

"Why didn't Al's supervisor counsel him and put him on a performance improvement plan?" Shannon asked immediately.

"Because the guy just kept moving from one department to the next, from one supervisor to the next. It's partially HUD's fault because no one wanted to document all the hours Al wasted and his poor performance. Al always went to the union to protect him when a supervisor started to take corrective action."

"And he's still with HUD?" Corey asked.

"Well, no, actually he's retired now. One of the field managers finally caught on to him and directed Al's immediate supervisor to take corrective performance action. But then human resources and legal got involved and actually engaged in all sorts of crazy and ongoing protracted union defense activity for Al. Human resources told the supervisor that Al was complaining through his union representative that he had never been trained properly for the job he was now assigned to do. Keep in mind the guy had been working for HUD for twenty-seven years."

"And he didn't know how to do his job?" Shannon's eyebrows raised in disbelief.

"It was just a ploy." The tan supervisor shook his head. "Al said that the handbook rules had changed and he needed time to learn how to implement the changes."

"Did other staff doing the same work as Al have delays or trouble implementing the new handbook changes?" Shannon asked skeptically. She was beginning to see a very broken-down system for dealing with nonperforming staff.

"Believe it or not, it took over a year to get Al retrained to do his job, and then he filed a reasonable accommodation claim saying that his doctor wouldn't let him leave the house due to his heart condition and that he needed to telework full time."

"But his job entailed doing field inspections, correct?" Shannon guessed.

"Yes, and when Al's supervisor would call him or e-mail him to inquire about report progress, Al wouldn't respond for days. And then the union complained the supervisor was harassing Al with too many communication attempts. And don't forget management is not allowed to instant message staff."

"So you couldn't communicate with Al about his lack of performance?" Corey frowned.

"Yep, then Al asked for HUD to provide him transportation to do his inspections, because he said he couldn't drive anymore. He wanted a driver. We had to work with our legal department and human resources on this, and finally management declined."

"And all this while Al was receiving his full salary?" Corey leaned forward and asked.

"Yes again. But finally, after two years of this, Al filed another reasonable accommodation, and this one was misplaced by the reasonable accommodation staff in Washington, DC, and the RA employee handling Al's case went on RA medical leave himself, so Al's case sat for over a year. The supervisor called the RA management, but nothing was done. Finally, the RA employee returned from a very long medical leave, the file was transferred, and we learned that Al had filed yet another RA *and* a hostile work environment claim against his supervisor."

"I can hardly wait," Shannon said incredulously. "What was the new reasonable accommodation for, and what happened next?"

The tan young supervisor couldn't wipe the ironic grin off his face. "Well, you see, this time the new reasonable accommodation was for him to go naked, not wear clothes, because he claimed he was a nudist and it was against his civil rights to compel and force him to wear clothes to do his work. And that a reasonable accommodation was due him to not wear clothes, but then he couldn't do his field work or go into the HUD office naked. And his hostile work environment was also based upon his claim that he was a nudist and was being treated in a hostile manner with his supervisor demanding him to and making him wear clothes to do his field work."

Shannon looked over at Corey, who was trying very hard to hold back a laugh. "This is for real?" she asked.

"You can't make stuff this good up," the young supervisor chuckled.

Shannon interrupted, "How many of these reasonable accommodations have been approved versus disapproved?" she asked.

"As far as I know, the HQ RA staff approves all reasonable accommodations they receive," the first supervisor answered, and the other ten supervisors in the room concurred.

Corey looked over at Shannon and addressed the room. "Does it seem that the RA process is being used to circumvent supervisors' and managers' decisions for advanced sick leave and telework denials?"

"You have that right!" the supervisors answered nearly in unison.

Corey and Shannon stood up to leave the reasonable accommodation concurrent session and asked, "Who will be your foreman, your spokesperson tomorrow for this session?"

A supervisor obviously from one of HUD's Southern offices answered, "Ah will be th' spokesperson for this here group."

Shannon smiled, and Corey chuckled. "All right, y'all, keep up the good work. And if you can get some solid figures from the reasonable accommodation division here in HQ regarding how many requests they approve or deny, that would be very useful."

Disciplinary Actions/Advanced Leave

BREAK OUT SESSION – Disciplinary Actions/ Advanced Leave

Shannon and Corey entered the next breakout session and stepped into a very spirited discussion on disciplinary actions, gone awry. A pretty black supervisor stood up and stretched her arms over her head, while the others were dictating to a supervisor writing notes on paper taped to the wall. All of them had an open bottle of water in front of them, and several had empty coffee cups. Shannon and Corey sat down in the back of the room again, observing and listening to the passionate discussions.

"So, how shall we present this extended leave situation?" the writer was asking the group.

"We have to make it clear that the employee left for a long holiday weekend and was gone four months; he never came back to work—that is, did not return to his office," a Hispanic male supervisor was saying.

"*How long* was he away from his office?" asked a surprised fortysomething female supervisor.

"About four months. But he kept calling in and e-mailing and asked to have his work sent to him about halfway across the nation."

"Excuse me," a gray-haired male supervisor said. "They stayed away from their duty station for four months? Did they have approved leave of some sort?"

"Yes and no," the Hispanic supervisor answered. "This is one of those situations where the employee had used up just about any annual or sick leave they had accrued and had been counseled for leave abuse, so there was very little available. The employee consistently called in with headaches, backaches, sore throats, and so on and missed work assignment deadlines. So when this employee's parent had a sudden medical issue, he felt he needed to stay and take care of them. So he demanded that his work be sent to his parents' house."

"Was this employee's work transportable?" the writer asked.

"Actually, what makes this case really complicated is that the employee's work up until the time he left on vacation was poor, but his supervisor had not sufficiently documented his poor performance, according to HR, and HR refused to take any disciplinary action, and he was just passed on to my office and left out there halfway across the nation. He had not been trained on any of our work product or procedures; in fact, he had never stepped a foot in my office."

"But he expected that you should just send him work to do for those four months?" the forty something supervisor inquired.

"Exactly."

"Did the employee request advanced sick leave?"

"Actually, yes; however, the supervisor did not approve it. The employee had used just about every hour he accrued immediately, and the likelihood of him not taking any leave for the next two and a half years in order to pay back the advance request was very, very slim; thus it was denied. And then he went to the labor union, who filed reasonable accommodation requests for him and more advanced sick leave requests for him, and it got really interesting. The labor union told him he had a right to have his work sent to him and began sending really aggressive and threatening e-mails to our supervisors, copying HQ managers. The next thing I knew I was getting calls from the assistant secretary asking me why I wasn't cooperating with the union."

The room full of supervisors erupted in conversation, and Shannon and Corey looked at each other.

"Seriously?" Shannon turned to Corey.

"Just leave on vacation and then file reasonable accommodation requests for four months through the union for work you've never been trained to do? Taking leave without pay might be acceptable…"

"Well, I feel sorry for anyone who needs to take care of their parents or their children, but..."

"Sure, we all do, and overall, I think HUD policies are pretty good about family leave. But HUD can't be paying salaries to employees who just take off and don't show up for work."

The Hispanic supervisor was looking through some notes and looked up at the group in front of him,

"So we wrote up this employee for disciplinary action, and the union immediately filed hostile work environment actions and an EEO action. The union went to HQ, so the assistant secretary called, and other top brass were involved. The amount of time and effort, not to mention the salary dollars of all the supervisors, managers, HR, RA, and attorneys in discussing this issue, is exorbitant."

"What was the outcome?" a supervisor asked.

"The employee eventually came back to work at his office after he was given an intent to terminate letter, and then asked for official time to work on his hostile work environment and EEO cases against management, which we are compelled to give him and pay his salary while he works on them."

"And HR affirmed the employee's time for working on complaints against management?"

"Yes. And the legal department confirmed it too. And in one of the employee's actions against management, he is demanding back pay for all the leave without pay he said he was forced to take."

Shannon asked from the back of the room,

"Was this a mid-grade 9,11 or 12 employee?"

"No, it was a grade 15, making over $150,000 a year."

"A manager?" she asked incredulously.

"No, just a senior employee who was hired with a high grade in HQ and then was immediately sent out to the field when he filed for a reasonable accommodation to move."

Before Corey or Shannon could ask another question, the pretty black supervisor said,

"I have an interesting case regarding disciplinary action," and the writer stepped back and taped a new piece of paper to the wall.

"OK, let's have it," he said.

"Well, in this case, I was a new supervisor and made a trip out of state to meet with one of my employees. I had been reviewing all the work files for my staff and noticed that his performance was less than any of my other field monitors and had particularly slowed down the past year. In fact, he was the lowest-producing person on my staff. He had also used his leave as soon as it was accrued and had been caught not at work when his previous supervisor called, but he hadn't put in any leave slip requests. He usually said he had left early or come in late and just forgotten to put in a leave slip. So I read his last five reports, and they were primarily 'no findings' letters, that is, he didn't note or document any violations in the program executions he was examining. Most findings letters are twelve to thirty pages long; his were three."

"OK, so how do you want to say that on here..."

"Let's start with documented lack of performance. Then No Findings."

"All right, I got it."

"So I went to visit him, he picked me up at the airport and drove me around to see the sites and then to the nearby mountains, which I thought was a little odd. But he was just proud to show me his newly remodeled lakefront house. And it was very nice. So he proceeded to tell me how he had done most of the work himself, and that it was very time consuming to do the updating and repair work by himself. He told me he had become obsessed with the rehabilitation project for his house. He said he would spend hours at several other local jobsites to see how they were handling certain repairs and talked to the construction crews and learned new techniques and tips from watching them. So I asked, 'How long did it take you to do all this rehabilitation work?' And he said nearly a year. So I asked him about his No Findings letters, and he pretty much stopped talking.

"It became apparent that he had met contractors, obtained bids, shopped for materials, gone to the city regarding permits, et cetera all during his work time. His Performance reviews had noted delayed assignments, wasted time, missed deadlines, missed extended deadlines, missing documentation, weak or unsupported reports, et cetera, and a series of e-mails were in his file about late assignments and being behind on his scheduled work. He had used all of his sick time and annual vacation time, and requested advanced leave, which was declined. When disciplinary action started, he went to the union, who called the HQ deputy secretary and requested a transfer to another division rather than to face disciplinary action."

"Ah, I'm beginning to see a correlation," the writer said as he made notes on the hanging sheet of paper.

"That's right."

"And where does the disciplinary part come in?" The writer paused.

"I came back and scheduled an appointment with HR."

"Oh, no," groaned the Hispanic supervisor.

"Oh, yes," she smiled sardonically. "And they said there wasn't enough documentation to take any suspension action, and that taking disciplinary action now for his poor performance during the entire year would be excessive and untimely. So as I was talking to him about his poor performance and outlining a performance improvement plan, I received a strange e-mail from HQ. It seems that this employee had jumped right over me and my manager and said he was being treated unfairly, he was alleging a hostile work environment, and he requested a transfer to another division, which HQ was informing me had been granted."

"So this guy got away with not working for a year and then gets transferred when he is found out?"

"That's right. I had some documentation to prove he was working on his house while falsifying his time reports, but HR and the legal department didn't want to take that disciplinary route. And in the end, he just got himself transferred and passed on to another supervisory to start over with him. There was never any consequence or remedy, he was just passed on to another division. And he still enjoys the house that he rebuilt on the federal government's time and salary."

"You know, I had an employee that I finally had suspended for ten days, but it took me over a year to do it," a young male supervisor shared with the group.

"Just a minute," the writer said, and he grabbed another sheet of paper, taped it to the wall, and began writing.

"Why did it take so long?"

"I had to work with HR and legal first, and it took them over six months to draft the letter I sent to the employee advising of the suspension. The union got involved, and that made the process longer. Then the employee had four weeks to appeal, or ask for an extension, which they did. That all had to go back through HR and legal, and then we had to respond."

The writer made abbreviated notes on the sheet and asked, "Does this timeline look right?"

"Yes. And then there's a process of considering the Weingarten points."

"What's that?" the writer asked, as he wrote "Weingarten" on the hanging paper.

"It's a required process where the supervisor has to look at the seriousness of the misconduct or performance issues and determine that the correlating amount of suspension time or other actions is warranted."

Corey looked over at Shannon. "Are you familiar with Weingarten?" he whispered.

"I am familiar with it," she whispered back.

"I've had to apply it a few times," Corey said, returning her whisper.

"So where does that fit into the timeline?" the writer asked.

"We look at it early on in order to write the Notice letter to the employee. And the attorneys and HR want to make sure we had sufficient documentation to support the disciplinary action we are taking."

The supervisors in the room continued with their discussions of their experiences with HUD disciplinary actions. As Shannon and Corey stood up to leave the session, the young black supervisor was saying,

"In our office, if a supervisor doesn't approve every employee request for advanced sick or annual leave, the union files a grievance and an EEO against that supervisor and sometimes his or her manger. Even though all the legal contracts between the labor unions and HUD say that advanced leave is only approved if there is a likelihood that the advanced leave will be repaid to HUD before the employee retires or leaves HUD, we know what is going to happen every time we decline a request."

Legal Actions

As they left the room, Corey signaled Shannon. "I would like to stop by the attorneys' session if you don't mind," he said as they proceeded down the hallway and saw the "Breakout Session—Legal Actions" sign on a door.

"Sure. We should learn something in this one too," Shannon agreed.

As they entered the ongoing session of attorneys and other managers, a colleague from HUD's northern office was just exclaiming, "You mean that HUD has been paying EEO claims up until now?"

Marcus, a new thirtysomething-year-old attorney from Headquarters who Shannon had met in previous management meetings, was answering,

"Yes, in the past, I said. In every lawsuit, legal staff prepares an opinion of merit, describing the case elements, the case law, and the percentage chance of winning or losing. Even if it seems like a winning case, the attorney has to include the cost of legal procedures, including interrogatories, depositions, discovery, court costs, office staff costs, travel, et cetera to see if it offsets the amount of the claim or exceeds it. HUD HQ has determined in most matters that it is cheaper to just pay a nominal claim or negotiate to a nominal amount to settle a claim rather than to litigate it."

"I think I'm afraid to ask, but what is considered nominal?" a manager from the northern region inquired.

"Well, in the past, HUD has paid twenty-five to thirty-five thousand dollars to settle these types of cases, because that was cheaper than the cost of litigation."

"Even if HUD was in the right, and the legal analysis showed HUD had not committed any labor violations?"

"I know that's really hard to understand, but it's just a business decision," the young attorney from HQ informed the group.

Shannon thought about this a minute and then asked,

"Don't you think that this business policy or decision to pay the claims is setting poor precedent for HUD? That is, the message is being communicated that it doesn't matter if you have a strong claim or a weak one, HUD is most likely going to pay some amount of money to make it go away."

"If you don't like that policy, wait until I tell you what the unions are doing now. One union leader stated in a meeting with several managers and attorneys present that … 'if the unions couldn't get any traction from grievances and unfair labor practices, they were going to start filing simultaneous equal employment opportunity suits, EEOs, and see how the Secretary and Assistant Secretary like that'."

Corey spoke up at that moment, "What's HUD's history with EEOs and payouts?" he asked.

"I don't have that information here with me, but I can tell you that an EEO can be very expensive."

"Aren't they very involved, and have lots of options on how to proceed with one?" Shannon asked.

"Yes, they can drag on for years and years. And that's often an advantage for the unions because HUD staff moves on or retires, and the chances of having the manager charged with the EEO available for a trial are slim. Also, initially there are time-consuming investigations, depositions, and interrogatories by an outside contractor, which can be expensive for HUD. Then if the claimant doesn't like the initial decision of merit, the claimant can start over again through a mediator, or go to court, or..."

"And the attorney's fees just continue to mount up? Sounds like this whole area of union activity is costing HUD a mint," Corey complained.

"More than a mint," the young attorney answered sourly. "As long as the current administration continues to send out directives saying that HUD has to cooperate with the labor unions, it isn't going to get any better."

Before Shannon or Corey could comment, a senior attorney stood up and said,

"There's one more thing we need to discuss, and that's the Labor Board." He walked over to the young man writing on the papers hanging on the wall and asked, "Can I have your marker, please, and fresh piece of paper?"

The young man taped up a new page for the senior attorney, who turned to Shannon and Corey and informed them,

"Any unresolved issue involving the union eventually gets elevated to the Labor Board for a hearing. Attorneys can be present, interrogatories and depositions occur, witnesses appear, just like in court. BUT, as its name implies, it is the *labor board*, and the deciding official is a union representative, not an impartial judge."

The senior attorney made these notes on his paper hanging on the wall.

"Why do we do that? Why would HUD agree to have their grievances decided by a party that is really a part of the plaintiff's group?" an Asian attorney questioned.

"Because once upon a time, HUD agreed to abide by the various unions' contracts, which provided for exactly that, the Labor Board as a determining and deciding entity for unresolved matters."

"And not an impartial judge?" the Asian attorney continued.

"There are various avenues a complaining employee can choose for elevating his complaint," the senior attorney explained. "The employee can elect to go through mediation, which is usually a compromise, or a court route, but the court route takes a lot longer, often years. Or the Labor Board. And as we said earlier, an employee can start down one avenue process and then change and start over through another avenue. If the employee doesn't like the pending decision and feels they are not going to win their case, they can change to one of the other avenues and start all over again. Often an action can run for three or four years or more, and by that time, the manager has transferred or retired. And the cost of these complaints is enormous, especially when the union changes avenues once or twice. As you can see, unless the employee is looking for large sums of punitive damages, the Labor Board is more of a direct and expeditious route for getting what they want."

"Doesn't HUD have to agree to the avenue process the employee selects?"

"Nope, they have no say in the process selection whatsoever. It's totally up to the employee."

Corey summed it up well. "Shit."

Shannon and Corey had had their eyes opened throughout the day in the breakout sessions. They were both quiet when the left the last session, each considering what they had learned today.

"See you tomorrow morning?" Corey asked Shannon. "I'm going to do a little more research on all this tonight."

"Wouldn't want to miss the report-outs," she smiled sardonically.

The next morning the Assistant Secretary was standing on the raised platform at the front of the auditorium, talking to his aides and two other division directors when Shannon and Corey entered the room. The room was lively with high-energy discussions among the managers and supervisors. Stand-up flip charts were arranged along the front of the room with the pages that had been taped to the walls during the breakout sessions. The Assistant Secretary finished his conversations with the division directors and addressed the audience.

"If you would all please find your seats, we will get started."

The managers and supervisors moved out of the aisles and into the rows of chairs facing the front of the room. The conversations quieted, and the rustling of papers and brief cases subsided.

"I have heard bits and pieces about some of the breakout sessions yesterday," the Assistant Secretary began. "Our intent in holding this meeting here in Headquarters is to discuss HUD's standing in the national federal employees' satisfaction survey and in discussing ways to improve our standing. The current executive office, President Obama's cabinet, and Chief of Staff are concerned with HUD's rankings on the Survey…"

There was a low rumbling from the managers and supervisors in the room.

"And so we are presenting a new training piece for all HUD managers and supervisors…" he trailed off as the lights were dimmed and a Power Point presentation came up in the front of the auditorium. It was titled, "Labor – Management Agreement, the LMA", and pictured two people shaking hands.

An unfamiliar voice accompanied the Power Point, as it advanced to the next screen.

"Listening to Labor" it read. And the voice announced that management and supervisors needed to make time for their local union leaders and stewards to vent their concerns and requests.

"Respect and Consideration" read the next slide, with the voice announcing that management and supervisors must show the union leaders and stewards due respect without interrupting them or arguing with them, to consider their requests and demands seriously without pushing back or rejecting their ideas.

"Meetings" came up next, instructing management to hold regular scheduled meetings with their local union officials, taking minutes and acting on any requested action items.

Several additional screens came up in which management and supervisors were directed to be cordial, polite, and accommodating with the local union leaders.

But then a slide came up depicting a manager bending backward over his desk while a union leader yelled in his face with his finger shaking at the manager. The unknown voice explained,

"Meetings and negotiations may become heated and passionate. It is recognized that there can be emotion and, at times, swearing and vulgar expressions due to the heightened passion of the issue. Recent rulings have found that union leaders can express themselves literally and forcefully, including swearing, as this slide depicts. Union leaders may become physically forceful as in this picture. HUD officials, managers, and supervisors will NOT respond in like kind. Managers and supervisors will maintain professional, courteous behavior at all times, restraining from aggressively pursuing the labor leaders and using rude or inflammatory retaliatory or responsive language."

The room full of HUD managers and supervisors had had enough. The protest from the managers and supervisors erupted and surprised the Assistant Secretary. He called for the lights to be turned back on, and he raised his voice over the din,

"We have received instructions from President Obama's Executive Office to cooperate with the federal employee unions. We think the accelerating amount of grievances, EEO actions, and claims are part of the poor showing HUD is experiencing in the Survey, it reflects the dissatisfaction of the employees. We know they are affecting our overall budget, and we need to discuss how we can improve both our budget line items for these claims and our survey standing..."

Suddenly, Corey Anderson stood up and asked, "Isn't this really about the recently released office memorandum from the Executive Office, from President Obama, about cooperating with the union's demands in order to assure smooth election activity for the current administration?"

The roomful of HUD managers and supervisors became silenced.

"President Obama's executive memo to all federal agencies states that... 'management should discuss and agree with the unions to the extent possible, *Pre Decisionally*, regarding all management actions pertaining to work programs, work processes, work assignments and staffing.' This is making it almost impossible to do our jobs. You might as well have the unions manage the federal agencies."

With that comment, the decibel level in the room increased to a near roar.

"Let me read to you something that was just published in the *Federal Times* about the unions," Corey continued,

… "' Official time' refers to a practice under which the federal government pays the salaries of federal employees who work as union representatives. In other words, the government pays a person to work on behalf of the union while still receiving salary as a federal employee"…

… "The official time practice strikes some as odd because it results in the *government spending money to pay union representatives to file grievances, unfair labor practices, or prepare various appeals or complaints from employees or from the union. After paying the union representatives' salaries, the government then spends large amounts of money to pay the salaries of lawyers, managers, human resources specialists and, of course, union representatives, in defending or prosecuting cases against the government* on behalf of individual employees. No one really knows the total cost of this system but we do know that it is a considerable amount of money being spent on the government's administrative expenses…

"The reality is that we do not know with any accuracy how much money the federal government spends on salaries for union management salaries. OPM stated that agencies reported 3,395,187 hours used in 2012… But, even with the hours that were reported to the Office of Personnel Management, the cost to the federal government was $156 million—a 12 percent increase over the previous year. OPM says that the increase in amount of official time used was because there are more employees represented by unions, more bargaining with unions in several large agencies, the growing use of labor-management forums and more emphasis "…on accurately documenting official time compared to previous years.'"

The room full of managers erupted in a cacophony of voices all talking at once about their recent union activity experience.

The Assistant Secretary signaled the group by motioning with his arms and hands to quiet down.

But Corey wasn't done yet.

"'Senators Rob Portland, Republican from Ohio, and Tom Coburn, Republican from Oklahoma, have introduced the Federal Employee Accountability Act to reduce the so-called 'official time' for union staff who are government employees who receive a federal salary and benefits but don't do any agency work, only union work. They say that many agencies allow their taxpayer-funded employees to focus their time and energy on full time *political union activities* that don't have anything to do with the agencies work tasks…and agencies like the IRS and VA have hundreds of employees on their payrolls that do nothing but full time union work paid for by taxpayer dollars.'

"The recent Training sent around called 'Managing Conflict in a Union Environment' even states… *'Remember, unions are political institutions…unions are democratic institutions and as such, are political entities which have their own constituency …'* There seems to be a real conflict here." Corey looked around the room at the nodding managers' heads, "As managers, we are tasked with running efficient, productive, and ethical programs, to be as businesslike as possible in terms of streamlining operations and saving costs for the taxpayers, but the unions are political entities, interested in power and control, with the federal agencies paying their way. Shouldn't at least the union staff's salaries be paid from their own funds from their union dues?"

There was a lot of agreement from the managers, chants of 'yes they should', and 'pay their own way' echoed around the room.

"The ethics and integrity in these HQ decisions and choices to enable the labor union activities while workloads, production and program performance is diminished is corrupt. I expect we will soon see an exodus of the best managers who just won't work anymore under these circumstances." With that said, Corey was finished and sat down.

The room was nearly in an uproar. The Assistant Secretary had walked over to talk to other HQ managers, the labor relations director, and the HR director seated on the raised platform at the front of the room. He came back to the podium and tried to calm and quiet the room.

"All right now, all right. Let's quiet down. We can't accomplish anything with everyone talking at one time." He held his arms out in front of himself and indicated for everyone to remain seated. "I can see that this subject is going to need another meeting. I will inform you each of the time and place. But for now, we need to hear the report-outs from yesterday's breakout sessions."

Shannon leaned over to Corey. "So this is all just a political situation, to support the current presidential administration, and to provide support and ongoing votes for the Democratic party, isn't it? It has nothing to do with waste or fraud or abuse or falsification of employee time records. Or agency efficiency and ethical spending of taxpayer budget money. It's another political game with taxpayer funds for the benefit of the current administration. And I am an Apolitical pawn in this political game."

23

Finding Balance

Dave called and asked Shannon if she would like to go ocean kayaking out through Baby Beach at the Dana Point marina.

"I have a two man kayak," he was telling her. "If we launch at Baby Beach, we can paddle down and look at all the boats on our way out to the ocean."

"Promise you won't tip me over?" she countered.

"Promise, but I don't control the whales and porpoises out there!"

"It sounds like fun. What should I bring?"

"I'll make us some snacks. If you want to bring water or soda, that would be great."

Saturday came swiftly, and this time Dave picked up Shannon at her house.

"Hey, nice to see you again," she smiled at him when he stepped into the entry hallway of her home, and she gave him a quick hug. *Hmmm, nice strong shoulders and chest*, she thought. *All much needed for a strong paddle push for the kayak.*

Dave took a look around the living room from the front door.

"Nice house," he complimented her. He took in the camel-color carpeting, the soft beige walls, and the floor-to-ceiling curtains in the living room. It had tall, squared-off, fourteen-foot ceilings with beautiful ceiling crown molding and pretty floor molding. The entry was a travertine that continued down the hallway to the left past the stairs. And he could see a view of trees and sky through the living room and dining room windows out through the backyard. "How long have you been here?"

"About five years," she answered. "I actually rented it out when I first bought it because I wasn't ready to try and manage this much house by myself. But now I really love it."

"How many bedrooms is it?"

"Three, all upstairs, and two and a half baths. Come on back to the family room. I'm just about ready," she said, inviting him in. She had dressed casually in shorts and a knit T-shirt and flip flops. She walked him back to the family room, and he looked over at the kitchen, where she had just refinished the cabinets in a soft, antique-butter yellow with light granite countertops.

"Looks like you've done a lot of work," he complimented her again. "It looks great." He walked over to the built-in maple bookshelves that were perpendicular to the fireplace, which was also faced in matching travertine. He scanned several shelves of her books and took a quick look at some of the pictures she had displayed. "Your kids?" he asked, as he looked at pictures of Toby and Jenny standing on rocks at the beach with her.

"Yes, we had a great time on the beach that day," she answered.

"I miss seeing my kids all the time," he began and then stopped quickly. She could see the hurt in his eyes. He had talked about his recent divorce and how much he missed his three daughters and son.

"You know, they grow up and don't need us so much," she said, trying to help him out.

"But mine are a little younger, and I want to be there to finish guiding them and helping them make great choices," he said quietly.

"I understand. But I can tell you that no matter what age, they are always our children, and we will worry about them, love them, and want to help them with any issues life brings their way. None of that ever changes." *That might seem a little heavy*, she thought, but it was so very true, and she wanted him to know it was OK to talk to her about his kids like that.

"Well, are you about ready to go now?" He changed the subject.

"I am," and she grabbed her sun visor and the chilled water and sodas she had on the counter.

"Then let's go." He led her out of the house and to his car, which had a massive two-person kayak strapped onto the top of the car.

"Wow, that thing looks heavy!" she exclaimed.

"Well, we don't want it to tip over in high seas!" he teased back at her.

"Yes, but how did you ever get that thing up on top of the car?"

"It takes a special skill and talent. There's only a few of us in the world that can do it!"

She had to giggle. He was so funny. "OK, then, I can't wait to get on the water. I haven't been kayaking for a while, and it's hot today. It should be fabulous. Did you happen to look at the tide or wave report?"

He smiled over at her. "Of course. It's three- to four-foot swells, and the current is going south. It should be perfect."

"Four-foot swells!," she wailed.

"Get in the car," he said patiently. "I won't let any little old swell ruin our day," and they drove off for the beach.

When they arrived, she watched Dave unstrap the big kayak and bring it down to the ground. *Very strong*, she thought. That was no light or easy feat to wrangle the heavy kayak by himself. Then she watched as he pulled a set of wheels from his trunk, which he attached to the back end of the kayak. He put a storage box with other equipment on top of the kayak and handed her a cooler.

"Careful with the cooler," he said. "It has our gourmet snacks."

"Hmmm, what is it?" She was curious.

"Hummus and pita, some chips and dip."

"Where did you get it?"

"I made it."

"What? You can make your own hummus?" She was impressed. *He just keeps getting more interesting*. She added that thought to her previous one about his strength.

"Yeah, I like to cook. Let's wait and see what you think after you taste it."

They rolled the kayak to the edge of the water. Dave opened the storage box and pulled out seats for the kayak and installed them, putting the wheels inside the kayak's belly. He gently pushed the kayak into the shallow water and held it still while she jumped into the front seat. He pushed the kayak out about waist deep and then jumped into the backseat. He handed her a paddle and began paddling with his own.

"Have you kayaked here before?" he asked. "I bring my daughters down here, and they share the front seat where you are," he told her.

"I come here a lot and bring my grandson, Westin. He's so much fun to kayak with, and he's beginning to play golf too."

"Do you single or double kayak with him?"

"We single. He likes to have his own kayak. We go up and down the slips and look at all the boats. I haven't taken him out in the ocean, though."

"So you really do enjoy kayaking?"

"Of course. Who wouldn't?" she looked back over her shoulder. "I kayaked at Lake Tahoe once; there were white caps on the water. And it was cold. But the movement in the water was fabulous, you could kind of do miniature surfing on the little waves in the kayak. It was a great day."

OK now, he thought. This is good. *She really is athletic, and isn't afraid of taking a little risk in sports. And she's even paddling fairly well, not just coasting.* He was surprised to again think that he hadn't had this much fun in a very long while. She had refused his offer of a life jacket, saying that it was too constricting. He would see if she changed her mind when they went out into the ocean.

They paddled through the harbor, looking at and talking about the different kinds of boats and the funny names on some of them like 'Hole in the Water', 'Second Mistress', and 'Rum Pirates'.

"Shannon, look at the tall ships coming in," Dave pointed to the beautiful tall masts of an old sailing vessel. "It's called *The Pilgrim*," he told her.

Shannon smiled to herself. Since she had been kayaking in Dana Point with her grandson for so long, she had seen *The*

Pilgrim several times. "It really is a beautiful ship," she said, "and I love the bow sprit."

"Yeah, it looks like you," he teased. But she didn't mind. It was a pretty, fair maiden with an admirable bosom.

They paddled up close to the pelicans on the jetty rocks and to the sea lions swimming around the bait barge. The cranes were graceful as they lifted off the rocks, and the seagulls were entertaining as they dove into the waves for fish. They finally paddled to the end of the jetty, and Dave said,

"Are you ready to go out in the ocean?"

"I am, let's go," she answered.

"Want a life jacket?" he offered.

"No, thanks, I can swim. Just don't tip us over."

"I would never do that, but the whales and porpoise..."

"Not worried."

So out they went, enjoying the gentle swells and avoiding as much of the boat bumps from the larger boats as they could. Dave was an excellent pilot, guiding the double kayak away from the jetty rocks on the ocean side, and he maneuvered at the correct angle on the waves made by the larger boats smoothly. She was happy, impressed with his skills, and enjoying the warmth of the sun and the motion of the ocean thoroughly. They paddled around for a while, and Dave called,

"Look back," and snapped Shannon's picture when she turned around smiling at him.

They put down their paddles and rested.

"How about some lunch?" Dave offered.

"Sounds perfect," she answered.

"I'm going to steer us over behind that cluster of rocks," he explained to her. "That way the waves and swells won't rock us so much while we're eating."

He maneuvered the kayak several yards ahead and then around an outcropping of small, shallow rocks about thirty feet away from the jetty. Shannon watched the water eddy around the rocks and make swirling motions in the water. She noticed the waves passing on either side and around them, as Dave had said they would do, as they were protected behind the rocks. Dave threw down an anchor he had pulled up from the kayak's belly. He pulled the cooler towards him and opened it, pulling out a plate with pita bread and cheese. He handed it to Shannon.

"Here, hold this," he instructed her. Then he pulled out a container with the most delicious-smelling hummus she had ever had.

"What's that in the hummus that smells so good?" she asked.

"It's half roasted garlic hummus and half red pepper garlic humus. See which one you like best," he said and passed the container to her.

She balanced the two containers on her legs and dipped the pita bread into each of the types of hummus and lavished in the rich flavor of the chickpeas, tahini, and olive oil. "I don't think I can choose just one," she smiled at him. "They are both excellent, and delicious too! I love them both."

He felt pretty proud of himself for giving her a great treat. When they had their fill of the hummus and cheese, he offered her some grapes. She took a few, to enjoy the juice.

"I brought the water and soda," she offered.

"Are you getting thirsty?" he asked.

"I am. Could you please pass over a bottle of water?"

He handed her a cold bottle and took one out for himself. They sat and talked for a while after eating, just enjoying the gentle rocking of the water and the warmth. After they finished their snack, he pulled up the anchor, stowed it, and turned the kayak back towards the marina. Just then a large boat came up behind them, creating a strong wake that picked them up and sent them sailing down a little wave. Shannon had had her eyes closed, enjoying the sun, and wasn't prepared. She dropped her paddle. Dave leaned out and rescued it.

"Sorry," she admitted, "I had my eyes closed for just a minute, taking in the sun and the motion of the ocean."

He smiled. She felt comfortable enough to close her eyes in the ocean, on a kayak. With him steering. Life was getting better.

They paddled up the marina, and Dave held the kayak still while Shannon hopped out in the shallow water. Then he jumped out and pulled the kayak out the rest of the way. They stowed the gear, and she watched as he pulled the kayak up onto the top of his car and secured it. *This man is different*, she decided. *He's strong, but he's gentle. He's confident, but not arrogant. He's smart but not showy. He's certainly athletic as evidenced by his golf and now kayaking.* After playing golf, she knew he was patient and had a great sense of humor. And he was fun—lots of fun. *And not to forget, he's a good cook!*

She was watching him finish his securing of the kayak when he said,

"I'm sorry, I have to get back home now, I have to pick up my kids."

Shannon understood his responsibilities and answered, "No problem. I've had such a great time today. I'm going to feel the rocking of the kayak when I go to sleep tonight."

She wished they could extend their day longer. She was surprised to realize she was a little disappointed that their time together wouldn't be longer today.

"I'm glad you enjoyed it," he smiled at her. "Why don't you take the hummus and keep it since you liked it so much?" It seemed that he wanted to say more but stopped. He then came around and opened her door for her to slip in.

They chatted on the way home, and when he walked her to her door, they hugged—not a passionate hug, but a very warm, happy, sweet hug. They said their good-byes, and Dave left to pick up his daughters, while Shannon hummed to herself as she went upstairs for a shower, thinking all the time about this very handsome, intelligent, and, yes, romantic man.

Two weeks later, on a Saturday morning, she woke up to beautiful sunshine slanting into her bedroom through the ivory voile curtains on her window, and the sound of birds awakening, with their unique squeaks, tweets and trills. The morning doves cooed as a backdrop. It was mid-summer, and the air was already warming.

Dave had called and asked Shannon to dinner Saturday night at Salerno's, a little Italian restaurant in Laguna Beach that he said he liked. Shannon was happy to be seeing Dave again, and the restaurant sounded charming.

She was especially glad he had asked her out again, since she had fallen asleep on him during their last dinner date a week before. Eyes still closed, she lay in bed and luxuriated over her thoughts about that previous date. She had flown in from Washington, DC on the day of their date. She hadn't had much sleep in Washington due to the time change from East to West Coast, and she was too excited to sleep on the flight home. So by the time Dave had picked her up at 7:00 p.m. for dinner, it felt like 10:00 p.m. to her body. Thus, she had promptly fallen asleep after dinner, mumbling something like,

"I'm feeling really sleepy and tired now. I think I should go home."

Dave later told her she was cute with her eyes closing and head falling forward at the dinner table. He had taken her to Sun Dried Tomatoes restaurant in Laguna Beach, and they had sat outside.

It had been another action-packed week at the office, with the typical congressional inquiries and urgent requests for information from Washington, DC. She thought for a moment about the reports and work she had brought home for the weekend, but put those thoughts out of her head for now. There was all day, all weekend really, to finish the work. She stretched lazily and then sat bolt upright! Dave! She was seeing Dave tonight. She didn't know what she would wear, or if the house was decent for him to see when he picked her up. What if one of the cats had produced a furball and left it on the carpet? Twenty-pound Jack, her Maine coon long-haired, orange-and-white male cat with the huge paws, often left her such surprises.

She bounced out of bed and threw on a short pink robe, determined to check out the downstairs for evidence of cat activity. She was greeted by Jack outside her bedroom door and bent down to scratch his ears, which immediately started some very loud purring. She proceeded down the stairs as Jack followed her, expecting to be fed and let outside. After determining that there was no cat damage to be repaired, she fed Jack and went outside to pick up the morning newspaper off her driveway and sat down for a little breakfast. She smiled to herself as she thought of her very feminine responses this morning to her date with Dave, worried about what she would wear in contrast to her much more reserved behavior at the office with her staff and Washington, DC management. She had worked very hard to climb up the corporate political ladder, and had strived to always maintain a polished, professional demeanor at the office, which had served her well. She realized she had far more corporate experience than personal dating experience. But she was ready to change that with Dave.

The day went quickly, and she even completed reviewing much of the work product and letters her staff had prepared for her review. She put the completed work into her briefcase and decided it was time to go upstairs and switch gears from a corporate director into a femme fatale, or as close to it as she could.

She stepped into her walk-in closet and realized that she didn't have any femme fatale fashion there but lots of navy, camel, and black suits and cream blouses with matching pumps. Not to be deterred, she padded across the upstairs hall into her guest room and looked into that closet and discovered two dresses that could work, one surplus wrap red and another ocean blue. *Or maybe the leopard print dress*, she considered. *Definitely the leopard print dress*, she decided. *Leopard always looks good on a blond*, she rationalized, and it had a lower-cut neckline. She was *not* going to be Miss Goody Two Shoes office director tonight!

She pulled the dress out of the closet and padded back into her dressing area. *Now for shoes*, she thought. Darn! She didn't have any black strappy heels, but she did have some higher black heels that would have to work, and she pulled them off her shoe shelf in the closet and put them on the floor in the dressing area. *Might as well pull out the pretty feminine and lacy black bra and panties too*, she thought, smiling. *He may not see them, but I will sure feel them,* she thought to herself as she went to her lingerie drawer and pulled out the pretty, soft delicacies.

She looked at the clock and decided she had time for a quick shower before she dressed for her date and started to turn on the hot water in the shower. Just then she heard the familiar haawwk!, not a sound she wanted to hear, because it meant Jack was leaving her evidence of his fur, and she reached under her sink for paper towel to clean it up. So much for feeling like a sensual woman, she thought and rolled her eyes. *Thanks, Jack, for bringing me back to reality.*

After the shower, still wearing a towel wrapped over her breasts, she blow dried her blond shoulder-length hair, realizing it had grown longer and she needed to schedule a trim. She didn't usually wear much makeup to the office, only mascara and lipstick, but tonight she applied eyeliner, a little soft eye shadow, *lots* of mascara, bronzer, and a soft coral lipstick. She stepped back in her robe and examined herself, turning her head to each side. *Not bad,* she thought. *If Dave liked me on the golf course and in a wet kayak, he should like this!*

She finished putting small, gold, pierced earrings on and slipped into her dress and heels. She picked up her purse, the big, heavy tote she carried to the office because she could fit lots of files and reports in it. *This will not work tonight,* she thought again, and went back into her walkin closet for a smaller black purse that would match her heels, and found a small clutch that was acceptable. She transferred only the basics, a hairbrush, lipstick and wallet, and proceeded down the stairs as the doorbell rang. It was Dave. She was surprised again that she felt butterflies in her chest. *Oh, come on!* she chastised herself. *Get a grip.*

She answered the door, and Dave stood there looking tall and handsome, just as she had remembered.

He smiled and asked,

"Wow! You look great! Are you ready? Our reservations are in about a half hour."

She reached for her purse, and they left for the restaurant.

Salerno's was a charming little Italian restaurant on a side street in Laguna Beach. He had arranged for a small private table for two in a corner nook by a front window, where they could people watch.

"You look beautiful tonight," Dave smiled across the white linen tablecloth at Shannon. She glowed at the compliment.

"It's nice to see you again tonight, too," she answered quietly.

The waitress arrived at their table and Dave ordered a white wine for her and a red wine for himself. *He remembered I don't like red wine*, she thought pleasantly.

After the waitress left to get their wine, he asked,

"How was your week? Not too much work, I hope."

"Hmmm", she began, "This week was typical, with congress-men wanting information on their constituents' mortgage loan status and reviewing my staff's letters on lender examinations."

"No new bad guys on the scene?"

"We did find a new website offering to 'rent the down pay-ment' money to borrowers."

"How does that work?"

"It seems that the principal puts the borrower's name and his own on a joint bank account, to make it appear that the borrowers have sufficient down payment funds to defraud the FHA lenders. After the borrowers are approved, he then loans them the down payment money at a pretty steep interest rate, so then the borrowers have two mortgages, the one with the bank and one with this principal person."

"Are you serious?"

"Afraid so. It amazes me how creative some of these people are."

"You never get bored, do you?"

"Not ever," she laughed softly. "I love what I do. It's not work; it's practicing what I really enjoy. And I especially enjoy and appreciate my staff."

They chatted a while longer and then ordered dinner and enjoyed being together and catching up. Toward the end of the dinner, Dave looked over at Shannon and seemed a bit uncomfortable with what he was about to say,

"You know, there's something I want to ask you, but your answer doesn't really matter." Shannon thought that was rather an odd comment.

"I don't care one way or another, I really don't, but because of how we met, on the golf course, I realize I don't know how old you are. And it really doesn't matter anyway, I guess I just thought I should know."

She didn't like his question. It just seemed almost rude. And it certainly ruined her warm, fuzzy romantic feelings at the moment. When she didn't immediately answer him, he continued,

"I guess someone asked me, and I realized I didn't know, and I thought that I probably should know."

She let him sit there uncomfortably for a few minutes while formulating her response, and he awkwardly said,

"I'm fifty-two. I'm sure you're a lot younger than me."

She thought about who she had recently dated and thought of John, who was seven years younger but who she had been with for several years until he moved to the East Coast. She thought about an anthropologist who had been interesting and who was also younger than her, and she realized that she had dated only one man who was older than her, and she had been too active for him. He had wanted her to slow down, which she had declined to do. All the rest had been younger, not intentionally, it had just worked out that way. So she looked at him directly with a sweet smile and said,

"Actually, Dave, you're a little old for me," and let him deal with that.

His face fell, his eyes seemed to sadden, and his shoulders appeared to drop slightly. He didn't have a response to that, and she felt a little bit sorry for him considering what she had said and how she had said it, so she continued,

"You're only three years younger than me, and I'm accustomed to dating much younger men."

He didn't quite understand immediately, but then his eyes narrowed, and he sat up much straighter and answered,

"Glad we got that over with."

The next weekend when he took her out to their first movie date together, he bought himself an adult ticket, and a senior ticket for her!

Touché!

Two years later, Shannon was sitting with Dave in her family room, looking out at the garden in the backyard. She smiled over at Dave and said,

"The market hit 14,000 today. Time to take your money out of the market, say good-bye to Wall Street, and go to cash." It was October 2007.

"You're sure about that?" Dave smiled back at Shannon. "The market is so hot, and it sure has been on a good run-up..."

Although she smiled, she shook her head, "Don't you know, it's all going to happen all over again? You have to get your money out of real estate, banks, REITS, anything related to finances, banking, or real estate. Houses will start to go into default, foreclosures will flood the market, the banks will have to take enormous write-downs that will cause hundreds of bank failures, and the FDIC will be back in action."

She then thought, *And all those government liens against the properties will evaporate into thin air, although they could have been collected if my government lien program had been implemented. We'll see if the government steps in and what they do this time...'* she smiled at him.

Dave pulled Shannon's hand to his lips, and kissed her palm. "You seem pretty sure of all that."

"I am one hundred percent certain," she smiled, not wanting to talk business but wanting to enjoy his attention and kisses instead. "I took all my investments and converted them to cash. We are heading into an economic downspin of epic proportions."

Dave smiled back at Shannon, picked up a strand of her blond hair in his fingers, and ran his fingers to the ends. "Tell me more."

"When there's no verification of the buyer's income or down payment requirements, disaster is the result."

"What else?"

"And then there's all the adjustable loans that are going to adjust, and the increased payments will cause an avalanche of defaults and foreclosures..."

He kissed her neck and said, "Won't they just refinance their adjustable loans?"

"No, they won't be able to because the appraised values won't hold up anymore, and they won't be able to document the false employment they reported on their initial liar loan."

He kissed her ear and said, "Keep going."

"Then the commercial market will crumble next," she said a little unsteadily, as his lips tickled her ear. "Just look around at all the vacant office buildings and the overabundance of new commercial space that has been built. At the FDIC, we used to call them 'see-through' buildings, because there was no office furniture or people working in them, and you could see right through the windows and out the other side. The glut of vacant space will decrease competitive rents, and the commercial property values will plummet. And we're talking million-dollar losses to the banks and savings and loans with the large commercial loans. It's like shattered glass, that cuts no matter how you try to step through it."

He stopped kissing her ear and looked at her, "Is there more?"

"Let me tell you all about the Wall Street and market fiasco that is coming due to the hundred-percent subprime financing, liar and NINJA loans, and failing loan portfolios..."

"NINJA?"

"No income, no jobs..... Did you know that some lenders are even making loans at 125% of the current appraised value for a house? They figure the property will continue to appreciate to cover the higher loan values. And of course they can charge higher fees for those loans, and the banks are just raking in the cash. Is that a ticking time bomb or what?" She shook her blond head.

"How can you know this?" and he turned her hand over and kissed the top.

She smiled into his blue eyes and replied, "Anyone that was alive in the 1980s and 1990s when all the banks and savings and loans failed should be able to see the signs. It's just like when I was at the FDIC and RTC all over again. The real estate crash will be even worse this time, because the loans are not just being held domestically in the United States, but have been bought by International funds. The economic fiasco about to occur will be historical, not just in the United States, but internationally. *It's going to be painful. It's going to be like dancing on shattered glass.*"

"Dancing on shattered glass...?"

"Yes, because ordinary people and investors will watch their savings and investments *bleed*. Every drop in the stock market will make a deeper cut into lifetime savings, pensions, investments like life blood dripping from working folks and investors. *The bankers and Wall Street will try and dance away from what they have done, but every way they step and turn will cut them too, and make their balance sheets bleed red ink.* Every step will be painful and cut deeper as the stock market crashes and real estate values collapse. The job losses in banking, real estate, construction and the financial industry will be staggering as those industries come to a standstill. The toxic mortgage dance will stop, and the bleeding will begin. *The industry will not be able to dance on the shattered glass any longer.* Companies will fail. Banks will fail. Lives will be shattered. The shattered glass will carve out and cause a deep and long recession."

He paused and cocked his head to one side, "You seem very certain."

"I am. I lived it already once through the FDIC and RTC not that long ago. And it is so easy to see that the residential real estate is foolishly overvalued and overmortgaged now, most purchased with self-stated income loans. When the appraised value on a house increases $10,000 to $20,000 per month, there's an inflated value that is unsupportable and unsustainable."

He thought about what she had said and nodded his head.

"Is there any good news?" he asked, and he looked at her seriously.

"Yes, for those who have moved their savings to cash, it will be a windfall to invest in all the newly devalued properties. There will be such a glut of foreclosures on the market, anyone can make a bundle of profit by buying the foreclosures and just holding them for a few years."

"I'm listening," he said and ran the back of his hand slowly up her cheek. "Did I ever tell you that I love it when you talk like this?"

She squirmed and tried to continue, "Then you'll love this. Did I ever tell you I once spoke before Congress about a Plan to recover billions, maybe trillions of dollars of government liens that are lost and the IRS can't account for?"

"Trillions?" he asked. "You are irresistible."

But then he moved closer and continued to kiss her lips until she couldn't remember her next point...

Shannon continued to discuss the anticipated meltdown in real estate and banking with family, friends, HUD staff, and colleagues; however, they hadn't been exposed to the failed banks the way Shannon had while at FDIC and RTC. They didn't see the imminent declines in all things real estate, finance, and banking quickly approaching. Shannon liquidated all her 401K holdings and other investments and converted them to cash. She waited, confident that she had protected her and her family's investments, and would buy back in after the market took the anticipated nosedive. It didn't take long for the epic meltdown to begin.

24

History Repeats Itself, Only Worse This Time

Although Congress proposed several bills and other legislation to regulate the subprime industry, the lending industry lobbyists insisted that the lending industry was monitoring
itself. They didn't want or need legislation, extra oversight, or
increased monitoring. That competition would keep rates and
loan terms reasonable, low, and affordable.

About one million residences had fallen into foreclosure
since 2006, and an additional 5.9 million were expected
over the next four years, reported *BusinessWeek*. The lending industry continued to thwart legislation and regulation.
A Homeownership Preservation Summit was held on April
18, 2007, behind closed doors in the Dirksen Senate Office
Building to address the foreclosure crisis with the heads of
the largest lending institutions across the country. A statement of principles with vague guidelines, including making
early contact with defaulting borrowers and offering modifications to the loan terms, resulted. However, the foreclosure
epidemic continued to worsen.

Treasury Secretary Henry Paulson then summoned the
executives back to Washington again in late 2007, and the

program du jour was entitled The Hope Now Alliance, a government-endorsed private-sector organization wherein lenders promised to cooperate with nonprofit credit counselors who would help borrowers prevent defaults. But the lenders participation and cooperation was voluntary. *BusinessWeek* reported that in a press release, Hope Now said it had prevented 2.2 million foreclosures during 2008; however, it didn't reveal that fully 53 percent of the consumers receiving loan modifications were again delinquent on their mortgages after six months. By early 2008, it was obvious that Hope now wasn't halting a significant percentage of foreclosures.

Democrats began gathering ideas for a government-sponsored remedy. Lobbyists were working to propose their own versions, each protecting the lending industry from government controls or oversight. Before long, the antiforeclosure provisions were being altered in ways the industry favored. Hope for Homeowners was approved by Congress on July 26, 2008. *BusinessWeek* reported that lobbyists gathered to lift plastic cups of wine in celebration. HUD reported that only twenty-five loans had been refinanced under this plan, it also, was a dismal failure.

Then the actual number of mortgage loans in default, with increasing past-due and overdue payments, began to surface. Foreclosure signs popped up in neighborhoods throughout the nation. Emergency meetings with the nation's banks were held in Washington, DC to determine the depth and breadth of the situation. FDIC and the Treasury were called in to discuss the failing balance sheets for the banks, due to the failing mortgage loans still on their books that they had not been able to unload or sell or put into portfolios for investors, and the ugly truth about the weakening banking system began to emerge. Foreclosures began to snowball. A record number of banks could soon be considered insolvent, and poised for failure and closure by the FDIC. Wall Street and the entire financial and insurance industry were in peril of failing. The country's entire financial system was on the brink of breaking. Or, unheard of and never before provided, the federal government and, the American taxpayer, could bail out the banks and other financial companies. As Shannon had said, *The bankers and Wall Street had tried to dance away from what they had done, but every way they stepped and turned, the shattered glass cut them too, and made their balance sheets begin to bleed red ink.* The toxic mortgage dance had stopped, and the bleeding had begun.

In early September 2008, the US government took control of mortgage finance giants Fannie Mae and Freddie Mac by injecting $200 Billion dollars into the mortgage backers, replacing their managements and agreeing to guarantee their debt.

The *USA Today* headline of September 17, 2008, shouted, "Fed to lend up to $85 Billion to AIG." "*...The Federal Reserve said it will lend up to $85 billion to American International Group (AIG) effectively putting the government in control of the flailing insurance giant, saying the move was necessary to protect the financial system and the economy...the action averts a bankruptcy filing by AIG, which has been struggling* *to raise capital after crippling losses on insurance policies sold to investors in mortgage-backed securities...AIG is so huge and its operations so intertwined in the financial system that the Fed feared an AIG failure could harm the broader economy..."*

"...If AIG had gone bankrupt and not been able to make payments the domino effect would have been devastating and unprecedented...

"...Nearly every Fortune 500 company has an AIG related policy and the average person has some exposure to AIG policies or firms..."

AIG faced the most difficult financial crisis in its history when a series of events unfolded in late 2008. The insurer had sold credit protection through its London unit in the credit default swaps (CDSs) on collateralized debt obligations (CDOs), but they had declined in value. The AIG Financial Products division, headed by Joseph Cassano in London, had entered into credit default swaps to insure $441 billion worth of securities originally rated AAA. Of those securities, $57.8 billion were structured debt securities backed by subprime loans. As a result, AIG's credit rating was downgraded and it was required to post additional collateral with its trading counter-parties, leading to a liquidity crisis that began on September 16, 2008, and essentially bankrupted all of AIG. The United States Federal Reserve Bank stepped in, announcing the creation of a secured credit facility of up to US $85 billion to prevent the company's collapse, enabling AIG to deliver additional collateral to its credit default swap trading partners. The credit facility was secured by the stock in AIG-owned subsidiaries in the form *of warrants for a 79.9% equity stake in the company and the right to suspend dividends to previously issued common and preferred stock. The AIG board accepted the terms of the Federal Reserve rescue package that same day, making it the largest government bailout of a private company in U.S. history—a $152 billion dollar bailout by the Federal Reserve for a 92% ownership.*

The *Los Angeles Times* ran bold headlines in mid-September 2008--"Current Crisis May Be Trickier Than S&L Mess."

"...This week's bailout of insurance giant American International Group, Inc, (AIG), for example, was crafted at the last minute in an atmosphere of impending catastrophe, as were the earlier rescues of investment bank Bear Stearns Co and mortgage giants Fannie Mae and Freddie Mac...

"...the Savings and Loans were regulated institutions and were taken over by the government...

"...the cleanup cost to the American taxpayer (from the S&L crisis) is an estimated $124 billion...

"...by contrast with the S&L crisis, a large portion of the distressed assets involved in the current Wall Street meltdown is held by investment banks, hedge funds and other institutions that operate outside federal regulations..."

The current situation was very different.

"...Today's troubled securities are much more complex than the S&L assets, with valuations that may not have yet hit rock bottom...

"...They're very hard to account for and their value is still a moving target," said Michael Greenberger, a law professor at the University of Maryland and a former official

at the Commodity Futures Trading Commission. *"Creating a bureaucracy that takes paper that has no value and tries to sell it is just going to look like more smoke and mirrors."*

USA *Today* on September 18, 2008, carried a leading story called "Snowballing Fears Set Us Up for a Fall."

"… Risk aversion skyrocketed Wednesday as investors still shaken by 500 point Dow plunge were rocked with another 450 point decline, one that wiped out another $700 billion in shareholder wealth and tested the nerves of even the most committed long term investors…

"…dive in the yield of the 3 month U.S. Treasury bill, considered one of the safest investments on the planet…closed at 0.05% down from 1.47% on September 12, 2008, its lowest since 1941…"

June 18, 2009, Treasury report says Office of Thrift Supervision failed to rein in the savings and loan's risky lending regarding California's Downey Savings and Loan....

"... a federal thrift regulator bungled its oversight of Downey Savings and Loan, allowing the Newport Beach thrift to pile on billions of dollars in high-risk mortgages and eventually collapse...

"*The regulators from the beleaguered Office of Thrift Supervision (OTS) also botched their oversight of Pomona California based PFF Bank and Trust, which collapsed along with Downey last fall (2008) according to reports issued this week by the U.S. Treasury Department's Inspector General, the internal auditing agency...The Obama administration proposed Wednesday that the OTS (the Office of Thrift Supervision), which has long been criticized as weak and ineffectual, be abolished...*

"*...FDIC spent $10.7 billion to back deposits at Pasadena's failed IndyMac Bank, while the Inspector General said that OTS examiners ignored repeated warning signs of trouble with exotic mortgages and allowed the thrift to backdate a cash infusion to make it seem stronger. The Downey Savings and Loan, in Irvine, California, failure attracted special attention because it was a major purveyor of one of the riskiest types of home loans: the pay-option-adjustable rate mortgage, which allowed borrowers to pay so little that their loan balances went up instead of down. These option arms, often written without checking borrowers' earnings or assets, emerged as a major contributor to the nation's foreclosure crisis...*

"*...By 2002 Downey was heavily involved in high risk loans according to the Treasury report, and examiners began warning Downey's management that year of potential problems. Yet despite the warnings, OTS examiners did not require Downey to limit concentrations in higher risk loan products. 'We believe that in light of the OTS's repeated expressions of concern and management's unresponsiveness* *to those concerns, the OTS should have been more forceful, at least by 2005,' the report said.*

"...The subprime lenders, initially applauded for increasing homeownership in America and for providing mortgages for buyers with weaker credit and lower FICO scores, although they charged for it in their fees and interest rates, were later named as villains of the melt down. 'Ameriquest Mortgage Company of Orange, California was the nation's largest subprime lender in the early part of the housing boom before an investigation by 49 state attorneys general looked into allegations of deceiving borrowers, falsifying loan documents and overstating home appraisals that led to a $325 million settlement,' the LA Times reported.

Countrywide, a subprime giant in Calabasas, California, pushed 80/20 loans that provided combined 100% financing for a home purchase at very lucrative fees to Countrywide. Chief legal officer, Sandor Samuels, was quoted in BusinessWeek as saying, ... "(Countrywide) vowed to continue selling loans with enticing introductory rates as well as those requiring minimal evidence of borrowers' income. We are going to keep making these loans until the last second they are legal."

Anthony Mozilo, Chief Executive Officer of Countrywide Financial Corporation, said that a "gold rush" mentality had taken over the nation, and that he got swept up in it as well. He later agreed to pay a $22.5 million fine to settle a government fraud lawsuit over the lender's near collapse.

Headquarters asked Shannon to attend a local meeting in California to meet with various Countrywide managers and executives to discuss the status of their FHA loan portfolio. The Obama administration continued to push HUD to refinance as many subprime loans as possible, which would take the pressure off of the banks and lenders but would shift the risk to HUD and, thus, the taxpayers.

When Shannon sat down with the Countrywide reports, she saw that the causes for delinquencies and inability to pay mortgage payments were staggering:

Curtailed income	60%
Loss of income provider	15%
Illness	5%
Divorce	10%
Miscellaneous	10%

Mozilo at a congressional hearing on the mortgage crisis in 2008

She wondered if the income on these loans had *ever* been verified, or was just part of the 'no documentation', 'no income - no job' NINJA craze.

It became clear after meeting with several lenders who were holding subprime loans, which the Obama administration wanted refinanced by HUD, that 60% of the loans in their portfolios had 'curtailed' income—that is, there likely never was any income, wasn't now and most likely there would never be. There was no basis or foundation for making these subprime stated income loans in the first place under customary credit underwriting rules, and there wasn't sufficient income now for an FHA refinance. But no one wanted to tell Congress, especially the lenders. If the lenders truly reported the condition of their loans, they would have to transfer balance sheet revenue to 'loan loss reserves'. Which may make them insolvent, and subject to seizure by the FDIC.

Brian Montgomery, the FHA commissioner, tried to tell Congress that FHA had income verification requirements that the lenders did not, and that many of the subprime loans could not be refinanced with FHA insurance. Shannon was shocked when the current presidential administration then told FHA to loosen their qualifying, or underwriting standards, so that the high-risk subprime refinances could go to FHA.

While the administration's intent to unburden the banks of their risky loans would shore up the banking industry and be good for the nation, it would transfer the risk to HUD and, ultimately, the taxpayers.

With the economy still stalling, the *Los Angeles Times* reported on June 19, 2009:

> ... *"President Obama's plan to increase the authority of the Federal Reserve is emerging...his overhaul of financial industry regulations. Obama wants the central bank*

to take on a key new job of regulating large financial institutions, beyond only banking firms, whose failure would pose a significant risk to the economy. But several members of the Senate Banking Committee pushed back on the idea of expanding the Fed's power. 'Your plan puts a lot of faith in the Federal Reserve's ability to spot risk and exercise its power to prevent the next crisis. However, if the Fed and other regulators had been doing their jobs and paying attention to what the banks and other firms were doing earlier this decade, they almost certainly could have prevented the mess,'" Sen. Jim Bunning (R-Ky) said.

"Other lawmakers are concerned that giving the Fed more of a regulatory role could impede its independence, which they say is crucial to keeping politics out of its responsibility for setting monetary policy.

"Several experts who criticized expanding the Fed's powers likened it to parents giving a teenager a bigger, faster car after he had crashed the family station wagon."

The Los Angeles Times article continued,

"...Challenges Obama faces in getting his regulatory overhaul passed into law...the plan, the most comprehensive since the Great Depression...would institute tough requirements on large companies that could damage the economy should they fall, add oversight of such complex financial instruments as derivatives, attempt to rein in executive compensation and create a new agency to oversee consumer financial products....most of the key provisions, including changes to the Fed's use last fall of extraordinary

emergency lending power to back JPMorgan Chase and Company's takeover of Bear Stearns and the bailout giant insurer American International Group Inc (AIG)... The Fed substantially increased its lending to help stabilize the financial system, and many lawmakers want more information about who is getting the billions in loans. The Fed does not disclose the recipients of loans to protect the confidence of depositors and investors in those institutions...

"Obama's overhaul also would create the Financial Services Oversight Council to identify emerging risk to the economy. The council would be headed by Geithner and include the Federal Reserve chairman and other financial regulators.

"At its core, President Obama's overhaul of regulations for the financial industry seeks a fundamental change: Make the federal bureaucracy work for consumers, not just Wall Street. And Wall Street, not surprisingly, doesn't like it."

The Los Angeles Times wrote on June 18, 2009... "'The most unfair practices will be banned,' Obama said. 'Those ridiculous contracts with pages of fine print that no one can figure out, those things will be a thing of the past, and enforcement will be the rule, not the exception.' But Wall Street firms that earn billions of dollars on consumer financial products quickly attacked the proposal, setting the stage for what is likely to be a hard fought legislative battle."

The *New York Times* reported on June 21, 2009, *"Obama Pushes Financial Regulatory Plan....President Obama said he would fight for a package on overhauling the financial regulatory system...* it is clear...an "epidemic of irresponsibility took hold from Wall Street to Washington to Main Street."

In February 2009, *BusinessWeek* printed a 'Political Generosity' chart, based on data from the Center for Responsive politics, U.S. Treasury Department, showing Senate and House leaders who had accepted significant contributions from financial services firms as campaign donations from 2007-2008:

Senate	House
Banking Committee Members:	Financial Services Committee:
Christopher J. Dodd, Chairman $5,948,568	Barney Frank, Chairman $ 984,148
Richard C. Shelby, Ranking Republican $ 565,399	Spencer Bachus, Ranking Republican $ 897,725
Appropriations, Financial Services Subcommittee:	Ways and Means Committee:
Dick Durbin, Chairman $1,325,383	Charles B. Rangel, Chairman $1,346,669
San Brownback, Ranking Republican $254,837	Eric Cantor, Member GOP Whip $1,008,937

Financial Lobbying

Spending on lobbying by financial institutions that eventually received federal bailout funds:

Company	Bailout Awards	2008	2007
AIG	$40 billion	$9,690,000	$11,379,000
Citigroup	$45 billion	$7,660,000	$8,480,000
JP Morgan Chase	$25 billion	$5,390,000	$5,535,000
Merrill Lynch	$10 billion	$4,700,000	$4,420,000
GMAC	$5 billion	$4,620,000	$1,460,000
Bank of America	$35 billion	$4,090,000	$3,220,000
Goldman Sachs	$10 billion	$3,280,000	$2,720,000
Morgan Stanley	$10 billion	$3,120,000	$2,760,000

The *Los Angeles Times* ran other headlines such as "Many Are Faulted in Credit Crisis."...

"A U.S. panel probing the meltdown assigns wide blame... A federal commission created to investigate the financial crisis is pointing the finger at nearly everyone, from over-extended homeowners to reckless executives and timid regulators...the crisis was the result of human action and inaction, not of Mother Nature or computer models gone haywire...The commission disclosed that Federal Reserve Chairman Ben S. Bernanke told in a private session that, during a two week period in the fall of 2008, twelve of the largest 13 financial institutions had been at risk of failure...the housing bubble ended badly, triggering a global credit crisis and the worst recession in decades..."

The report ultimately said *that"... the near meltdown didn't have to happen...."*

"*We never thought we'd see home prices go down,*" *Jamie Dimon said, JP Morgan Chase, chairman...*

"The Financial Crisis Inquiry Commission was made up of six Democrats and four Republicans and chaired by former California Treasurer Phil Angelides. They released their 633 page report stating... *"The collapse was utterly foreseeable—there was no shortage of warnings from bankers, analysts and others in the credit and stock markets—but managements of major financial institutions and their regulators were unable or unwilling to act to halt or moderate imprudent behavior...instead, the carousing banks were overseen by... fellow party animals...*

"Another cause...is that credit rating firms such as Moody's and Standard & Poor's 'erroneously' rated bundled up mortgage garbage too highly. The key here is that it was the securities' packagers that paid the rating firms' fees, which gave the latter an incentive to shower even the foulest product with glitter. The rating firms sought lucre by turning themselves into assembly lines for triple-A ratings. On the average working day in 2006, Moody's delivered its top rating to 30 mortgage backed securities. About 83% of them were eventually downgraded."

There was much discussion on enforcing laws currently on the books and passing new legislation. However, the report was crystal clear in its conclusion,

"Mortal flaws like greed and hubris, can't be legislated away, especially on Wall Street, where money clouds men's minds."

The *New York Times* headline from February 2009 shouted.... "FDIC Struggles to Unload Toxic Assets from Banks—Bad Loans Sold via Auction Sites...."

"...When regulators took over First National Bank of Nevada last year, they faced a showdown with the Terrible Herbst, the mustachioed cowboy who boasts of being the "best badman in the west." This was no real gunslinger, but the name and logo of a chain of gas stations and convenience stores in Nevada that feature slot machines beside candy and beer. Auditors at the Federal Deposit Insurance Corporation concluded that the family-owned Herbst chain did not generate enough sales at its Reno-area gas stations to support the repayment of a loan, leaving auditors with three bad choices: take over those stations and put the government in the gambling business, cut off any flow of additional loan money, or sell the loan at a steep loss.

"The FDIC faces tough choices like this every day as it struggles to manage $15 billion worth of loans and property left from failed banks....and is selling hundreds of millions of dollars' worth of loans through eBay-like auction sites...

"And in the most closely watched tactic, the FDIC is negotiating a series of billion dollar deals with private-equity partners who will take over huge batches of loans in exchange for a chunk of the sales proceeds..."

And as Shannon read the next article in the *Federal Times*, she couldn't help thinking about the government lien collection program she had developed, knowing that much of the lost revenue could have been recovered during the boom years of 2004 to 2008 and with more recoveries during the 2009 and forward foreclosures. Liens that would be ignored. Liens that had been lost. And that sadly, billions and trillions of dollars were going uncollected as properties went through the foreclosure process, wiping out billions and trillions of dollars due to the IRS, states and other agencies. Instead of satisfying those debts with the real estate, the agencies would now pursue the tax payers for ten to twenty years, garnishing their wages, seizing their bank accounts, and attaching liens to new assets, and the government would be going further into debt.

The *Federal Times* reported on June 1, 2009, "IRS Tax Revenues Drop 34%."

*"**Federal tax revenue plunged $ 138 billion, or 34% in April versus a year ago**—the biggest April drop since 1981, a study released last week by the American Institute for Economic Research says. When the economy slumps, so does tax revenue, and this recession has been no different, said Kerry Lynch, senior fellow at the AIER and author of the study. It illustrates how severe the recession has been.*

"...For example, 6 million people lost jobs in the 12 months ended in April 09—and that means far fewer dollars from income taxes. Income tax revenue dropped 44 percent from a year ago. 'These are staggering numbers,'

Lynch said. Big revenue losses mean that the U.S. Budget deficit may be larger than predicted this year and in future years. 'It's one of the drivers of the ongoing expansion of the federal budget deficit', said John Lonski, chief economist for Moody's Investors Service. The Congressional Budget Office projects a $1.7 trillion budget deficit for fiscal 2009. The other deficit driver is government spending, which AIER's report says is the main culprit for the federal budget deficit. The White House thinks that tax revenue will increase in 2011, thanks in part to the stimulus package says the report from AIER, an independent economic research institute. But it warns, 'Even if that does happen, the administration also projects that government spending will be so much higher each year that large deficits will continue, and the national debt held by the public will double over the next 10 years'. The government may have a hard time trimming spending to reduce the deficit when the recession ends. The 77 million baby boomers—those born in 1946 to 1964—will start tapping their federal retirement benefits soon, which means increased government outlays for Social Security and Medicare."

By September 12, 2009, FDIC reported that 92 banks had failed. By the end of the Wall Street meltdown and resulting real estate collapse, from 2008 to 2013, more than 400 banks failed.

New HUD Leadership

HUD was an old federal agency, and had the highest number of long-term employees, more than any other agency. They had often promoted managers from the rank-and-file tenure employees, which ensured that most of the same old ways were carried on—same old ways of thinking, measuring, and performing, without having the opportunity to bring in new methods and updated thinking from other agencies or the private industry.

Finally, with the mortgage financial crisis, and the conventional lenders stepping back away from making new home loans and FHA stepping up with making home loans, FHA was swelling with loan activity, and new thinking had to be found to lead HUD through an unparalleled crisis. New leadership that looked at HUD operations differently, asked questions, and evaluated the ongoing operations for their efficiency and effectiveness was needed. No longer could standard operational procedures, – SOP – be accepted.

Charles Coulter and Kathleen Zadareky were hired in 2011 and 2012, respectively, from outside HUD, to bring in the much-needed leadership, vision, and proven alternative methods for managing staggering portfolios of real estate and loans, both performing and underperforming. Charles's position was the deputy assistant secretary, known as the 'DAS', and Kathleen was his associate deputy assistant secretary, 'ADAS', both highly placed and responsible positions over the single-family divisions of HUD, answering to FHA Commissioner Carol Galante and then-Secretary Shaun Donovan.

Coulter and Zadareky reformatted the single-family operations and analyzed the FHA mortgage process step by step. Their objectives included change management, business transformation, updated technology, quality control, and challenge. Joy Hadley, Director of Quality Assurance and FHA Lender Approval, and her deputy, Justin Burch, worked closely in headquarters with Charles and Kathleen to include their visions of updating FHA and rebalancing the credit risks while ensuring a cohesive implementation of technical platforms for the business transformation. Their combined approach was to look at every process, credit policy, credit risk, and loss mitigation. They analyzed data and met with industry partners and leaders to query what was working within the FHA arena and what was not. They talked with other lenders, mortgage brokers, real estate brokers, underwriters, appraisers and more. They wanted to know how the end user, the FHA lenders, and borrowers, perceived the FHA programs.

They listened, considered, analyzed, reported to the Commissioner and then acted. They were concerned that FHA was out of step with the industry, seriously in need of updating. They brought in analysts from the lending industry to discuss policy and technology, looking for those that could think differently and improve the FHA and HUD process.

They asked staff to review and streamline every process, to increase accuracy and results.

They formed teams to evaluate risk tolerance and pricing and to balance anticipated loan losses with the pricing for FHA mortgage insurance premiums.

And they assigned teams to analyze and evaluate every credit policy and communication from FHA to the lending industry, for applicability, soundness, clarity and consistency.

Handbooks giving guidance and requirements for FHA lenders to follow when making FHA loans had not been updated for over twelve years, while changes or modifications to the old handbooks were made piecemeal by mortgagee letters to the industry. The industry had greatly changed, and staff was challenged to accomplish making updated industry handbooks.

The handbooks were scheduled to be living documents online, so that updates or modifications would be readily and consistently available to all FHA industry groups.

They intended to change the way HUD communicated with the lending industry, by providing written questions and answers that accompanied new policy statements and announced new policies in industrywide conference calls, further providing access to HUD staff for consistent and timely answers to inquiries.

It was recognized early in their tenure that FHA loans that were foreclosed and became HUD homes or real estate owned (REO), as the industry called it, were a costly way for HUD to recover funds for the FHA insurance fund. Instead, Coulter and Zadareky began to focus on loss mitigation, requiring FHA lenders to process a failing loan through several steps before foreclosing, including trial payment plans to catch up mortgage payments, loan modifications, deeds in lieu of foreclosure and other programs.

Focus was not just on making new loans and refinancing subprime loans where possible, but on loss mitigation and holding lenders accountable for not making more REO.

They constantly evaluated revised policies to ensure alignment to risk tolerance.

They developed Sharepoint sites for staff to track program progress and next steps and changed HUD staff's performance rating criteria, updating a very old and dated pass-fail system. Charles worked constantly with industry groups and Kathleen worked endlessly, usually 7:00 a.m. to 8:00 p.m. daily and more, always very positive, supportive, encouraging, and constantly demonstrating leadership that was much overdue at HUD.

Shannon had the opportunity work with these two new HUD leaders at length and with Joy Hadley and Justin Burch, to accomplish their long list of improvements and changes to bring the FHA into the current world of mortgage banking. They, and others, had been charged with thinking differently and improving the vast amount of credit decision making for the new FHA program.

25

OPM; The Federal Government's Office of Personnel Management and Social Security

Trying to Retire, but OPM Computers Broken—Can't Get Out

Shannon looked around her corner office on the ninth floor of the Santa Ana, California, HUD office and took in the Secretary's Award on her wall, Exemplary Service Awards from HUD, RTC, and FDIC, and other plaques and certificates for outstanding service throughout her lengthy career.

She had enjoyed working with the new leadership in Washington, DC and helping change the way HUD did business. She was pleased to have had the opportunity to effect change and to share her findings and suggestions to improve high-risk programs. But she had now come to the decision that it was time to extricate herself from the government arena.

She would miss the stimulation, energetic discussions with her staff, challenges, and satisfaction of knowing that some fraud had been stopped, some restitution made, and some new statutory rules had been put in place to protect consumers by her division.

On a personal level, she appreciated her staff and respected them and continued to acknowledge their professional performance, knowledge, skills, and work products. Every day she enjoyed talking with her employees about their current projects, the latest scams, and lawsuits. She enjoyed celebrating their successes and working with them on their challenges. She cared about them.

She would not miss the HUD, FDIC or RTC managers that were more interested in their political careers for their own gain rather than in managing their departments and divisions toward successful goals and accomplishments. She was disappointed in the empire building and gerrymandering by various government leaders to expand their staff but not expand the work or responsibility performed by their divisions, and in federal government managers who would not take the appropriate and necessary steps to remove a nonperforming employee because it was too hard, took too long, it would mean a visible fight with the local union, and it might make the manager look bad to the other staff and people at headquarters who wanted to support the Obama administration edict to cooperate with the unions in exchange for their votes.

She would not miss the arguments with the HUD attorneys over written rules and regulations that they interpreted as unenforceable, although they were the ones who rewrote the rules and legislation after they were submitted by HUD's program offices. HUD's field staff, including Shannon, often identified weaknesses in HUD's rules and guidance, and wrote revised rules and guidance to provide industry partners with clear information and program descriptions. However, the attorneys would modify the new rules, codes of federal regulations, and other handbooks such that they were difficult to support and enforce, ambiguous and confusing, often lead-ing to cases of fraud and abuse of government programs to go unresolved.

She would not miss the inefficient human resources di-vision at HUD that couldn't handle their workload so they reduced it by conducting a sort of lottery by which they se-lected an odd or even number and then only processed the job applications with social security numbers that ended with the selected odd or even number for that job, until the HUD human resources workload was transferred to the Treasury Department's human resources group, which didn't fare much better, where applications were only reviewed until a qualified candidate was identified, and then the remainder of the appli-cations were not even considered.

Social Security, Supplemental Social Security, and Disability

Shannon made an appointment at the local Social Security Office in Mission Viejo, California. As she entered the lobby of the Social Security Office, she noticed that nearly all the chairs in the waiting area were full with about seventy people. The average age of the people waiting seemed to be in their thirties or forties, with several children sitting or playing near their apparent parents. There were a few elderly, but not many. She found a chair at the end of the long room and settled in for what appeared to be a long wait.

She noticed that there were several windows along one wall at which the social security staff sat and called the names of the people waiting in the lobby, who would gather their papers and sit in front of the window, speaking in low voices. Often the government staff person would leave and come back with a second government person, who appeared to be a translator or could speak the language of the person appearing at the window.

Before Shannon could observe any more, her name was called, and instead of directing her to one of the windows, she was asked to come into the back office for her appointment.

As Shannon sat down at the indicated desk, a young woman came and sat next to her and said in English, "Do you require the services of a translator? What languages do you speak?"

Shannon was taken aback, with this being the first question she was asked, but then she quickly realized that the majority of people in the lobby waiting area had been speaking a multitude of languages other than English.

"English primarily," Shannon answered, "and some Spanish."

"OK, then, you will be fine speaking with Agent Maria Mooring today." Before Shannon could ask another question, the young woman left her alone at the desk.

Shannon quickly looked around the interior office area. It looked like a typical government office, with aging gray cubicles separating desks. The carpet was some sort of a gray pattern of carpet tiles that could be replaced as needed if there was a spill or it became heavily soiled. Several of the carpet tiles needed immediate replacing. Each gray metal desk had two well-worn visitor chairs in front of it, and there were enclosed offices down one wall made from glass so the light from outside could light up the gray interior of the Social Security Office. Shannon could see the wall of windows where the people waiting in the lobby area were called up to present their paperwork, and noticed the rolling file carts next to each employee working at the windows. As she was completing her visual assessment of the interior office area, a second young woman approached the desk where Shannon waited and extended her hand.

"Hello, I'm Agent Maria Mooring," she said by way of introduction. The agent quickly shook Shannon's hand and immediately sat down across the desk without smiling. Before Shannon could say anything, the young woman continued while looking down at her file on her desk,

"So, your appointment information says you are here today to discuss your available social security benefits," and she pushed a sheet of paper across the desk to Shannon without looking up. "This report lists your quarterly contributions paid into social security based upon your earnings. I need you to look at this report and tell me if there are any inaccuracies or mistakes."

Shannon looked at the young woman, taking in her short brown hair tucked around her glasses and ears, guessing she was about thirty-five years old. She was wearing brown slacks and a flowered blouse. Shannon glanced at the report and answered the young woman,

"Without having my own records with me, I can't guarantee that these figures are correct, however, they do appear to be reasonable."

"That's all right," she replied without looking up. "If you do find a mistake, you can notify me within ten days, and I will make that correction."

At that moment, there was a commotion out in the waiting room area, and Shannon saw a young man working at one of the windows stand up and take a step back from the window. She couldn't understand what was being said as she didn't recognize the language, but she could determine that there was a disagreement of some sort taking place.

Shannon asked, "There are a lot of people sitting out in the waiting lobby, but I was brought back here. Am I being taken out of order?"

At that question, the young woman finally looked up at Shannon.

"No, you are just about the only person here today that made an appointment. The ones waiting in the lobby are walk-ins."

"Oh, so making an appointment is definitely more efficient." Shannon tried to strike up a conversation with the young social security agent.

"Not exactly," she answered without a smile. "You see, you are the only appointment so far today to discuss the social security benefits you have earned by working for"...and she looked down at her file again, ... "over thirty-five years in the United States."

"Excuse me, I don't understand." Shannon was confused by her comments. After all, this was the Social Security Office, and Shannon's understanding was that the program had been developed to provide income at the end of a person's working life as he or she entered retirement. That's why a portion of her salary had been set aside and matched by her employers over the thirty-five years she had held a career. It was a bedrock program, it had been a constant requirement to contribute into the program, and it reflected the time and work performed during a lifetime.

The young woman paused, looked up at Shannon, and, without a smile, answered, "The people in the lobby are here without an appointment because they are here to bring in doctor's letters explaining why they can't work, but why they should receive supplemental social security or disability payments."

"I thought Disability was for someone injured while working?" Shannon asked.

"Yes, but the program was expanded, and now Disability covers a very broad range of conditions."

Shannon took in this information, but before she could respond, the young woman continued.

"The public has learned that they can receive government benefits if they provide a doctor's letter stating that they cannot work for physical, mental, or medical reasons."

Shannon listened to the social security employee's information and then asked,

"You said I'm the only person who made an appointment to discuss social security benefits thus far today?"

"Yes, that's right. Yours is the normal retirement benefits appointment after you have completed working in the social security system and paying into it for the length of your career. And there are about fifty to sixty walk-ins today for SSI, that's short for supplemental social security or disability in the lobby this morning."

"Is this a typical day?"

The young woman paused again before saying, "Yes, it really is." She hesitated and then continued, "There are about fourteen million people now receiving a monthly Disability check from the government. The number has roughly doubled every fifteen years."

"I'm not very knowledgeable about SSI or Disability benefits," Shannon responded. "Do people have to work a certain length of time to collect supplemental social security, like the normal social security?"

"No, SSI benefits are not based on prior work or family members' prior work history. SSI is usually for those disabled, blind, or age sixty-five or older with limited resources and incomes. Additionally there's SSI for kids with learning disabilities. If you are eligible for SSI, you can usually get medical coverage and sometimes food assistance, except in California."

The agent opened a drawer to her desk and removed two government pamphlets, entitled, "Disability Benefits" and "Do You Qualify for SSI?" and handed them to Shannon.

"The disability program began in the 1950s, and the government's definition of disability included heart disease, cancer, basically lots of severe illnesses that often killed pretty quickly, and there were pretty easy tests for these diseases. But then in 1984, Congress changed the definition of disability and made it more vague, and added things like depression and back pain, things that are very hard to determine with standard tests."

Shannon thought about the staggering numbers the young woman was describing and asked, "Is the SSI and disability paid for with social security funds?"

"No, they are paid for from our personal income taxes, corporate, and other taxes."

"How long does a person normally stay on disability?" Shannon asked.

The agent shook her head. "About one or two percent come off disability. You have to understand that once a person is found eligible for disability benefits, they automatically receive health insurance, Medicare. It's a package."

"Do you have any idea what this program costs annually?"

The young woman sat back in her chair and answered quietly,

"Disability alone costs about *a quarter of a trillion dollars a year*."

"Oh, my gosh!" Shannon exclaimed. "I hope there's a good audit program. My background is in government enforcement. Does the social security administration have an audit team, a group who verifies the doctor letters and the integrity of the medical issues?"

"Well, I can tell you that there is an appeals system, where someone denied disability can go before an administrative judge and appeal to receive benefits."

"And is there a significant pool of Defense attorneys for these hearings?"

The young agent stifled a smile,

"Actually, there are NO attorneys for the government present at these appeal hearings. Just an attorney for the plaintiff seeking benefits, and the administrative judge. That's it."

"Then there must be a serious audit program to verify medical letters, frequency of use by certain doctors…"

The social security agent sighed, "No, not really. Congress doesn't give us the budget money for sufficiently auditing the claims."

Shannon couldn't accept that so much money was being given out without any check-and-balance or extensive audit of the program. "There must be some review of the claims," she questioned the agent.

"Maybe one tenth of one percent of the claims get a second look," she offered weakly. "But there is no broad review or audit of the claims."

"Is there a review of the doctors to determine if their diagnosis or support for a person being unable to work and recommendation for SSI or Disability payments is valid?"

"Occasionally there's a tip from the public that someone is receiving Disability who is not disabled, and the inspector general might get involved, but, no, there's no budget for any broad audits or reviews."

"Not even a statistical analysis or capture of the doctor's names to see which doctors are issuing these letters?"

"None. Occasionally there will be an administrative action against a physician, but not very often."

"There has to be some control of the SSI and Disability payments," Shannon began, in complete disbelief. "With such large sums of money and number of payments being distributed, there has to be some government controls…"

The young woman interrupted tiredly, "There is just no money from Congress for broad controls or audits. In fact, the disability fund is just about out of money. Congress keeps increasing the budget for the benefit payments, but none for controls or file reviews."

"There needs to be."

Shannon thought about the reports she had read recently about the social security fund running precariously low, and now understood some of the underlying but not overtly discussed reasons why.

Shannon glanced down at the pamphlet the Social Security agent had given her, and noticed that it clearly stated the payments were made by the federal government, not the state.

She asked the young agent,

"So, are the fourteen million people receiving Disability benefits included in the unemployment figures we continue to watch?|"

"Oh, no," she answered. "They are expressly excluded. They are kind of invisible non-workers, not counted in the states' unemployment figures. We've seen people file for disability after their unemployment benefits expire. You see, the state pays welfare, but the federal government pays Disability. There are companies who are paid a fee to move people off of welfare and onto Disability to save the states money. There is no diagnosis called disability. Back pain and depression are among the fastest-growing causes of disability, both of which are difficult to test. It's become a discretionary decision of a physician…"

"For which there is little chance of an audit because there's no budget for it," Shannon finished for her.

OPM—Office of Personnel Management
Shannon returned to the office, pulled the retirement papers she had requested toward her, opened her current pay statement, and immediately noticed a discrepancy. The total years she had worked attributed toward her retirement had been changed! By about four years! For the last six years, she had been monitoring her accumulating years toward retirement, and now four years had been removed without a letter of explanation, without notice; it simply was a change on her pay statement. Shannon had received preretirement estimates on her planned end of service and saw now that all the calculations and figures had been changed.

She picked up the phone and called the HUD PBRC or Pay, Benefits, and Retirement Center. When they finally answered, she inquired,

"There has been a change in my most recent pay statement in the years attributable to retirement. Can you explain this to me?" She was cordial and gave the PBRC woman her identifying information.

The woman on the other end of the phone advised Shannon, "It looks like you have three or four years here that were included in your total years of federal service that have been removed."

Shannon listened carefully and asked, "And why has that happened?"

"Because it appears you didn't pay into the retirement system during those years."

"There were about three years that I wasn't in management at the beginning of my career," Shannon began to explain, "and I didn't contribute to the retirement plan during those early years. However, after moving into management, the office of personnel management, OPM, sent me a letter allowing me to pay back the retirement deposits for those early years, and I did just that."

"Well, then you need to get a statement from OPM showing that you have paid all retirement contributions, and then I can change your retirement calculations again."

Shannon called the office of personnel management, OPM.

"I need to get a statement of all my government service for retirement purposes," she began. "My agency, HUD, doesn't have an accurate total of all the time I've worked for the federal government, and they advised me to call OPM for a revised and current statement."

"We're kind of busy," was the answer. "If you can hold a while, I can look into it for you."

Shannon thought that it might take a while for the information to be gathered and then organized, so she offered, "Why don't you take your time and call me when you have all the information you need?"

The person on the other end of the phone sighed and said, "I'll put it in my pile of problem files," and hung up.

After about seven days, Shannon had not received a response from the OPM, and she called again.

"I would like to discuss a change in my years of service, please," she began. This time, the woman on the phone didn't even pretend to be interested or concerned and just said, "Our computers are broken. We can't tell you anything. You'll just have to wait," and the woman hung up.

Then Shannon saw the article a colleague had just left on her desk from *The Federal Times*, June 1, 2009, "Right Call on Annuity Calculator."

> *"The (federal) government so far spent $ 100 million on efforts to develop an accurate method for calculating pension benefits. In fact, the federal project is a scandal...There's no excuse for something so simple and non-controversial to have dragged on so long. The fact that a retiring federal employee can wait six months or more after retiring before knowing exactly what his or her monthly benefit will amount to is outrageous. Some 600,000 federal workers are projected to retire by 2016 and there are fewer and fewer people who know how to (manually) operate and maintain the current antiquated paper based system. And there is a real risk of system meltdown. 'If it failed tomorrow, we could not pay our retirees', new OPM Directory John Berry said. Berry is right on the money in his call to scrap a planned online retirement calculator for employees in favor of creating a new, reliable system for quickly calculating annuities for new retirees."*

Shannon called OPM right back. This time, another person answered. After Shannon explained her question and asked about the computer problem, the OPM person began explaining in a very tired voice,

"Well, you see, last year we moved, and then our computers failed. Well, actually, they've been broken for almost a year now, and we think they'll be fixed soon. But I can't look in the computer now to see how much time you've accrued for retirement or anything like that. And we can't really accurately calculate your retirement manually because of all the changing interest rates and stuff like that. Heck, we couldn't even put the right interest rates into the computers so they could compute retirement rates, or annuities, or benefits. So if the computers can't do it, we sure can't."

Shannon said to the tired woman, "In order to file my retirement request and to provide the correct number of years I've worked in the federal government, I need to have a statement from OPM."

"Yes, I know that," the tired woman said slowly. "But I can't look into my computer, and I can't generate a computer report or statement for you until the computers are fixed."

Shannon asked again, "You must have some way of providing information to other government agencies about the number of years someone has worked so that they can prepare for retirement."

The very tired woman said, "You can have your people in your retirement section call me, and I'll tell them your service years from some old statements."

Shannon asked, "Will you send them a letter to confirm the years of service?"

"No. I can't write anything or send a computer statement. But I can give them a verbal answer. There are a few of us here that can remember how to do it manually, but our computers can't."

"I don't think HUD will accept just a verbal answer from OPM to calculate and activate my retirement amounts," Shannon countered.

The woman only said, "That's all I can do right now, because our computers are still broken. You'll just have to wait."

26

Deeper Inside HUD: One Last Promotion and the Federal Government Shutdown

As Shannon sat stunned once again at the very broken government system, this time OPM, she received a call from the Deputy Assistant Secretary Charles Coulter, asking her to accept another promotion, this time to the Director of the Santa Ana Homeownership Center, managing upwards of 175 staff throughout the eight (8) western states.

"I just had the most interesting and frightening conversation with the Office of Personnel Management," Shannon said to Charles sarcastically.

"Frightening how?"

"OPM still seems to have broken computers, and can't provide retirement information. It's now been at least two years that their computers have been broken and they can't provide a retirement estimate."

"I've heard about their fiascos from other staff recently."

"Charles, *this is the personnel agency for the entire United States federal government*, for all federal employees, and they can't answer any questions about an employee's retirement plans, years worked, benefits..."

"And they are classically broken..."

"It's more like classic *insanity*. Nowhere in the real world would ineptness of this kind be tolerated. Management would be removed, and people fired, but it is accepted from a federal agency."

"I hear they are struggling to get things under control..."

"For over two years?" she exclaimed. "I can't even talk with them to get reliable retirement figures..."

"Oh, you don't want to talk with them about that right now..." Charles chuckled.

"But I do. You know that I'm thinking about retirement..."

"No, you really don't want to do that either," he continued. "I need you to do this one last thing for me."

"Charles, remember when I was in your office in DC a few weeks ago and I said I was finally looking forward to enjoying my personal life? I told you I was looking forward to rertirement, working out regularly and generally enjoying the next chapter in my life, away from HUD? "

"This is a promotion you well deserve and I need you to handle the next two years."

"I've given you outstanding results since I've been at HUD. I've developed some great teams and programs, and developed national training, staff and new leaders..."

"And those new leaders will support you in your work as the new Executive Homeownership Director. Shannon, you are different from the other three homeownership directors. They have all been with HUD for their entire careers and are accustomed to doing things the same way they have seen them done all throughout their careers. I don't want a continuation of the same processes, the same old reports and programs. I want a fresh look, a fresh approach, and I think you can provide that."

"I know you. What else is it you need me to do?" she asked skeptically. Charles was great at providing vast amounts of flattery, just before he asked for a big favor or challenging project.

"Glad you asked," he chuckled again. "I want to know your perspective on how the general economy and housing market will look in the near future. How HUD can position itself best in the upcoming market. We've talked about your anticipation of the 2008 mortgage meltdown, how you saw the signals to the financial fiasco and how you protected your investments. Now I need you to take a look at the other government entities, Fannie Mae, Freddie Mac, the Veterans Administration. Compare and contrast our structures and pricing. Look at our policies and procedures. Is HUD balancing policy and risk? Where can we streamline, save time, be more efficient?"

"Is that all?" she countered sarcastically.

"Well, there is one more thing. I need you to outline a whole new HUD staffing approach. You and I talked about it some time ago when you were suggesting using contract employees as well as career federal employees."

"Yes, to balance the ebbs and flows of the real estate and financial markets."

"Well, I want you to expand on your thoughts, explain the changing markets, what we should expect, and how HUD can react to those coming changes. Draw a word picture for me of how HUD can be different, and better."

"What's your timeline?" Shannon inquired.

"Start as soon as possible. You're a national figure with HUD now for how you successfully managed the lender oversight quality management division and received the Secretary's CMIT Award. The discoveries you and your team made on the mistakes with the HECM home equity loans have saved the agency millions, and you were the one that discovered and implemented the first look at our FHA servicing lender operations to detail the extensive errors and lack of compliance with loan modifications that we are now requiring the FHA lenders to do. Your work was the beginning and foundation of the HUD legal actions for restitution with the servicing lenders. And you saw the weaknesses in the seller-funded down payment assistance program. I need you to take this new position on to help us with what's coming next."

"What's coming that you need me to handle? What are your terms? I want to retire now but can't get a retirement estimate that is reliable from OPM. I will want to retire in two years. Maybe you need someone else who wants to stay with HUD longer."

Charles Coulter answered, "There will be some tough situations coming up for HUD in the next two years. We are closing smaller offices, consolidating staff, and splitting up the program support division with a portion of the work going into the new office of housing counseling. We may be facing a sequester budget, including mandatory unpaid days off and a possible federal governmentwide shutdown. The local union is also ramping up to challenge some of these actions, so we need your skill and expertise to manage these challenges, and you are our choice to do it. Can you stay and handle the West Coast for us, please?"

"And staffing for this Directors office?" she countered.

"Hire what you need. I'll make sure it happens."

She had planned well during her career and positioned herself well for the day she would retire. She had rarely thought of each day as work, but as challenges and experiences she enjoyed. She had more than enjoyed her staff in the Quality

Assurance lender oversight division as she had genuine affection for the staff, and appreciated and respected the work that they did. Each one of them was unique, and had outstanding skills that had made her job a pleasure.

She didn't need another plaque or award for another project, she would rather sponsor and facilitate her staff now to watch them succeed. Could retirement wait another two years? Evidentially! She smiled to herself since OPM couldn't get its act together. Shannon thought, *Why not? With the broken OPM agency computers, I can't even get out with a reliable retirement figure.* So she said,

"Thank you for your confidence, Charles. I will do my best for you," and it was done.

The new Executive Director's position came with new political exposure and extensive contact with senators and congressmen inquiring about FHA business on behalf of their respective constituents throughout the eight Western states and often beyond. She came into the office with a secretary and a deputy director, who primarily handled administrative matters.

She was constantly preparing talking points and speech data for HQ officials as they made presentations to the U.S. Congress, the financial, real estate and lending industry groups. She gave congressional briefings, met with legislators at local FHA and HUD outreach events, and worked on training local staff to handle the increasing request for HUD speakers at their industry trade conferences.

Washington, DC wanted increased face-to-face time with the FHA lenders, nonprofits, and other HUD partners to hear what was working well within HUD and where processes could be improved. These meetings were called round tables.

Carol Galante, the current FHA Commissioner located in Washington, DC, had scheduled a round table meeting with several California FHA lenders and nonprofits, as well as local congressional staff, to be hosted by Shannon's California office to discuss current HUD programs, rules, and regulations as well as upcoming potential changes to these programs.

Shannon arrived at the office on the day of the round table meeting and her secretary came into her office. Sara was a beautiful black woman in her midsixties with a beautiful smile that lit up a room. Sara always had something good to say about everyone and had a gentle spirit about her.

"Good morning Boss. Looking forward to the big meet and greet today?" She smiled.

Shannon had been sorting her mail and returned her smile, "Yes, I'm actually looking forward to it. HUD tries hard to measure risk against profitable loan originations, and I always enjoy hearing from the lenders how we stack up against the conventional lending world with our rules. It can get rather spirited in these meetings."

"Have you met the Commissioner before?"

"I have, and I like her very much. She's sharp, she's very focused on making HUD a more efficient organization, and she's approachable. I really do enjoy her."

"Well, this will be my first time to meet her in person, and I'm looking forward to it too. Sometimes I wish I weren't getting ready to retire soon so I could experience this new phase of HUD where women like you, and the Commissioner are the new leaders."

"Thank you, Sara. But are you sure you really want to retire? Won't you miss all the pressure and busy phones and the reports?..."

"And the lines outside your door, and the never-ending meetings, and messages, and conference calls…"

"But think about the donuts, and the staff parties, and …"

"And the calories, and the pounds! No, thank you! I've had enough sweets to last me the rest of my life. I'm going to start a walking program and get in shape!" Sara laughed.

Shannon smiled again at her friend and colleague. Sara was a part of the large number of HUD staff that were eligible to retire.

"Sara, I have to ask you to be ready to meet the Commissioner downstairs in the lobby when she arrives and escort her up here to the 9th floor conference room, or to my office if she's early. I will assign some additional staff to meet with the invited lenders and others and bring them up to the conference room as well."

"I'll be happy to. Like I said, I'm glad I get to meet her today. I'll let you know when I leave to go downstairs."

"Perfect, I appreciate it," Shannon answered, as she pulled a stack of letters toward her that Sara had handed her for signatures. "Is the conference room all set up for the Round Table today?"

"Yes, our facilities people have set up the tables and chairs the way the Commissioner indicated in her e-mail. Cold water chilling and coffee ready to brew. It was nice of you to buy the coffee and water; it makes for a nicer meeting."

"The federal government is not generous when it comes to providing refreshments for the thousands of meetings they conduct. I can manage the refreshments once in a while," she smiled.

Sara left Shannon's office and closed her boss's door halfway. "So maybe you can get those letters signed before the line starts to form," she laughed softly.

The morning was progressing nicely with Shannon signing letters and taking phone calls while Sara took messages for those that came in while Shannon was on another line, which was typical at just about any time of the day. In between calls, various division directors would tap on her half-open door and come in to brief Shannon on the latest updates for their departments. It was around one o'clock when Shannon stood up and began to contemplate finding some lunch when Sara marched in,

"We have a problem," she said rapidly.

"And it is...?"

"The elevators are broken. We have the Commissioner coming in about thirty minutes, and all those lenders and nonprofits she has invited. They will have to walk up nine flights of stairs..."

Shannon quickly forgot about lunch and instructed Sara, "All right, then, let's see if we can find an alternative meeting room on a lower floor."

"That's a great idea."

"Will you please look at all the other divisions' meeting space calendars and let me know what you find?"

"Right away."

Shannon picked up her phone and called the building maintenance office,

"Hello, Jason, I understand the elevators are down, again," she said in an exasperated voice, since one or more of the four elevators had been out of operation for several weeks due to certain parts that had been ordered but had not arrived. "Can you tell me when you expect them to come back up?"

"Um, yeah, I thought it was just one or two of the elevators that went down, but I guess it's all four now."

"That's not helping. When do you expect at least one to be operating? Soon, I hope?"

"Well, uh, I have a couple guys looking at the operational panels now, and I'm going down to see how they are doing."

"OK, will you please call me within the next ten minutes with an update, please? I just need to know if you think you can have one or more elevators back on line soon. I have some visitors from Washington, DC arriving in about thirty minutes, and I need to know if they will be able to use the elevators or if I need to make some alternate plans for them."

"Yeah, sure, I will call you."

They hung up. Shannon walked out of her office to her secretary's cubicle and waited while Sara finished her call.

"It looks like the third floor has a conference room we can use," she informed Shannon. "It will accommodate about fifty people. I will get the water and coffee ready to move down there. I'll have to set up the folders, name tents, and sign-in sheets again."

"Great. Can you ask how the room is configured, classroom or roundtable style? I don't want you having to climb up and down six flights of stairs."

Sara grinned. "I can still do it. I just have to go really slow."

Shannon reached over and squeezed Sara's shoulder. "I know you can. But let's ask our facility and operations people to handle it for us. I need you up here until we know how this is going to play out."

"Hey, what's that noise?" Sara exclaimed, turning and moving toward the window to look out. "Oh, my, when it rains, it pours."

"What do you mean?" Shannon asked warily.

"I'm sorry to inform you, Boss, but it looks like there's another demonstration or protest starting outside by the front doors and going around the building."

"A demonstration? How many people this time?" Shannon put her head back and massaged her temple, which was starting to ache, probably from not eating lunch again as much as from all the last-minute issues.

The building that the Santa Ana HUD office occupied was shared with other federal agencies, including the Department of Defense and ICE, the Immigration and Control Enforcement Office. ICE held prisoners in the cells in the basement when they were awaiting trial, since the building was across the courtyard from the federal courthouse. There had been increasing picket lines and demonstrations due to the pending immigration reform legislation that was being worked on by both state and federal legislators. Previously, the demonstrators had lain down in the street and handcuffed their wrists together so they would be difficult to remove when the police came. Other times, there were hundreds of demonstrators marching around the entire federal square, with several standing on the steps of the HUD building, demanding a stop of all deportations and other ICE activity. The advantage of sharing an office building with other federal agencies was shared expenses and lower costs, but the disadvantage was sharing their issues, problems, and, now, pickets.

"I can't tell how many are out there," Sara sounded alarmed. "But the ones I can see are loud and have bullhorns this time and banners."

"Can you hear what they're saying? What they're picketing about this time?"

"Looks like immigration and deportation banners."

"All right, I'll call the police and see if this is a rally that has a permit or what it is…"

She quickly left Sara's cubicle for her own office. As she dialed the number for the local police unit, she heard voices outside her office.

Jason stuck his head in the door, not noticing she was on the phone, "Uh, Shannon, two of the elevators are back up now. It was just a glitch in the programming system, and the other ones will be up in about an hour."

Shannon held up one finger to indicate that she would be a minute and for Jason to wait. "OK, uh-huh, I see, all right, I understand, thank you." She hung up the phone. "Two elevators are working now?" she repeated to Jason.

"That's right. All set to go now."

"Thank you for the update. I appreciate it," she said quickly as she walked toward Jason and the door. "When are those elevator parts expected to arrive so all this elevator downtime will stop?"

"Uh, I can check on that and let you know."

"Not now," she answered brusquely. "Later this week will be fine. Just keep those two that are operating now up."

"OK, I get it," he answered weakly.

Shannon walked around Jason and back to Sara's desk. "I just spoke with the police, and they will be disbursing the crowd momentarily. They don't have a permit this time, and it seems that the prisoner they are picketing about was just taken over to the court for his hearing, so they are following him there."

"Then it should get a little quieter soon," Sara answered.

"Yes, I hope so." Shannon shook her head. "And we will have the Commissioner and guests in the ninth-floor conference room since two elevators are now working. But thank you for your fast work in locating alternate space for today."

"No problem, Boss. I'm glad to help."

"So we have about ten minutes left until the Commissioner arrives…"

"Right, and I will go on downstairs to greet her and bring her up."

Somali Pirates

As Shannon was sitting at her desk reading over reports from Washington, DC, Riker Tucker, her REO division director, tapped on her door and stuck his head in,

"Got a minute?"

"Sure," she set aside her reports and invited Riker into her office.

"I have to tell you about my crisis de jour," he chuckled.

Shannon was accustomed to ongoing real estate issues because they were tangible and affected people's living options and conditions.

"I just received a call from the police in Avondale, Arizona, who said they have been contacted by King Azeem Basil El Bey about occupying certain HUD properties."

"Excuse me?"

"Remember how I told you our property management contractor told us that there seemed to be some squatters in a few of our houses down in Arizona, and they were trying to determine who the squatters were?"

"Yes, sure, I remember we talked about that last week. So, who are they?"

"Well, you're going to love this," and Riker paused for dramatic affect... "They are Somali Pirates, or rather, ancient relatives or descendants of Somali pirates."

Shannon's eyebrows shot up, and her eyes sparkled, "What? Are you kidding?"

"I'm not kidding," he chuckled again. "And they are taking back our HUD properties as proper payment that was due them from a previous treaty with the United States not to attack American ships, over 100 years ago."

She smiled and said, "Gee, I guess I'm not totally familiar with that treaty."

Riker handed a letter to Shannon, "It's from *the King*."

Shannon scanned the letter, and then read it out loud,

"From the Moorish National Republic, Moorish Divine and National Movement of the World;

"Aboriginal and Indigenous natural peoples of the Land—Northwest Amexem/North America;

"Public and Legal Notice, Allodial title, to the US Department of Housing and Urban Development...;

"I, King Azeem Basil El Bey, a Moorish American National Aboriginal and Indigenous Natural Person......;

"Make this a legal and public notice of land inheritance to the ancestral estate claim effective immediately..."

The letter then listed its' reference authority,

... "Treaty of Peace and Friendship, Constitution of the USA North American Amendment IV, the Zodiac Constitution Article #4,

Rights of Indigenous People Part II, Land and more..."

She looked up at Riker, who was grinning at her.

"So you said the Arizona police just called about this?"

"Yes, they wanted to know if we had given permission to the King to occupy the properties or if we were going to give him the properties as payment to the ancient treaty."

"I see," she couldn't stop smiling.

"I think the United States entered into some sort of an agreement or Treaty many, many years ago because American ships were being attacked by pirates...Anyway, the people in the Arizona properties have told the police that they are seizing the HUD homes as payment long overdue for the treaty."

"And have you spoken to Legal about this yet?"

"Yes, and I have a meeting with them later today. I'll brief you more after my meeting this afternoon."

"I can hardly wait."

"Well, at least the King also sent a copy of our letter to Janet Napolitano with the Department of Homeland Security, the Maricopa County Sheriff in Arizona, the Honorable Janice Brewer, Arizona Governor, and to the United Nations, Geneva Switzerland Committee of twenty-four. The last one I'm not too sure about."

"Glad that he was thorough."

"Oh, and the FBI are active in this one, too. I guess the Arizona police called them in since this has the implications of an international nature. I'll keep you posted as things transpire."

"I can hardly wait to see how this one wraps up," she continued to smile, and Riker left her office for his meeting with the legal division.

A New Business Model

When she closed her office door, she worked on the future business model for a modernized HUD structure. Shannon detailed the changes that she anticipated would occur in the real estate and FHA home loan arena after the 2008 economic collapse and world market financial explosion. She projected a model for increasing FHA loan activity due to the exodus of conventional and subprime lenders from the lending market. She also projected that other financial underwriters and private mortgage insurance companies would flee from the real estate home loan world, and FHA would step in to provide a reliable source of financing for home purchases.

Because this increase in FHA loan production activity would be relatively short-lived for three to five years, she recommended that two-year contract employees be hired rather than lifetime career employees, to avoid the need for a future reduction in force (RIF) effort when loan demand would significantly decrease. She also made recommendations for actions against the FHA lenders that consciously broke the rules for FHA loan originations and foreclosure avoidance. She recommended that more apprentice level staff be hired instead of high-level, high-grade senior staff, and have a mentoring, training program by the journeymen staff for the newly hired lower-grade staff. HUD was very top heavy with highly graded staff because they had worked for the federal government for so long and had advanced up the grade ladder over time, leaving HUD with a very aging staff and few younger and lower-graded employees. Out of 175 employees, Shannon had less than seven employees under the age of forty at lower grades. HUD had the most senior level, highly graded staff of all the other federal agencies. HUD was paying higher-graded staff to do lower-graded work, which was highly inefficient and costing the taxpayers unnecessarily. She emphasized the need to bring in two-year-contract, lower-graded staff. This suggested hiring methodology would have a significant savings impact on the HUD budget going forward.

She extended her projections forward, predicting that the conventional lenders would reenter the market at the end of 2012 and 2013, and FHA loan activity would decrease correspondingly; thus, HUD/FHA staffing demand should decrease. Alternatively, FHA insurance claims reviews could increase, somewhat due to the higher-risk loans the White House administration had asked FHA to refinance and the corresponding easing in loan terms also directed by the White House. And she drew a word picture detailing the large number of HUD staff that would be retiring from 2012 to 2016. HUD had the largest number of senior employees of any of the federal agencies, with over 60% retirement eligible during 2013–2016. This would then lead to the need for immediate leadership and management training, recruiting, and mentoring of newer employees before the retirement wave crescendoed.

The Government Accounting Office (GAO) had recently released a report entitled Recent Trends in Federal Civilian Employment and Compensation, indicating that… "a mass exodus of agency program managers was anticipated… about 31 percent of all non-postal federal employees in the workforce as of September 2012 will be eligible to retire by September 2017, and 56 percent of the workforce working for midsized agencies (between 1,000–14,999 employees, including HUD) involved in Program Management will be eligible to retire by September 2017…by 2017, the GAO report said, nearly 600,000 employees would be eligible for retirement and require consideration for replacement." The projections were staggering.

Office space was expensive and becoming more expensive, and she wrote into her plan recommendations for utilizing the 'hoteling' concept where teleworking staff would work from any open and available cubicle space in their division when they came into the office. The unions had been advocating that employees could keep their work space permanently, regardless of whether they were in the office full time or only one day a week. This would be an area that could greatly reduce budget outlay.

She worked on a workflow project with HQ staff and another homeownership director on examining historical records on productivity and levels of staffing, determining optimum staffing numbers and appropriate grades for a more efficient future HUD model. Not only was the current structure inefficient, but the underlying processes, such as hiring and grade level designations, were in dire need of improvement. Federal government agencies relied on a 'grade' philosophy, whereas if an employee was a certain grade, the employee's skills were transmutable to any department, regardless of his or her knowledge or experience with a new division. Often, managers were moved into new departments because there was an opening and the person had the right 'grade', but not the knowledge, skills, or any experience in the new area.

Shannon leaned back in her chair after reviewing her final report and felt very pleased with her analysis and recommendations for business transformation to improve the HUD staffing Plan and structure. It had been both a labor of love and dislike. Love, because she deeply cared about making HUD and all federal agencies more efficient, since she had worked for several agencies and had noted best practices but also inefficiencies and waste in them all. Love, because she could clearly see how the recommendations were easily doable and necessary to improve a pedantic government system.

Dislike because she knew change was difficult in the federal government arena. She had friends who called the federal employment system a 'White Collar Welfare' system that carried nonproducing staff that would otherwise have been fired in the real world. Dislike because she knew intimately that the world of federal agencies was controlled by politics, not efficiencies or best efforts and returns. It was a world of processes, not profits.

Love, because she had dedicated her career to the federal government, trying to run her divisions more like a business, with measurable goals and results. She cared for her staff and their success. She had set some good examples, and truly believed she could make a real difference by example and by design. She had strived to effect positive change and improvements within her own areas of responsibility, that could be replicated and implemented immediately to stem the tide of waste, and restore dignity, trust and faith in the federal government arena.

She remembered how she had cried when she had to terminate several employees, even though they had earned their terminations by falsifying records and abusing several federal programs. She waited until she had escorted them from the building, and then stopped in the ladies' restroom to cry quietly for their mistakes and circumstances. She had also celebrated her staff's successes, to her delight and enjoyment. With each of their successes, she knew she had made a contribution. She signed her final Plan and sent it off to Washington, DC.

Apache Trails, Arizona Project

Shannon came into her office around 7:30 a.m., as she did most days, to her ringing telephone. She unceremoniously dropped her purse and briefcase and leaned across her desk,

"Hello, US Department of Housing and Urban Development," she greeted the caller as she walked around her desk and turned on her computer.

"Hello, Ms. O'Toole," the caller answered. "You are the top Executive Director in your office, correct?"

"Who am I speaking to?" she asked.

"This is Fox News. I am trying to verify the facts surrounding the Arizona Deaf Senior Citizens project."

"That project is a multifamily project and not managed from this office. I can give you the contact information in Los Angeles for it..."

"Are you aware of the situation at the Apache ASL Trails senior and deaf project?"

Shannon knew that HUD had made it into the headlines again in October 2013. Fox News had reported that HUD provided the Arizona Deaf Senior Citizens Coalition and its developer with $2.6 million in funds and tax credits to build the apartment complex in 2008. Apache ASL Trails was designed specifically for the hearing impaired. Every unit accommodated wheelchairs, blinking lights to indicate when doorbells rang and when utilities were on and even video phones that let residents "talk" to their friends via sign language. There was also a large events room where many residents met daily to watch television, play games and communicate with sign language. It was now fully occupied, with 69 of the 74 units rented to deaf and deaf-blind residents. But now, HUD was saying that Apache ASL Trails violated civil rights laws, because it showed a preference for the hearing-impaired.

When Shannon didn't immediately answer the reporter, he continued. "Are you aware that the Department of Housing and Urban Development is now saying that Apache ASL Trails violates civil rights laws by essentially discriminating against others who do NOT have a hearing impairment?"

Shannon was painfully aware of the pending situation. She knew that in 2005 a federal study had found that the United States had virtually no affordable housing for the deaf. So the federal government, HUD, had helped build the Apache ASL Trails apartment building in Tempe, Arizona, designed specifically for the deaf.

"I understand that there are some current issues with the property," she tried to answer honestly but without admission of the potential outcomes.

"Are you aware that when HUD approved and helped fund the project in 2008, it did so knowing that the property was specifically designed for seniors who are deaf, hard of hearing and deaf blind? Senator Jeff Flake of Arizona has been attempting to negotiate these matters, and has been quoted in the news as saying, 'I think it's the most ridiculous thing I've heard in a while', and that the National Association for the Deaf has also stepped in, calling HUD's actions 'atrocious' and ' a tragic irony'?"

It was clear to Shannon that this reporter had done his homework and had most of the facts surrounding the project. Although she felt strongly that the project had been conceived and developed in good faith and filled an important need, she couldn't express her personal thoughts and feelings to the reporter. She started to answer, "I…" but the reporter interrupted.

"Did you know that HUD is threatening to pull all federal housing aid to Arizona unless it limits the number of hearing-impaired residents to eighteen people?"

Shannon cringed. She had not heard that HUD had threatened other Arizona projects. She had heard that HUD did not intend to forcibly remove any current tenants in the Apache Trails project, but was arm twisting to have units blocked off to deaf residents in the future once they left. She had read the current HUD attorney's opinion stating that '… a preference or priority based on a particular diagnosis or disability and excluding others with different disabilities is explicitly prohibited by HUD's Section 504 regulations…'

"Arizona state taxpayers and the apartment's developer have now spent $500,000 so far fighting HUD." The reporter was not trying to hide his contempt for HUD any longer. "The Arizona State Housing Director has said that the attorneys he dealt with at HUD he characterized as ignorant and arrogant, and much worse, they are powerful. He also said that if they worked for him, he would have fired them a long time ago."

Shannon waited a moment to see if the reporter was finished, but he continued.

"The Arizona State Housing Director, Michael Trailor, told Fox News that after two years of negotiation, he met with your HUD Secretary, Donovan, hoping to resolve the dispute. Trailor told us Donovan looked him in the eye and said, … ' if you say we have taken too long to resolve this, you are right. If you say we haven't handled this very well, you're right. We are committed to solving this ---but to do so, can you be patient?' It's been another five months now since that conversation."

It seemed to Shannon that the reporter was running out of steam, though she agreed with his passion for what seemed like an unjust situation. She would have very much liked to agree with him and discuss the merits of his position. She felt that he and the state of Arizona were justified in their actions, ethically, morally, and legally. However, she also knew that in her position, she was not able to comment.

"I understand your frustration," she offered the reporter.

He hung up.

Shannon closed her eyes and hung up the phone. *Nice way to start the day*, she thought to herself, and then turned to scan her computer to see what else would challenge her day.

The South Korean Presentation

The phone was ringing when she came into the office later that week in the morning. She picked it up as she shrugged off her trench coat and laid it across the back of her chair. It was the political regional manager calling from San Francisco. Her responsibilities were to maintain excellent relationships with HUD partners, congressional leaders, nonprofit organizations and others, and did not run too deeply into FHA or other HUD programs.

"Hello, Shannon, good morning. Hope you had an easy drive in this morning."

"Much easier than your commute in San Francisco," Shannon smiled. She enjoyed the easy banter with the Regional Administrator, who was responsible more for political matters than program issues.

"Definitely true, but at least we have some public transportation," she countered.

"Ah, yes, you do have that."

"Listen, I have an interesting opportunity I would like to bring your way."

Shannon sat down in her chair and turned on her computer, "And what would that be?" she said casually.

"Well, I've just been informed by HQ that the South Korean government would like to send over a group of delegates to discuss and learn about the HUD Reverse Mortgage

Program, how it is structured, how it works, et cetera. I thought you would be the ideal person to meet with them and introduce our program."

Shannon was pleased to have been tapped as the person for this prestigious opportunity, and answered the regional manager, "I would like that. I would enjoy demonstrating how the federal insurance system works and more specifically, how the reverse mortgage program can assist seniors. It's a great program if it is handled correctly."

"All good and all true. So, the Korean contingent will be coming in about thirty days. I think they are also considering going into Headquarters, but I don't know all the details yet."

"That sounds fine to me."

"Is thirty days enough for you to prepare your presentation?"

"More than enough. I'll work on some tangible handout materials for them to take with them for reference. This will be a pleasure," she smiled into the phone.

"I thought you would enjoy it. So let me know how you are progressing on this, and I'll send you more details as I get them."

"Perfect," she answered.

"We'll talk more later."

Shannon added this latest project to her busy calendar.

Shannon had invited her reverse mortgage specialist, Yoli Ngo, to also be present at the meeting with the South Koreans. She reflected on the many good opportunities for senior homeowners the reverse mortgage offered, but also on the areas of concern she had previously brought to headquarters' attention, including the removal of a younger spouse from title to the property. She couldn't fathom removing someone from title who may have resided in and coowned the property for decades and then removing that person during the course of the reverse mortgage processing. Since the algorithm for calculating the amount of money that could be taken out of the senior's real estate was based on the youngest person's age that was on title to the property, the senior borrowers often wanted to pull out the maximum amount possible, and that resulted in the younger spouse being taken off title, without a thorough understanding of the consequences. Shannon was discussing this issue with Yoli,

"When we make this presentation to the South Korean contingent, I want to emphasize the algorithm terms, so they can see how the age of the seniors affects the amount of cash they can pull out of their homes and the related actuarial charts we use. I want them to see how FHA considers the seniors age and anticipated life expectancy when determining their available funds."

"Sure, I have the tables and charts right here to include in their handouts."

"Great, and I want to carefully discuss the determination of equity that provides the amount of money the seniors can draw down."

"I have a couple of examples right here," Yoli answered, and pulled out three worksheets.

"That will really help", Shannon thanked her. "I want to present the various ways the seniors can pull their available funds out, such as the credit line, the monthly stipend, or the full amount and how they can often pay off their existing mortgage and then have no more house payments, ever."

"Right."

"And we will need to discuss the importance of the seniors continuing to make their property tax and insurance payments timely," Shannon added. "Right now HUD is dealing with this situation, and it is very awkward, to say the least."

"I know," Yoli agreed. "To tell a senior that their reverse mortgage loan is about to be foreclosed on because they failed to pay their property taxes is not pleasant."

"We can suggest to the South Koreans that a requirement to have an impound sort of account for all reverse mortgages to avoid the unpaid property tax and insurance issue would be a good conversation to have."

"True, and we can tell them that we have seen these sorts of issues with our current book of reverse mortgage business, and are considering those requirements for impounded taxes and insurance for all new reverse mortgages in the future."

"All right then. I have a few charts and examples I want to give them to study and use when considering their own reverse mortgage program. I'm not completely familiar with South Korean property rights and forms of holding title, but I want to impress upon them the consequences if a senior is removed from title. I want them to understand that the senior would have to move out and vacate the property if the older senior passes away, and that can be a hardship on someone who has been living in the property for a long period of time."

"This question has been bandied about in Washington, DC for a while now," Yoli explained. "Unfortunately, there has been no movement to change our policy at this time."

"I really think the HUD reverse mortgage program and policy affecting the youngest spouse will have to be addressed, and soon," Shannon added.

"Didn't you send a policy analysis to Headquarters on this issue already?" Yoli asked.

"I did, and I continue to bring it up in policy meetings."

"Well, I sure hope HQ will act on it soon, before HUD has to inform any more seniors that since their spouse died, they now have to move out of their home."

"All true," Shannon agreed. "I want to very carefully explain to the South Koreans how the reverse mortgage payments come out of the equity in the property, that's why HUD is so careful in determining equity and value."

"I have those portions of the reverse mortgage handbook copied and in their handouts too," Yoli answered.

"Both the adjustable-rate and fixed-rate rules?" Shannon queried. "The adjustable loans can be somewhat complicated."

"That's true, and I will have specific worksheets for the adjustable-rate loans."

"That's great." Shannon smiled. "Just leave your handouts with me. I would like to add some more material for our guests and then will have the documents copied and prepared in presentation binders. I have a chart that shows that lenders and banks, not HUD, actually process and make the reverse mortgage loans, but HUD insures the lenders against loss as long as the lenders have followed all of HUD/FHA's program rules."

"That sounds like a good plan," Yoli agreed and stood up to leave Shannon's office. "I really enjoy working with you," she said to Shannon. "You give staff a chance to step up and experience new opportunities, and I appreciate that."

Shannon continued to smile at the younger woman. "I appreciate your knowledge and expertise with the reverse mortgage program, and I want this presentation to be accurate and useful if the South Koreans decide to implement a program similar to ours."

Yoli continued to smile as she turned and left Shannon's office. Shannon turned to a new stack of files on her desk and started to work on her next project.

The Korean presentation date came quickly, and the three delegates from South Korea bowed slightly as introductions were made to Shannon, Yoli, and the political San Francisco regional manager and staff. The San Francisco manager's deputy had also provided written material for the meeting that was used in the introductions.

"I am Chang-Ryoung Cheon, Executive Director and member of the Korea Housing Financing Corporation board of directors. I serve at the pleasure of the President and CEO, Jong Dae Seo, of the Korea Housing Financing Corporation, who is appointed by the President of South Korea.

"The mission of housing finance is to 'ensure stable housing for the public, promote a robust housing market, and advance the nation's housing finance system.' "Our vision statement is that the Korea Housing Finance Corporation is a lifetime financial partner for low- and moderate-income people," he said, reading the prepared statements.

Shannon's research had provided general economic information detailing that the Korean domestic economy had slowed down in all segments in 2011 largely due to the fiscal crisis in Europe and the economic downturn in the United States.

The housing market was on an upward trend in the first half of 2011 on growing demand for housing amid rising Chonsei price and an extended shortage of small and midsized houses particularly in nonmetropolitan areas. Chonsei is a unique Korean lease contract in which the tenant pays an upfront deposit, typically about 40 to 80% of the value of the property, with no requirement for periodic rent payments. At the contract maturation, the landlord then returns the nominal value of the deposit. Since there is no legal obligation on the part of the landlord to deposit the money in an escrow account, the principal default risk associated with the Chonsei contract falls on the tenant. The number of houses for installment sale sold in 2011 totaled 285,000 units, up 41.8 percent from the previous year. In metropolitan areas, 120,000 units were sold, while 165,000 units were sold in nonmetropolitan areas. At the end of 2011, the number of unsold new houses totaled seventy thousand.

"We want to understand how American can make loans with so little down payment," the South Korean representative said. "The old-age senior loans are of most interest to us. How can old-age seniors buy houses and make NO payments?"

When it was Shannon's turn to present the reverse mortgage, HECM, loan program, the South Koreans listened closely. They had submitted several questions to Shannon before the presentation so she could cover their concerns and interests. Shannon turned the page on a flip chart and drew three circles.

"The top circle is the homeowner," she said and drew two figures in the circle.

"The second circle is the bank, or lender," she instructed, and drew a columned building.

"The third circle is HUD or FHA, the insurance company," and she wrote "FHA" into the circle.

"The homeowner completes an application with the lender, who makes the reserve mortgage based on the value of the property, the equity, and the age of the homeowner. Any questions so far?"

One of the South Koreans asked, "How do you determine the equity?"

"Good question," Shannon answered. "An appraisal is done to determine the market value of the property, and then any liens or loans against the property are deducted, leaving the estimated equity in the property."

"OK, I understand," the gentleman said politely.

"We look at the age of the homeowners," Shannon continued, "and determine how much of their equity we can release based upon their life expectancy and actuarial tables."

"Actuarial tables?"

"Um, yes, that measure the estimated length of life. Insurance companies typically create these tables. It defines anticipated Life expectancy."

"I think ours is very long." He smiled at Shannon.

She returned his smile, "Yes, I think so, too."

"No smoking, careful with food, much exercise, stay lean."

She laughed softly, and answered, "All very good habits."

He nodded his head.

"Please note that HUD or FHA does not make the reverse mortgage, the lender does. FHA only *insures* the loan, so that if it does not perform FHA will pay the lender and take back the loan."

"But why does the senior not make payments?"

"Because the lender only gives the senior *a portion* of their equity; the rest is set aside to make the house payments for the estimated life expectancy."

"When the senior dies at end of life expectancy, what happens?"

"The next-ofkin or whomever the senior designated as their end-of-life beneficiary or contact has the option to purchase the house, or leave it with the bank. If they purchase the house, the lender is paid off. If they don't, usually the lender assigns the loan and property to HUD, and HUD pays off the loan to the lender. Then HUD sells the property to recover their money."

The rest of the presentation went very well with good exchanges, questions and answers. Yoli went over the reverse mortgage handbook and pointed out some of the highlights Shannon had asked her to identify.

About two weeks after the meeting, Shannon received a T-shirt that read "Dance Gangnam Style," noting the new international South Korean dance craze that was making its way around the globe, started by Psy, a South Korean rapper and pop star.

A Pending Election Strategy

The Obama administration continued to want HUD to help all the borrowers who had been hurt by the Great Recession and to help other struggling low-income borrowers, by changing the FHA underwriting policies. HUD has previously demonstrated that their existing credit standards and requirements were such that these loans could not be refinanced because most had been made as 'no document' NINJA loans. Now, politically, these presidentially mandated changes in FHA rules and credit requirements were timely for the upcoming elections. The direction coming down to HUD from "the Hill", from the presidential administration, was for HUD to help those subprime borrowers that were struggling or in early default by refinancing them into a new FHA loan even if they had missed a house payment, had been late, or had filed for bankruptcy. Once again, it was intended to transfer the risk from the conventional lenders to FHA. That way, the banks that had originally made the high-risk loans were off the hook, and they were no longer in danger of having their balance sheets affected by defaulting liar loans or loans with weak credit value. It would shore up the banks. Instead, FHA, and the taxpayers, would shoulder the risk, and it would benefit the borrowers with better loan terms. This time $300 billion was marked for this strategy.

Obama sent HUD Secretary Shaun Donovan on a multistate trip to promote the new legislation. Donovan appeared on the *CBS This Morning* show to talk about President Obama's plan to help save people struggling with foreclosures, and met with Los Angeles Mayor Antonio Villaraigosa, Senator Dianne Feinstein, and other leaders sponsoring three refinance bills backed by the President. Donovan was quoted as saying, "Frankly were it not for an election...and an interest of some members to just stand in the President's way on everything...I think we'd see this (legislation) passed easily."

HUD prepared a draft *"Back to Work"* policy change mortgagee letter to FHAapproved lenders pertaining to foreclosures, bankruptcies, alternative credit, and reduction in wage-earner income, allowing borrowers to purchase a new home within a year of their foreclosures—until then, unheard of in the mortgage industry. Shannon and other managers spent hours on conference calls to discuss how this new presidentially directed rule would be made and implemented, and discussed the associated risks. Across the nation, the enforcement divisions, including

Shannon's Quality Assurance group, pushed back with the proposed changes to allow any homeowner who had a change in their household incomes to purchase again within a year of foreclosure as too great a risk. As the draft was written, any change in household income would include additional unverified or rental income from casual or transient renters or boarders, friends or relatives, or anyone else residing at the property, not just the borrower and coborrower's income used to qualify for the loans. The draft was too lenient, and the net it cast was much too broad and not credit worthy. More refined rules were recommended, stating that if anyone on the mortgage loan had a change in income due to loss of job, illness, divorce, and so on and could verify that the income loss was corrected, it would be considered when the borrower reapplied for a new FHA mortgage.

It was determined that the rule change would be temporarily withdrawn and reworked. In August 2013, HUD published new mortgage credit rules, *"Back to Work-Extenuating Circumstances"* that would allow borrowers who experienced a foreclosure to purchase a new home with an FHA mortgage loan <u>after only 12 months from the date of their foreclosure</u>. Until now, borrowers had to wait several years before reapplying for a mortgage after a bankruptcy or foreclosure. Under these new HUD rules, the borrowers had to demonstrate an *economic event*, such as loss of twenty percent or more of the income for the borrowers who had qualified for and signed on the failed/foreclosing loan and that the economic event had lasted for a period of at least six months; that the borrower had recovered from the economic event and reestablished satisfactory credit for twelve months, and that the borrower and coborrowers were living at the foreclosing property. The borrowers had to attend housing counseling. The Back to Work final rule was not what the Obama administration had wanted, however, it was more acceptable now to HUD's own enforcement divisions.

The Obama Administration also wanted lenders to take writeoffs, reducing the principal loan amount by up to $50,000 so the refinanced loan would have a lower house payment and perhaps reflect the reduced value of the property to help with the 'under water' home loans, where the mortgage amounts were greater than the current reduced appraised value. At the same time, the Obama administration was dealt another setback when Acting Director Edward DeMarco of FHFA confirmed he would not allow Fannie Mae and Freddie Mac to offer principal reductions to underwater homeowners. That would damage the holders of the loans who had bought the loan portfolios, with reduced mortgage-note values.

Some called these Obama strategies election-year stunts, HUD Secretary Donovan called them... "the opposite of a bailout"...

A HUD Bailout

The liberal underwriting changes to FHA loans finally began affecting the FHA Insurance Fund.

Housing Wire magazine dated May 2013 ran its headline "Billion Dollar Question, Facing FHA Commissioner Carol Galante ..."

> "...How to shore up the FHA's mutual mortgage insurance fund, whose capital reserve ratio fell into negative territory last year. On April 10, President Obama's budget predicted

a $943 Million government bailout for the FHA would be required....

"...It's a critical time for the agency. If it takes a subsidy from the Treasury, it will be the first time in the agency's nearly 80-year history....

"...U.S. Rep. Jeb Hensarling, R-Texas, chairs the House Financial Services Committee where a series of hearings are under way on the FHA's financial conundrum... **'If the FHA were a private financial institution, likely somebody would be fired, somebody would be fined and the institution would find itself in receivership," said Hensarling...** 'Instead, it is merely and merrily on its way to becoming the recipient of the next great taxpayer bailout."

The *Housing Wire* report stated that serving first-time home-buyers, the low-to-moderate-income population, including minority/ethnic populations, is referred to as the FHA's core mission. The article continued to state that (HUD/FHA) efforts to date included a tighter credit policy that eliminated seller-funded down payment assistance programs, which cost the FHA Mutual Mortgage Insurance (MMI) fund more than $15 Billion in economic value. It also increased down payment requirements to 10 percent for borrowers with credit scores below 580, although the agency (HUD) admits banks and non-bank mortgage companies have shied away from lending to borrowers with FICO scores below 620.

However, Anthony Sanders with George Mason University countered that ... "loans below a 600 credit score, or even below a 640 credit score are 'Political Loans'...The fact that lenders are unwilling to lend to borrowers with credit scores below 620, for example, should signal to FHA that perhaps it shouldn't be in that market...If there was a taste in the marketplace for very low-income households or very low credit score households, the market would respond. Multifamily is where people with low incomes and low credit scores belong. I don't know why the FHA thinks on the ownership side they have to fund that, other than for political reasons." The risk was simply too great. The lower FICO scores indicated irresponsible credit behavior.

Galante responded, "We've made lots of changes and I think all of them have made a large impact on the current and future trajectory of the (FHA) MMI fund...I feel that we are in a good place right now," Galante continued. "I always say we have to work hard at the right balance between facilitating access to credit, helping the economy recover and ensuring we are taking on risk appropriately."

After much posturing, debates, actuarial reports, and dart throwing, HUD did accept funds from the US Treasury. HUD defended itself by pointing to statutory rules that stated HUD was required to have 2 percent of its insurance in force in re-serves and admitted that they had fallen to approximately one half of 1 percent due to the book of bad loans they were deal-ing with from the mortgage financial crisis and refinancing they had done at the direction of the Obama administration in 2008. However, the actuarial reports that damned HUD had not taken into consideration all the premiums and thus refill-ing of the FHA insurance fund from future business that HUD said would eventually put the agency back into compliance.

Budget Talks

The budget talks in Washington, DC in 2013 were not go-ing well, with the Democrats still wanting to extend benefits to the long-term unemployed, Obamacare, spending money on increased food stamps and other assistance programs. The Obama administration still wanted to reduce 'under water' mortgages by up to $50,000. The Republicans wanted less government, less unemployment and other benefits, and lower taxes.

As the deadlines for the national budget approached, it became clear that a government shutdown or sequester would become a reality that most everyone hoped would be avoided. Shannon was summoned back to Washington, DC again. The frequent trips to HQ continued to be difficult. She had to go to the early meetings without coffee like everyone else was sipping and that smelled so good. She had always loved the smell of coffee. But even a couple of small sips would affect her heart. She still rationalized that chocolate was acceptable.

Shannon had arrived at the Reagan Airport in Washington, DC at about quarter to eleven the night before, had pulled her tapestry luggage off the conveyor belt, and hailed a taxi at the airport to take her to the hotel. She had arrived at the hotel around eleven-thirty. Although it was only eight-thirty to her West Coast body clock, she was still weary from traveling and changing to connecting flights in Texas along the way, and dealing with the inevitable delays with the flight and overcrowded seats. As she was unpacking, she pulled out a crimson blouse she hadn't remembered packing and then a gray suit. As she was hanging up the clothes, she saw an unfamiliar robe in the suitcase. She quickly looked through the rest of the suitcase and then squeezed her eyes shut,

"Oh, crap, I hope she wears my size." This wasn't Shannon's suitcase. There must have been an identical piece of tapestry luggage on the luggage carousel. Someone must have accidentally taken her suitcase, and left Shannon hers. Since there was no other tapestry suitcase, she had taken this one, and now she had discovered it wasn't hers.

She stopped unpacking, but she did take a peek at the size on the suit and blouse just in case her own luggage was lost, and went to the phone to call the airlines to report the luggage switch. She had had to wait up until 2:30 a.m. to have the airline pick up her suitcase from the other passenger and bring it to Shannon and then take the wrong piece that Shannon had picked up and return it to the other passenger. There was no real sleep that night, only a short nap before she had to get up and get ready for the day's meetings.

Shannon dressed as warmly as her California wardrobe would provide, with a plum wool pantsuit and black heels. She wore her long blond hair down, and added small diamond-stud earrings. Her makeup was conservative, with light eyeliner and mascara and a light coral lipstick. She didn't wear face makeup and depended on her California tan to suffice. She picked up her black shoulder purse and briefcase.

As she went downstairs to the hotel lobby to catch a taxi, she looked over at three other managers who had called her name.

"Want to share a taxi?" a round woman in her fifties with short red hair asked. There was another woman and a muscular bald gentleman standing with her, who Shannon recognized as managers from another division on the East Coast.

"Sure, that would be great," she answered, envying the hot cups of Starbucks coffee each of the other three managers held. She tried not to be obvious about sniffing the delicious aromas from the coffee, but didn't succeed.

"No coffee for you?" the muscular manager asked Shannon. "You know there's a Starbucks across the lobby, that serves the hotel as well as pedestrians."

She remembered that she had been to previous meetings with these three managers, and was pleased to have colleagues to share the taxi with to and from the HQ meetings.

"No, I don't think she drinks coffee," the red-haired woman answered for her.

"That's correct," Shannon sighed, "But it sure does smell good this morning."

"How much sleep have you had?" the male colleague asked, looking at Shannon sympathetically.

"Not much. About three hours."

"Ouch. That's tough," he smiled. "Well here then," he said and held his hot coffee out toward her. "Take a whiff of this morning brew, maybe it will help."

"Thanks." She smiled back. To change the subject, Shannon asked the group, "Has anyone seen an Agenda yet?"

The third woman, a tall brunette also in her fifties answered, "No, not yet. We don't usually see an Agenda before we get to the meetings. I think HQ doesn't finish modifying the subjects until the last minute."

The red-haired woman concurred, "Yes, I think you're right."

Shannon spoke up, "I understand we'll be discussing the coming year's budget, and the possible need for staff furloughs."

"Yep, and the probably-it-won't-happen federal government shutdown," the male colleague added.

"Right. I was with HUD when the last government shutdown happened," the red-haired woman became animated with her story. "We were all sent home except for a very small handful of what was called 'essential staff,' who were kept working to endorse new FHA loans. We all thought we were not going to be paid, but we were! We received a big fat check for all the days we were forced to stay home. It was really kind of a nice paid vacation if you ask me!"

Just then, a taxi pulled up, and the group of four piled into the car for the ride to HUD headquarters, with the round, red-haired woman getting into the front seat.

"Hey, I just pulled up the agenda on my Blackberry," the muscular male colleague advised the others. "It's just like we guessed: the budget, staffing, furloughs, and possible federal governmentwide shutdown. Oh, and related union notice and negotiations."

"Oh, my favorite", the brunette said. "More union relations matters."

"Are you having many issues with the unions in your office?" he queried her.

"All the time now," she responded and shook her head. "It seems that they are constantly filing grievances and now hostile work environment complaints because management tries to take corrective action for an employee who is not performing, and we all have to spend hours justifying our management decisions and actions. I hope HQ is going to start supporting us soon. It might just help."

The conversation continued until they reached the HUD headquarters building and entered through the security doors. As Shannon started down the hallway on the first floor to the large conference room, a pretty Hispanic woman fell into step with her.

"Good morning, Shannon," she said with a grin. She was a busty, bright-eyed, curvaceous woman with shiny brown curly hair and a beautiful smile. "How was your flight?"

Shannon was pleased to see her friend Carly, short for Carmelita. "It was smooth. I only had a slight delay this time. I had to connect through Dallas, and there were a few thunderstorms, but I still arrived in DC around ten-thirty last night. Has it been cold here? I checked the Weather Channel, and it said you're in a cooling trend." Shannon had been stalled at airports enough to last a lifetime due to weather, mechanical problems, or flight cancelations, especially in Chicago.

"We expect to have snow by the weekend. Hopefully you weel get out before the weather really turns cold." Shannon loved the slight accent and melody in her friend's voice.

"It's so good to see you. It's been a while. Did you ever get away for that scuba diving vacation you were planning?"

"I deed," she answered happily. "And it was sooo beauteeful! The water was so clear and warm! I loved it. I deedn't want to come home."

"And did that new gentlemen you were with want to come home?" Shannon teased her friend.

"Ahhh, si, he came back home so he could see more of me!" she laughed. "He knows what's good for heem!"

They came to the double doors for the large conference room and greeted others entering the room. They were each handed a folder with the agenda and other handout materials and looked around to find seats.

The first morning's meetings were attended by all the HUD executive managers across the nation from all divisions, including Shannon's Single-Family division, the Multifamily group, Nursing Homes, Public and Indian housing, the legal division, the environmental group, and more. An assistant secretary was standing on the small stage at the speaker's podium with additional headquarters managers from the various program divisions seated to his left.

The audience of executive managers settled in and the early-morning hellos and greetings died down as the Assistant Secretary stood and approached the podium.

"Good morning, all," he greeted the audience. "We hope you all had an easy flight or train ride or walk into the office this morning," he said pleasantly. "We know this is a little early for you West Coasters, and we appreciate you adjusting your schedules accordingly."

As the rest of the audience softly moaned or laughed, Carly nudged Shannon's elbow and said, "Yes, very nice of you, Shannon." Shannon shot her a dirty look.

The Assistant Secretary continued...

"At the time the sequester budget was developed, it was never thought that it would have to be implemented. The terms are so severe it was thought that it would encourage a compromise on the national budget negotiations and it would never have to be implemented. However, as we now know, a satisfactory compromise has not been reached, and the sequester budget has now come into effect. Each agency must in turn revise and adjust their budget requests with necessary cuts to meet the terms of the sequester."

There was a long murmur that moved through the room full of directors, as they heard the word 'cuts' again, which would mean lack of program funding, lack of hiring much needed employees because of continuing retirements, continuing vacancies, and more.

"I can hear your concerns," he smiled as he spoke. "We've been working around the clock here in Headquarters trying to decide how best to approach these challenges. I have each one of the program area headquarters directors up here with me, and each will speak to you about recommendations they have proposed to me to deal with the sequester requirements. After lunch today, you will all break out into your respective program areas with your Headquarters director to discuss the details and hopefully to discuss additional thoughts, ideas and recommendations you will have…

"Listen," he said quietly and paused, "I understand the difficulties and hardships that are involved here. There will probably be some delayed projects, definitely delayed hiring and equipment purchases. Our goals will be extended or modified. But the most important matter here is our employees. They, as well as ourselves, are going to feel the impact of possible sequester/furlough days off. It will affect their financial situation. It will greatly affect morale. In headquarters here, we have gleaned our open contracts, shaving off as much contract dollars and future projects as legal and possible. We have put new contracts on the back burner. You all know this already, because you were asked last week to list what contract work could be delayed in your respective offices, and you responded quickly."

There was a little murmuring in the audience as the managers recalled their exercise in deleting planned contracting actions and adjustments to program goals.

"We have reduced the HUD budget as much as possible here from Washington. But there will still be some necessary furlough days for all staff to meet the sequester requirements."

"Will some staff remain and work during the furlough days?" A question came from the audience.

"No, I'll explain that. Any furlough day means that all federal government staff is off. No one works, no managers, no staff. That's because the money to pay salaries on that day will not be spent, thus helping to reduce the federal national budget expenditures."

"Can we or our staff work on a volunteer basis?" Another question came from the managers.

"No. Absolutely not. There is an implied basis that if a federal employee works, he will get paid. And we cannot accrue any salary dollars during furlough days off."

The room full of managers talked among themselves as the assistant secretary walked over to his program managers on the stage, and then he returned to the podium.

"I will be making an all staff teleconference call next week to announce the sequester and furlough situation and how it will affect our staff. I will be sending out more information on this by the end of the week. I ask you not to try and inform your staff of this situation before my teleconference because I think there could be some confusion and initial misunderstandings. I want all of our staff to get the same information at the same time from me." He paused, clearly feeling the responsibility of the current situation.

"And now I am going to advise you that in addition to the furlough days, and we don't know just how many there will be, between five and ten depending on how our final budget works out; we could also be facing a complete federal government shut down."

At this news, the room actually sat quiet.

"As I said earlier this morning, no one believed that we would ever get to this point, and that the terms of the sequester would ever be activated. But, here we are. Our legislators are at opposing ends of the national budget field. We still don't know if this will happen, but we need to prepare ourselves in the event it does. In the event of a federal government shutdown, we will allow essential staff to work, and you will have to let each of your program managers know who that would be and what function they would be performing. In headquarters, we have been talking about this possibility all week, and have an idea of what essential staff would look like and be needed to keep basic HUD and FHA operations going so we don't impact the public more than absolutely necessary.

"I think it is time now for each of your program managers to tell you what they have proposed in terms of cuts to meet the sequester requirements. I look forward to hearing what other thoughts or suggestions you have to help reduce our HUD budget." He then left the stage after introducing the next speaker with the audience listening to the program area dire reports.

The Assistant Secretary for HUD called an all staff teleconference for all employees across the nation. Shannon went downstairs to the large eighth-floor conference room with her staff to watch the presentation with them. She knew the announcements that were coming from the assistant secretary about the unpaid furlough days would not be a pleasant task. It caused unknown hardships on many of the federal employees. Loss of pay could make the difference in being late on a car payment or rent. It seemed that Congress had spent budget money on unlimited benefits and aid and had taken it now from the federal staff. Very few staff members would welcome the time off, although unpaid.

She did not agree with how the entire Wall Street meltdown had been handled by the Federal Reserve or congress, with their selected bailouts and extended social benefits. Food stamps had nearly doubled across the country, unemployment benefits had been extended several times, and requests for housing and rental assistance had skyrocketed. But now the federal employees would pay for some of those bailouts and benefits with furlough days, so their salaries could be used for other federal expenses. She had lived through the FDIC and RTC banking and savings and loan crisis, and felt strongly that the players that had caused the Great Recession should be held responsible. However, they had continued to receive their pay and take outrageous bonuses and other perks, while now the federal employee paid with their earnings.

She did pause and consider that the good news was that the federal staff still were employed, whereas a staggering number of private citizens had been laid off and were no longer able to meet their financial obligations. However, there were really no good feelings about the current situation that was about to be explained to her staff.

Soon after the furlough days were completed, the Assistant Secretary made another difficult call to all staff.

As it had been discussed in Washington, DC that the furloughs were not the end of the budget impasse with the US Congress and President Obama, and now a federal government shutdown was looming.

The Assistant Secretary had sent an e-mail to all HUD staff, this time advising them of the seriousness of the state of the nation's budget impasse, and advising them that there would soon be a mandated federal governmentwide sequester and shutdown. This closure was for an unknown period of time. It would last until the Washington, DC elected officials and the President of the United States agreed on a working budget. This time the staff didn't know how much salary they would lose, and expressed their frustration over not being able to budget or plan for their immediate expenses. They asked if it was allowable for them to take another job during the interim, and still be able to return to HUD when the shutdown was lifted. Or to keep the second job while working at HUD to make up for lost wages.

The federal government shutdown began in October 2013. Only those employees deemed to be 'essential' were allowed to come into the office, and they were not paid. HUD essential services included continuing rental assistance vouchers, insuring FHA loans, and paying contractors for services rendered while HUD staff was off. In the event the budget was finally passed and had sufficient funds, the essential staff could receive payment for their essential time, however, it was not guaranteed or promised.

Shannon had only a handful of essential staff to process the real estate contractor invoices and to approve other health and safety repairs. Additional invoices for required vendor services had to be reviewed and certified for payment, and new loans had to be processed for insurance by a contractor with oversight from HUD.

Shannon came into the office each day. It was like walking into a ghost town, with no staff on her floor, no phones ringing, no faxes, no conversations. She went down to other floors to check on her essential staff and to determine if they were able to keep up with the essential workload, and she pitched in to verify and process invoices and loan oversight. She knew that if and when the federal government shutdown finally ended, the backlog and time to catch up would be enormous. It was eerie to not have any contact with Washington, DC management, no e-mails, no phone calls. No communication.

She finally received a call from the associate deputy assistant secretary to see how the essential operations were going, and she brought her up to speed. Other than that, it was silence from the outside.

The Obama administration reached a stop-gap spending bill agreement that ended the 16 day federal government shutdown close to midnight and the back-to-work summons was issued to all federal employees to return to work the next day. After more than two weeks of the federal government shutdown, staff was beginning to return to work, some thankful that the shutdown was over, some anticipating the work that had piled up, many still resentful that they had been forced to suffer both unpaid furlough days and now the entire federal shut down for two weeks.

Managers were grappling with the consequences of the shutdown including lost or forgotten passwords, overdue reports, getting a reading on project schedules and delayed actions. Washington DC was asking for backlog reports.

Shannon was working on reports at her desk when her Deputy tapped on the door and stepped in.

"Did you see where the union is filing a lawsuit against HUD to get back pay for all the staff for the sequester days off?"

"I find that interesting," Shannon answered. "I thought that HUD staff had all been paid back for any days off the last time the federal government shutdown, so I'm not really surprised."

"Well, the staff is all hopeful that that will happen again this time, and I am too."

"Don't you think it's a little awkward that the staff all had two and a half weeks off work, didn't have to get up and get ready then drive to work, answer phones all day, respond to customers and constituents, and now be paid for staying home?"

"I don't have a problem with that."

"You don't think that the optics of this whole matter will be perceived by the public as another government freebie, paying workers for two weeks to stay home and not work?"

"I don't have a problem with that either."

"You don't think there will be backlash for this government shutdown and payment to staff?"

"It won't have any effect on me."

"Seriously?"

"I have a vacation to plan. I just want the pay, that's all," and she turned and left Shannon's office.

Sometimes Shannon envied a more simple approach.

Another conference call with Headquarters was scheduled, this time with the Deputy Assistant Secretary for HUD Single Family, Charles Coulter. He had scheduled a conference call with senior managers to discuss the small office closings project. Shannon walked into her office with a full glass of ice water and a small salad for lunch as she settled into her chair to prepare for the meeting, followed by her Deputy. She opened up her computer and scanned the agenda. She was still scanning the agenda as she called into the conference call.

"Hello, this is Shannon," she announced herself.

"Hello, Shannon," she heard in response from several others on the line.

"How's it out there in California?" a familiar voice asked.

"Beautiful as usual," she answered. "Palm trees are swaying, sky is blue..."

"And the smog is bountiful," her friend Damien from HQ was baiting her.

"I'll trade a little smog for your ice and snow," she bantered.

"Yeah, but tell me one thing good about your smog."

"It makes for beautiful sunsets!" she teased.

"Oh, is *that* what makes your sunsets orange!"

As her Deputy smiled, the rest of the managers on the line laughed good naturedly, and Charles came on the line.

"Hello, all," he began. That was his favorite salutation and how he always opened his conference calls. "I'm glad you could all carve time out of your busy schedules to make this call happen." He paused and then continued. "You may have heard pieces of what I am about to tell you, but I want us all to have a chance to discuss it here today so we can make this plan work as smoothly as possible.

"As you know, many of our field offices have become smaller in terms of staffing and workload due to our accelerated retirements and changing demographics. We actually have offices being manned by only one or two employees. It doesn't make sense to pay the overhead for office space for these smaller offices. And in light of the recent budget issues and furlough days, it makes sense to close some of these smaller offices at this time."

There was a little murmuring on the line as the managers spoke quietly to deputies in their office also listening to the call.

"So I am going to give you a proposed list of small offices in your jurisdiction and ask you if you think it would be fiscally responsible to close it or not. And if you do, to give me your plan to move any workload to another office or location. Any questions so far?"

"What about the staff in the closing offices?" an East Coast manager asked.

"Our plan details that they will be offered a buyout, which will be attractive to those near and ready for retirement. Others will be transferred to the next closest office or possibly be given a choice as to where they might want to go. Of course, we have to look at all the administrative and moving costs associated with their choices and the available workload at the receiving office to see if it supports another full-time employee."

"What is the timeline for this program?" Shannon asked.

"We will start with closing the identified small East Coast offices first," Charles informed all the managers. "Then we will progress across the country, ending in Shannon's area."

There was some general discussion then about the efficiencies of the small office closings and the overall impact it would have on workload balancing and staffing.

"I will send out the list of offices later this afternoon." Charles was speaking again. "If you would get back to me this week on your suggestions or alternatives, I will appreciate it."

The conference call was soon completed.

"So," Shannon said to her Deputy, "what are your initial thoughts on the small offices in our area targeted for closing?"

Shannon thought it was a good plan and had spoken to Charles and other Assistant Secretaries about saving millions of dollars in expensive rents and overhead. Especially with the volume of FHA loan activity decreasing now in 2013 due to the reemergence of the conventional lending market, it was no longer feasible or fiscally responsible to continue to provide

HUD offices in areas with shrinking demands for HUD and FHA services and minimal staffing.

"I don't think it will ever happen. HUD has tried to close offices before to save money, but they never did it."

"Why is that?" Shannon queried.

"Because in the past, the local government leaders, congressmen, senators, mayors, and such lobbied HUD headquarters and demanded that the local small HUD offices stay open to service their constituents. They felt it bought them votes."

"That model just doesn't work anymore," Shannon responded. "We can't justify a fifteen-hundred- to three-thousand-square-foot office space for one or two employees anymore, especially when they telework two or three days a week!"

"I'm just saying that I don't expect to see any offices closing, not now, not ever."

Another simple approach, Shannon thought. "HUD has some interesting history."

The unions were pushing back on the small office closings project. Their position was that they supported the rights of the affected employees to stay in their present offices, and they were fighting against the inconvenience and hardships any relocations would create. They went so far as to file motions to delay the closings and demanded evidence that Congress had appropriated sufficient funds to HUD to handle the reassignments and relocations. With the federal government's fiscal budget ending in September, a new budget not being passed, and a federal government shutdown looming for October 2013, the unions pushed many of the small office closings off for over nine months into 2014. HUD continued to pay millions of dollars in nearly vacant small office space due to these delays.

HUD labor relations tiptoed around the unions as the unions stalked the halls in Washington, DC to demand that HUD abide by the Obama administration's edict to listen to the union's demand and predecisionally discuss any management actions.

Some of the unions then demanded to negotiate additional terms for the small office closings, and submitted their terms to permit all affected small office employees to telework from home full time until 2017. That would be about three years without going into a HUD office.

By mid-2014, the designated smaller offices had finally closed, the affected staff was given approximately three months of telework and more time to relocate, and HUD could reduce its line item by many millions of dollars in the budget for office space.

The Hatch Act of 1939 and 2014

The Hatch Act had been passed to prohibit political activity, rallying, campaigning or influential activities in the federal workplace. Officially, the Hatch Act was defined as an act to prevent pernicious political activities and is a United States federal law whose main provision prohibits employees in the executive branch of the federal government, except the president, vice president, and certain designated high-level officials of that branch, from engaging in some forms of political activity.

Each year, the HUD legal department circulated a reminder that Hatch Act activities were prohibited, especially during election period cycles. The statutory prohibitions on agency lobbying include federal statutes and appropriation restrictions contained within the Consolidated Appropriations Act 2012, retained in the Consolidated and Further Continuing Appropriations Act 2013. The conflict-of-interest problem is obvious. If your boss suggests that you take a political stand on an issue, you might legitimately wonder if your job or advancement opportunities depend on complying.

In February 2014, the United States House of Representatives, Committee on Financial Services in Washington, DC issued a memorandum regarding an oversight and investigative subcommittee hearing entitled "Inspector General Report: Allegations of Improper Lobbying and Obstruction at the Department of Housing and Urban Development". The Memorandum further stated that... "the HUD Inspector General will provide testimony on his office's investigation of improper lobbying and the efforts of officials at the Department of Housing and Urban Development to obstruct the investigation and conceal their improper activities."

Congress called Housing and Urban Development officials to testify before Congress over a Hatch Act scandal at HUD. The Subcommittee on Oversight and Investigation chairman, Rep. Patrick McHenry (R-NC), called on the Department of Housing and Urban Development to provide key current and former officials for testimony at the upcoming hearing on February 26, 2014, on the alleged scandal at the HUD agency.

An inspector general's report said senior HUD officials allegedly engaged in inappropriate lobbying that violated federal statutes and attempted to obstruct the office's investigation of the matter. The HUD inspector general testified that certain

HUD officials failed to comply with Federal law and HUD policies prohibiting lobbying, as well as efforts by certain HUD officials to obstruct the investigation of those matters

Earlier, HUD's inspector general uncovered alleged improper lobbying activity undertaken by a former HUD deputy secretary, Maurice Jones, and a whole host of other HUD figures. According to the inspector general's reports, e-mails had been sent to over one thousand recipients, including many of his staff, asking them to contact several U.S. senators and encouraging them to vote in favor of procedural motions to advance Senate consideration of S. 1243, a bill making appropriations for transportation, housing and urban development and related agencies ("THUD"). The e-mail communication urged recipients to oppose certain amendments and suggested that recipients encourage named Senators to support final passage of the bill.

The e-mail read... *"I am humbly asking you to let your Senators especially the ones listed below know how important it is that the cloture motion passes so that the Senate THUD bill MOVES FORWARD to a vote and TO VOTE for the Senate THUD bill...it is critical that your Senator hears from you NOW. Specifically, we need to maintain the current level of Republican support for the Senate THUD FY14 appropriations bill, acquire other Republican supporters and ensure vocal and active support from Democratic Senators. Please ask them (the listed Senators):*

- *To vote YES tomorrow on the cloture motion to end the debate and to vote YES on the merits of the bill when it comes up for a vote;*

- *To defend against efforts by some Republicans to prevent the underlying bill from coming up for a vote or to enact harmful amendments such as those that would cut some of the important funding in the bill;*
- *For example, Senators should vote "No" against Senator Coburn's Amendment 1754 which would have a devastating effect on our homeless population."*

The IG report stated, "His e-mail violated Federal law, as well as HUD internal policy, prohibiting federal employees from lobbying …"The Committee on Financial Services Memorandum stated … "The directness and specificity of the email communication appeared to violate well established federal restrictions on lobbying by federal agencies…"

Jones was able to provide information indicating that internal HUD legal resources had approved the e-mails and assured him they were not in violation of Hatch. However, Jones moved on to become the commerce secretary for the newly elected Virginia Democratic Governor, Terry McAuliffe.

The financial services memo continued to state, "Other HUD officials, including Elliot Mincberg, attempted to withhold information from Congress and the IG and claimed he was doing so at the direction of and in 'coordination' with top layers from President Obama's White House."

The *Washington Times, Reverse Mortgage Daily, Breitbart News*, and others reported that the alleged White House involvement in obstructing the pertinent investigation was buried on page nineteen of the inspector general's report.

Senator Chuck Grassley (R-IA) told *Breitbart News*,

"If an employee is trying to withhold information from or obstruct an investigation of the Inspector General or member of Congress, that's alarming. The appropriate entities, including law enforcement as necessary, need to get to the bottom of it."

The White House Administration had also asked HUD officials, managers, and staff to tout certain pending pieces of legislation when they were meeting with industry partners and the public, to make them aware of the pending legislation and to gain their support in contacting their local congressional representatives to push the passage of several pending bills.

The Menendez-Barbara Boxer 'Responsible Homeowner Refinancing Act of 2012' would eliminate certain upfront fees on Freddie Mac and Fannie Mae refinances, eliminate appraisal fees, and penalize second lien holders who unreasonably blocked a refinance.

The Senator Feinstein bill would create a new six-billion-dollar FHA fund to provide insurance on federally backed loans and to homeowners who owed more on their home mortgage than their home's value, also known as underwater mortgages. This proposal was modeled after a plan presented by President Obama in his February State of the Union Address. The Feinstein bill would also increase the acceptable loan to value to 140 percent to encourage more homeowners to refinance with FHA. This would move the loans and credit risks associated with those loans away from conventional mortgage lenders and transfer the risk of loss to HUD.

Senator Merkley had proposed a bill to encourage shorter-term loan refinances with no closing costs for underwater borrowers, and with no need to qualify for the monthly payments.

Its intent was to help homeowners build up their equity by paying down their loans sooner.

And Senator Jack Reid from Nevada proposed a bill called 'Rebuilding Neighborhoods: Project Rebuild and Distressed Asset Stabilization Program', designed to stabilize hardest hit neighborhoods with the highest number of foreclosures.

The current White House wanted HUD to do everything possible to save homeowners from foreclosure, to prevent an increasing avalanche of foreclosures in hardest hit areas and across the nation, and to use housing as a tool to restart the economy after the 2008 mortgage meltdown.

The risk to the FHA fund in refinancing the underwater loans was calculated by the current administration as tolerable, with the infusion of more money into the FHA insurance fund to provide cash for anticipated foreclosures and losses to FHA.

Shannon paused after reading all of above the memos and reports. She had thought about the fact that any outside company, special-interest group, or contractor could and did approach their congressmen, senators, and heads of agencies to tout their availability, willingness, and interest in doing business with the government. In fact, many politicians and lobbyists had their offices very near the White House on Ave K. Ave K was the code word for lobbyists, special-interest groups, and other companies that could pay to have their lobbyist represent their companies to their colleagues, old congressional acquaintances, and friends in federal government.

The HUD marketing and management contractors had lobbied hard and long in Washington, DC saying that they could do the job of managing and selling foreclosures better than HUD staff, which eventually resulted in the mega-multimillion-dollar HUD M&M contract work. Technical companies and accounting firms constantly lobbied HUD and just about all the other government agencies in Washington, DC, offering their superior brand of data mining, business analysis, and accounting services. Auctioneers, loan servicers, escrow companies, title companies, property inspection companies, and thousands of other vendors continually passed through the halls of HUD and the other federal agencies, and Congress to solicit business, and it was legal.

So why couldn't government employees lobby for themselves, for their own benefit, offsetting the private-sector lobbying? The private sector constantly pushed and bragged that the private sector could do the work better than government employees. Why was it so wrong for federal employees to respond in kind? Because there were rules, obviously, and laws to prevent such activity. But the one-sidedness of the situation continued to remain on Shannon's mind.

HECM in the Headlines

The home equity conversion mortgage, or HECM reverse mortgage, was in trouble. *Pratt v HUD* was another lawsuit from unhappy HECM seniors, but this time it was a class-action suit from a nonborrowing spouse alleging that the HUD program and lender had misguided and misinformed the nonborrowing spouse to be removed from title in order to obtain a HECM reverse mortgage, never discussing the consequences: foreclosure and eviction. Instead, the lenders had focused on how the seniors could draw the equity out of their homes and possibly never have to make a house payment ever again.

The *Washington Post* ran a leading story on February 27, 2014:

> **"...Surviving spouses sue HUD over reverse mortgage rules that leave them in the cold (Washington DC)...**Four surviving spouses of people who had taken out reverse mortgages on their houses filed a class-action lawsuit Thursday against the U.S. Department of Housing and Urban Development, saying HUD had failed to protect them from displacement and foreclosure as required by federal law.
>
> "...The suit comes nearly five months after a federal court ruled that HUD regulations, which allow banks to foreclose on surviving spouses who are not on the reverse mortgage or force them to pay it off, contradict a federal statute designed to protect them.

"...HUD declined to comment on the suit.

> "...A reverse mortgage provides cash to homeowners who are 62 or over in exchange for equity in their homes, either as a lump sum or in monthly disbursements. Payment of the loan is deferred until they die, sell, or move out of the house, at which point their heirs can sell the home to pay off the mortgage. The amount of the mortgage can compound to surpass the value of the property. Most reverse mortgages are insured by HUD.
> "...One factor in approving a reverse mortgage is the age of the buyer, and brokers tell couples that they can get more money if only one borrower, almost always

the older one, is listed, said Craig Briskin, an attorney with Mehri & Skalet PLLC who is a co-counsel in both suits. To get the loan, the non-borrowing spouse must also be removed from the title.

"They don't tell them that you're not protected if you die," he said.

"...Although reverse mortgages have been around since 1988, they were not widespread until the 2000s; there are now 600,000 outstanding reverse mortgages, according to Jean Constantine-Davis, a senior attorney with AARP Foundation Litigation and a co-counsel in both suits.

"The problems for surviving spouses arose after the 2008 housing collapse, when many homes lost equity," Briskin said. "They didn't treat the spouse as a home-owner at all."

"...The plaintiffs in the suit live in Nevada, Massachusetts, Florida, and California. It is unclear how many additional surviving spouses are in this situation, but it is "likely thousands," Constantine-Davis said.

Reverse Mortgage Daily ran another headline:

Local NBC News Profiles Reverse Mortgage Non-Borrowing Spouse Case (Reverse Mortgages),
February 2014:
"A local Baltimore NBC News outlet this week looked into the potential implications faced by non-borrowing reverse mortgage spouses when they are removed from the title of their homes.

"The coverage from local WBAL TV-11 focuses on one couple, Mr. and Mrs. Breeden, who took out a reverse mortgage on their Baltimore County home in 2007 and are now fearing the loss of their home should the borrower named on the title and reverse mortgage need to move into full time care.

"The Breedens went through U.S. Department of Housing and Urban Development-required counseling before taking the reverse mortgage, but they said the issue of taking Charlotte off the title didn't come up, and they didn't truly understand what could happen," WBAL TV-11 said.

"HUD now requires all non borrowing spouses to attend reverse mortgage counseling, per a 2011 mortgagee letter.

The news segment borrowed some insight from National Reverse Mortgage Lenders Association President and CEO Peter Bell, on why couples might consider removing one spouse from the home title when taking out a reverse mortgage.

"It's something that's generally done when people have existing indebtedness on the property and other expenses that need to be paid, and they can't get enough money if the loan is underwritten to the younger age," Bell said.

Also mentioned in the segment is the case of Robert Bennet, who is represented by the AARP Foundation in a lawsuit against HUD that claims the agency violated federal law by making surviving spouses vulnerable to foreclosure.

A Washington, D.C. court ruled against HUD in the October-September lawsuit in favor of two reverse mortgage non-borrowing spouses, however, HUD filed a notice of appeal regarding the lawsuit.

Shannon had brought this area of risk up in Headquarters previously; however, there had been no mitigating action taken at that time. Now with the headlines and pressure on HUD to change their HECM rules, Shannon leaned into Washington to work on the team to make the appropriate modifications to the HECM program. She felt personally rewarded to see this issue finally coming to resolution.

TOTAL – Technology Open to All Lenders, or How to Fake It until You Make It, Faking out FHA Credit Requirements

Shannon was running lender-default reports again and noticed an uptick in defaults for several lenders in the southwest area. She ordered the files and, when they arrived, saw that the lenders' underwriters had submitted the loans through FHA's automated credit scoring program, TOTAL, for Technology Open to All Lenders. This automated scoring system had been created by HUD to provide lenders with an efficient and consistent method for inputting borrower income and liability information for the purpose of determining acceptable credit and loan approval. Loans could be manually underwritten; however, that proved to be time consuming, and the automated system was primarily used for determining eligibility.

However, Shannon became concerned when she looked closely at the files and saw that the loan applications had been submitted to TOTAL often up to eighteen times! She discovered seventeen declines and then, finally, an acceptance on the eighteenth attempt. Some of the loans were only submitted six or seven times, each receiving declines until the final submission. She assigned staff to the loan files and waited for their draft report. Her staff found that the underwriters tweaked the credit information in each one of the defaulted files just enough to get the loan through the automated approval process. Sometimes they had pushed up the income just enough to get the loan through or, more often, dropped a liability, thus changing the income to house payment ratios.

But just as serious, she saw loans that were being approved by the TOTAL system at 55%, instead of the customary 32%-34% of income to house payment ratios. FHA credit risk analysis had proved that the higher the percentage of income used for mortgage payments, the higher the risk of default and foreclosure. FHA provided that a purchaser's house payment should be no more than 32-34% of their income, not 55%. There were several approvals even higher, that made it through the TOTAL system at 65%. Years of financial risk analysis had developed the 32%-34% house payment to income as a reasonable and sustainable ratio, giving the homeowner a solid opportunity to make their regular house payments and not lose their house to foreclosure.

She spread the loan files on her desk and turned to her computer, commencing a memo to Washington, DC detailing her discovery and recommending that the algorithm controlling the approval process be corrected.

She was contacted by HUD Washington, DC and asked to attend a Senior Executive discussion on the TOTAL issue. She flew to Washington DC and walked into the meeting with three Assistant Associate Secretaries and various credit Directors, and was handed the agenda for the day.

"Good to see you, Shannon," an Assistant Associate Secretary greeted her. "Glad you could make it."

"It's good to see everyone again," Shannon responded with a quiet smile.

"This is going to be a lively meeting."

"Why is that?" she inquired.

"Well, the Director from the FHEO, Fair Housing and Equal Opportunity, group is going to be here shortly, and explain why changing the TOTAL algorithm is not supported by their group or the President's administration, because it would decline loans on too many low income and minority borrowers. Their group has been trying to get our credit divisions to loosen up the algorithm, not tighten it."

Shannon frowned for a moment, "And what about our FHA manuals and rules that state the ratios should be close to 32% for mortgage to income ratios and 43% for all liabilities to income? Those are stated underwriting rules. And the number of defaults we are experiencing because of the higher credit ratio loan approvals? Have they considered the increasing defaults we are seeing again, after all the problems with the subprime loans and Wall Street fiascos with the liar loans?"

"I don't think they care."

"I should think they cared about the FHA claim fund that is taking major hits and payouts because of these over encumbered loans that never should have been made. I've been in meetings where they discussed raising the insurance premiums again to offset these losses."

"The political pressure is heavy and getting heavier all the time," the Assistant Associate Secretary whispered. "It's all about getting votes, increasing homeownership, and making headlines, staging media opportunities."

"But FHA just resisted taking a taxpayer bailout because of the shrinking mortgage insurance premium fund."

"I know, but now FHA is also going to ignore collection accounts when credit qualifying borrowers."

"Unpaid collection accounts have always had a negative effect on a borrower's credit and perceived ability and responsibility in paying their mortgage. It's an indication of the borrower's previous credit behavior if they paid their debts. Good underwriting has always required the borrower to pay the collection accounts or at least arrange for a payment plan to pay them off," Shannon stated.

"Uh-huh, but this is all part of the Presidents' plan to increase homeownership. There are elections coming up."

The meeting was called to order, and Shannon took a seat next to the Assistant Associate Director.

After many hours of discussion, reports being passed around, several power point presentations, and speakers, it was agreed that the TOTAL automated credit scoring program would be adjusted to reduce the maximum ratio that would be approved for FHA loans, but it wasn't adjusted down to the 34% recommended margin. It was allowed to remain significantly higher to satisfy the FHEO, EEO and presidential administration's targeted priority goals. Additional concession was given in the form of ignoring collection accounts, which conventional lenders attributed to more risky loans.

Notice to FHA lenders toward the end of October 2013 stated,... "FHA does not require collection accounts to be paid off as a condition of mortgage approval...FHA is requiring the lender to follow the guidelines on collection accounts with an aggregate balance less than $2,000...the lender is NOT required to consider or evaluate collection accounts...." Other directions to FHA lenders stated, ... "All medical collections and charge-offs are excluded and...do not require resolution,"... a concession to making FHA more accessible for administration purposes.

California

Back in the office again in California, Shannon and her Real Estate division Director, Riker, had poured over recent REO reports, looking at demographic and geographic concentrations and current market performance information. The western area markets in Shannon's jurisdiction were improving, and the HUD Homes real estate operation was prepared and poised. She and Riker had implemented an automated valuation method for establishing a current market value for each property. Combined with a customary appraisal and broker opinion of value, the properties were listed at the current market value and sold quickly They had determined that a real estate auction would be an efficient and cost-saving strategy for selling larger concentrations of properties at one time. Including the auctions, Shannon's office sold over 15,381 properties in 2013, decreasing holding time by 10% and improved recovery rate by over 11%. Over 125,600 HUD homes were sold throughout the nation.

In 2013, under Shannon's guidance, in spite of the Federal Governmentwide shutdown, her office endorsed 289,203 new FHA mortgage loans; 118,646 to first-time homebuyers. Over one million new FHA loans were originated in 2013 throughout the nation, and the 2014 loan production figures were on track to mirror the previous year. Although other areas in the nation might have originated and insured more loans, her dollar volume was the highest in the nation due to the market value of the real estate in the western states including Hawaii. Thus, Shannon's operation brought in a very significant portion of insurance premiums to bolster the FHA fund, and the default and claim rates were among the lowest.

She had been an invited public speaker at hundreds of events, meetings, and conferences, including the National Association of Real Estate Brokers (NAREB), Mortgage Broker's Association (MBA), National Association of Hispanic Realtors, National Reverse Mortgage Lenders Association (NRMLA), Women in Banking groups, Professional Mortgage Women's meetings, events with local politicians and other government agencies, and had written speaking points for other HUD officials' speeches.

Shannon had been taking a close look at HUD operations, programs and processes, completing a mental checklist of the policy changes and process changes she felt needed to be completed before she would feel she had completed what she had set out to do when she accepted the homeownership executive director position. She had worked on the HECM reverse mortgage policy modifications, FHA loan credit policies, the seller-funded down payment programs, worked on the TOTAL automated loan approval program and had written the recommendations for the Single Family office structure and hiring plan. She had enjoyed directing staff in stopping fraud, waste, and abuse in the FHA lender industry. The furloughs and government shutdown were over. She had closed small offices that could no longer be justified. The promises she had made when she accepted the promotion to the top HUD Executive Director position had been ful-filled—and more.

A New Look at Government Lien Collections, IRS Liens, and HUD

It was Monday morning, and HUD headquarters called its weekly management meeting via conference call with Shannon and the three other homeownership directors. Shannon also invited her five Program Directors to the meeting to keep them informed of any new programs or policies that headquarters was rolling out.

Headquarters had decided to add a little humor to the meeting and asked the directors to tune into a YouTube skit on conference calls.

It began with the committee moderator welcoming all the callers to the conference call and began a roll call, however, the first caller had so much noise in the background with dogs barking and children crying that he couldn't fully announce his name; The second caller's line went dead halfway through announcing his name;

The third caller had noise from a backing-up truck, and then a siren went by, and she never could finish announcing her name; A fourth caller called in, but it was for the wrong meeting;

The second caller called again, but his line went dead, again;

A fifth caller announced her name but then rattled papers so loudly that no one could hear anything further;

A sixth caller announced their name and forgot to put the phone on mute so that everyone had to listen to her private conversation with someone else about picking up groceries for dinner that night;

The second caller called in again, this time apologizing for his phone line going dead, twice;

And the seventh caller announced his name, and then water running—hopefully not flushing—was all that was heard.

As the Directors chuckled at the scenario, Charles added,

"OK, this one was funny, but how much of it was familiar to us, and have we had to deal with similar situations? I just wanted to point out that this is what we want to avoid. So let's get on with our call now...."

As the meeting began to close, Shannon looked at her notes and turned to her Real Estate Director.

"Riker, has FEMA paid HUD yet for all the Katrina victim rental properties we prepared and gave them to use?"

Riker chuckled and answered, "Nope, not yet. They still owe us at least $52 million dollars for repairs and rent."

"What's the latest we have from them?"

"Well, FEMA provided HUD with a list of disaster victims names, and HUD cross indexed the names with those people already receiving public assistance, Section 8 rental housing assistance and public housing and found quite a few duplicate names. HUD asked FEMA to resort their list of eligible persons removing the duplicate names of those that were already living in HUD public housing. FEMA resorted the list, but only the column with the alphabetical names, not the pertinent rows of information pertaining to social security numbers, addresses, phone numbers, et cetera. Thus, none of the contact information was usable."

"You're kidding!"

"I'm not. We've been chasing that money for a long time, and here we are in 2014. I wonder if we have any new liens on those properties now. They were clear when we gave them to FEMA, but it's been a long time, and additional new liens could have been applied for lack of maintenance, taxes, and other levies if FEMA didn't pay them too."

Shannon began to think about the GLIC program, the Government Lien/ IRS Collection program she had presented to Congress, and how HUD might be involved, if it had ever had any HUD homes redeemed by the IRS, or if the IRS liens and other government liens filed against HUD home loans had all been extinguished at the time of the foreclosure. Or had the government agencies with liens against the HUD home loans ever received notice that their liens were being foreclosed? Did any of the agencies ever act on the notices? Had HUD also been a player in the lack of notice or action on the unpaid government liens?

After the headquarters call ended, Shannon turned to Riker,

"Would you see me in my office after this meeting for a minute, please."

"Sure," Riker answered with a nod.

Shannon closed the meeting, and he followed her into her office near the conference room.

Riker took a chair and looked at Shannon expectantly. Shannon went around her desk and settled into her chair. She smiled at the real estate manager and asked,

"What do you know about government liens that may have been filed against our HUD homes?"

"What do you mean?", he frowned.

"I've been thinking about government liens that may have been placed against HUD/FHA properties prior to foreclosure."

"And…?"

"Well, you know how a government agency can file a lien against a piece of real estate for an unpaid debt or unpaid income taxes, and supposedly if the property is sold, the lien has to be paid off to clear the legal title for the new buyer."

"Right, so...?"

"So, what about our HUD foreclosures? If there was a lien filed by, say, the IRS, for unpaid income taxes, do you know if the IRS received notice that their lien was about to be foreclosed on and the property become a HUD home?"

"Well, no, we wouldn't know that," he answered slowly.

"From what I can tell so far, none of our data systems would show any government liens prior to the foreclosure action. We are only going to see the loan origination credit information, loan terms, and payment history, correct?"

"Correct."

"So, we would have to look at the FHA approved lenders' files or title company files to see if they had sent required notices to the government agencies when there were filed liens prior to initiating the foreclosures."

"I guess so," he responded, not really concerned. "That wouldn't be our job, it would be the lenders' job. We just want to make sure we have clear title when the property comes to us."

Well, that sounded familiar to Shannon, an echo of the FDIC discussions.

"So, then, let me ask you this," she began on another tack. "Has HUD ever had an REO reclaimed or redeemed by a government entity that had a lien position to protect?"

Riker thought a minute and then answered,

"The only time I can think of a property being redeemed was in Kansas or one of those states that has an owner redemption period, like up to six months or so, to come back and buy back their home from the new owners. But never anything like that from the IRS or any other government agency or taxing authority."

"And how many pieces of real estate has HUD received through the foreclosure process, say, in the last ten years or so?"

"Well, this office alone transferred over 25,000 HUD homes to the M&M contractors in 1999, and the other three HUD offices transferred similar or larger amounts of foreclosures to the M&Ms at the same time. Then our foreclosure activity decreased for a few years when the subprime conventional market increased their market share and FHA lending was reduced. But our HUD Homes inventory increased again when the White House asked HUD to refinance those subprime loans, even if they were delinquent, after the market collapse and mortgage meltdown in 2008."

"Right. Most of that is historical. But I'm trying to get at the fact that with over a half of a million pieces of foreclosed real estate properties, probably more, you have never seen one redeemed or bought back by the IRS?"

"No, not one."

⌘

It had been two long years for Shannon as the executive director for the HUD Homeownership Center in California. The great retirement wave had begun, and staff had been reduced from 175 to 140 employees, with an estimated ten percent more leaving each year for the next four years. The program support division had yielded staff to the new office of housing counseling, the smaller offices had been consolidated to save budget money for HUD, and she had handled all the small office closings and reassigned staff. She had streamlined every program and procedure in her office.

Shannon slowly smiled as she thought about her career accomplishments and her genuine enjoyment and appreciation for much of her staff. She celebrated the different personalities and each of their special skills and knowledge. She had never really felt that she was 'working', but instead doing what she enjoyed so much, identifying and improving systems and processes, mentoring capable people, and encouraging those who needed a little extra help. She enjoyed writing and contributing to legislation and rule making. She enjoyed public speaking and the exchange of ideas. Making presentations to the business industry and her staff was a pleasure. And she especially had enjoyed all the challenges and opportunities to do things no one had ever done before, like resolve failed banks and their remaining assets, including finding a purchaser for 1330 timeshares in Olympic Village, Tahoe, California, or hiring two hundred new staff for a government real estate start-up business, or writing training manuals for FDIC and HUD staff. None of it had been thought of as 'work', but instead as that day's challenge and opportunity to make a difference, to learn something new, and to improve the task at hand. And now she thought, *I think it's time for something else new.*

She once again pulled out her retirement plans and wrote to HUD's retirement department.

Later that week she received an estimate of her retirement pension amount, with the proviso…"Congratulations on your retirement! Your application for Retirement has been forwarded to OPM….This is only an estimate, the actual amount of your retirement pension will be generated by the Office of

Personnel Management, OPM. *At a minimum, please allow 4–10 months for final processing of your retirement application by OPM."*

She thought, only in the government can you get away with something like this. Some things never change, …but they need to.

27

A Whale's Tail

Shannon was walking in the door from visiting her daughter, Jennifer. She was stepping around her two cats, who were winding around her legs as best as a twenty-pound tabby could wind, happy to greet her, when her cell phone rang.

"I'll pet you in just a minute," she whispered to the cats, quickly scratching their heads, and reached into her tote bag purse to find her phone, while fumbling to hang her sweater on a door knob,

"Hello?" she said with a smile, still warm from talking with her daughter.

She hadn't seen Jennifer for a few weeks and had truly enjoyed catching up and sharing lunch with her. Her daughter was working hard at the University of Southern California, San Diego, while her husband was attending law school at the University of San Diego. She admired her daughter's tenacity to push forward with her own career while Jason pursued his own. She worried sometimes about how hard Jennifer worked, but her daughter assured her that she had plenty of time to run on the beach, which was a stone's throw from their apartment in LaJolla, and to enjoy the beautiful hiking venues at Torrey Pines Park, taking in the ocean views from several of the resting plateaus. Jennifer still wore her blond hair long, almost to her waist, and was as slender now as when she was a cheerleader in high school. To Shannon, she still looked like she was sixteen.

It seemed that her family all loved the ocean and the beach, with her son, Toby, now into scuba diving and anything water. He still had his broad, strong, swimmer's shoulders and wonderful sense of humor. He and his new wife had just returned from a vacation in the Caribbean, where they swam, snorkeled and dove every day. Most of the pictures he had shared with her were of 'fish butts', because by the time he swam up to the fish, they turned and swam the other way!

Shannon had taken her two children to the beach every summer, taught them to swim early, and had shared with them her love of the ocean.

She focused back on the telephone call and was happy to hear Dave's voice.

"Hi, you're home," he greeted Shannon. "How was your visit with Jennifer?"

"Wonderful." She continued to smile. "We shared a great lunch and got caught up."

"Did you go to Old Town Café for lunch?" he teased her, knowing she loved the old restaurant with the women making hand-rolled tortillas in the front window.

"We did!" Shannon enthusiastically replied. "It's just sooo good, I can't go near San Diego without stopping by."

"Did you bring some home?" he laughed.

"Of course! And some delicious refried beans."

"Enough to share?"

"Always!" she laughed.

Dave smiled into the phone, enjoying her happiness and letting it seep through the phone lines to him. She never ceased to amaze him—her endless energy, her ability to find fun in everything and, at the same time, to be deeply involved in her career and government issues. They were together now, most of the time, and he always felt a glow when he thought about her or was with her.

"Well, do you have time to slip away to the beach with me tonight?" he asked softly.

"Of course," she answered easily. "But does that mean you want to come over and share some of my tortillas and beans tonight?"

They had made tentative plans to get together that evening, but hadn't decided what they wanted to do. The beach, as always, sounded heavenly.

"Why don't you pack them and we'll take them to the beach?" he countered. "I'll bring the liquid refreshments."

"Will the refreshments have bubbles?" she laughed softly.

He knew exactly what she meant, "Yes, my love, I will bring you champagne."

Dave came by the house around five o'clock, tapped on the front door, and let himself in. Shannon was coming down the stairs, dressed in white jeans and a short, soft-blue sweater. She smiled at this most important, intelligent, handsome man in her life. She had been surprised when she realized that the one thing that was very different with Dave from the other men she had dated was that she respected him. He was honest and honored his responsibilities, both professional and personal. He was wonderful with his children. He was ethical—and fun, sexy, and tender, of course.

She remembered being surprised when she first put those thoughts into words.

"You look like a mermaid." He smiled and leaned over to kiss her hello as she stood on the bottom step of the staircase.

"You're just saying that to get my tortillas," she kissed him back and smiled at him.

"Hmmm, tortillas and champagne. Maybe we should re-think this," he teased her.

"Well, perhaps, but they are two of my most favorite things, so I'm game," she laughed and ducked under his arm to go into the kitchen and get her beach bag.

He followed her around, gently took the bag from her hand, and ushered her out to his car.

When they reached their favorite beach location, Crystal Cove in south Newport Beach, they parked and walked slowly down the steep cliff. The sun was still up, the air still a sweet and warm seventy-two degrees. The view of the ocean that revealed itself as they descended the path was breathtaking. Sparkling sun diamonds on the ocean. Crystal-clear waters, beautiful exposed tide pools and rocks. The sun seemed to be shining through the waves, creating the most beautiful soft greens and teal colors. The kelp decorated parts of the beach with twining branches and pods. The waves were breaking on some of the rock formations, sending salt spray up into the warm evening air and sending the sea foam running onto the sand. A few seagulls floated above, and the smaller sandpipers were skittering along the beach. The pelicans flew in perfect formations above.

They took off their shoes, and Dave tucked them into his beach bag. He took Shannon's hand in his, and they began to walk toward the sun, enjoying and appreciating the reflection of the sun's rays on the wet sand, as the waves pushed the sea foam onto the beach until it stopped and ran back to the next wave, tickling their feet. They explored the exposed tide pools, always looking for starfish and watching the crabs walk sideways along the shallow shelves. Shannon enjoyed finding unusual seashells, left by sea creatures no longer present. Dave enjoyed identifying several uncommon sea animals that Shannon would look at but not touch, as Dave laughed at her squeamishness.

To both of them, the ocean was a magical place of beauty, peace, and renewal. Always changing. A constant energy. A place with limitless distances. A place to meditate. A place to rest. A place to celebrate the sunshine, the warmth, and endless possibilities.

"Look! A spout!" Dave said excitedly.

"What? Where? What is it?" Shannon looked out to the ocean where Dave was pointing.

"It's a whale!"

"No way, I've lived here all my life and have never seen a whale."

"Well, you have now."

"Are you sure?"

"Just watch," he said. "It will come back up again, and you can see the next spout in just a minute."

"This is wild! I've been swimming in the ocean since I was twelve and have never, ever seen a whale spout before."

"Look, there it is again!"

Sure enough, the whale surfaced again about one hundred yards offshore. The plume was iridescent against the darker blue water, and its' back a dark dome above the smaller waves.

"Oh my gosh!" she exclaimed excitedly. "I've seen dolphins often, but this is a first!"

They continued to watch as the whale moved silently along the shore.

Dave slipped his arm around Shannon and pulled her close. "She is the ocean, I am the sea, wherever she is, I want to be," Dave unexpectedly recited to her.

She looked up at Dave and smiled. "What is that? It sounds like a poem."

"It's something that I wrote. There's more."

"Oh, can I read it?"

"Yes, later you can."

They looked back out at the whale and saw its' final spout as it took a deep breath and dove, flipping its' magnificent tail in the air.

As they turned to walk back down the beach, Dave was feeling unexplainably happy that he had shown Shannon her first whale and spout. He enjoyed sharing new experiences with her, and this was one they wouldn't soon forget. He realized that it was great to experience something new, but so much better to share the new experience with her. He had been thinking about all that they shared, and more that he wanted to share in the future.

He guided Shannon over to a rock formation they had climbed several times before.

"Let's go up here again," he suggested. "I'll bring the picnic bag up with us."

He easily swung both his bag and hers over his shoulder as he began the twelve-foot climb and reached back to take Shannon's hand. There was a small plateau on the top of the rocks where they often sat and watched the sun set. Dave pulled a beach towel from his bag and spread in down for them to sit on, and they settled themselves facing the sun, now edging toward its' decent.

"Look at the colors in the sand when the water runs back out!" Shannon said happily. "The reflection in the wet sand is beautiful. It reflects the sunset," and they looked at the elongated sun beams of yellow and pink and orange.

"I know we've seen the sun set from here before, but it seems especially beautiful tonight," she looked over at Dave and smiled.

Dave leaned over and kissed her. "It looks like a pathway," he murmured to her.

"It does, and it is, a beautiful pathway, a pathway to tomorrow," she answered quietly.

Dave looked at Shannon for a moment without talking, and then said,

"Would you like to marry me?"

She turned and looked at him. She was surprised, she hadn't expected anything like this, not now. They had been to Europe together, and struggled to learn fifty words of French between them just to survive, and they just recently went to Hawaii. If he hadn't asked her to marry him in those romantic locations, she certainly hadn't anticipated a proposal sitting on these rocks. He hadn't hinted at anything. She looked at him, and said quietly, "Say that again."

"Would you like to marry me? But before you answer.... I should tell you that I can sometimes get kind of quiet and moody...."

"Dave, I've known you for three years now, and I've never known you to be quiet or moody," she laughed. "You're fun, and thoughtful, and I love being with you. I love You." She was thrilled.

He thought about that for a moment and realized that, with her, he never was quiet or moody any longer. He was happy, and hopeful, both in the moment and with thoughts of the future. Surprised with himself, he said,

"You're right. I'm not that person anymore. I'm so happy with you, and I just can't wait to see you again, to talk to you, to share with you, to plan things with you. To hear your voice. I love you, and I want to be with you, and ..."

She interrupted with, "Yes! Yes, I want to marry you!"

He leaned over and kissed her again, and again. They just looked at each other with wide smiles. She was so excited, and happy, and still trying to comprehend that he had proposed.

"I think we should name this place Besame Rock, because we always seem to be kissing when we are up here," he smiled. "I wanted to ask you here because then we can always come back here to remember."

"It's in my heart now."

"So we're getting married!"

She asked, "When?"

"Soon."

"How 'soon' ?"

"I'd like to get married next month or the one after that," he continued to surprise her.

That more than surprised Shannon, as she repeated his request,

"You want to get married in the next few weeks?" she couldn't believe his words. "That's awfully fast."

She was hardly getting used to the fact that he wanted to get married, but in just a few weeks?

"Yes, I want to get married soon."

She wasn't sure why he felt this way, but needed to tell him, "Planning a wedding usually takes several months, not weeks."

"We don't have that much to plan."

"Well, maybe not, but I would still like to enjoy the planning process, and I think you would too."

He seemed to think about that, and then asked, "Well, how much time do you need?"

She wasn't sure how to respond, so she offered what she did know. "I will be in Washington, DC and at several of the HUD offices on the East Coast for the next few weeks. I have several huge national projects I have to work on and finish at the office, I would like to get those done, and then we can focus on us and our planning."

She didn't want to have him think she was delaying, because she loved this man and was excited about marrying him. "I love you, and want to be able to commit all of me and my time to us."

He didn't answer right away, and she thought she might have offended him, but he said, "OK, how about three or four months?"

"OK, I'll take four," she answered, and they shared a long, sweet, passionate kiss. When they pulled apart, he brought out the champagne and poured it into two long-stemmed champagne flutes.

"To us," he toasted.

"Yes, to us," she repeated, and leaned in to kiss him to seal the thought.

After sitting for a few minutes, basking in the sinking sunlight and warm ocean breezes, she turned to him and asked, "Will you read more of your poem to me?"

He smiled at her, took her hand to his lips for a kiss, and said, "Yes, I will. It's really a haiku more than a poem." He reached into his pants pocket and pulled out a folded piece of paper.

He began.

"*Links meet, a bowl of soup,*
Eyes that shone, hair glowed in the light
Diffusing through the trees,
Smart, knowledge, thoughtful, creative ideas.

Starfish nibbles, a shout under water,
Snorkel in the storm, a strange sea creature.
Dolphins tickling the feet, brave to be first,
Fearless inside.

Golf, kayaking the surf and not turning over,
Champagne bubbles on the tongue,
Appreciating the moments in every one.

Dreaming, redreaming,
Pictures packing the savored moments,
So many in a short time.

More to share, more to learn,
Sharing the future, catching up on the past,
Events shaping us and putting some pieces together.

A puzzle worth placing each shape an adventure,
A laugh, a friend, a conversation.
More beaches to savor, hands touch in the warmth.
Bubbles a theme, travel with gusto.

Reading the mind, complex and wondrous.
Nights in a castle, ancient and powerful.
Finding our way, people with passion.
Beseme, mi amore, and more.

Beach here and new beach, seize each one,
Whales, turtles, stick fish and angels.
Roads less traveled, rain, sun and vistas,
Sunsets that render paintings for always.

An era begins, beginning all over.
Time is forever.
Planning the next step, adventures to treasure.
Unknowns to discover, surprises are always,
Je voudrais vous, it seems so amazing, yet simple too,
I love you."

She was speechless. She was deeply moved. She continued to be amazed at the depth of this man she loved. Her eyes teared.

"When did you write this?" she asked in a whisper.

"When I knew."

They were married four months later, on a bluff overlooking the Pacific Ocean, celebrating with their friends and family and a few locals who became caught up in the joy and beauty of the day and moment.

28

Denouement

Shannon completed her professional responsibilities and promises, and proceeded with her efforts to retire, in spite of the Office of Personnel Management delays.

The country had survived the worst recession since the Great Depression era of the 1940s. The present executive administration in Washington, DC had pushed through health reform legislation that would cost the taxpayers billions. Unemployment benefits had been extended due to the loss of jobs from the recessionary weakened economy, resources for food stamps and housing assistance were depleted.

The US House Committee on Oversight and Government Reform held hearings at which Tom Coburn (R.-Oklahoma), author of the '*Wastebook*', which identified over $30 billion in frivolous and wasteful government spending, testified, "We have 679 renewable energy programs from 23 different agencies costing $15 billion dollars a year," Coburn said. "Can anyone logically say why we need 679 programs?"

Thomas Schatz, the president of Citizens Against Government Waste, testified as to the numerous overlaps in federal programs regarding forty-seven job training programs across nine agencies, which was costing about $18 billion in 2009. Thirteen agencies administered 209 science, technology, engineering, and math (STEM) programs totaling $3.1 billion in fiscal year 2010. Most absurdly, there were 56 programs from 20 different agencies devoted to promoting financial literacy 'intending to improve the fiscal acumen of the American people'. Fifteen of those programs cost $30.7 million in 2010.

"While it would be funny if it wasn't so sad, a government that itself is going broke should not be spending any money trying to teach others how to balance their checkbook," Schatz said.

All this fraud, waste and abuse is more shattered glass, growing even deeper, spreading further, Shannon reflected. *Our government agencies are not just inefficient but tragically broken, cutting deeper and causing more personal and financial bleeding. It seemed that it was becoming impossible to step out of the broken glass, and the taxpayers were being recklessly cut.*

Wall Street firms and banks had been taken to task for their roles in the toxic mortgage activity that had nearly destroyed the stock market and the global economy. The *Los Angeles Times* reported that a settlement was pending in which...

"Goldman Sachs Group, Inc. will pay roughly $5 billion to settle federal and state investigations of its role in the sale of shoddy mortgages in the years leading to the housing bubble and subsequent financial crisis..."Wells Fargo agrees to pay $1.2 billion to settle claims that it duped the federal government into insuring thousands of risky mortgages in the years leading up to the housing crash if approved by a federal judge...

"Bank of America, JP Morgan, Chase and others reached larger, more substantial settlements in 2014 and 2015..."

By January 2015, after a crushing Republican victory in November 2014, during the midterm elections, where the GOP took the majority of the seats in both the Senate and the House of Representatives, the Obama Administration was looking for ways to ensure that the Democrats fared better in the upcoming 2016 Presidential election and hopefully restore some of the congressional seats they lost to the GOP.

Obama went on a tour in early 2015 announcing his new plan to provide a free college education for any students attending a two-year community college, spending over $60 Billion over ten years. His platform promised that anyone who wanted a two-year college education could have one for free. His administration was posturing to bring in as much of the new, young, voting population as possible to make them Democrats before they were exposed to politics.

The Obama administration had announced the immigration reform platform without congressional participation or approval, providing safe residency for millions of illegal immigrants and for them to apply for temporary legal work permits. Thus, they would become full tax-paying contributors receiving immediate benefits and hopefully indebted to the Democratic party, which was trying to bring in as much of the new immigrant vote as possible to the Democratic Party.

The Presidential administration huddled with HUD to develop new programs that would make it easier for first-time home-buyers and those who had lost their homes during the Great Recession or had impaired credit to purchase a new home. Obama's team worked with HUD to push down the FHA insurance premium to nearly half of what HUD had determined was necessary to float their foreclosure and claim fund so it would cost less to obtain an FHA loan. FHA had previously been very careful with their insurance premiums to avoid being forced to take an additional taxpayer bailout. The Presidential administration also pushed HUD to change its credit requirements to make it easier for purchasers who had experienced a foreclosure or deed in lieu, where they handed back the keys to the house to the bank, to buy a new home again within a year, instead of waiting for several years to clear up their credit as had been the customary practice in the real estate industry. The Presidential administration pushed HUD hard to change its requirements to permit FHA purchasers with lower FICO scores, no FICO scores, or poor credit to purchase a home, insuring an additional new group of voters for the Democratic party.

The housing industry had sunk to new lows, only recently re-bounding in 2013 and still struggling in 2015. Some home-owners had been handed up to $50,000 to pay toward their 'upside down' loans in economically hardest-hit areas, when their loan balance exceeded the market value of their house, paid for by the taxpayers. Loan modifications and free money had been handed out to countless homeowners who had over-borrowed or had suffered decreased equity, and how was all this being paid for?

The country needed a new source of revenue. And Shannon thought she knew where it was: *Her Government Lien/IRS Collections recovery plan. It would curtail some of the broken glass of government over-spending and provide a pathway out of the bleeding without further cuts.*

She wrote a clearly worded letter to the IRS and Treasury, seeking information pertaining to the number of liens placed against real property in the fifty United States; and the number of those liens that had been redeemed, or paid. She prepared the letter pursuant to FOIA (Freedom of Information Act) rules.

She immediately received a response letter from the IRS, requesting her social security number and picture identification.

"That's not what I expected," she thought sardonically, and sent another letter requesting the same FOIA information. She waited.

She actually received several phone calls from the Treasury after her new FOIA request was received.

"Hello, Ms. O'Toole. This is Daniel from the IRS office in Pennsylvania. I have a few questions for you regarding your FOIA. Please return my call."

Shannon was pleased to have made contact with a live body at the IRS, and returned the call.

"Hello, this is Daniel. I will be out of the office for the next two weeks in training. Please don't leave any messages on this line. You can contact me when I return.....in two weeks."

Shannon narrowed her eyes and shook her head.

Another two-week delay, Shannon complained to herself.

When the time was up, she picked up the phone to call Daniel.

"Hello, this is Daniel. I am out on annual leave vacation and will be returning in two weeks. You can leave a message, which I will return when I come back into the office."

When Daniel finally returned from his vacation, he called Shannon and left a message,

"I have some questions about your FOIA. You know there's some privacy issues here. We can't divulge taxpayer lien information; that's personal. Please call me back and we can discuss this."

Shannon called back,

"Hello, this is Daniel. I will be out of the office until May twenty-fifth, I'm on medical leave. Please don't leave any messages on this phone. Call back when I return."

Shannon tried calling the same number as Daniel's and changed the last number, theorizing that the extensions for other staff could be consecutive. She could not reach another live body. Shannon continued trying other departments, other extensions, and could only reach voice mails.

About two weeks later, Shannon received another call from someone with a deep smoker's voice. "Hello, Ms. O'Toole. This is Stephanie with the U.S. Treasury. I'm calling you about your FOIA request. I'm taking over some files for a colleague. Please return my call so we can discuss it."

Shannon immediately called the number left by Stephanie, and received her voicemail. "I'm not at my desk right now. I'll call you back if you leave your phone number." So Shannon left her contact number for Stephanie.

Two days later, the phone rang, and Shannon answered. "Hello, Ms. O'Toole, this is Stephanie with the U.S. Treasury. I have your FOIA here for your GLIC project and need to ask you a couple of questions." Shannon was delighted that she had finally made contact! But GLIC?

"Excuse me, did you say GLIC?

"Yes, your Government Lien IRS Collections FOIA. The government likes to use acronums instead all of them big long program names."

Shannon chuckled to herself. "Yes, what do you need?" Shannon asked.

"Well, you are asking for liens from the IRS for the last ten years, is that correct?"

"It is, and I was requesting the number of liens placed against real property broken down by state. I'm assuming there is such a report?" Shannon knew that FOIA requests only had to provide available information, data or reports, that agencies had on hand, and were not required to create such reports if they were not already available.

"Well, um, I'm not sure. I will have to find out. I just wanted to make sure I understood what you were asking."

"I see," Shannon answered patiently. "I would expect that the IRS would have a report on the liens they placed against taxpayers' property."

Stephanie didn't answer quickly. "I don't know, I will have to ask my manager."

"All right," Shannon responded, and the call ended with Stephanie agreeing to call back after she talked with her supervisor.

When Shannon hadn't heard back from Stephanie, she placed two calls and left a message. The next week, Stephanie returned Shannon's calls. "Hello, Ms. O'Toole. This is Stephanie, calling about your FOIA. That information is protected under the privacy act, the liens against taxpayers is private data."

Shannon quickly replied, "Stephanie, I don't want to know the individual liens or against whom they were placed. I'm simply requesting an aggregate number of liens, the aggregate amount, the total number of liens in the various fifty states. There's no privacy issue with that."

"Oh, I don't know about that. I guess I could ask my supervisor again."

"Yes, or, better yet, why don't I speak with your supervisor? That might help move this forward more easily."

"I will let you know." Stephanie disappeared from the call.

On May 26, 2015, Shannon received a letter from the IRS stating they were unable to send the information requested in the FOIA within the twenty-business-day period allowed by law...

"The FOIA (process) allows an additional ten day statutory extension in certain circumstances. To complete your request I require additional time to: Consult with business submitters. We have extended the statutory response date to June 10, 2015 after which you can file suit... your complaint will be treated according to the Federal Rules of Civil Procedure applicable to actions against an agency of the United States..."

Shannon read the letter and closed her eyes. *Sue the IRS! Crap, they aren't going to make this easy*, she thought to herself. Since she had worked for the government, she knew how tightly controlled information was prior to releasing it for a FOIA and how the government generally provided the least amount of data or information possible, when they were forced to do it at all. She was disappointed. Was the IRS saying they still didn't track the liens they placed on taxpayers' properties, as she suspected? Shannon had been trying to get to the bottom on this subject ever since she spoke to Congress about it, and here she was, being blocked and delayed again.

The next letter from the IRS was no more encouraging. The June 10, 2015, letter started:
"This is our final response to your Freedom of Information Act (FOIA) request...you asked for:

(1) The number and dollar amount of tax liens IRS has placed against any real property within the United States including Hawaii and Alaska for the last ten years broken down by year and state.
(2) The dollar amount that has been redeemed or collected from those liens against real property by year and state, for the last ten years.

The IRS does not compile tax lien information in the format you requested above. The FOIA does not require agencies to respond to questions, create records not already in existence in some format, or engage in doctrinal discussions with requesters.

Please be advised that individual tax liens are protected from disclose under FOIA exemptions (b)(6) and (b)(7)(C). Only business tax liens are subject to disclosure from the Automated Lien System (ALS) database...."

Shannon rolled her head back and rubbed her neck after reading the last letter. She couldn't determine if the IRS actually did have a report on the individual liens, but was refusing to give her a cumulative total, not the individual details that were protected by privacy rules, or if they did not have an automated tracking method for the liens.

The last letter from the IRS had been signed by Cara Carlson, directing her to call Sharon Richards if she had any further questions. Shannon still had questions, and placed a call to her,

"Hello, this is Sharon Richards. I am not able to get to my phone at this time. Please leave a detailed message and I will return your call."

Not surprised to reach her voicemail, Shannon left her message,

"Hello, Ms. Richards, this is Shannon O'Toole concerning recent correspondence you sent me. I would like to discuss my FOIA request for a cumulative total number of liens IRS has placed against real property, the total number of those liens, and the total amount. This is not private or protected information, as it does not identify any individual person or taxpayer or their location. If you would return my call, we can discuss this further."

She sat back in her chair and massaged her temples. She knew that foreclosures were public information, with paper notices nailed to the front door or taped to the front window of a property going into foreclosure, and foreclosure notices were posted in the local newspapers. It was all public information. And liens placed against real estate become public information once they were filed with the local county offices. Any person could look at the county records and review the liens placed against any property. All public records, all public information.

Two days later, on July 1, 2015, Shannon received Ms. Richard's return call.

"Hello, Ms. O'Toole. We only have an automated lien database for commercial IRS liens, and you can obtain that database for one hundred and thirty dollars."

"Do you also have an automated lien database for individual taxpayer liens?" Shannon queried, anxious to learn if there was a database for the billions and possibly trillions of dollars against individual taxpayers' homes and real estate.

"IRS only has an automated database for commercial IRS liens, and you can obtain that database for one hundred and thirty dollars."

Shannon was pleased to have received a return call, but couldn't determine from the woman's scripted answers if there were any reports that would list the information she wanted.

"I'm trying to understand the IRS process for placing liens and then for redeeming property against which the lien was placed. Can you explain that to me?"

"Um, no, I don't do that."

"Then can you transfer me to another department that does that kind of activity?"

"No, I don't know who that is."

"Do you have a directory that would help us find the right division or department that redeems the liens?"

"No."

Frustrated now with the unhelpful IRS person Shannon asked, "Are you an employee of the U.S. Treasury or a contractor?" thinking that maybe a contractor had not been given a sufficient script to answer these questions but that an employee should know their own organizational structure.

The woman hesitated and then answered, "I'm an employee."

"And you can't explain the process or transfer me to the department that works on the taxpayer liens and payments and collections?"

"Yes, that's right. I can't. I don't know."

"And you don't know of any reports that collect information on the individual taxpayer liens against their real property?"

"IRS maintains an automated list of commercial liens you can obtain for one hundred and thirty..."

"But not for the individual, residential liens, correct?" Shannon finished her sentence for her.

If not, it would explain why the IRS liens were not redeemed when a property went into foreclosure. The IRS couldn't match the foreclosure notice to the lien. The agency didn't have an automated database, or a process for receiving the lien notices and matching them up with their liens, or a process for determining if there was sufficient equity in the property to pay all or a portion of the lien amount. If the liens were not collected or paid, then the taxpayers suffered seizure of their other assets and properties, wage garnishment, and bank account seizures for ten to twenty years.

Through 2015 and 2016, Shannon continued her discussions and FOIA activity with the IRS. She was able to have a lengthy discussion with an IRS tax specialist, Marcia, in May of 2016. Marcia sent Shannon the latest tax gap report, which determined the amount of unpaid taxes to the IRS; however, it was dated 2006. When Shannon questioned this report as being unacceptably dated, the IRS tax specialist replied,

"Yes, well, we don't have the funding to do another updated report. Our budget continues to be cut. When we have people leave the IRS, and we can't replace them. We are shrinking,

shrinking continually. We don't have the people anymore to do these tax gap and other reports, so we look at the older reports and estimate what the current amount might be."

Shannon was stunned, "The 2006 unpaid *tax gap report shows a gross $450 Billion dollars in unpaid taxes.*"

"Yes, that's correct."

"But that is before the mortgage crash and great recession the economy went through in 2007-2012."

"Yes, right again. We know there are more unpaid taxes due to the IRS, but we don't have the resources to do an updated gap analysis."

"How can the IRS determine its strategy for collecting on these unpaid taxes if it doesn't know the actual amount that is owed?"

"We have to look at the unpaid taxes with a higher dollar amounts and put our resources toward those higher amounts. And we use our more experienced agents to collect the higher-dollar amount of unpaid taxes, except we are losing many of those experienced agents to retirement and they can't be replaced."

"So then what happens?"

"The uncollected taxes have to wait. We are doing the best we can, but our budget continues to be cut, and we have to adjust."

"And the liens that are placed against a person's home for unpaid taxes? Can you tell me how many liens have been filed against homeowners in California?"

"No, we don't keep records of the unpaid taxes by state. Since we are a federal agency, we just look at the unpaid taxes in a lump sum. Your recent FOIA asks for the breakdown of liens by state, but we don't keep those kinds of records. We can't give that information to you."

Shannon tried another approach. "If the IRS could collect on the unpaid taxes, wouldn't that make a huge difference in our national budget?"

"Oh, yes, it would! Our individual taxes would be much lower! If people would pay what they owe, we would have a very different economy today. Our tax rates would be much lower, and, frankly, we wouldn't need so many government employees and government attorneys trying to collect the unpaid taxes. But, that's not the way it is."

"So what about the unpaid tax liens that are filed against people's homes, are they ever collected?"

"I'm in the tax specialty department, that would come under the collections department."

"Do you have a contact person I could talk to there?"

"No, their staff has been cut way back too."

Shannon reflected back to her discussion with Riker Tucker at HUD, about his comments regarding the complete lack of lien redemptions by IRS on a half of a million HUD foreclosures. And her much earlier conversations with title companies in California, in which they told Shannon that they sent notices to the IRS and other government agencies when their liens showed up as public records on foreclosure sales, but that the agencies had *never* redeemed the properties to recover their lien money.

It appeared to Shannon that the IRS did not have a system for receiving the lien notices pending foreclosure, or a method for taking appropriate action to recover billions and now trillions of dollars that the Treasury and economy sorely needed.

Nothing appeared to have changed with the lack of IRS lien recoveries since Shannon had appeared before Congress and the IRS commissioner had agreed that Shannon's plan 'had merit'. IRS had not been able to design, develop or implement its own in-house program for lien recoveries or redemptions. It continued to levy wage garnishments and seize bank accounts, other property, and assets from taxpayers while allowing the real estate to go through foreclosure without any action by the IRS.

The IRS still didn't have an automated database of liens to match to foreclosing lien notices. She thought of the newspaper headlines about failed IRS computer systems and millions of wasted dollars on broken data systems. According to the last telephone call with the IRS tax specialist, staffing continued to be decreased, with less resources than before for collecting unpaid taxes, while the unpaid taxes increased. But the IRS protected its turf and wouldn't let anyone else handle the liens under their connotation of 'private information'.

Shannon was confident that the lien information, once filed against a piece of real property, was no longer private, it became of public record. The IRS was hiding behind a shield of privacy laws, which in all reality, did not apply.

The economy had been in the worst condition since the Depression in the 1930s and 1940s and was beginning to recover. It certainly could use an infusion of revenue from the Government Lien/ IRS Collection recovery program that Shannon had in mind. The government lien program could change all that, by providing the much-needed revenue to pull the country out of the doldrums. The federal income tax rates were burdensomely high, but the spending during the Great Recession had put the country into the largest deficient status in history. Congress continued to increase the outstanding national debt and the nation's debt limit for spending on social benefits and interest payments.

Shannon had worked for the federal government for most of her successful career. Her accomplishments and outstanding ability to grasp organizational structures and develop streamlined procedures or efficiencies for otherwise stale and unworkable processes had been recognized and rewarded. She had managed real estate and loan operations for the FDIC, RTC and HUD, and understood what would be necessary to implement a program to collect the lost government liens.

She understood the internal posturing and maneuvering many government agencies practiced. And now, once again, she was looking into agency politics, where the IRS was protecting its policies and hiding behind privacy rules that did not apply to the overall summary of information she was pursuing.

The public was churning with dissatisfaction from government ineptness, waste and constantly increasing taxes. There was a building wave of public demand for change. And that included correction of the broken IRS system, where billions and now trillions of dollars were being lost every year from unrecovered liens. A large swell was beginning to build and carry her into the oncoming tides of political change. It was the next wave in a sea of political turbulence in which she, as an apolitical woman, would be swimming.

She couldn't move forward with her Government Lien/IRS Collection recovery plans as an Executive Director for HUD, but she could when she stepped away.

She had climbed the broken ladders of government at the FDIC, the RTC, and HUD. There was one more rung to climb, the broken rung at IRS. She thought through a new process that would ensure that all foreclosure notices would be given a thorough consideration and evaluation to determine if there was sufficient equity value to satisfy all or part of an IRS lien, thus removing that portion of the debt off the taxpayer's back, and putting revenue into the United States Treasury. A win-win situation, for Democrats and Republicans alike.

Shannon wanted to see the Government as it was intended to be. A limited, transparent government, with reduced regulations, low taxes, and a strong national defense, for a country with personal freedoms, letting people prosper, grow and follow their individual dreams. And for Shannon, it meant becoming a Washington Siren, to warn of the dangers of allowing broken government agencies to crash upon the rocks of fraud, waste and corruption.

Her Government Lien/ IRS Collection recovery program could provide the pathway out of the shattered glass from broken political and government agencies, it could stop the continued bleeding and spreading of fraud, waste and abuse. It would stop the Dancing on Shattered glass.

Shannon prepared detailed information on her Government Lien/ IRS Collection – GLIC recovery program and prepared packages to send to the current Congressional Committee on Government Oversight, The House Budget Committee, and the House Financial Services Committee, and to the newly elected U.S. President and his cabinet members. They needed to hear and understand the Government Lien/ IRS Collection Recovery Plan.

Like a Washington Siren, observing the turbulent economic storm from crashing waves of increasing national debt, she would provide a safe harbor and soft landing. She would warn of the dangers in ignoring the turbulent budget crisis, and implement a plan to calm the swelling tides of ineffective and wasteful government agencies. It was time to change the tide.

A Few Words from the Author

This story is an Insider's view and nonfiction account of a maze of scathing scandals in broken government programs. Although names and scenes have been changed, the public needs to hear this and demand that their elected officials take action for correction and change.

This is about your government. You deserve effective, efficient, honest politics and government programs that You are paying for.

If we know of these scandals and don't demand action to correct them, we are then giving tacit agreement to continue with the waste, fraud, and abuse that continues to increase our national debt and thus hand down the debt to our children and generations to follow.

The book is softened with a love story and humorous views into flawed characters, intended to demonstrate that we are, above all, human, but not at all above the law.

READ this book, TALK about it, WRITE a LETTER

Author Shannon O'Toole

Shannon O'Toole began her career with the Federal Deposit Insurance Corporation (FDIC) and advanced to executive director for the US Department of Housing and Urban Development (HUD) where she managed over 175 staff in five divisions. O'Toole worked extensively to identify fraud in multiple government programs. She received countless accolades and honors for her achievements and finally the prestigious HUD Secretary's Award for her work.

O'Toole presented the National Government Lien Recovery Program to Congress describing billions of wasted taxpayer dollars. She developed a pilot plan for government lien recoveries for the US Treasury and the California State Treasury.

O'Toole lives in Laguna Beach, California, with her husband. She enjoys golfing and kayaking.